Breaking the Glass Armor

Kristin Thompson

BREAKING

THE GLASS

ARMOR

Neoformalist Film
Analysis

PRINCETON UNIVERSITY PRESS, PRINCETON, NEW JERSEY

Library of Congress Cataloging in Publication Data will be found
on the last printed page of this book

ISBN 0-691-06724-4
ISBN 0-691-01453-1 (pbk.)

This book has been composed in Linotron Caledonia Type

Clothbound editions of Princeton University Press books are printed
on acid-free paper, and binding materials are chosen for
strength and durability. Paperbacks, although satisfactory
for personal collections, are not usually suitable
for library rebinding

Printed in the United States of America

9 8 7 6 5 4 3 2

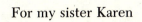For my sister Karen

Contents

Preface and Acknowledgments

THIS VOLUME follows up on the type of critical analysis I used in *Eisenstein's Ivan the Terrible: A Neoformalist Analysis*. Here, however, a series of essays on a variety of films demonstrates more of the range of the neoformalist approach.

Five of these essays are revised versions of articles previously published. Among them are some of the earliest pieces I ever wrote for publication, and inevitably I had begun to be somewhat dissatisfied with them over the years. Extending the life of one's older writings through revision and republication is one of the greatest luxuries a writer can have, and I am grateful to *Wide Angle* (the *Les Vacances de Monsieur Hulot*, *Tout va bien*, and *Play Time* chapters) and *Film Reader* (the *Stage Fright* and *Laura* chapters) for publishing the originals and for giving permission to reprint them. Seven of the chapters have not been published previously; they were written at intervals during the period from 1981 to 1985, partly as an excuse to leave the microfilm room and various historical projects at intervals for a few weeks of intensive viewing and writing. The reason for the choice of most of the films was that they seemed intriguing and challenging; in a few cases, I chose films specifically in order to explore methodological issues. In no case was a film chosen because it seemed "appropriate" to neoformalism, or neoformalism "appropriate" to it.

A number of people and institutions have kindly given me help along the way. Thanks to Richard Maltby, Darrell Davis, David Rodowick, Annette Kuhn, Michael Drozewski, and Janet Staiger. The Wisconsin Center for Film and Theater Research and its archivist, Maxine Fleckner, have for years made it possible for me to do this sort of close analysis in congenial circumstances. New Yorker Films—in particular Jose Lopez—and Janus Films, through Jonathan B. Turell, have given permission for the use of prints and frame enlargements. Jon Gartenberg of the Museum of Modern Art and Jacques Ledoux of the Cinémathéque Royale de Belgique have facilitated some of these analyses. Edward Branigan and Mary Beth Haralovich read individual chapters and offered invaluable suggestions, many of which I have adopted. The comments of Herbert Eagle and Stuart Liebman, as press readers, were extremely useful. Thanks also to Joanna Hitchcock, Sue Bishop, and Janet Stern of Princeton University Press. Finally, David Bordwell has contributed far more to this volume than I could possibly acknowledge in the footnotes that refer to him here and there.

June 28, 1987

The fate of the works of old artists of the word is exactly the same as the fate of the word itself. They are completing the journey from poetry to prose. They cease to be seen and begin to be recognised. Classical works have for us become covered with the glassy armour of familiarity—we remember them too well, we have heard them from childhood, we have read them in books, thrown out quotations from them in the course of conversation, and now we have callouses on our souls—we no longer sense them.

—Victor Shklovsky, "The Resurrection of the Word," 1914

PART ONE

A Neoformalist
Approach to Film
Analysis

1

Neoformalist Film Analysis: One Approach, Many Methods

GOALS OF FILM ANALYSIS

THERE IS no such thing as film analysis without an approach. Critics do not go to films only to gather facts which they convey in pristine fashion to others. What we take to be the "facts" about a film will partly depend on what we assume films to consist of, how we assume people watch films, how we believe films relate to the world as a whole, and what we take the purposes of analysis to be. If we have not thought over our assumptions, our approach may be random and self-contradictory. But if we examine our assumptions, we have at least a chance of creating a reasonably systematic approach to analysis. An aesthetic *approach*, then, as I am using the term here, refers to a set of assumptions about traits shared by different artworks, about procedures spectators go through in understanding all artworks, and about ways in which artworks relate to society. These assumptions are capable of being generalized and hence constitute at least a rough theory of art. The approach thus helps the analyst to be consistent in studying more than one artwork. I will consider a *method* to be something more specific: a set of procedures employed in the actual analytical process.

The approach which a critic adopts or devises often depends on why he or she wishes to analyze films at all. There are, it would seem, two general ways analysts typically decide to work on a film—one centered on an approach, one on the film itself.

One can decide to look at a film in order to demonstrate an approach and its attendant method (since in most approaches there is generally only one method). This is currently a common strategy in academic film studies. The critic begins with an analytical method, often derived from approaches in literary studies, psychoanalysis, linguistics, or philosophy; she or he then selects a film that seems suited to displaying that method. When I first began doing film analysis in the early 1970s, this kind of impetus for film criticism seemed almost self-evidently the way to go about things. Method was paramount, and if one were not

3

seen to have a method before beginning an analysis, one risked appearing naive and muddled.

Yet now such an attitude seems to me to present considerable pitfalls. The critic could, of course, truly use the analysis of a film as an actual *test* of the method, to challenge and perhaps change it. But all too often in the analyses written in the past fifteen years or so, the choice of a film simply serves to confirm the method. That psychoanalytic film readings can be done of films like *Spellbound* and *Vertigo* is hardly surprising; such an analysis offers little challenge to a method. But can a psychoanalytic method deal equally well with *The Great Train Robbery* or *Singin' in the Rain*—without forcing the film into a simplistic and distorted reading?

Here we encounter a second problem with the imposed-method tactic. Preconceived methods, applied simply for demonstrative purposes, often end by reducing the complexity of films. Because the method exists before the choice of film and the process of analysis, its assumptions must be broad enough to accommodate any film. Every film must then be considered in some way "the same" in order to make it conform to the method, and the method's broad assumptions will tend to iron out differences. If every film simply plays out an Oedipal drama, then our analyses will inevitably begin to resemble each other. The result is that the critic makes films seem dull and unintriguing—yet I take it that the critic's task is, at least in part, to emphasize the intriguing aspects of films.

Such homogeneity in the treatment of films furthermore suggests that, by choosing a single method and pressing it down, like a cookie cutter, on each film in the same way, we risk losing any sense of challenge in analysis. The films we use as examples are those appropriate to the method, with the result that our approach becomes perpetually self-confirming. There can be no difficulty for the system, and ease will discourage revision. Indeed, revision, for critics who develop a method and then apply it in order to prove it, tends to come from outside the field of film. Developments in linguistics or psychoanalysis may alter the method, but the medium of cinema usually has little effect on it. (This is often because in such cases the original approach itself—psychoanalysis, linguistics, etc.—lies outside the field of aesthetic studies.)

In years of dealing with films, I have gradually moved away from this notion of applying a preexisting method in order to demonstrate it. Rather, I will be assuming here that we usually analyze a film because it is intriguing. In other words, there is something about it which we *cannot* explain on the basis of our approach's existing assumptions. It remains elusive and puzzling after viewing. This is not to say that we begin with no approach at all. Rather, our general approach will not dictate fully how we would analyze any given film. Since artistic conventions are constantly changing and there are infinite possible variations within existing conventions at any given moment, we could hardly expect that one approach could anticipate every possibility. When we find films that challenge us, that is a sure sign that they warrant analysis, and that the analysis may help to expand or modify the approach. Alternatively, we may sense a lack in the approach as it stands and thus deliberately look for a film that seems to offer it difficulties in that weak area. I have selected a few of the films in this volume for this reason. For example, a formalist method is thought to be most appropriate to highly stylized or unusual films. I have chosen *Terror By Night* to lead off my analyses precisely because it is a fairly ordinary classical film. Moreover, many would consider realism a challenge to a formalist approach, and I have analyzed two of the most widely accepted examples of cinematic realism—*The Rules of the Game* and *Bicycle Thieves*—to show how neoformalism can treat realism as a style.

I believe that analysis involves an extended, careful viewing of a film—a viewing that gives the analyst a chance to examine in leisurely fashion those structures and materials that intrigued him or her on initial and subsequent viewings. In a manner of speaking, the film itself can push us to do such a viewing; that is, some disparity emerges between the viewing skills we bring to the film and the film's structures as we experience them. We are confronted by something that we had not expected to find. (Again, this problematic quality can surface in the approach itself: we may realize that something we had hoped the approach would contain is in fact missing, and we will then seek a film or films that can help us to fill in that gap.)

When the film piques our interest, we analyze it in order to explain, in formal and historical terms, what is going on in the work that would cue such a response. Similarly, when an issue arises in the approach that eludes specification, our first response should be to turn to a diverse group of actual films in order to understand how the approach would deal with issues they raised. We then pass the results of close viewing along to others who may also have found this or similar films intriguing, or who at least have been intrigued by the issues raised by analysis—for ultimately we write and read criticism as much for the issues raised as for the explication of a single film. Theory and criticism thus become two different aspects of the same give-and-take process.

Neoformalism is an approach to aesthetic analysis based fairly closely on the work of the Russian Formalist literary theoretician-critics. They worked in Russia in the period from the mid-1910s to about 1930 before being forced by official pressure to modify their views. In my previous book of analysis, *Eisenstein's Ivan the Terrible*, I presented an explication of how the original Formalists' assumptions could be adapted to film. Here I shall not be retracing this ground; rather, I shall lay out the neoformalist approach itself, with less frequent references to the Russian Formalists' writings—bringing them in primarily when they seem to offer the clearest definition of a given term or concept.[1] In this book, I am interested in how neoformalism applies to film analysis, but the approach is based upon many assumptions about the general nature of art. Hence I will feel free to bring in examples from artworks in other media as well.

Neoformalist analysis has the potential to raise theoretical issues. And unless we wish to deal with the same theoretical material over and over, we must have an approach that is flexible enough to respond to and incorporate the results of those issues. This approach must be able to suit each film, and it must build into itself the need to be constantly challenged and thus changed. Each analysis should tell us something not only about the film in question, but about the possibilities of film as an art. Neoformalism builds into itself this need for constant modification. It implies a two-way interchange between theory and criticism. It is *not*, as I have already suggested, a method as such. Neoformalism as an approach does offer a series of broad assumptions about how artworks are constructed and how they operate in cueing audience response. But neoformalism does not prescribe *how* these assumptions are embodied in individual films. Rather, the basic assumptions can be used to construct a method specific to the problems raised by each film. In 1924, Boris Eikhenbaum stressed this limited meaning of the word "method."

The word "method" must be reinvested with its previous modest meaning of a device used for the study of any concrete problem. The methods of the study of form may be as varied as is wished, while holding to a single principle, depending on the theme, the material and the way the question is put. Methods of the study of the text, methods of study of verse, methods of study of a particular period, and so on—these are the natural uses of the word "method" . . . We are dealing not with methods but with a principle. You can think up as many methods as you like, but the best method will be the one which can

[1] For explications of Russian Formalism as an approach, see my *Eisenstein's Ivan the Terrible: A Neoformalist Analysis* (Princeton: Princeton University Press, 1981), chap. 1, and Victor Erlich, *Russian Formalism: History—Doctrine*, (3d ed.)(The Hague: Mouton, 1969).

be relied upon most to lead to the goal. We ourselves have an infinite number of methods. But there can be no question of peaceful coexistence between ten different principles, there cannot be even two principles. The principle which establishes the content or the object of a specific science must stand alone. Our principle is the study of literature as a specific category of phenomena.[2]

In effect, what Eikhenbaum calls the "principle," and what I am calling the "approach," is what allows us to judge which of the many (indeed, infinite) questions we could ask about a work are the most useful and interesting ones. The method then becomes an instrument we devise to answer these questions. Because the questions are (at least slightly) different for each work, the method will also be different. Of course, we could make things easy for ourselves (as busy academics) by asking the same question every time, choosing the same types of film, and using the same method. But this would defeat the purpose, which is to discover what is intriguing or challenging in each new work; moreover, it would not modify and illuminate our approach with each new study.

By assuming an overall approach that dictates modification or complete change of the method for each new analysis, neoformalist film criticism avoids the problem inherent in the typical self-confirming method. It does not assume that the text harbors a fixed pattern which the analyst goes in and finds. After all, if we assume at the outset that the text contains something, we are likely to find it. Thus neoformalism sidesteps cliché and tedium by using analysis as a means to test itself against actual films.

THE NATURE OF THE ARTWORK

Neoformalism jettisons a communications model of art. In such a model, three components are generally distinguished: sender, medium, and receiver. The main activity involved is assumed to be the passing of a message from sender to receiver through the medium (e.g., speech, television images, Morse code). Hence the medium serves a practical function, and its effectiveness is judged by how efficiently and clearly it conveys that message.

Many approaches to artworks assume that art communicates in a similar way: the artist sends a message (meanings or a theme) via the artwork, to the receiver (i.e., the reader, viewer, or listener). The implication here is that the artwork, too, should be judged by how well

---

[2] B. M. Eykhenbaum, "Concerning the Question of the Formalists," in *The Futurists, the Formalists and the Marxist Critique*, trans. and ed. Chris Pike (London: Ink Links, 1979), pp. 51–52.

it conveys its meanings. Moreover, the artwork should usually serve a directly practical purpose in our lives, since communication is a practical activity. As a result, many critical traditions have treated artworks as valuable only if they convey significant themes or philosophical ideas. "Merely entertaining" works are not as valuable, since they are seen as performing no useful service for us. From this basic assumption has come the traditional distinction between "high" and "low" art.

One way of avoiding a communications model of art traditionally has been the adoption of "art for art's sake" position. Art is assumed not to communicate ideas, but to exist for the pleasure we experience in our reaction to it. Beauty, intensity of emotion, and similar qualities would be the criteria for judging works. Again, a certain elitist distinction between high and low art would tend to inform this position, since the aesthetic experience becomes the province of aesthetes, with superior taste, who can appreciate the attractions of well-made works, while the average person can only cope with the crudities of popular art.

Though it is frequently assumed that the Russian Formalists advocated an art-for-art's-sake position, this was not at all the case. Rather, they found an alternative to a communications model of art—and avoided a high/low art split as well—by distinguishing between practical, everyday perception and specifically aesthetic, non-practical perception. For neoformalists, then, art is a realm separate from all other types of cultural artifacts because it presents a unique set of perceptual requirements. Art is set apart from the everyday world, in which we use our perception for practical ends. We perceive the world so as to filter from it those elements that are relevant to our immediate actions. Standing at a street corner, for example, we may ignore a myriad of sights, sounds, and smells, focusing upon a small traffic signal for the moment when it turns green, indicating that we may proceed toward our actual goal, an appointment a few blocks beyond. For such purposes, our mental processes must be focused down, factoring out other stimuli. If we noticed every perceptual item within our ken, we would have no time to make decisions concerning our most pressing needs, like not stepping out in front of a bus. Our brains have become well adapted to concentrating on only those aspects of our environment that affect us practically; other items are kept peripheral.

Films and other artworks, on the contrary, plunge us into a nonpractical, playful type of interaction. They renew our perceptions and other mental processes because they hold no immediate practical implications for us. If we see the hero or heroine in danger on screen, we do not leap forward ready to act as rescuer. Rather, we enter the film-watching process as an experience completely separate from our everyday existence. This is not to say that films have no effect on us. As with all artworks, they are of vital importance in our lives. The nature of practical perception means that our faculties become dulled by the repetitive and habitual activities inherent in much of daily life. Thus art, by renewing our perceptions and thoughts, may be said to act as a sort of mental exercise, parallel to the way sports is an exercise for the body. Indeed, individuals' use of artworks is often comparable to their use of non-exercise games—chess, for example—and to the aesthetic contemplation of nature for its own sake. Art fits into the class of things that people do for recreation—to "re-create" a sense of freshness or play eroded by habitual tasks and the strains of practical existence. Often the renewed or expanded perceptions we gain from artworks can carry over to and affect our perception of everyday objects and events and ideas. As with physical exercise, the experience of artworks can, over a period of time, have considerable impact on our lives in general. And because playfully entertaining films can engage our perceptions as complexly as can films dealing with serious, difficult themes, neoformalism does not distinguish between "high" and "low" art in films.

Neoformalism's assumption of an aesthetic realm distinct from (though dependent upon) a nonaesthetic realm goes against a major trend in contemporary film theory. Both Marxist and psychoanalytic film theory depend on large-scale explanations of how people and society work. These approaches are not concerned with the specificity of the aesthetic realm. Yet the Russian Formalists were "specifiers," as Eikhenbaum put it. They singled out the aesthetic realm as their object of interest, realizing full well that it was a limited—though important—one. They started from the specificity of art and then moved toward a general theory of mind and society that was consistent with their basic assumptions and helpful in explaining the work and how people reacted to it in real, historical contexts. Marxism and psychoanalysis work from the top down, arriving at the artwork with a huge body of major assumptions already made and proponents of such theories must in effect find an ontology and aesthetic of art to fit.

This is not to say that neoformalism takes art to be a permanent, fixed realm. It is culturally determined and relative, but it is distinctive. All cultures seem to have had art, and they all recognize the aesthetic as a realm apart. Neoformalism is a modest approach, seeking only to explain that realm and its relation to the world. It does not seek to explain the world as a whole, with art as a corner of that world.

This difference in aims, more than anything else, makes it difficult to reconcile neoformalism with these other current approaches.

Before neoformalism is condemned as conservative, however, it should be noted that its view of the purpose of art avoids the traditional concept of aesthetic contemplation as passive. The spectator's relationship to the artwork becomes active. Nelson Goodman has characterized the aesthetic attitude: "restless, searching, testing—[it] is less attitude than action: creation and re-creation."[3] The viewer actively seeks cues in the work and responds to them with viewing skills acquired through experience of other artworks and of everyday life. The spectator is involved on the levels of perception, emotion, and cognition, all of which are inextricably bound up together. As Goodman puts it, "In aesthetic experience *the emotions function cognitively*. The work of art is comprehended through the feelings as well as through the senses."[4] Thus the neoformalist critic does not treat aesthetic contemplation as involving an emotional response that no type of object other than artworks can elicit. Rather, artworks engage us at every level and change our ways of perceiving, feeling, and reasoning. (I shall usually speak of "perception," a simplified formula in which I assume that emotion and cognition are also functioning.)

Artworks achieve their renewing effects on our mental processes through an aesthetic play the Russian Formalists termed *defamiliarization*. Our nonpractical perception allows us to see everything in the artwork differently from the way we would see it in reality, because it seems strange in its new context. Victor Shklovsky's famous passage on defamiliarization probably provides the best definition of the term:

If we start to examine the general laws of perception, we see that as perception becomes habitual, it becomes automatic. . . . Such habituation explains the principles by which, in ordinary speech, we leave phrases unfinished and words half expressed. . . . The object, perceived in the manner of prose perception, fades and does not leave even a first impression; ultimately even the essence of what it was is forgotten. . . . Habitualization devours work, clothes, furniture, one's wife, and the fear of war. . . . And Art exists that one may recover the sensation of life; it exists to make one feel things, to make the stone *stony*. The purpose of art is to impart the sensation of things as they are perceived, and not as they are known. The technique of art is to make objects "unfamiliar," to make forms difficult, to increase the difficulty and length of perception because the process of perception is an aesthetic end in itself and must be prolonged.[5]

[3] Nelson Goodman, *Languages of Art* (Indianapolis: Bobbs-Merrill, 1968), p. 242.
[4] Ibid., p. 248.
[5] Victor Shklovsky, "Art as Technique," in *Russian Formalist Criticism: Four Essays*,

Art defamiliarizes our habitual perceptions of the everyday world, of ideology ("the fear of war"), of other artworks, and so on by taking material from these sources and transforming them. The transformation takes place through their placement in a new context and their participation in unaccustomed formal patterns. But if a series of artworks uses the same means over and over, the defamiliarizing capability of those means diminishes; the strangeness ebbs away over time. By that point, the defamiliarized has become familiar, and the artistic approach is largely automatized. The frequent changes that artists introduce into their new works over time reflect attempts to avoid automatization, and to seek new means to defamiliarize those works' formal element. Defamiliarization, then, is the general neoformalist term for the basic purpose of art in our lives. The purpose itself remains consistent over history, but the constant need to avoid automatization also explains why artworks change in relation to their historical contexts and why defamiliarization can be achieved in an infinite number of ways.

Defamiliarization must be present for an object to function for the spectator as art; yet it can be present to vastly varying degrees. Automatization may nearly wipe out the defamiliarizing capacities of ordinary, unoriginal artworks, such as B westerns. Such ordinary works tend not to defamiliarize the conventions of their genre of classical Hollywood filmmaking. Yet even an unoriginal genre film is, in its subject matter, minimally different from other, similar films. Thus it is slightly defamiliarizing in its use of nature and history. Indeed, we can assume that all art at least defamiliarizes ordinary reality. Even in a conventional work, the events are ordered and purposeful in a way that differs from reality. The works that we single out as most original and that are taken to be the most valuable tend to be those that either defamiliarize reality more strongly or defamiliarize the conventions established by previous art works—or a combination of the two. Yet if we single out an ordinary film and submit it to the same scrutiny that we afford more original works, its automatized elements can shed their familiarity and become intriguing—as we shall see when we examine such a film in the next chapter. Defamiliarization is thus an element in all artworks, but its means and degree will vary considerably, and the defamiliarizing powers of a single work will change over history.

These assumptions about defamiliarization and automatization allow neoformalism to eliminate a common feature of most aesthetic theo-

---

trans. and ed. Lee T. Lemon and Marion J. Reis (Lincoln: University of Nebraska Press, 1965), pp. 11–12.

11

ries: the form-content split. Meaning is not the end result of an art-work, but one of its formal components. The artist builds a work out of, among other things, meanings. Meaning here is taken to be the work's system of cues for denotations and connotations. (Some of those cues will be existing meanings that the work uses as its basic material; clichés and stereotypes are obvious examples of preexistent meanings brought in by the artwork, though these may serve a variety of functions within the work.) We can distinguish among four basic levels of meaning. Denotation can involve *referential* meaning, in which the spectator simply recognizes the identity of those aspects of the real world that the work includes. For example, we understand that *Ivan the Terrible*'s hero represents an actual tsar who lived in Russia in the sixteenth century, and that the plot of *The Wizard of Oz* involves a lengthy dream. Beyond this, films often state more abstract ideas out-right, and this type of meaning we may designate as *explicit*. Because the General in *The Rules of the Game* keeps lamenting that upper-class values are becoming rare, we may assume that the film explicitly sets forth the notion, as one pattern in its formal system, that that class is in decline. Since these types of meaning are laid out in the film, we comprehend them or not, according to our prior experience of art-works and the world.

Connotative meanings move us to a level where we must interpret to understand. Connotations may be *implicit* meanings cued by the work. We tend to look for referential and explicit meanings first, and, when we cannot account for a meaning in this straightforward way, we then move to the level of interpretation. At the end of *Eclipse*, for example, we are unlikely to assume that Antonioni shows us seven minutes of empty streets simply to refer to the streets—the lengthy time span and privileged placement at the end of the film work against such an assumption. Similarly, the explicit meaning—that neither Vit-toria nor Piero has shown up for their rendezvous—seems inadequate to explain the sequence thoroughly. The ending of *Eclipse* encourages us to think back over the couple's relationship and environment, and to come to additional conclusions about them—most likely something about the sterility of their lives and of modern society. We also use interpretation to create meanings that go beyond the level of the in-dividual work, and that help define its relation to the world. When we speak of a film's non-explicit ideology, or of the film as a reflection of social tendencies, or of the film as suggestive of the mental states of large groups of people, then we are interpreting its *symptomatic* meanings. Siegfried Kracauer's discussion of German silent films as

12

indicative of the population's collective desire to surrender to the authority of the Nazi regime would be a symptomatic interpretation.[6]

All of these types of meaning—referential, explicit, implicit, and symptomatic—can contribute to the defamiliarizing effect of a film. On the one hand, familiar meanings may themselves be defamiliarized by striking treatments. Indeed, most meanings that are used in films will of necessity be existing ones. Truly new ideas rarely appear in philosophy or economics or the natural sciences, and we can hardly expect great artists to be great and original thinkers as well. (Of course, some critics do expect the artist to be a sort of philosopher, with a vision of the world; this assumption underpins auteurist criticism in particular. The Russian Formalists, however, viewed the makers of art as skilled craftspeople working at a particularly complex craft.) Rather, artists usually deal with existing ideas and make them seem new through defamiliarization. The ideas in Ozu's *Tokyo Story* boil down to one explicitly stated theme: "Be kind to your parents while they are alive." This idea is hardly earthshaking in its originality, yet few people would deny that this film's treatment of it is extremely affecting.

Meanings do not exist in artworks only to be defamiliarized. They can help in defamiliarizing other elements. Meanings can play the part of justifying the inclusion of stylistic elements which themselves will be the main focus of interest. The rather simple, almost clichéd notions in Tati's films about how modern society affects people serve in part as a pretext for unifying a string of highly original, perceptually challenging, comic bits.

Because neoformalism does not view art as communication, interpretation becomes one tool among many for the neoformalist critic. Each analysis uses a method adapted to the film and the issues at hand, and interpretation will not always be used in the same way. It may be crucial or incidental, according to whether the work concentrates on implicit or explicit meanings. Depending on the analyst's purpose, interpretation may emphasize meanings within the work or the work's relation to society.

In this way neoformalism differs considerably from other critical approaches, most of which stress interpretation as the analyst's central—often only—activity. Interpretive methods usually assume that how one interprets meanings remains constant from film to film. Such a method may have to be quite general, since it will need to force all films into a similar pattern. Tzvetan Todorov has differentiated be-

[6] Siegfried Kracauer, *From Caligari to Hitler* (Princeton: Princeton University Press, 1947).

tween two broad types of interpretive strategies in common use: "operational," which places constraints on the process of interpretation, and "finalist," which places constraints on the results of the interpretive process. As examples of the latter, he cites Marxism and Freudianism:

> In both the former and the latter, the point of arrival is known beforehand, and cannot be modified: it is the principles derived from the work of Marx or of Freud (it is significant that these types of criticism bear the names of their inspirers; it is impossible to modify the text produced without violating the doctrine, and hence without abandoning it).[7]

Referring specifically to Freudian interpretation, Todorov declares:

> If psychoanalysis is really a specific strategy (as I believe), it can only be such, on the contrary, through an a priori codification of the results to be obtained. Psychoanalytical interpretation can only be defined as an interpretation that discovers in the objects analyzed a content in harmony with psychoanalytical doctrine; . . . it is foreknowledge of the meaning to be discovered that guides the interpretation.

As an instance of this guidance, Todorov cites Freud's declaration that the vast majority of symbols in dreams are sexual in nature.[8]

Such pre-determined patterns have become quite common in film studies. For example, recently some critics have claimed to find a "family romance" (based on Freudian notions of the Oedipus complex) in all classical narrative films. Another interpretive template dictates that the analyst sort out eyeline directions for the various characters, determining through them who has the "look" and therefore is more powerful. Such reductive schemata are tautological, since they assume that any film will fit these patterns, and the patterns are simple enough that any film can be made to fit them. (Or, if a film seems not to fit, the analyst can find its meaning ironic.) Alternatively, many Freudian critics deal with symptomatic meanings, finding in a film symptoms of psychic repression or ideological conflicts. Such a method, while more complex, still ends up dictating a narrow range of meanings ahead of time, which the analyst will necessarily find present in the film. Such systems are impossible to attack or defend, since no conceivable evidence could confirm or deny them.

Another problem with an exclusive concentration on interpretation is that even if the film makes its meanings very explicit indeed, the

[7] Tzvetan Todorov, *Symbolisme et interprétation* (Paris: Editions du Seuil, 1978), pp. 160–161.

[8] Tzvetan Todorov, *Theories of the Symbol*, trans. Catherine Porter (Ithaca: Cornell University Press, 1982), pp. 253–254.

critic has to deal with them as if they were implicit or symptomatic—otherwise, what would he or she have to talk about?

Neoformalism assumes that meaning differs from film to film because it, like any other aspect of the film, is a device. The word *device* indicates any single element or structure that plays a role in the artwork—a camera movement, a frame story, a repeated word, a costume, a theme, and so on. For the neoformalist, all devices of the medium and of formal organization are equal in their potential for defamiliarization and for being used to build up a filmic system. As Eikhenbaum pointed out, the older aesthetic tradition treated the elements of the work as the "expression" of the author; the Russian Formalists looked upon these elements as artistic devices.[9] The structure of devices is seen as organized not solely in order to express meaning, but to create defamiliarization. We can analyze devices using the concepts of function and motivation.

Yuri Tynjanov defined *function* as "the interrelationship of each element with every other in a literary work and with the whole literary system."[10] It is the purpose served by the presence of any given device. Function is crucial to understanding the unique qualities of a given artwork, for, while many works may use the same device, that device's function may be different in each work. It is risky to assume that a given device has a fixed function from film to film. For example, to use two of the clichés of film studies, bar-like shadows do not always symbolize that a character is "imprisoned," and verticals in a composition do not automatically suggest that characters on either side are isolated from each other. Any given device serves different functions according to the context of the work, and one of the analyst's main jobs is to find the device's functions in this or that context. Functions are also important in relating the work to history. Devices themselves become automatized quite easily, and the artist may replace them with new devices that are more defamiliarizing. But functions tend to remain more stable, since they are renewed by a change of device, and they persist longer historically than do individual devices. We may call different devices that serve the same function *functional equivalents*. As Eikhenbaum pointed out, the function of the device in context is usually more important for the analyst than is the device as such.[11]

[9] Boris Eikhenbaum, "Sur la théorie de la prose," in *Théorie de la littérature*, trans. and ed. Tzvetan Todorov (Paris: Editions du Seuil, 1969), p. 228.

[10] Yuri Tynjanov, "On Literary Evolution," trans. C. A. Luplow, in *Readings in Russian Poetics*, ed. Ladislav Matejka and Krystyna Pomorska (Cambridge, Mass.: MIT Press, 1971), p. 68.

[11] Boris M. Èjxenbaum, "The Theory of the Formal Method," trans. I. R. Titunik, in *Readings in Russian Poetics*, p. 29.

Devices perform functions in artworks, but the work must also provide some reason for including the device to begin with. The reason the work suggests for the presence of any given device is its *motivation*. Motivation is, in effect, a cue given by the work that prompts us to decide what could justify the inclusion of the device; motivation, then, operates as an interaction between the work's structures and the spectator's activity. There are four basic types of motivation: compositional, realistic, transtextual, and artistic.[12]

Briefly, *compositional motivation* justifies the inclusion of any device that is necessary for the construction of narrative causality, space, or time. Most frequently, compositional motivation involves the "planting" of information early on which we will need to know later. For example, in P. G. Wodehouse's *The Girl in Blue*, a lazy secretary fails to pass on a message to her boss that a friend has placed his valuable Gainsborough portrait in a drawer; as a result, the latter assumes that the painting has been stolen. The novel's entire series of comic misunderstandings follows from the motivation provided by one event—the secretary's blunder. As a result, we anticipate that the mix-up will be resolved by the finding of the portrait in the drawer. Often compositional motivation does not promote plausibility, but we are willing to overlook this for the sake of having the story continue. As Shklovsky put it, "To the question of Tolstoi: 'Why does Lear not recognise Kent and Kent—Edgar' one may answer: because this is necessary for the creation of the drama, and the unreality disturbed Shakespeare no more than the question 'Why cannot a knight move straight?' disturbs a chess player."[13] Indeed, compositional motivations act to create a kind of internal set of rules for the individual artwork.

Plausibility falls within the realm of *realistic motivation*, which is a type of cue in the work leading us to appeal to notions from the real world to justify the presence of a device. For example, when Phineas Fogg makes his bet to travel around the world in eighty days at the beginning of Verne's novel, we realize that he is wealthy, and hence able to drop everything in order to travel; moreover, he can pay for all

[12] The Russian Formalists differentiated only three, and transtextual is not included in Boris Tomashevsky's seminal exploration of motivation in his "Thematics," in *Russian Formalist Criticism: Four Essays*, pp. 78–87. David Bordwell borrowed the term *transtextual* from Gerard Genette to account for how artworks appeal directly to the conventions established by other artworks—a type of appeal not explicitly covered in the original three categories. See Bordwell's *Narration in the Fiction Film* (Madison: University of Wisconsin Press, 1985), p. 36.

[13] Viktor Shklovsky, "On the Connection Between Devices of *Syuzhet* Construction and General Stylistic Devices," trans. Jane Knox, in *Russian Formalism*, ed. Stephen Bann and John E. Bowlt (New York: Harper and Row, 1973), p. 65.

the different vehicles he employs along the way. (A similar realistic motivation of wealth underpins Dorothy L. Sayers' Lord Peter Wimsey novels and many screwball-comedy films of the 1930s.) Our ideas about reality are not direct, natural knowledge of the world, but are culturally determined in various ways. Thus realistic motivation can appeal to two broad areas of our knowledge: on the one hand, our knowledge of everyday life gained by direct interaction with nature and society; on the other, our awareness of prevailing aesthetic canons of realism in a given period of an art form's stylistic change. We shall see both types of realistic motivation at work in *Bicycle Thieves* (Chapter 7) and in *The Rules of the Game* (Chapter 8).

Since realistic motivation is an appeal to ideas about reality, rather than an imitation of reality as such, its means can be extremely varied, even within a single work. For most of Mozart's *Le Nozze di Figaro*, the fact that the characters sing instead of speak is motivated transtextually by genre: people do sing in operas, even though they are not always represented as "singing" within the narrative's world. Yet occasionally realistic motivation does "justify" their singing. Cherubino's first aria, "Non so piu cosa son, cosa faccio," functions simply as a way for the boy to tell Susanna about his feelings. Later, however, Susanna accompanies on a guitar Cherubino's song to the Countess, "Voi che sapete che cosa e amor," and the two women praise his singing voice. The introduction of an "actual" song amid the rest of the singing in an opera is common enough (e.g., Pasquale's comic serenade "Ecco spiano" in Haydn's *Orlando Paladrino*). But a completely different type of realistic motivation appears in the duet "Canzonetta sull'aria," in which the Countess dictates to Susanna a letter in the form of a poem. Ordinarily in a duet, the singers repeat and pass back and forth the same lines, or parts of lines, and that practice is motivated by the genre of opera. Here that practice is realistically motivated as Susanna's repetition of the last word or phrase of the Countess's previous line of dictation, to check if she has written it correctly. Thus:

> Countess: "A gentle zephyr . . ."
> Susanna: ". . . zephyr . . ."
> Countess: ". . . will sigh tonight . . ."
> Susanna: ". . . will sigh tonight . . ."
> Countess: ". . . 'neath the pines in the copse . . ."
> Susanna: " 'Neath the pines?"
> Countess: ". . . 'neath the pines in the copse . . ."
> Susanna (writing): ". . . 'neath the pines in the
>   copse . . ."

17

Moreover, in the first go-through, there is a musical passage between each line as Susanna writes, and at the "pines" line she gets behind and has to ask about the phrasing, thus motivating further repetition. In the second part of the duet, the two women read over the letter, and now they sing in counterpoint, with no pauses for writing—as if checking or revising the letter. (At the end of the whole thing Susanna declares, "The letter is ready.") As these examples from *Le Nozze di Figaro* indicate, a mixture of types of motivation can be defamiliarizing. Indeed, "inconsistent" motivation of this type (the duet does not *need* to be realistically motivated in the way it is) is the privilege of art, and audiences are usually prepared to accept it.

Transtextual motivation, the third of our four types, involves any appeal to conventions of other artworks, and hence it can be as varied as the historical circumstances allow. In effect, the work introduces a device that is not motivated adequately within its own terms, but that depends on our recognition of the device from past experience. In film, types of transtextual motivation most commonly depend on our knowledge of usage within the same genre, our knowledge of the star, or our knowledge of similar conventions in other art forms. For example, the lengthy buildup to the shoot-out in Sergio Leone's *The Good, the Bad, and the Ugly* is certainly not realistic, nor is it necessary for the narrative (a quick exchange of gunfire would settle the issue at hand in seconds). But from having watched countless westerns, we realize that the shoot-out has become a ritual of the genre, and Leone treats it as such. Similarly, a familiar star carries many associations which the film can exploit. When Chance (played by John Wayne) first appears in *Rio Bravo*, we need not be told that he is the protagonist, and he can get down to business with no exposition to set him up; his behavior is also consistent with the way we know John Wayne's characters ordinarily behave. And an example of a convention in film coming from another art form is the "cliffhanger" ending, which was adopted into film serials in the 1910s, having been established through the nineteenth-century publishing practice of issuing novels in installments.

Our expectations about transtextual conventions are so pervasive that we probably accept them fairly automatically in many cases; yet it is also easy for the artwork to play with our assumptions by violating genre conventions, casting actors against type, and so on. Although the Russian Formalists did not designate a separate type of motivation of this transtextual sort, they did tacitly recognize its existence. Eikhenbaum mentions both the familiar nature of this motivation and its violation in his discussion of Lermontov's use of the Republic of Georgia as a lyrical element in a poem.

Georgia appears as something intrinsically poetic, as an exotic element which does not require special motivation. After innumerable Caucasian poems and tales had made the Caucasus a fixed literary decoration (which Tolstoy later destroyed with such irony), there was no need to motivate the choice of Georgia.[14]

Transtextual motivation, then, is a special type which preexists the artwork, and upon which the artist may draw in a straightforward or playful way. (A work that depends heavily on the violation of transtextual motivations of a specific type will most likely be perceived as parodic.)

Artistic motivation is the most difficult type to define. In one sense, every device in an artwork has an artistic motivation, since it functions in part to contribute to the creation of the work's abstract, overall shape—its form. Yet many, probably most, devices have an additional, more prominent compositional, realistic, or transtextual motivation, and in these cases artistic motivation is not particularly noticeable—though we can deliberately shift our attention to the aesthetic qualities of the work's texture even if it is densely motivated. Yet in another sense, artistic motivation is present in a really noticeable and significant way only when the other three types of motivation are withheld. Its pervasive quality sets artistic motivation apart. As Meir Sternberg puts it, "Behind every quasi-mimetic motivation there is an aesthetic motivation . . . though not vice-versa."[15] That is, artistic motivation can exist by itself, without the other types, but they never can exist independently from it. Some films foreground artistic motivation at intervals by withholding the other three types, and in such cases we sense the overall motivation as "thin" or inadequate and strive to discover abstract relations among devices.

Some aesthetic modes—for example, non-programmatic music, decorative and abstract painting, abstract films—are almost completely organized around artistic motivation, and their audiences will be aware of that fact. Yet even in a narrative film, I would argue, artistic motivation can be systematically foregrounded. When this happens, and artistic patterns compete for our attention with the narrative functions of devices, the result is parametric form. In such films, cer-

---

[14] Boris Eikhenbaum, *Lermontov*, trans. Ray Parrott and Henry Weber (Ann Arbor: Ardis, 1981), p. 101.
[15] Meir Sternberg, *Expositional Modes & Temporal Ordering in Fiction* (Baltimore: The John Hopkins University Press, 1978), pp. 251–252.

tain devices, such as colors, camera movements, sonic motifs, will be repeated and varied across the entire work's form; these devices become parameters. They may contribute to the narrative's meaning— for example, by creating parallelisms or contrasts—but their abstract functions exceed their contribution to meaning and draw our attention more. Because artistic motivation and parametric form are difficult concepts, and because they hold such potential for defamiliarizing automatized narrative and genre conventions, I shall spend a considerable portion of this book, the last four chapters, on this topic.

A special, "strong" case of artistic motivation comes with the *baring of the device*. Here artistic motivation foregrounds the formal function of a given device or structure in the work. In a classical or realist work that draws heavily upon the other three types of motivation, the device will be bared only occasionally. (We shall see, for example, how *Bicycle Thieves* foregrounds its own realism by referring ironically at intervals to the glamor of classical entertainment films.) But some artworks make device-baring a central structure. Shklovsky's analysis of Sterne's *Tristram Shandy* finds that the novel flaunts its own delaying tactics as arbitrary and playful, to the point at which real progression of the narrative action becomes a side issue.[16] A highly original artwork will tend to bare the device a good deal to help cue spectators as to how to adjust their viewing skills to cope with the new and difficult devices in use. The concept of baring the device should become clearer in the course of this book, since we shall encounter it often.

Thus formal devices serve a variety of functions, and their presence can be motivated in one or more of the four possible ways. Devices can serve the narrative, can appeal to similar devices familiar from other artworks, can imply verisimilitude, and can defamiliarize the structures of the artwork itself. Meaning, as a device, may also serve any of these functions. Some artworks foreground meanings and invite us to interpret them. The works of Ingmar Bergman, especially those of the 1960s and 1970s, contain obscure imagery that cannot be understood without considerable interpretation. In a different way, Jean-Luc Godard's films elicit interpretation as a major viewing strategy, as we shall see with *Sauve qui peut (la vie)*, in which even the film's basic referential level is made obscure so as to guide us toward implicit meanings. Yet, as I have suggested, meaning in a film may be very simple and obvious; it may serve as a motivating device around which defamiliarizing systems of style are structured, as we shall see in such

[16] Victor Shklovsky, "Sterne's *Tristram Shandy*: Stylistic Commentary," in *Russian Formalist Criticism: Four Essays*, pp. 25–57.

films as *Play Time* and *Late Spring*. The analyst, in formulating an appropriate method, must decide what type and degree of interpretation is appropriate to the overall analysis. But analysis of function and motivation will always remain the analyst's central goal, and it will subsume interpretation.

THE FILM IN HISTORY

Given that film sets up a renewing playfulness for the spectator through defamiliarization, how can the analyst determine what method is appropriate to a specific work? Neoformalism resolves this question in party by insisting that the film can never be taken as an abstract object outside the context of history. Every viewing occurs in a specific situation, and the spectator cannot engage with the film except by using viewing skills learned in encounters with other artworks and in everyday experience. Neoformalism therefore grounds analysis of individual films in historical context based upon a concept of norms and deviations. Our most frequent and typical experiences form our perceptual norms, and idiosyncratic, defamiliarizing experiences stand out in contrast.

Neoformalism calls norms of prior experience *backgrounds*, since we see individual films within the larger context of such prior experience. There are three basic types of background. First, there is the everyday world. Without a knowledge of it, we could not recognize referential meaning, and it would be impossible to comprehend stories, character behavior, and other basic devices of films; moreover, we need everyday knowledge to comprehend how films create symptomatic meanings in relation to society. A second type of background involves other artworks. From a very young age we see and hear a great many artworks and come to understand their conventions. We are not born understanding how to follow plots, how to grasp filmic space from shot to shot, how to notice the return of a musical theme in a symphony, and so on. Third, we recognize how films are used for practical purposes (advertising, reportage, rhetorical persuasion, and so on), and we see the artistic use of cinema as something apart from such usage. Thus when we watch an aesthetic film, we perceive it as deviating from reality, from other artworks, and from practical usage in certain distinct ways. The film's adherence to and departure from its background norms are the subjects of the analyst's work, and the historical context provided by the backgrounds gives the analyst cues for constructing an appropriate method. Those methods that privilege interpretation, on the other hand, often have no way to treat differently films of different periods and sources; all will be forced into the same pattern of meaning. For neoformalism the film's functions and motivations can only be understood historically.

This is not to imply that neoformalism simply reconstructs the viewing circumstances of the film's original audiences. The work does not exist only at the moment of its creation and first screenings. Many artworks continue to exist and are seen in different circumstances. Indeed, it would be impossible to reconstruct fully the original viewing circumstances of most films. We shall probably never know precisely who saw pre-1909 films and under what circumstances. We can still find primitive films interesting and enjoyable, but we can never be sure we understand them in at all the same way as their first audiences did. We no longer have access to the original backgrounds, and critics and historians almost invariably must analyze these early films against the background of later, classical filmmaking. (I am not suggesting that we should avoid historical research into the original contexts of films, but we should realize that our perspective inevitably will be colored by more recent developments.) To take another example, many Japanese films made in the 1930s and early 1940s contain implicit or explicit militarist propaganda. Western audiences looking at these films today do not accept this ideology in the way original audiences would have in Japan; indeed, modern Japanese viewers, particularly those living in the United States, seem to find such films difficult to enjoy thoroughly. Yet, because they present striking similarities to and differences from the more familiar Western films of the same era, and because many are skillfully made, with interesting narratives, these films still intrigue audiences for whom the original backgrounds are irrecoverable.

Even a relatively recent example demonstrates how quickly changing backgrounds can alter our perception of a film. When *Bonnie and Clyde* was released in 1967, its astonishing amount of violence and particularly its advertising campaign ("They're young. They're in love. They kill people") aroused a great deal of controversy. In the intervening two decades, the use of violence in films has become so commonplace that *Bonnie and Clyde* and its ads seem tame. A new background has automatized the film's devices to a considerable extent. Audiences will probably never be able to watch it with the sense of shock felt by 1967 viewers.

As these examples suggest, referential and symptomatic meanings tend to be the most difficult types for audiences to recover outside the original context. Explicit and implicit meanings, on the other hand, are to a greater extent created by the work's internal structures and thus they will be more apparent to later audiences. In judging what sorts of reality backgrounds it may be useful to discuss, we should determine what types of meanings the film at hand emphasizes. To enable ourselves to do this, we should avoid using a method that predetermines the meanings to be found, but should instead pay attention to those aspects of the film that may be difficult to interpret. Such difficulties are, in effect, cues within the work directing us to move beyond obvious levels of meaning. In the next section of this chapter, we shall see how historical norms help the critic determine what a film's meanings might consist of in a specific context.

Some films depend extensively on a knowledge of historical, social backgrounds, while others create more self-contained systems that encourage us to view them primarily against other artworks. *Lancelot du Lac* provides an example of a film that downplays the importance of realistic backgrounds. The burden of proof would fall to the critic who claimed that an extensive familiarity with French society of the early 1970s would help us understand the film better (the way it would with a Godard film of the same period). *Lancelot's* meanings are largely explicit and implicit. On the other hand, by comparing *Lancelot* with other films representing the same distinctive modernist system of filmmaking—parametric form—we can perhaps better grasp the film's peculiar formal strategies.

In choosing what type of background to use, the neoformalist critic also makes assumptions about whether his or her reader will be familiar with various backgrounds relevant to the film. In this book, for example, I decided that to analyze *Late Spring* for a largely Western readership, it would be helpful if I examined the ideology of family and marriage practices in postwar Japan; looking at Ozu's films against an ethnocentric background of recent Western ideology distorts them, as we shall see in Chapter 12. Stylistically, however, *Late Spring* plays upon deviations from the norms of classical Western filmmaking; thus the latter provides a relevant background as well. Other films utilize much more familiar backgrounds of reality, as in *Play Time*. It is hardly necessary to harp on that film's satirization of modern life; rather, I shall be examining its perceptual challenges in terms of traditional comic gag structures. It may also be useful to place some films against a variety of backgrounds. Audience perceptions of *The Rules of the Game* have changed radically over the decades since it was made— changes we can explain by comparing different backgrounds with each other. Altered reactions to *Rules* will help demonstrate, in Chapter 8, that the perception of realism as a style is a historically based reaction.

As is indicated by my frequent references to the classical cinema,

23

both here and in the individual analyses, I consider it one of the most pervasive and helpful backgrounds against which we can examine many films. Historically, the type of filmmaking associated with Hollywood from the mid-1910s to the present has been widely seen by audiences and widely imitated by other filmmaking nations all over the world.[17] As a result, vast numbers of viewers have developed their most normative viewing skills by watching classical films. Moreover, many filmmakers who have worked in original ways have set up formal systems that play off and challenge those normative skills. Chapter 2 will examine an ordinary Hollywood film, and I will frequently make reference to such films as backgrounds for the less classical films discussed in other chapters.[18]

The notion of backgrounds does not mean that neoformalism is doomed to complete relativism. For one thing, appropriate backgrounds are not infinite in number. Because neoformalist analysis depends upon an understanding of historical context, some backgrounds will clearly be more relevant than others. For example, there has been a trend in the past decade to look at primitive (pre-1909) films against the background of modern experimental cinema. As a result, analysts sometimes ascribe some sort of radical form and ideology to these early films. Yet such a proceeding is arbitrary, since it ignores the differences in norms between the two periods. Early filmmakers were experimenting with an new medium in which norms did not exist, except as borrowed from the established arts; over the first two decades, specifically cinematic norms were themselves established. But by the time modern experimental filmmakers began working, the norms had been in existence for a long time, and the filmmakers were reacting specifically against them. Hence to equate these two types of film simply remains an intriguing game, not an historically valid method of comparison. The notion of backgrounds does not legitimate any whim of the analyst. The current fashion (resulting from an ahistorical approach to analysis) of an "infinite play of readings" cannot be justified by using a vast group of different backgrounds for the same

---

[17] I have examined how the American cinema's hegemony was achieved during World War I and how it was perpetuated in the postwar era in my *Exporting Entertainment: America in the World Film Market 1907–1934* (London: British Film Institute, 1985).

[18] There is no space here to deal with the classical cinema thoroughly. For a basic account of classical film style, see David Bordwell and Kristin Thompson, *Film Art: An Introduction* 2d ed. (New York: Alfred A. Knopf, 1985); for more theoretical and historical discussions, see David Bordwell, Janet Staiger, and Kristin Thompson, *The Classical Hollywood Cinema: Film Style and Mode of Production to 1960* (New York: Columbia University Press, 1985), and David Bordwell, *Narration in the Fiction Film*, chap. 9.

film. Since there are a finite number of reading conventions at any given moment, we may assume that they can produce a variety of "readings," but not an infinite number of them.

Precisely because backgrounds give neoformalist analysis a historical basis, they make possible an examination of how defamiliarization occurs. Defamiliarization depends on historical context; devices that may be new and defamiliarizing will decline in effectiveness with repetition. Our *Bonnie and Clyde* example has already suggested how this happens. Highly original artworks tend to foster imitation, and devices are introduced, used, and dropped. As the original background becomes more remote, an older artwork may once again seem unfamiliar to a new generation of audiences. We constantly see examples of artworks going through cycles of popularity, being revived as norms and perceptions change. Nineteenth-century American realist painting, for example, was long considered of little interest; yet recently it has become more "respectable" through major exhibitions and publications. Film serials provide an interesting example of a form that has gone through cycles. In the teens, serials were taken quite seriously; they were the equivalent of "A" pictures. During the 1920s and 1930s they declined in status and became cheap "B" products. Finally, in the 1950s, television took over the function of providing continuing narratives, and serial production ended. But in the later 1970s and the 1980s, a number of filmmakers who grew up watching "B" serials have revived some of their conventions, and we see very popular and prestigious classical films—*Raiders of the Lost Ark*, the *Star Wars* and *Star Trek* series, and so on—once again drawing upon the tradition. Similarly, French intellectuals of the 1920s held such popular filmmakers as Louis Feuillade and Léonce Perret in utter contempt; yet decades later, the works of these two filmmakers have garnered increasing respect. The concepts of defamiliarization, automatization, and changing backgrounds can help account for such cycles in film viewing.

THE SPECTATOR'S ROLE

Because the work exists in constantly changing circumstances, audiences' perceptions of it will differ over time. Hence we cannot assume that the meanings and patterns we notice and interpret are completely there in the work, immutable for all time. Rather, the work's devices constitute a set of cues that can encourage us to perform certain viewing activities; the actual form those activities take, however, inevitably depends on the work's interaction with its and the viewer's historical contexts. In analyzing a film, therefore, the neoformalist critic will not treat its devices as fixed and self-contained structures that exist independent of our perception of them. The film exists physically in its can when we are not watching it, of course, but all those qualities that are of interest to the analyst—its unity; its repetitions and variations; its representation of action, space, and time; its meanings—result from the interaction between the work's formal structures and the mental operations we perform in response to them.

As we have seen, perception, emotion, and cognition are central to the neoformalist critic's view of how film's formal qualities function. That view does not treat the spectator as being wholly "in the text," since this would imply a static view; backgrounds changing over time would be incapable of affecting our understanding of films if we as spectators were constructed entirely by the work's internal form. Yet the spectator is not "ideal" either, since that traditional view also implies that the work and the spectator exist in a constant relationship untouched by history. But in accounting for the effects of history on spectators, critics need not go to the opposite extreme of dealing only with the reactions of actual people. (They need not resort to audience surveys, for example, to find out how people watch films, or plunge into complete subjectivity, taking their own reactions as the only accessible ones.) The notion of norms and deviations allows critics to make assumptions about how viewers would be likely to understand a given device.

In the neoformalist approach, viewers are not passive "subjects," as current Marxist and psychoanalytic approaches would have it. Rather, viewers are largely active, contributing substantially to the final effect of the work. They go through a series of activities, some physiological, some preconscious, some conscious, and some presumably unconscious. *Physiological* processes involve those automatic responses that viewers do not control, such as perceiving movement across a succession of static film images, differentiating colors, or hearing a series of sound waves as sounds. Such perceptions are automatic and mandatory; we cannot determine by introspection how we are aware of them, nor can we by conscious willing make them otherwise (e.g., we can never see the motion-picture image as a series of still pictures separated by black moments). The medium of film depends upon these automatic abilities of the human brain and senses, but in many cases in film criticism, they are so self-evident as to be of little immediate interest; the critic can assume them as givens and go on to the preconscious and conscious activities. (Some films, and particularly modern experimental genres, play with our physiological responses and make us aware of them; for example, Stan Brakhage's *Mothlight* draws our attention to the flicker effect and the perception of apparent motion.)

Preconscious activities are of more general interest to the analyst, for these involve easy, nearly automatic processing of information in ways that are so familiar that we do not need to think about them. Much object recognition is preconscious, as when we realize that the same person appears in shot A and shot B (as in a match on action) or that in a crane upward it is the camera that moves, not the landscape that suddenly "falls away" (even though the latter may be the perceptual effect on the screen). Such mental processes differ from physiological activities in that they are available to our conscious mind. We can, if we think about it, realize how we went about recognizing continuous action over a cut or the stability of the ground in the crane shot. We can at will think of these stylistic flourishes as abstract patterns. Much of our reaction to stylistic devices may be preconscious in that we learn cutting, camera movement, and other techniques from classical films, and we learn them so well that we usually no longer need to think about them, even after only a few visits to the cinema. (It is instructive, by the way, to watch a film intended for children and listen to young audience members asking their parents questions; they are, in effect, in the process of learning skills that will later become preconscious.) Object recognition and other activities will be preconscious or conscious, depending upon the degree of familiarity involved. Familiar objects will be recognized without conscious effort, while we may have to struggle to cope with the novel devices with which a film may confront us.

Conscious processes—those activities of which we are aware—also play a major role in our viewing of films. Many cognitive skills involved in film viewing are conscious: we struggle to understand a story, to interpret certain meanings, to explain to ourselves why a strange camera movement is present, and so on. For the neoformalist critic, conscious processes are usually the most important ones, since it is here that the artwork can challenge most strongly our habitual ways of perceiving and thinking and can make us aware of our habitual ways of coping with the world. In a sense, for the neoformalist, the aim of original art is to put any or all of our thought processes onto this conscious level.

There is a fourth level of mental processes, the *unconscious*. Much of recent film theory and analysis has been devoted to an application of psychoanalytic methods of various stripes, in an effort to explain film viewing as an activity primarily carried on in the viewer's unconscious. For neoformalists, however, the unconscious level is largely an unnecessary construct. For one thing, the textual cues that psychoanalytic criticism points to—the repetition and variation of motifs, the use of glances, patterns of symmetry in narrative structure—are wholly available to neoformalism as well. The psychoanalytic argument hinges upon the interpretations that can be produced from these cues, but these tend to be of the cookie-cutter variety, whereby every film enacts the castration complex or the rule "he who has the look has the power." Moreover, it can be argued that contemporary psychoanalytic criticism, despite its claim to offer a theory of "spectatorship," is in fact not particularly concerned with the viewer. Most psychoanalytic studies of films simply employ a Freudian or Lacanian model of the text's internal operations (in which the film is taken as analagous to the discourse of the psychoanalytic patient) in order to interpret the film as an isolated object. The viewer becomes a passive receiver of textual structures. Furthermore, psychoanalytic criticism has posited that viewer as existing largely outside history. If the spectator performs no significant conscious activities in viewing, then he or she is not using experience gained in the world and from other artworks. Hence there can be nothing comparable to what I have been calling backgrounds, and historical circumstances cannot affect the viewing. One could posit that perhaps backgrounds affect the unconscious— though how could we ever know this?—but in the practice of film analysis, categories used to characterize the viewer's unconscious have been general and static ones. If the experience of moviegoing perpetually replays for us the mirror phase of entering into the imaginary, or imitates dreaming, or reminds us of the mother's breast in our infancy (all explanations put forth in recent theory), then it presumably does so in the same way for all viewers and in the same way at all viewings throughout the individual spectator's life. We would have to assume, therefore, that all the effects of the film are created by structures within the film itself, and that it exists unchanging, outside history. Certainly many psychoanalytic "readings" treat the film as just such an ahistorical object. (This is not to say that psychoanalytic concepts can never be used by the neoformalist critic as part of a method for analyzing a specific film, as we shall see in examining *Laura* in Chapter 6.)

It is for such reasons that Dana B. Polan is, I believe, in error when he proposes a synthesis of neoformalist poetics and Marxist-psychoanalytic theory. He writes of how "psychoanalysis and materialism . . . have come more and more to realize the necessity for a theory of form and therefore for a dialogue with Formalism."[19] While I appreciate the

[19] Dana B. Polan, "Terminable and Interminable Analysis: Formalism and Film Theory," *Quarterly Review of Film Studies* 8, no. 4 (Fall 1983): 76.

friendly gesture, I take this to be wishful thinking. For a successful blend of approaches to be possible, psychoanalysis would have to provide an epistemology compatible with Formalism's ontology and aesthetic—and it clearly does not. Psychoanalysis is not concerned with perception and everyday cognitive processes in the way that neoformalism must be in order to retain its concern with defamiliarization, backgrounds, and the like. This is not to say that neoformalism is at present a complete theory, since much more reflection and research needs to be done. But the point is that neoformalism offers a reasonable sketch of an ontology, epistemology, and aesthetic for answering the questions it poses, and these are not commensurable with the presuppositions of the Saussurean-Lacanian-Althusserian paradigm.

A merger with other versions of Marxism is more conceivable, since Marxism is basically a socioeconomic theory, not concerned with the aesthetic realm at all. Marxists concerned with analyzing how artworks relate ideologically to society might well use neoformalist analysis as a basic approach to the formal properties of art objects, concentrating on those functions of formal devices that link art to society. But those breeds of Marxism that are tied to a psychoanalytic epistemology would seem not to be compatible with neoformalism.

Neoformalism posits that viewers are active—that they perform operations. Contrary to psychoanalytic criticism, I assume that film viewing is composed mostly of nonconscious, preconscious, and conscious activities. Indeed, we may define the viewer as a hypothetical entity who responds actively to cues within the film on the basis of automatic perceptual processes and on the basis of experience. Since historical contexts make the protocols of these responses inter-subjective, we may analyze films without resorting to subjectivity. David Bordwell has argued that recent Constructivist theories of psychological activity offer the most viable model of spectatorship for an approach derived from Russian Formalism. (Constructivist theories have been the dominant view in cognitive and perceptual psychology since the 1960s.) In such a theory, perceiving and thinking are active, goal-oriented processes. According to Bordwell, "The organism constructs a perceptual judgment on the basis of nonconscious inferences."[20] For example, we recognize that shapes on the flat cinema screen represent three-dimensional space because we can rapidly process depth cues; unless the film plays with our perception by introducing difficult or contradictory cues, we will not consciously have to think about how to grasp the spatial representation. Similarly, we tend automatically to register the passage of represented time, unless the film uses a complex tem-

[20] Bordwell, *Narration in the Fiction Film*, p. 31.

poral layout that skips over, repeats, or otherwise juggles events, in which case we begin a conscious sorting-out process.

We are able to understand such aspects of most films because we have had vast experience in coping with similar situations. Other artworks, everyday life, film theory and criticism—all provide us with countless *schemata*, learned mental patterns against which we check individual devices and situations in films. As we watch a film, we use these schemata to form hypotheses continually—hypotheses about a character's actions, about the space offscreen, about the source of a sound, about every local and large-scale device that we notice. As the film goes on, we find our hypotheses confirmed or disconfirmed; if the latter, we form a new hypothesis, and so on. The concept of hypothesis-forming helps explain the constant activity of the spectator, and the parallel concept of schemata suggests why that activity is based in history: schemata change over time. In effect, what I have called "backgrounds" are large clusters of historical schemata organized by the analyst for the purpose of making statements about viewer responses.

According to Bordwell, "The artwork is made so as to encourage the application of certain schemata, even if these must eventually be discarded in the course of the perceiver's activity."[21] This is why we can say that the work *cues* us in our responses. The analyst's task becomes to point out the cues and on the basis of them to discuss what responses would reasonably result, given a knowledge of backgrounds on the part of the viewer. The neoformalist critic thus analyzes not a set of static formal structures (as an "empty" formalist or "art for art's sake" position might dictate), but rather, a dynamic interaction between those structures and a hypothetical viewer's response to them.

Because we are dealing with aesthetic films, we must remember that the viewer's skills will be employed for non-practical ends:

What is nonconscious in everyday mental life becomes consciously attended to. Our schemata get shaped, stretched, and transgressed; a delay in hypothesis-confirmation can be prolonged for its own sake. And like all psychological activities, aesthetic activity has long-range effects. Art may reinforce, or modify, or even assault our normal perceptual-cognitive repertoire.[22]

If an artwork largely reinforces our existing viewing skills, we are not likely to notice how we employ schemata and form hypotheses. Thus certain films seem simple to watch, and we may assume that we are "naturally" able to view such films. (Even while watching the most familiar films, of course, we go through very complex operations in

21 Ibid., p. 32.
22 Ibid.

30

order to understand structures of causality, time, and space.) Other films, however, challenge our experience more strongly; if we are unable to account for what we see on the screen, we become aware of being puzzled and of having our expectations delayed, or even permanently frustrated.

The films that we value highly for their complexity and originality are exactly those that challenge our expectations and habitual viewing skills. *Last Year at Marienbad* is a famous example of a film that induces us to keep forming different hypotheses concerning its causal, temporal, and spatial contradictions; finally it leads us to the conclusion that there is no satisfactory way of reconciling them (or to a perpetual wrangling among viewers who insist on forcing the film into a familiar pattern: the heroine is insane, or the narrator is insane, or they are both ghosts, and so on).[23] Other, perhaps more subtle examples are Ozu's films; he almost constantly plays with our familiar notions of how space is laid out from shot to shot in continuity-style films. We shall see how in *Late Spring* he cheats our expectations about character position repeatedly by reversing continuity guidelines. Similarly, Tati's refusal to furnish the payoff in certain gags forces us to fill in the rest ourselves; here, by cueing us to create hypotheses and then failing to confirm or deny them, Tati encourages active participation by the viewer.

The notions of historical cues and backgrounds enable us to specify the goals of film analysis. The viewer can respond actively to a film only to the degree that he or she notices its cues, and only if he or she has viewing skills developed enough to respond to these cues. The analyst can help in both areas: by pointing out the cues and by suggesting how the viewer might cope with them. Such an approach would work on everything from complex, challenging works to ordinary, highly familiar ones. The viewer may find an original work incomprehensible because he or she lacks familiarity with the viewing conventions appropriate to it. On the other hand, faced with a film that sticks closely to the norms, the viewer may employ familiarized skills automatically and thus, through lack of interest, coast over many of the film's cues.

For these tasks of pointing out cues or suggesting new perspectives on films, the critic need not have more refined tastes or greater intelligence than the reader. Rather, the analyst seeks to uncover the historical circumstances that would suggest viewing skills relevant to the

---

[23] For an analysis of *Last Year at Marienbad*'s unresolvable contradictions, see Bordwell and Thompson, *Film Art: An Introduction*, pp. 304–308.

film. The analyst also tries to become as aware as possible of how he or she applies those skills in the extended viewing upon which analysis is based. The resulting discussion can then point out additional, less noticeable cues and patterns within the work—things that more casual viewers might find of interest but have not been able to ferret out for themselves. Such an approach can be equally valuable for familiar, less original sorts of films. Neoformalism often deals with highly original, challenging works, but its goal is also to take familiar, even clichéd films and create a new interest for them—to "re-defamiliarize" them. As Shklovsky put it, "The aim of the formalist method, or at least one of its aims, is not to explain the work, but to call attention to it, to restore that 'orientation towards form' which is characteristic of a work of art."[24] In this sense, the neoformalist critic can take a familiar film and point out its underlying strategies—strategies usually camouflaged by motivating devices. The analyst can thus encourage the viewer to perceive the film in a more active fashion than the film would seem at first to warrant. (As we have seen, the film may also have been highly original at one point, but become automatized by many imitations or by repeated viewings. This, I think, is to some degree the case with *Bicycle Thieves*, for example.)

At first, the neoformalist approach may seem rather "elitist," in that it favors those highly original films that may be inaccessible to mass audiences. But I would contend that this is not the case. For one thing, as we shall see in Chapter 2 with *Terror By Night*, neoformalism can and does concern itself with popularly oriented films. (We take popular films seriously, not by taking the fun out of them, but by treating them with the same respect we would accord any other film.) But, more important, neoformalism treats audience response as a matter of education about and awareness of norms, not as a matter of passive acceptance of norms imposed by the makers of popular films. Much of contemporary theory treats the viewer (read "ordinary spectator") as a passive subject taken in by whatever ideology and formal patterns the popular cinema cares to impose upon the public. Such an approach implies that the critic should be an arbiter of tastes by pointing out the advantages of avant-garde cinema, and by treating the classical cinema as an ideological machine that uses conventional approaches to seduce a mass audience.

Neoformalism assumes that spectators are, to a large extent, *active*, and that they can cope with films to the degree that they have learned

[24] Viktor Shklovski, "Pushkin and Sterne: *Eugene Onegin*," trans. James M. Holquist, in *20th Century Russian Literary Criticism*, ed. Victor Erlich (New Haven: Yale University Press, 1975), p. 68.

the norms appropriate to those films, and also to the degree that they have learned to be aware of and question those norms. The neoformalist concepts of backgrounds and defamiliarized perception are not neutral in this sense. They imply that the critic is not an arbiter of tastes, but an educator who places at the disposal of the spectators certain skills—skills that allow them to become more aware of the strategies by which films encourage spectators to respond to them. The neoformalist critic assumes that spectators are able to think for themselves, and that criticism is simply a tool for helping them to do it better in the area of the arts, by widening the range of their viewing abilities. In the case of familiar films, this process can consist of pointing out in the work additional cues and patterns as the potential objects of a more active understanding. For more difficult films, the neoformalist critic can help develop new viewing skills. A combination of these goals is most appropriate to very difficult or highly original films. If a viewer has few viewing skills appropriate to, say, a film by Jean-Luc Godard, the sudden confrontation with such a film can be discouraging. The building up of viewing experience takes time, and we may need to see a number of films of a given type before we begin to be comfortable with their challenges. Indeed, people who have been nurtured on an almost-exclusive diet of classical films may simply reject the notion that film viewing should be challenging and even difficult. In such cases, film analysis can help give them the knowledge needed to build up these new viewing skills more quickly, allowing them to find these difficult films more interesting. This is not to say that the neoformalist critic simplifies these films for the less-experienced viewer. Rather, analysis should try as much as possible to point out and preserve the difficulties and complexities of the film, but should suggest at the same time the perceptual and formal functions of the problematic aspects. Neoformalism does not want to explain the film, but to send the reader back to it and to other films like it with a better set of viewing skills.

Moreover, even the most experienced viewers will not have time to watch every complex film with equal care, and the reading of criticism can help such viewers to learn more about the films and about viewing skills. We return here to the idea that we read criticism as much for the issues it raises as for knowledge of specific films. I would presume that we never reach a saturation point in our viewing skills. There is always more to learn, and as our viewing skills become habitual, we also need to rethink and renew them. Analyses of all types of films should be capable of challenging viewers, however much experience they may have. This is another reason why we cannot settle for simple "readings" that skim the same sorts of things off every film and summarize them in simplified ways. The analyst must take the trouble to watch a film very closely indeed, and to present his or her readers with new questions, not with predigested answers.

In this sense, the current notion of "infinite readings" is again shown to be inappropriate to the neoformalist critic. Some analysts would say that we can use mental play to generate more and more readings, more meanings, without limitation. Again, this is an ahistorical claim, making the untenable assumption that we could go on dealing with the same film forever without its becoming automatized for us. But in practical terms, the film would necessarily become automatized if we simply went over and over it with the same goal each time, of doing a different "reading." As we went on, the memory of the sum of previous readings would make new ones more and more difficult to find. Moreover, each new reading would have to resort to less appropriate schemata to explain devices in the work, and the later readings would seem increasingly silly and far-fetched and ultimately uninteresting.[25]

The only way to keep a work reasonably fresh upon many repeated viewings is to look for different things in it each time—more subtle and complex things, seen in new ways. And this means developing new viewing skills that will allow us to form different kinds of hypotheses about all formal relationships—not just meanings. We do this, as we have seen, by studying films themselves, forcing ourselves to expand and modify our overall approach on the basis of the method demanded by each new work. This book is an exercise in that process. Five of these analyses were written and published over a period spanning the mid- to late 1970s; the other six were written later, specifically for this volume. The differences in method should be obvious from one analysis to the next. In doing the later analyses, I was drawn to certain conclusions that influenced my revision of the earlier pieces. Moreover, since the earlier essays were written, both David Bordwell and I have done work on structures of narration; his book on that subject has influenced a number of the later analyses in this volume. This kind of ongoing work, though it makes one perpetually dissatisfied with one's earlier analyses, aids, I believe, in renewing and multiplying the ways one can look at familiar films.

The result is not infinite readings, but increasingly detailed and

---

[25] Neoformalism does not do "readings" of films. For one thing, films are not written texts and do not need to be read. For another, "reading" has come to equal "interpretation," and, as we have seen, for the neoformalist, interpretation is only one part of analysis. The main critical activity, therefore, is "analysis."

complex analyses. The analyst focuses on more of the work's formal subtleties and tackles the work from more than one standpoint. An analysis of narration, for example, stresses different aspects than those emphasized by an analysis of character traits and their effects on causality. To discuss how the critic goes about finding such varied traits in a film, we need to examine what analytical tools are available in a neoformalist approach.

THE BASIC TOOLS OF ANALYSIS

Neoformalism makes two broad, complementary assumptions about how aesthetic films are constructed: that films are artificial constructs, and that they involve a specifically aesthetic, non-practical type of perception. These assumptions help determine how the most specific and localized sorts of analyses are carried out.

First, films are constructs that have no natural qualities. In terms of any absolute or permanent logic, the choice of the devices that will go toward creation of the film will inevitably be largely arbitrary. (This assumption simply states in another way the idea that art works respond to historical pressures rather than to eternal *vérités*.) Even the devices that go into works seeking to imitate reality as closely as possible will vary from era to era and from film to film; realism, like all viewing norms, is an historically based notion. There are certainly pressures that help determine aesthetic choice, and these come from factors extrinsic to the individual work. Ideological pressures, the historical situation of film and the other arts at the time of creation, the artist's decisions about how to recombine and modify devices to achieve defamiliarization—all contribute to making artworks respond to the forces of culture rather than of nature. In every work, then, we must expect a tension between the conventions that preexist in that culture and whatever degree of inventiveness the filmmaker brings to the individual form of the film.

In passing, I want to make clear that neoformalism's stress on inventiveness and originality does not place us back in the "Great Man" theory of history, which would assume that the individual's inspirations are the source of all innovations in art. Neoformalism assumes that artists are rational agents, making choices they judge appropriate to an end they have in view. Artists have intentions, even if the results they achieve are often unintentional. One step in judging those results (not the intentions themselves) may be the reconstruction of the artist's choice situation. As one step in that judgment, we should realize that inventiveness is itself a convention in many modern aesthetic traditions. Our culture values originality, and some artists do create highly innovative works. Yet those innovations cannot come independent of all cultural influences. This is true of a highly distinctive artist like Godard as well as of a conventional one like Lloyd Bacon. Yet at any given moment, any artist will have a broad range of possible choices open to him or her, within the limitations imposed by the cultural context.

Since films are made in response to cultural rather than natural principles, the critic should eschew a notion of analyzing films according to a set of assumptions about mimesis. It is never "just natural" that a filmmaker would put any given device into a work, no matter how realistic a film may seem. Here the concepts of motivation and function become central. We can always ask why a device is present; usually we will find that a great many of a film's devices function to create and perpetuate the film's own structures. Repetition may foster an impression of unity, may form narrative parallelisms, or may even call attention to a stylistic flourish. Any film's first task is to engage our attention as forcefully as possible, and many, if not most, of its motivations and functions will serve that purpose, among others. Art's main concern is to *be* aesthetic.

Beyond the idea that films are arbitrary rather than natural constructs, neoformalist analysis makes a second broad assumption derived from the notion of defamiliarization. Because everyday perception is habitual and strives for a maximum of efficiency and ease, aesthetic perception does the opposite. Films seek to defamiliarize conventional devices of narrative, ideology, style, and genre. Since everyday perception is efficient and easy, the aesthetic film seeks to prolong and roughen our experience—to induce us to concentrate on the processes of perception and cognition in and of themselves, rather than for some practical end. (Again, there may be a practical result, in that our viewing skills, and hence our perceptual-cognitive abilities in general, will be challenged and changed. Any one film is not likely to change our perception greatly, but the process is cumulative.) *Roughened form* and *delays* are two important concepts in the neoformalist approach. Since such structures pervade art works, they will take different forms in different films, and hence the methods used to analyze them will change. But in approaching any film the analyst will assume that they are present in some shape. Most films will contain a tension between those strategies that are included to make the form easily perceptible and comprehensible and those that are used to impede perception and understanding.

Roughened form, the more general of the two concepts, encompasses all types of devices and relations among devices that would tend to make perception and understanding less easy. For example, D. W. Griffith's decision to intercut the four epochs in *Intolerance* roughens the form of the film, even though the total film may be the same length it would have been if told through successive stories. Luis Buñuel's apparently unmotivated use of two actresses to play a single role in *That Obscure Object of Desire* provides another example of roughened form. A given device may be used consistently across the entire structure of a work, as in these cases, or it may enter only in isolated portions, as in the "white-on-white" prison sequence of George Lucas's *THX-1138*, where spatial orientation is temporarily minimized.

Roughened form can function to create an infinite variety of effects, but one of the most common types of roughened form involves the creation of delays. On the level of a film's overall formal organization, length is arbitrary. This book will be dealing exclusively with narrative, feature-length films, and we will see how causal material can be added to delay the progress toward the end of the narrative. Similarly, the same events can be presented in a more or less compressed way; expansion will also cause delay.[26] The same set of narrative events can be presented in quick summary form or can be strung out in leisurely fashion into a lengthy work. One of the narrative film's most important sets of devices is that group which functions to hold off an ending until a point appropriate to the overall design. All but the shortest narrative films are likely to have some delaying structures.

The overall pattern of such delays is called *stairstep construction*. This metaphorical term implies stretches of action in which the events progress toward the ending alternating with other stretches in which digressions and delays deflect the action from its direct path. As Shklovsky noted, there is an unlimited possibility for additional delay: "I have noticed in particular a type [of storytelling] where the themes are accumulated in steps. These accumulations are, by their very nature, infinite, just as those adventure novels are infinite which are built upon them." He cites the case of sequels, in which authors use continuing characters to string together new sets of adventures—for example, Dumas, with his *Dix ans après* and *Vingt ans après*, and Twain, with his series of Tom Sawyer–Huck Finn novels.[27] (Even the death of an author need not shut off the process of expansion, as we

---

[26] These same principles can inform non-narrative formal structure as well. For a discussion of four types of non-narrative formal organizational principles, see Bordwell and Thompson, *Film Art: An Introduction*, chaps. 3 and 9.

[27] Victor Chklovski, *Sur la théorie de la prose*, trans. Guy Verret (Lausanne: Editions l'Age d'homme, 1973), pp. 81–82.

have seen in our century with the fad for non-Doyle Sherlock Holmes books, Fred Saberhagen's Dracula series, and post-Fleming James Bond adventures; similarly, several comic strips have been continued after the deaths of their creators. Radio and television soap operas have indicated the potential of a narrative to last longer than the lives of some of its audience members.) Practically speaking, however, most narrative works are relatively short and self-contained; feature-length films accommodate themselves to a single evening's entertainment. But this length is culturally determined, and we should approach such films with the knowledge that they are constructed specifically to fit this basic length.

The concept of stairstep construction implies that some materials are more crucial to the narrative progression than others. Those actions that move us toward the end are necessary to the overall narrative, and we can call them *bound motifs*. The digressions, or "landings of the staircase" are there to delay the ending, and they are likely to be tangential actions that could be altered or eliminated or replaced without changing the basic causal line. These delaying devices we will term *free motifs*. As with any device, delays can be more or less thoroughly motivated. Extensive compositional and realistic motivation may make the free motifs seem as important to the narrative as are the bound ones, and in that case we will not notice the digressions as such; we will see this happening in *Terror By Night*. But delays can be left evident to the viewer through artistic motivation, and we shall find examples of this in *Les Vacances de Monsieur Hulot, Late Spring, Sauve qui peut(la vie)*, and other films. (Note that free motifs are as functionally important as bound ones, since art depends upon delay for its aesthetic effect.) Roughened form, stairstep construction, and bound and free motifs, then, are the general components of a film's overall form, but how does the critic go about analyzing their functions in a variety of narrative films?

ANALYZING THE NARRATIVE FILM

One of the most valuable methodological procedures devised by the Russian Formalists for analyzing narratives has been the fabula-syuzhet distinction.[28] Basically, the *syuzhet* is the structured set of all

[28] This methodological procedure has been translated widely as the story-plot distinction, and there is a temptation to use these English terms for simplicity's sake—as indeed I have done in the past. But the English terms also carry the burden of all the other senses in which non-Formalist critics have used them, while fabula and syuzhet relate only to the Russian Formalists' definitions. Hence for presentation of the neofor-

causal events as we see and hear them presented in the film itself. Typically some events will be presented directly and others only mentioned; also, events often will be given to us out of chronological order, as when flashbacks occur or when a character tells us of earlier events which we did not witness. Our understanding of these syuzhet events often involves rearranging them mentally into chronological order. Even when the film simply presents events in their 1–2–3 order, we need to grasp their causal connections actively. This mental construction of chronologically, causally linked material is the *fabula*. Such rearrangement is a viewing skill we learn thoroughly from watching narrative films and from dealing with other narrative artworks as well. For most films, we are able to construct the fabula without great difficulty. But the differences between fabula and syuzhet can be manipulated in an infinite number of ways, and thus the distinction between the two allows the analyst to deal with one of the narrative film's strongest means of defamiliarization.

A useful pair of concepts for analyzing the syuzhet is the distinction between the proairetic and hermeneutic lines.[29] The *proairetic* aspect of the narrative is the chain of causality that allows us to understand how one action is linked logically to others. The *hermeneutic* line consists of the set of enigmas the narrative poses by withholding information. The interaction of these two forces is important for maintaining our interest in the narrative. By working to grasp the proairetic line, we feel satisfaction in understanding actions, but the ongoing questions posed by the hermeneutic material pique our interest and keep us oriented toward hypothesis formation. Thus these two aspects of the syuzhet are important in their encouraging an active perception on the part of the spectator. The different functions of the proairetic and hermeneutic lines are responsible for much of the narrative's forward impetus. Most crucially, they function to spur us into constructing the fabula. Without the interaction of causality and enigma, events would merely be strung together, one after another, and would lack an overall sense of dynamism.

Every narrative film has a beginning and an ending. Those points are not casual parts of the overall syuzhet. The beginning tends to

malist position, I have decided to stick to the original terms at the risk of adding some extra terminological weight. Bordwell's *Narration in the Fiction Film* also uses these terms extensively.

[29] I have borrowed the idea of the proairetic and hermeneutic lines from Roland Barthes's *S/Z*, trans. Richard Miller (New York: Hill and Wang, 1974), p. 19 passim. Barthes terms them the proairetic and hermeneutic "codes," but as this suggests that there is some sort of preexistent function for each, I have chosen to treat them as structures, or "lines," running through the work and varying in each context.

provide us with the crucial information from which we form our strongest and most lingering hypotheses about the fabula. And the ending is essentially the moment when the most important information which the narration has been withholding from us is finally revealed—or at least when we find out that we will never be given the crucial information; the hermeneutic line is thus very important in giving us a sense of when the narrative ends. Not all narratives emphasize beginnings and endings so forcefully. Shklovsky suggested that a simple narrative might use stairstep construction merely to string together a series of events, constituting what we typically think of as a picaresque narrative; such a work (e.g., *The Decameron*) could be prolonged or shortened by adding or taking away episodes without significantly affecting the construction of the whole. But when the beginning sets up a proairetic or hermeneutic whose answer or completion is delayed throughout the whole narrative until the end, then we perceive the whole syuzhet as being unified around a sequence of interrelated events. Shklovsky termed this the "buckle" construction, for the end reverses and refers to the beginning in some way: we sense the end as such because it echoes the situation of the beginning. Shklovsky gives as examples *Oedipus Rex* and *Macbeth*, both of which revolve around the main characters' attempts to elude prophecies; each ends when the prophecy is completely fulfilled.[30] Those narratives that provide all the information needed to answer an enigma, and that make clear the effects of all the causal action I will assume are "closed"; they achieve closure, coming full circle to complete the buckle structure. Some narratives do not provide this kind of closure. A film that leaves dangling causes and does not provide a complete solution to the enigma has an "open" narrative.

The main agents that carry through the various causal events of the narrative are, as I have mentioned, *characters* (though social and natural forces can provide some causal material as well). For the neoformalist, characters are not real people, but collections of *semes*, or character traits. Because "traits" are qualities that we take real people to have, I will be using Roland Barthes's term "semes" here, meaning devices that characterize the figures in a narrative.[31] Since characters are not people, we do not necessarily judge them by the standards of everyday behavior and psychology. Rather, as with all devices and collections of devices, characters must be analyzed in terms of their functions in the work as a whole. Some characters may be fairly neutral,

---

[30] Chklovski, *Sur la théorie de la prose*, pp. 82, 84.
[31] Tomashevsky, "Thematics," p. 88; Barthes, *S/Z*, p. 68.

existing primarily to hold together a series of picaresque imbedded narratives; Shklovsky remarked that "Gil Blas is not a man; it is the thread which connects the episodes of the novel, and that thread is gray."[32] Even in a more unified, psychologically oriented narrative we can find various functions for characters: providing information, providing the means for withholding information, creating parallels, embodying shapes and colors that participate in shot compositions, moving about to motivate tracking shots, and any number of others. Shklovsky has found that Watson, in the Sherlock Holmes series, has three main functions: (1) he tells us what Holmes does and keeps us interested in the solution (he creates, in other words, an uncommunicative narration, since Holmes only gives him bits of information at intervals); (2) he plays the "perpetual idiot," since he gives us clues without being able to place a significance on them—even suggesting false solutions; and (3) he keeps the conversation going, as "sort of ball boy who permits Sherlock Holmes to play."[33]

Characters may be presented in great depth, with a great many traits, but these do not necessarily conform to real psychological patterns. Characterization can provide the main focus of a work (though this does not make the characters any less artificial and device-bound). However much they may strike us as being like "real people," we can always trace that impression back to a set of specific, character-creating devices.

The process whereby the syuzhet presents and withholds fabula information in a certain order is *narration*. Narration thus continually cues our hypothesis-forming about fabula events throughout the course of viewing the film. (Some theorists and critics have assumed that narrative artworks always have a narrator, whom they regard as the person through whom information is filtered. Here I will assume that narration is a process, not a person, and that the only times films have narrators as such is when a voice, either diegetic or non-diegetic, speaks to give us information.) David Bordwell has laid out three basic properties that can be used in analyzing any narration: its degrees of knowledgeability, self-consciousness, and communicativeness.[34]

The apparent *knowledgeability* of the narration is characterized first, by the *range* of fabula information to which it seems to have access. Frequently, by restricting us to one or a few characters' understandings of the situation, the narration is able to withhold other infor-

[32] Victor Chklovski, "La Construction de la nouvelle et du roman," in *Théorie de la littérature*, p. 190.

[33] Chklovski, *Sur la théorie de la prose*, p. 152.

[34] Bordwell, *Narration in the Fiction Film*, pp. 57–61.

mation. Such a pattern is common in those detective films, for example, in which the narration concentrates on what the investigators learn but seems not to know anything that only the criminals would know. The narration's knowledgeability is characterized, second, by its *depth*—that is, by the extent to which it provides us access to characters' mental states. The range and depth of narration are independent variables; a film could present us with a great deal of objective information without telling us much about the characters' reactions to events.

Narration may be more or less *self-conscious*, in that the film acknowledges to a greater or lesser extent that it is directing its narrative information at an audience. Direct address on the part of a character, the use of "you" or other similar terms by a voice-over narrator, a nonsubjective track-in to reveal an important detail—with these and similar devices, the narration may betray some degree of self-consciousness. Conversely, thorough motivation for the revelation of each piece of information may gloss over the process of narration. If all the exposition is motivated by certain characters giving information in dialogue to other characters, we are less likely to notice the narration as such— it is less self-conscious.

Finally, the narration may be more or less *communicative*. This property is distinct from its knowledgeability, since the narration may demonstrate that it has certain information but is withholding it from us. For instance, if we have been waiting to learn the identity of a mysterious masked character, and the scene fades out just as that person strips the mask off, the narration is flaunting its own refusal to communicate information it could potentially reveal to us. This example suggests that the more self-conscious the narration is, the more likely we are to notice a lack of knowledgeability or communicativeness. Indeed, since all narratives need to withhold a certain amount of fabula information (if only what will happen next), the narration of any film is likely to be at least slightly restricted in either its knowledgeability or its communicativeness. Yet we are often unlikely to notice such restrictions unless the narration is fairly self-conscious. There are, of course, many possible combinations for film narration. We shall see with *The Rules of the Game*, for example, that the impression of realism it gives depends to a considerable extent on a narration that is fairly knowledgeable and largely communicative, but that withholds a few crucial bits of fabula information from us—in a way we are unlikely to notice, since the narration is not particularly self-conscious. In a narrative film, the process of narration is likely to affect a great many of the motivations and functions of the individual devices.

Narrative is an important structure in many films, but every narrative presented in a film will be created by the use of techniques of that medium. We can speak of the characteristic, repeated use a film makes of these techniques as its *style*. I do not propose to deal with the medium here, since that would properly be the province of an introductory film textbook. Suffice it to say that what I mean here are filmic techniques as they are used to create:

1. *Space*—the representation of three dimensions and of offscreen space.
2. *Time*—an interplay of fabula and syuzhet times.
3. *Abstract play among the non-narrative spatial, temporal, and visual aspects of film*—the graphic, sonic, and rhythmic qualities of the image and sound tracks.

Filmic techniques all have their motivations and functions in a film, and all can serve the narrative or exist alongside it to create non-narrative structures that are of interest in their own right.

On the level of stylistic structures, the work's ways of relating individual devices to each other are also arbitrary and depend on the motivation and function chosen for each. Stylistic devices can be made subservient to the narrative line through thorough-going compositional motivation. In such a case, defamiliarization is likely to be going on mainly on the narrative level. (Such an approach is characteristic of the classical cinema.) The techniques of the medium, however, can be used as impeding material, drawing our attention to themselves partially or intermittently, and thus complicating our sense of the narrative (as we shall see with Godard and Renoir). At an extreme point, through extensive artistic motivation, style for its own sake can create a complete perceptual play that constantly challenges the narrative line for our attention (e.g., *Lancelot du Lac, Late Spring*).

Defamiliarization is an effect of the work, rather than a structure. To analyze the specific form it takes in each work, the neoformalist critic uses the concept of the *dominant*—the main formal principal a work or group of works uses to organize devices into a whole. The dominant determines which devices and functions will come forward as important defamiliarizing traits, and which will be less important. The dominant will pervade the work, governing and linking small-scale devices to large-scale ones; through the dominant, the stylistic, narrative, and thematic levels will relate to each other.

Finding the dominant is important for the analyst, since it is the main indication of what specific method is suitable to the film or group of films. The work cues us as to its dominant by *foregrounding* certain devices and placing others less prominently. We can begin by isolating those devices that seem to be the most intriguing and important; in a highly original film, these will tend to be the most unusual and challenging, while in a more standard film, they will be the most typical and recognizable. A list of devices does not equal the dominant, but if we can find a common structure of functions running through them all, we can assume that this structure forms or relates closely to the dominant. Finding the dominant provides a beginning for analysis. Since this is such an important concept, I will be discussing it in more detail in Part Three, with examples from two films: *Les Vacances de Monsieur Hulot* and *Tout va bien*. Subsequent chapters will not contain so explicit a discussion, but notions of the dominant undergird the entire book.

THE FILMS

The remainder of this book is devoted to analyses of eleven films. The choice of titles may at first seem a bit disparate, but taken together they do display a range of the possibilities for applying neoformalism. The early chapters demonstrate specific concepts inherent in the approach—stairstep construction and motivation in *Terror By Night*, the dominant in *Les Vacances de Monsieur Hulot* and *Tout va bien*. But in the course of the book, the discussions of neoformalist terms become less explicit. The later chapters are intended less as explications of neoformalism than as simply analyses of the films at hand—though they do deal with methodological issues, as the part titles indicate.

Since norms are of such importance to this approach, I thought it useful to start off by analyzing an ordinary classical film, *Terror By Night*. Chapter 2, then, serves the double purpose of showing how delay is motivated and suggesting how the classical film subordinates style to narrative. All the other films discussed play with or depart from this norm in some significant way.

The dominant is a difficult concept to apply in practical analysis, and the two analyses in Part Three show how a single structure can be isolated and used as a tool for teasing out the formal relationships in various levels of the work—stylistic, narrative, and thematic. This is a process through which the analyst, to some degree, necessarily goes when formulating a method specific to the film, though again the discussion of the dominant as such need not be as explicit as it is here, in the *Les Vacances de Monsieur Hulot* chapter.

Part Four deals with two films that explore the limits of the classical Hollywood norm: *Stage Fright* and *Laura*. Each contains an idiosyncratic device—*Stage Fright* a lying "flashback," and *Laura* an ambiguous cue for a dream—that challenges the critic to explain to what extent it actually violates canons of classicism. Each film, in fact, motivates its troublesome device thoroughly. *Stage Fright* does so using a play with the hermeneutic line and a great deal of conventional "poetic" imagery relating to lying and theatrical deception. *Laura*'s dominant involves considerable manipulation of point of view, and I have used Chapter 6 as an opportunity to explore ways of talking about point of view in relation to filmic narrative.

Typically, the word "formalism" conjures up notions of bizarre, highly stylized films, but since neoformalism takes all devices within a work to be part of its form, realistic films can be analyzed for their formal structures as well. Part Five sets out to demonstrate this, with a brief theoretical discussion of realism as a formal trait. Then, taking two films generally considered to be realistic, *Bicycle Thieves* and *The Rules of the Game*, I look at how each has different ways of cueing the spectator to perceive its motivations as realistic. Given that these two films are familiar classics, I hope to show also that neoformalism, by examining works from a new perspective, can defamiliarize such well-known films.

As I have suggested in this chapter, neoformalism also seeks to make accessible those films demanding viewing skills that lie outside the accustomed norms. The last four chapters deal with films which, though perhaps familiar, offer considerable perceptual challenges, largely through the use of parametric form. *Play Time* and *Sauve qui peut (la vie)* both throw a great quantity of material at the viewer in a short time, creating a sort of perceptual overload. Not only can critical study point out more of what is going on in such films, but also it can explore some of the large-scale effects that such an overload has on the film's structures. Certainly, in order to keep up with such films, the viewer's perception must become very active indeed.

Yet the opposite strategy can also elicit an active viewing. By withholding many of the normal devices used by other films, and by paring down style and narrative to a minimum, a sparse film can force our attention to more and more minute stylistic variations on devices that usually remain subordinated to narrative function. Such strategies of sparseness occur in *Lancelot du Lac* and *Late Spring*; using these two films, I shall be discussing the issue of sparse, parametric cinema.

In closing, I would like to point out that any critical approach is only as good as the actual analyses it is capable of fostering.[35] It is an ab-

---

[35] A few reviews of my previous book of neoformalist analysis—*Eisenstein's Ivan the Terrible*—praised the analysis itself but found fault with the approach (described in the first chapter), as being either problematic or unnecessary (Polan, "Terminable and In-

stract system until it is applied to individual films. Each analysis confirms certain aspects of the approach and stretches or amends others. I hope that this book's range of films and the variety of results obtained will provide evidence of the usefulness of neoformalism as a general approach.

---

terminable Analysis," pp. 70–71; *Choice* [May 1982]: 261). Yet the results of my analysis there, as in the current volume, are inseparable from the neoformalist approach, and one cannot judge them in isolation, as if somehow the discussion of the films could have been done in an identical way without the approach.

PART TWO

The Ordinary Film

2

"No, Lestrade, in This Case Nothing Was Left to Chance": Motivation and Delay in *Terror By Night*

ANALYZING THE AVERAGE FILM

"Terror By Night?" I hear you asking yourself, as you search your memory. A quick check in Maltin's *TV Movies* directs you to "SEE: Sherlock Holmes series," conjuring up vague recollections. "Is that the one with the train?" It is indeed. Released in 1946, it is next to last in the dozen Universal Basil Rathbone/Holmes films.

My reasons for choosing this film are less bizarre than they might at first appear. I am not a secret Holmes-series fan, out to convince you that *Terror By Night* is another undiscovered masterpiece from the vaults of Hollywood. Roy William Neill, though a competent, even slightly stylish, director of low-budget films, will not stand forth here as a candidate for Andrew Sarris's Pantheon, or even for the Far Side of Paradise (Likely Likable at best). Quite the contrary, I picked *Terror By Night* because it seems to me unexceptional in terms of quality: certainly not the best that Hollywood has to offer, but similarly far from the worst.

Such a choice is appropriate here, since my purpose in this section of the book is to show that neoformalism can account for structures, materials, processes, and backgrounds in the average film. Many people may have the impression that Formalism, by its very nature, tends to favor those films that are formally daring and unusual, and it is true that essays by the Russian Formalists often singled out highly distinctive works. That is also true, however, of most other types of criticism. Critics have tended to choose films for close analysis on the basis of assumed quality—deciding whether an artwork is "worth" close study. And since one of the most traditional evaluative criteria of high quality has been originality, critics have gravitated toward those works that are different. (Critics who deal with ordinary films often do so as part of a more general approach, like cultural studies.) Yet a critical

49

theory could apply just as easily to an average work; moreover, I would argue that neoformalism is as suited to the study of such works as it is to more exceptional films.

Given the goal of demonstrating this idea, I found the choice of a film difficult. Ideally I would hope that the reader of this volume would have seen whatever film I decided to analyze, or at least would have relatively easy access to it. But most Hollywood films that circulate widely are not average; they usually include major stars, major directors, high production values, or other ingredients that would take them out of the "average" category in some way. A relatively good B picture from a series seemed the solution.[1] The Holmes movies are commonly available (having recently come into public domain and been released on videotape), show up frequently on television, and are among the more familiar of the B films. Basil Rathbone's Holmes and Neill's direction help raise these movies slightly above the level of most B's. In short, they are of average quality. *Terror By Night* is, in my opinion, neither among the best of that series (e.g., *The Scarlet Claw* and *Sherlock Holmes Faces Death*) nor among the worst (e.g., *Sherlock Holmes in Washington* and the notorious *Pursuit to Algiers*).

I am not claiming, incidentally, that *Terror By Night* is typical of all Hollywood movies. There is such a tremendous range of possibilities within the classical Hollywood norm that no one film could utilize them all.[2] *Terror By Night*'s short syuzhet time span and limited setting make it somewhat unusual, but there are certainly other familiar groups of Hollywood films—the stormy night-in-an-old-dark-house thriller, other train films—that share these traits. Yet, while *Terror By Night* is not broadly representative, it is average in quality, and it utilizes many familiar devices of conventional filmmaking.

By applying concepts derived from Russian Formalism, the critic can make such films more interesting. Ordinarily, the average Holly-

---

[1] This is not to claim that B films are inevitably of lower quality than A's. The films of Jacques Tourneur for the Val Lewton unit at RKO, and many works of Edgar G. Ulmer, Samuel Fuller, Joseph H. Lewis, and others, demonstrate the contrary. But short shooting schedules and limited budgets allowed less flexibility in technical and design choices and promoted a greater standardization of style. Perhaps more important, studios tended to use their B units as a sort of training ground, and the more talented performers and technicians often graduated to A production—unless, as with the directors mentioned above, they specialized in B-film genres. I am assuming, then, that although there was a wide range of quality in both A and B production, the classical mode of filmmaking would make lower quality more *likely* in a larger number of the B films.

[2] For an analysis of Hollywood's formal paradigm based on a survey of many types of films, see David Bordwell, Janet Staiger, and Kristin Thompson, *The Classical Hollywood Cinema: Film Style and Mode of Production to 1960* (New York: Columbia University Press, 1985).

wood film is largely automatized, remaining part of that undifferen-
tiated mass that we have come to think of as the classical cinema. In
such a case, the critic's job could be to re-defamiliarize the film—indeed,
to defamiliarize it more than it would have been on its first appearance. Genre films of this kind were created to elicit culturally defined
attitudes that were familiar and ordinary to audiences of the time. B
production in the 1940s in particular dealt in minimal variation from
film to film, in order to appeal to a specific, habitual audience. (*Terror
By Night* would originally have been seen mainly by men and boys.)
Such films played on the second half of double features, mostly in
theaters that did not have first-run status.[3]

Yet an analysis of a film like *Terror By Night* need not simply try to
determine what the audience of 1946 was supposed to notice and understand about the film. Such a discussion would merely accept the
film's original cultural terms and reiterate the conventional way of
viewing; this would imply an acceptance of the intentions of the original makers. Rather, in dealing with a highly automatized film, neoformalist analysis can show how the conventions themselves are used as
formal devices to guide our perception of the film. Such a perspective
is not dependent on valorizing films as "outstanding" or "great."

Because classical Hollywood films are so numerous and so familiar,
we tend to assume that they are simple in their formal strategies.
Complexity as a concept seems to apply more to the films of directors
like Jean Renoir or Michelangelo Antonioni. The apparent simplicity
of average films suggests another reason why analysts may avoid them:
what could there be to say about them? But it seems equally possible
that, although such films may lack notable originality, they have their
own type of complexity, automatized though they may be. (Similarly,
riding a bicycle requires an elaborate interaction of physical movements, but once we are past the learning stage, we usually do not have
to think consciously about making these separate gestures.) That complexity has to do with the classical film's need to motivate its devices
thoroughly to serve the narrative in a way that at least appears to the
viewer to be unified. Yuri Tynjanov discussed the fact that highly motivated artworks (of which the classical film would be one type) are
difficult to use in a study of general theoretical principles:[4] "From this

---

[3] For a discussion of the Holmes series as a product of studio policy, see Mary Beth
Haralovich, "Sherlock Holmes: Genre and Industrial Practice," *Journal of the University Film Association* 31, no. 2 (Spring 1979): 53–57.

[4] Tynjanov's distinction here between motivated and unmotivated art was based on
Russian Formalist usage in the early 1920s; the distinction I made in Chapter 1 among
different types of motivation was a later development by Tomashevsky. By "motivated,"

point of view, the outwardly easy and simple area of *motivated art* turns out to be quite complex and *unfavorable* material for study." But the principles that Tynjanov found unfavorable for a theoretical study are exactly those that help us to grasp the hidden complexities of the "ordinary" film.

Each factor is motivated by its connection with everything else.

The deformation of factors brought about by this is carried out evenly. The inner motivation, which occurs on the constructive level of the work, smooths over, as it were, their *specifica*, making art "light" and acceptable. Motivated art is deceptive. Karamzin suggested that "old words be given a new sense, offered in a new form, but so skillfully as to deceive the reader and conceal from him the unusualness of the expression."

But precisely for this reason, the study of the functions of any one factor is even more difficult to conduct on light art. The investigation of these functions does not mean the investigation of what is quantitatively typical, but rather what is qualitatively characteristic of the general elements in relation to other fields of intellectual activity. This is to find the specific "plus" of art. Therefore in motivated works of art, what is characteristic is the very motivation (the concealment of this "plus"), which is a distinctive negative characteristic (V. Shklovsky), rather than a positive one.[5]

The implication here is that highly motivated artworks must operate by the same principles as do other artworks. Their narratives, for example, will contain a play between fabula and syuzhet, and will depend on delay, roughened form, buckle structures, and so on. But these structures, which unmotivated works (i.e., those that use considerable artistic motivation) leave apparent for the perceiver's attention, will, in a motivated work, be hidden (by realistic, compositional, or transtextual motivation, all of which appeal in some way to "other fields of intellectual activity," i.e., our knowledge of the real world, systems of causality and temporality, other works in other media, and so on). The motivated artwork thus has two major formal patterns: on the one hand, the devices relating to the creation and sustainment of the narrative (e.g., stairstep construction); on the other, the motivations overlaid on these devices and having the overall function of concealing their operations. This double layering of motivation is what makes classical films complex, while at the same time lending them an appearance of simplicity (or "lightness," as Tynjanov characterizes it).

In analyzing *Terror By Night*, then, my strategy will be to distin-

Tynjanov is referring essentially to what I call realistic, transtextual, and especially compositional motivation; by "unmotivated," he means what I define as artistic motivation.

[5] Yuri Tynianov, *The Problem of Verse Language*, trans. and ed. Michael Sosa and Brent Harvey (Ann Arbor: Ardis, 1981), p. 36.

guish between these two patterns—to determine which devices are part of the basic progression/delay structure of the narrative causality and which are simply inserted to conceal the mechanisms of the narrative's workings. Furthermore, since the narrative line almost invariably determines the stylistic patterns, I will be looking at how devices like framing and set design are thoroughly subordinated, through motivation, to serve the ongoing action.

NARRATIVE: STAIRSTEP CONSTRUCTION

Critics and historians in film studies have recently assumed that classical Hollywood films are realistic, and that their narratives are linear (defined by these writers as simple). The first assumption is questionable, the second needs qualification.

On the whole, purely realistic motivation is not the main type employed in Hollywood films. Most actions are justified not, primarily, by an appeal to cultural beliefs about the real world, but by a seemingly necessary causal relationship to other actions within the film. Realistic motivation works as a backup justification in most cases, and where realistic and compositional motivations are at odds, compositional will almost invariably win out. For example, in the second scene of *Terror By Night*, Sherlock Holmes is walking along a train platform talking to his new client, young Carstairs, about the famous diamond he has been hired to guard. As the camera tracks with them, various people bustle along the platform within easy hearing range, and the pair speak loudly about matters that they presumably want kept secret. As Holmes is saying "the fact that your mother owns the famous diamond," a woman passes between him and the camera; clearly, if we can hear him, she can (in realistic terms), but she passes on without a glance. Holmes continues, "is common knowledge," and we might, if we are paying attention to such things, be tempted to mutter, "It is now, Holmes." But ordinarily we do not notice such contradictions between realism and narrative necessity, since in Hollywood films narrative necessity is so overwhelmingly dominant, from the largest- to the smallest-scale devices. Realism usually enters as the primary type of motivation only for limited purposes. One such purpose stems from the invariable need to cut off the causal chain extending back into the past, before the syuzhet's beginning; films must have certain initial fabula causes which are simply given as such, and which themselves are not traceable back to earlier causes. In *Terror By Night*, for example, the narrative depends on the fact that Lady Carstairs, living in Scotland, brought her famous diamond to London when she attended a reception at Buckingham Palace. No reason is given for this action in the cause-effect chain, but it provides the most basic compositional motivation for the rest of the narrative. To understand why she transported the jewel, we must fall back on realistic motivation: she is an aristocrat, and we assume that such people simply would wear their best jewelry when visiting royalty. But there are relatively few such moments in any one Hollywood film. Usually we can account for virtually any device by seeing how it arises from a cause within the narrative, and by seeing further how it creates other effects—in other words, we grasp its compositional motivation.

Assuredly there is a considerable amount of simple realism used as a secondary motivating force, a backup to the main compositional justification. Given that certain characters are necessary to the narrative, they will tend to wear costumes that are appropriate to their social statuses and personalities. A failure of realism would presumably divert the spectator's attention from the narrative. The Hollywood studios have been willing to invest in design experts who are expected to provide historically and geographically accurate settings and costumes. Except in those cases in which these elements come forward to create spectacle, realistic motivation primarily provides a steady, unobtrusive background to the more important syuzhet events. As I have suggested, however, realism rarely takes precedence over other types of motivation.

The classical film may not be primarily realistic, but is *is* linear in its narrative progression; that is, the basic narrative causality will be clear, with few or no gaps left in the chain of cause and effect (except by accident or lack of skill among the filmmakers). The narrative achieves closure, and along the way it keeps us fairly aware of how one scene links up to those that precede and follow it. But that does not mean that a Hollywood narrative avoids introducing considerable extraneous delaying material; quite the contrary, stairstep construction exists here as in the most radically avant-garde of works. The famous linearity may be hidden by a syuzhet that introduces digressions and delays, even while the film takes care to cue us to those events that are most important to our understanding of the fabula.

Here Boris Tomashevsky's distinction between "bound" and "free" motifs proves useful. As we saw in Chapter 1, a bound motif is necessary to the presentation of a narrative; its elimination would damage the clear linearity of narrative progression. (A film like Resnais's *Muriel* deliberately creates confusion by withholding information about important bound motifs; it can serve as an example of the nonlinear narrative. *Terror By Night*, on the other hand, provides us with everything we need to know about its bound motifs, though we may realize the importance of the information only retrospectively.) A free motif is one that could be omitted from the causal chain, even though it does play one or more formal roles in the work. Tomashevsky adds that "usually the introduction of a free motif occurs as a development of a previously introduced motif which is inherently bound up with the story."[6] That is, a free motif will have one or more functions relating to the bound motifs. For example, a nightclub chanteuse's number in a gangster film may be unnecessary in itself, but it may create atmosphere, provide a motivation for a conversation at a nearby table, help characterize the villain as lecherous, and so on. Thorough-going motivation will tend to blur the distinction between bound and free motifs by making the free ones seem more necessary than they are. Using this distinction between bound and free motifs, the critic can go a long way toward separating out the motivating patterns of the work from the more basic, camouflaged narrative structure. Clearly, the analysis of a narrative's stairstep construction depends on this idea of bound and free motifs. Devices causing the deflections away from straightforward linearity will usually be free motifs, while the bound motifs will pull the narrative back onto a path of progression toward closure— creating the metaphorical zigzag "steps."

Typically a film must strike a balance between supplying too little and too much material; it displays causal events in an arrangement that denies the spectator that specific body of information that would bring the film to a halt. Theoretically, without any external constraints, the story motifs could be suggested to us briefly (as I am about to do in a synoptic segmentation of *Terror By Night*) or in a more leisurely fashion, through the introduction of more incidental details. But narratives are never created outside of any sort of conventional modes. The Formalists stressed the effects of an artwork's length upon the types of structures it would need to contain. Eikhenbaum noted that the short story differs from the novel in more than length; the novel's larger structure needs to contain a much greater proportion of retarding material.[7] Given that *Terror By Night* was made in a tightly controlled

---

[6] Boris Tomashevsky, "Thematics," in *Russian Formalist Criticism: Four Essays*, trans. and ed. Lee T. Lemon and Marion J. Reis (Lincoln: University of Nebraska Press, 1965), pp. 68–69. The concepts of bound and free motifs are similar to Roland Barthes's "functions" and "catalyses" in his "An Introduction to the Structural Analysis of Narrative," in *Image, Music, Text*, trans. and ed. Stephen Heath (New York: Hill and Wang, 1977), pp. 79–124, an essay highly influenced by the Formalists.

[7] Boris M. Èjxenbaum, "The Theory of the Formal Method," trans. I. R. Titunik, in *Readings in Russian Poetics*, ed. Ladislav Matejka and Krystyna Pomorska (Cambridge, Mass.: MIT Press, 1971), p. 232.

institutional situation—a well-established Universal B series—its screen time was preordained within loose limits. At sixty minutes, it happens to be the shortest of the twelve Universal Holmes films (just barely, with the others ranging from sixty-two to seventy-four minutes). Given this outside constraint, the script could potentially involve a great many bound motifs, compressed by such devices as crosscutting to fit the length; an example of such a strategy is *Intolerance*, with its lengthy time span and multiple actions. Conversely, a skeletal set of bound motifs could be padded with a whole series of free motifs. One common type of free motif for a Hollywood B, for example, involves incidental scenes with comic characters, and *Terror By Night* has some of these. In an action genre, the succession of motifs, whether bound or free, has to move along at a brisk pace.

To study the film's delays, we need a description of its major motifs. Following is a segmentation summarizing the main actions in *Terror By Night*, in syuzhet order:

I. A montage sequence, with a documentary-style description of the discovery of the diamond, the "Star of Rhodesia"; we are told that every owner of the gem has met with a violent death.

II. A fashionably dressed young woman, Vivian Vedders, visits a coffin-maker's shop and arranges to have a coffin delivered to a funeral home, saying she is taking her mother's body to Scotland by the Edinburgh train leaving Euston Station at 7:30 that night.

III. At 7:15, a van delivers the coffin at the station, and Vedders boards the train. As the coffin is being loaded, a rich young man, Carstairs, greets Holmes on the platform and thanks him for agreeing to make the trip to Scotland; Holmes has already realized that his job is to guard Lady Margaret Carstairs's famous jewel, the Star of Rhodesia, because an attempt was made in London to steal it. Carstairs enters the carriage, which is a daycoach added that day to accommodate a large demand for tickets. Holmes waits for Watson on the platform and sees both Lestrade (who is pretending to be on a fishing trip) and Professor Kilbain enter the car. Watson arrives just in time, having been delayed by a chance meeting with an old friend, Duncan Bleek, who is also taking the train. Holmes and Watson meet with Carstairs and his mother in their compartment and examine the jewel. An elderly lady, Mrs. Shelcross, informs her husband that police are aboard the train, and he reacts nervously.

IV. Holmes joins Bleek and Watson in the dining car, finds a note warning him off the case, and sees Lady Carstairs come in to dinner alone.

v. Young Carstairs is killed in his compartment and the jewel case left empty. Lestrade, Holmes, and Watson investigate, but Watson contradicts Holmes's assumption of murder, reporting no sign of violence on the body. Lady Carstairs is taken to another compartment, and Holmes has the carriage sealed off. Holmes, Lestrade, and Watson confer with the conductor, who reveals that the luggage car behind the carriage is kept locked at all times. Holmes suggests that Carstairs was killed with poison. Lestrade gets a passenger list and goes with Holmes to search Vedders's compartment, Holmes having proposed to Watson that he conduct some inquiries himself. Watson "questions" Professor Kilbain to no effect.

vi. Meanwhile, Lestrade and Holmes fail to get information from Vedders, and Holmes suggests searching the coffin.

vii. Holmes breaks up Watson's argument with Professor Kilbain and sends Watson to question the Shelcross couple. Shelcross tells Watson that he "did it," and Watson rushes off to interrupt Holmes and Lestrade in their investigation of the luggage car. They come and hear Shelcross confess to having stolen a hotel teapot. Watson goes off to drink in Bleek's compartment while Holmes and Lestrade question Professor Kilbain.

viii. Bleek acts oddly as he chats with Watson over cards. Holmes learns that Professor Kilbain is a mathematics professor, then catches Lady Carstairs trying to sneak back into her original compartment; she claims she is after a suitcase.

ix. Bleek and Watson tell Holmes that they think Lady Carstairs may have committed the crime for the insurance money. Holmes studies Bleek and remarks on his doodling.

x. Lestrade and Holmes confer, the latter musing that Colonel Sebastian Moran, a master jewel thief he has never seen, is interested in mathematics. Lestrade runs through the list of suspects and decides to question Lady Carstairs. Holmes goes to his own compartment and spies on Professor Kilbain, who passes in the corridor.

xi. A dark figure in the corridor pushes Holmes out the train door, then locks it. Holmes clings outside and manages to pull himself back into the train. He and Watson go to the luggage car, find a suspicious looking guard, and investigate the coffin, discovering a hidden compartment in which the killer had apparently concealed himself. They show Lestrade this, and Holmes says there are two criminals, Moran and an accomplice.

57

xii. They confront Vedders with news of the coffin discovery. She says a man paid her £100 to take the coffin to Edinburgh, but she denies further knowledge. Bleek enters, and Holmes asks Vedders if he was the man who hired her, than reassures Bleek that he does not suspect him. Revealing that he had substituted a fake diamond for the Star, Holmes gives the real one to Lestrade, with Bleek looking on. Lestrade arrests Vedders as an accomplice.

xiii. Watson and Holmes go to the luggage car and find the guard dead, with a small poisoned-dart wound. The killer slips out unseen.

xiv. The killer throttles the carriage attendant and goes to Bleek (now revealed as Moran); the killer, a hired thug, now learns that the stone he had stolen is fake. The killer knocks Lestrade out and takes the real Star; Moran kills his accomplice and takes the stone. Watson and Holmes discover the body and revive Lestrade. The train stops; two policemen and Inspector MacDonald get on and take over the case, saying they have jurisdiction now that the train is in Scotland.

xv. MacDonald questions Vedders in the dining car, with Holmes, Lestrade, and Watson present; she leaves, and Holmes tells MacDonald that Bleek is really Moran. Moran is brought in and searched by MacDonald, who finds a gun and the Star. Moran grabs the gun and pulls the emergency brake. The lights go out and a chaotic struggle ensues, ending with Holmes turning over a muffled figure to MacDonald, who leaves the train with the other police. Holmes shows Watson that Moran, handcuffed, is under a table; he says that MacDonald and the others were imposters, set up by Moran as a means of escape. Meanwhile Lestrade, who was the muffled figure, arrests the gang. Holmes telegraphs to the real police; it turns out he is acquainted with the real Inspector MacDonald.

Genre conventions typically provide specific types of transtextual motivation for the withholding of crucial story information. At first, *Terror By Night* and the other Holmes films appear to be straightforward detective/mystery narratives. Probably the most common means for delaying the disclosure of information in the detective genre is for the syuzhet to begin well along in the series of events. We then mentally reconstruct those events into the chronological and causal order of the fabula. Typically, the narration first presents us with either the murder, the discovery of the body, or the moment at which the protagonist-detective is called in (the latter usually being a signal that the narration's point of view [POV] will be largely restricted to the detective or his assistant, as in the Nero Wolfe series or the original Sherlock Holmes pieces). The detective then sifts through a series of clues and suspects to find the killer. Next, he reconstructs for us a lengthy series of fabula events that occurred earlier than the first events we saw for ourselves in the early stages of the syuzhet. Thus, typically, the tactics for delaying the final revelation of the detective narrative involve a considerable amount of scrambling of fabula chronology; reconstruction of early fabula events becomes the basis for later action. (Even those detective narratives that begin substantially before the crime will usually manipulate POV to restrict reader knowledge, and the reconstruction of early events will be withheld until the end.)

These general tactics, however, are not the main basis for the delays in *Terror By Night*. Here there is relatively little reordering of events except on a local level. For example, in Segment V we do not see the murderer get out of the coffin compartment to kill Carstairs, nor do we see him return to it. But in Segment XI, when Holmes examines the coffin, we are able to fill in these events. Other reordering is even more short-term, as in Segment XV, when Holmes substitutes Lestrade for Moran, and we learn about the switch only moments later when he reveals it to Watson. By dividing the action summarized above into a list of bound and free motifs, I came up with approximately sixty-three separate actions. (This number is, of course, arbitrary, since one could divide each action up into smaller actions, but for the level of detail at which I wish to work, a subsegment such as a single conversation qualifies as an action.) Of these, the earliest fabula and syuzhet events are identical: the discovery of the Star of Rhodesia diamond and the deaths of its earlier owners by violence. This would appear to be a single bound motif, but it is actually a free one; that is, because we learn that Lady Carstairs owns the diamond, we would have assumed that it must have been discovered at some point: the opening montage is largely redundant. The characterization of the diamond as inevitably fatal to its owners is even misleading, since the owner, Lady Carstairs, is not one of the murder victims. The opening montage acts as a sort of prologue to assure us that violent action will figure in the syuzhet; it establishes atmosphere but is in no way vital to the narrative.

Leaving aside this prologue, the earliest syuzhet action we witness is Vedders making the coffin arrangement; there are six events that definitely occur before this in the fabula and two that occur at about the same time. Of these eight motifs, six are bound and two free. In chronological order, these eight motifs are:

1. *Bound motif*—Twenty-five years ago, Lady Carstairs received the Star of Rhodesia from her husband. (Revealed by her to Holmes and Watson late in Segment III.)
2. *Bound motif*—At an unspecified time, Watson and Duncan Bleek became friends, having both been in India and, later, members of the same club. (Watson tells Holmes about India while introducing Bleek in Segment III; in Segment XII he says, "I've known him for years," and mentions the club.)
3. *Bound motif*—At unspecified times, Colonel Sebastian Moran has made three attempts to kill Holmes. (Holmes tells Lestrade this in Segment X.)
4. *Bound motif*—Recently, Lady Carstairs and her son came to London; she attended a reception at Buckingham Palace and wore the Star of Rhodesia. An attempt was made to steal it during their stay. (Holmes, Carstairs, and Lady Carstairs discuss these events in Segment III, and Watson remarks that he read of the Palace reception in "last week's" paper.)
5. *Free motif*—Also recently, the Shelcrosses and Professor Kilbain traveled from their homes in Edinburgh to London. (Implied in questioning in Segments VII and VIII.)
6. *Bound motif*—Recently, Moran arranged his scheme by approaching Vedders about transporting the coffin, hiring the killer to travel with him, and getting the fake police to meet the train. (The coffin portion is revealed by Vedders in Segment XII, the rest at the end of Segment XV.)
7. *Bound motif*—Carstairs hired Holmes recently to accompany him and his mother to Edinburgh. (Revealed early in Segment III.)
8. *Free motif*—An extra day-coach has been added to the 7:30 Edinburgh train due to heavy booking. (Revealed by Carstairs in Segment III and reiterated by the attendant later in the same segment.)

Of the free motifs, motif 5 simply motivates the introduction of the conventional "red herring" suspects and comic figures to delay the plot progression. The addition of the day-coach (motif 8) enhances this pattern of digression and delay, serving at least three functions: it motivates putting all the characters together in the same carriage; it suggests that they all booked compartments at the last minute, and hence any one of them might have done so because Lady Carstairs did; and it insures that none will be able to go to bed, leaving them free to move about all night in a suspicious fashion, acting as red herrings. Almost none of the six bound motifs involves a mystery about the villain. They simply set up the basic situation that allows the narrative to occur at all. Most narratives presuppose at least a few earlier fabula events that are revealed through exposition, often early in the syuzhet. Again leaving aside the opening montage, in *Terror By Night* we learn of five of the eight pre-syuzhet events (motifs 1, 2, 4, 7, and 8) during the lengthy Segment III, which involves the gathering of the characters into the train for the journey. *Terror By Night* follows closely the standard five-part structure of the classical narrative: preliminary exposition, complicating action, development, climax, and denouement. Segments II and III correspond to the preliminary exposition phase, with the brief Segment IV leading up to the main complicating action, Carstairs's death early in Segment V. The functions of most of these eight early motifs are obvious. The gift of the diamond and its presence in London (motifs 1 and 4) provide the most basic motivation for the crimes and investigations. In itself the diamond has no significance; we have no particular sympathy for either Carstairs or his mother, and we are anxious to see it returned only because a failure would blot Holmes's reputation. (Note how Lady Carstairs and others scoff at him for having permitted the theft to occur.) When Holmes finally has Moran in custody and the Star in his possession at the end, he is satisfied, completely unconcerned that his client has been killed along the way. Watson's familiarity with Bleek (motif 2) permits Moran to deflect suspicion from himself—both Lestrade's and, for a time, ours. Motif 7, the hiring of Holmes, is, like the existence of the diamond itself, a sine qua non for the narrative and needs no causal justification within the film. It is realistically and transtextually motivated: Carstairs would of course hire the most famous detective in Great Britain, and we are familiar enough with Holmes as a character to know this without having to be told.

Motif 6, dealing with Moran's setting up of his scheme, is the only one actually central to the solution of any mystery, and that indeed is revealed in the conventional position at the end of the syuzhet, when Holmes explains to Watson how Moran managed the crime. But there is no elaborate assembling of the suspects by the detective in order for him to describe the crime and finger the guilty party. (Such a gathering was not typical of the original Holmes stories, but neither was the use of groups of red-herring suspects.) Holmes simply clears up the details for Watson in a few sentences. (Here the film contrasts even more sharply with the Doyle narratives, in which Holmes typically would spend the last scene explaining his solution in detail to Watson.)

But we have actually had our eye on Bleek for much of the syuzhet's unfolding. As early as Segment VIII, we see him playing cards with Watson, who reveals that Carstairs was killed with poison "from South America, probably, or India." Bleek, who up to now has been a pleasant and slightly comic fellow, a sort of restrained version of Watson, suddenly begins to look a bit sinister; his usual slight smile fades, and he stares at Watson intently as he says, in a meaning manner, *"I've been to India. So've you."* Presumably this is motivated as his testing of Watson to see if the latter is suspicious of his old pal. When Watson takes this as a joke, Bleek relaxes into his old manner. (Moran/Bleek is played by Alan Mowbray, a Hollywood actor associated equally with comic and villainous roles; thus a spectator would most likely take him as a Watson figure initially but would find his suspicious traits equally plausible here.) Events continue to suggest that Bleek is the real villain. In Segment XII Holmes asks Vedders if Bleek is the man who hired her, then asks Bleek if the name of Colonel Sebastian Moran means anything to him. Now we will be almost certain that he is at least the second villain, if not Moran himself—even though Holmes immediately assures him, "You have the perfect alibi—Dr. Watson." Finally, in Segment XIV, we leave Holmes's and Watson's POVs altogether and witness the killer's meeting with Moran. We therefore know the truth before the detective does and simply wait to discover if Moran will make good his escape with the real Star of Rhodesia.

Thus a film that started as an apparent murder mystery gradually drains the puzzle elements away, and in its second half it becomes more oriented toward suspense; we wonder not, who is the murderer, but, will the detective find out who he is in time. Alfred Hitchcock's familiar distinction between surprise and suspense is relevant here; while surprise involves withholding knowledge from the spectator (i.e., scrambling a fabula order in the syuzhet), suspense arises when the spectator knows more than does any one character. An example of suspense is the famous scene in *Sabotage*, in which we know the heroine's brother is carrying a time bomb, but he and the people he encounters are unaware of it. Hitchcock builds up suspense by introducing delaying tactics, as when the boy stops to help a sidewalk peddler demonstrate toothpaste.[8] In short, suspense usually involves stairstep construction, with complicating material—often, as in *Sabotage*, a series of free motifs—inserted at intervals. The situation does not remain wholly static, but we may be making progress toward a resolution only sporadically and in small steps.

[8] François Truffaut, *Hitchcock* (New York: Simon and Schuster, 1967), pp. 50–51, 76.

This, I would argue, is the case with *Terror By Night*. It is basically a suspense film, but it disguises its delaying devices by motivating them as part of the investigation of a mystery. We are unlikely to notice that most of the investigatory action comes to little—that it has in fact primarily *delayed*, rather than promoted, a solution. The film begins with the convention of a murder committed in a sealed area which contains a small number of people, and at first most of them seem possible suspects. After the murder of Carstairs, the narrative moves into the investigation phase (in conventional terms, the development); Holmes and Watson are closeted with Lestrade in the latter's compartment. (During their conversation, Holmes speaks the line that I have used as the title of this chapter; his claim that "nothing was left to chance" suggests that all the information given to us will eventually fit neatly together to solve the crime.) Here it appears that they will all work together, and they do at times join in questioning certain suspects, all three parting and meeting again in various combinations through the course of the action, until they all cooperate in the final fight in the dining car. But in between, Holmes, Lestrade, and Watson actually carry on three distinct lines of investigation, two of which provide the delaying material for the third one—which is, of course, Holmes's.

The Holmes-Lestrade-Watson conference in Segment v sums up the basic premises: the carriage is sealed (apparently), and no one left it after the murder; this is attested to by the fact that the locked luggage car is at the rear, and the attendant at the front, by the dining car, saw no one leave that way. The conductor gives Lestrade a list of the passengers. This list identifies some of them by name for the first time, though we saw all of them in Segment iii. Moreover, it gives a layout of where each one is, listing them in order by the letter of their compartments. Indeed, from this point on, the narrative takes on a schematic quality; the set, with its row of lettered compartments, becomes almost a static grid helping us to keep track of the main characters and the situation. A schematic overhead view of the set is shown in the diagram on page 64.

Lestrade takes the list he receives as a program for action; at intervals, particularly when he is at a loss, he pulls out the list and picks out a suspect to question. Indeed, in Segment x, when Holmes is trying to convince him that Moran is behind the murder, Lestrade goes through the list again. As he reads it, we see a montage of shots of each suspect in turn. The shots are of Kilbain, Vedders, Lady Carstairs, and Bleek; once again, the suspects are lined up for us in the order of their compartments, this time from rear to front. Lestrade

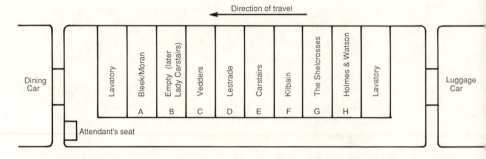

decides to go off and question Lady Carstairs, a rather arbitrary choice. Lestrade's investigation generally works along the lines of the mystery-story convention of questioning a series of suspects, and the fact that Lestrade is constantly held up to ridicule throughout the film confirms that this is the wrong way to go about things. Yet, for the first half of the film at least, this method seems on the surface to constitute the main line of action. The Holmes of this film does not behave as Doyle's Holmes would; that is, he does not conduct a minute search for physical clues in the compartment where the murder occurred. Rather, he seems to formulate no strategy at all, but simply accompanies Lestrade, apparently cooperating with him in the questioning. Yet almost nothing in this portion of the film contributes to his eventual solution of the mystery. We have no access to Holmes's thought processes and can only infer that in fact he is working independently of Lestrade, and along quite different lines.

In effect, Lestrade's investigation serves primarily as delaying material to pad the syuzhet. To solve the crime, the detectives first need to search the coffin in the luggage car. The discovery of a hidden compartment in the coffin reveals that there are two villains, one of whom is not a passenger. (Hence Bleek's alibi of having been with Watson is no alibi at all.) The stages by which Holmes's investigation of the crime progresses are few and simple. Because Vedders acts suspiciously when Lestrade and Holmes question her in Segment VI, Holmes decides that it would be a good idea to examine the coffin. He and Lestrade move to do so, but they are interrupted by Watson's news of Mr. Shelcross's "confession." This deflects the whole coffin issue for the time being and provides one of the major digressions in the film's stairstep construction. After the interruption, Holmes makes no apparent progress toward a solution for a while, but simply trails along with Lestrade again until Segment X, when he announces that he thinks Colonel Sebastian Moran is responsible; this was apparently suggested to him by the discovery that Professor Kilbain is a mathematics expert. (Moran's hobby is mathematics.) For some time Holmes seems to suspect that Kilbain may be Moran. In fact, Holmes is correct about Moran's being on board, but only later does he figure out which passenger he is. Since it is pure coincidence that Kilbain also happens to be interested in mathematics, Holmes's discovery of the criminal's identity remains on the level of intuition. This is peculiar, since the script could easily have introduced one crucial link that would have made Holmes's solution less intuitive—the dart gun. Had Holmes mentioned that Moran had tried in the past to kill him with a poisoned dart, the reasoning process would have been filled in. Here we would seem to have a gap in motivation due simply to "accident" or "lack of skill," as I suggested earlier.

After this introduction of Moran's name, Lestrade and Holmes split up, and Holmes's investigation takes precedence. In the second half of the film there is less delaying material, and it is here that Holmes does all the real detective work. After the brief delaying strategy of the attempt on Holmes's life in Segment XI, he finally goes back to his original plan from Segment VI and examines the coffin. Immediately after, he confronts Vedders with Bleek and asks the latter if he knows who Moran is. This question implies that Holmes has largely discerned the truth by this point, although there is very little in the film to suggest how he knows Bleek, and not Kilbain, is the master criminal. There is one rather strange moment in Segment IX, a short sequence in which Holmes joins Bleek and Watson in Bleek's compartment. Bleek and Watson offer the possibility that Lady Carstairs has herself committed the crime for the insurance money. On Bleek's part, this presumably is to be interpreted as an attempt to throw Holmes off the scent; Watson simply takes it as a reasonable theory. During the dialogue, Holmes stares intently at Bleek and remarks on his doodling. This doodling, which we see in a close shot, seems to have little significance: a man playing cricket and an ambulance, for example. But Holmes seems again to have intuited something from it. Indeed, throughout the film, Holmes tends to stare into people's faces, rather than to scan their clothes and belongings for clues, as Doyle's Holmes would do. The Holmes of *Terror By Night* operates in a more mysterious way, keeping things from Watson even at the end. Although Watson is here *not* a major POV character, the narration gives us no privileged insight into Holmes's mental processes at any point. His solutions are largely of this intuitive kind, and much of the film's motivational patterning is designed to conceal this fact. This lack of emphasis on Holmes's detecting skill is another element that makes *Terror By Night* more a thriller than a murder mystery.

When Holmes confronts Vedders with Bleek in Segment XII, the mystery seems largely solved. After this point, Holmes learns nothing more about Moran and his methods that is relevant to discovering the identity of the master criminal. When the killer is murdered later and his body found, the side issue of the accomplice is obviously cleared up. But still the film needs to delay closure, so it once again drops Holmes's investigation and concentrates on the thriller elements. For no apparent reason, Holmes, after reassuring Bleek that he is not a serious suspect, reveals in front of him that the real Star has not been stolen. Holmes had replaced it with a fake and now hands the real Star to Lestrade. We might assume that Holmes wants to catch Bleek in the act of stealing it, but in fact Holmes does not keep an eye on either Bleek or Lestrade; rather, he returns to the luggage car. There he finds the guard dead, with a poisoned dart in his neck. This may seem an important clue at the time, but Holmes already knows Carstairs was killed by poison, and nothing ever comes of this scene with the guard's body; it simply motivates the fact that Moran and his accomplice have a clear field in which to knock out Lestrade and take the real Star. Indeed, Holmes has carelessly put Lestrade's life in danger and allowed the real Star to be stolen. (Holmes here repeats the mistake he made with Carstairs. There it had not mattered that the stone was a fake, for as long as the thief thought it was real, he had a motive to kill Carstairs. Holmes should have been guarding his client rather than getting outside a steak-and-kidney pudding.) All this happens not because Holmes needs any more information to complete his investigation, but simply because the film needs one more large delaying device to avoid an ending. The delay provides the opportunity for more thrills as well. After Holmes boards the train and goes on duty, a whole series of violent events occurs: three separate murders, one attempted murder (with Holmes being pushed out the door), and two assaults (by the killer on the attendant and on Lestrade). The conventions of the thriller genre are dominant in this film, keeping the mystery elements subordinated. Action of this sort is ultimately more central to the film's appeal than are Holmes's mental calisthenics.

Holmes's final actions come once the false Inspector MacDonald boards the train. He reveals to MacDonald that Moran is on the train, under the name of Bleek. Then, when Moran tries to escape, Holmes deftly substitutes Lestrade for him and the fake Star once more for the real one. Holmes's intuitions and his agility have contributed as much to the successful outcome of his investigation as has his detective ability (again in keeping with the thriller orientation of the film).

Those moments when Holmes actually moves toward a solution are thus exceedingly simple: the examination of the coffin, the intuition of Moran's participation, and the later intuition of Moran's alias. In order to insert the thriller material that is actually its main element, the film spreads out these few bound motifs. We have already seen some of the motivating strategies, such as the apparent combination of Holmes's investigation (based on figuring out the method of the crime) with Lestrade's (based on questioning suspects who happen by chance to be present). But I mentioned that there is a third investigation being carried on by Watson, and here it becomes more obvious how free motifs create stairsteps in the syuzhet progression.

The 20th Century–Fox/Universal series is notorious among Holmes fans for its exaggeration of Watson's comic traits in comparison with the way Watson was portrayed in the original Doyle stories.[9] Nigel Bruce's mumbling delivery, double takes, and pauses before grasping Holmes's simplest statements suggest downright stupidity. In Doyle, Watson was a man of average intelligence, who as narrator could serve as a POV figure and suggest, through contrast, the nearly superhuman genius of the detective. The Watson of *Terror By Night* is not a POV figure; we are distanced from him because we understand far more than he does, and we see how very obtuse he is. In terms of B detective-series films, he and Lestrade fulfill the function of the standard comic-relief characters, such as the variously numbered sons in the Charlie Chan series, who try incompetently to emulate their father's skills. Beyond this, however, it must be said that of all the Universal Holmes films, *Terror By Night* probably places the greatest emphasis upon the stupidity of both Lestrade and Watson. In this case, the narrative depends extensively on their interference to provide delaying material.

As we have seen, *Terror By Night* begins with a conventional exposition section (Segments II and III). Once the complication arises with Carstairs's death, Lestrade, Holmes, and Watson sit down and lay out for us the elements which that death has introduced. As Lestrade and Holmes move to investigate Vedders, Watson, complaining because Holmes seems to be allowing Lestrade to run the investigation, remarks, "Could do it better myself." Holmes then replies, "Why don't you, old fellow?" and turns to join Lestrade in Vedders's

---

[9] David Stuart Davies, *Holmes of the Movies* (New York: Bramhall House, 1976), p. 60; Chris Steinbrunner and Norman Michaels, *The Films of Sherlock Holmes* (Secaucus: Citadel Press, 1978), p. 59.

compartment. This prompting leads to a series of short comic scenes of Watson's investigation, alternating with scenes of Lestrade and Holmes's. Watson initially questions Professor Kilbain, who manages to turn the inquiry back against Watson; by the beginning of Segment VII, Watson is on the defensive, feebly denying that he committed the murder, as Professor Kilbain towers accusingly over him. Holmes stops by Kilbain's compartment on his way to examine the coffin, just in time to rescue Watson from this situation.

As Watson joins Holmes in the corridor, the latter asks him, with quiet sarcasm, "Did you discover anything, Watson?" Throughout *Terror By Night*, Holmes taunts both Lestrade and Watson for their stupidity, and this running joke, casual though it seems, motivates his goading them both into searching along false paths. These wrong-headed lines of investigation in turn motivate deflections from our own concentration on Holmes's inquiries. Here we find a good instance of trivial free motifs masking major structural principles.

After Watson's failure with Professor Kilbain, Holmes sends him off again to try his luck with the Shelcross couple. Rather than moving on with Holmes toward the luggage compartment, the narration stays with Watson. Mr. Shelcross, assuming Watson to be a policeman, nervously declares, "It's all right, Inspector, I confess," at which point Watson jumps to conclusions and rushes off to fetch Holmes. He finds him with Lestrade, just about to open the luggage-car door. Holmes and Lestrade abandon this action to go and hear Mr. Shelcross's confession of the theft of the teapot. After this second failure, Watson gives up and goes off with Bleek to drink and play cards. From here on, Watson's role is relatively minor, up to the point in the final scene when he helps in the fight against Moran.

Watson's investigation, which appears to be a simple comic-relief device, actually comes at the exact point when Holmes is about to examine the one major tangible clue—the coffin. The Shelcross confession deflects the action entirely away from this, since neither Lestrade nor Holmes goes back to the luggage car after it ends. They go instead to question Professor Kilbain, and we are sidetracked from Holmes's investigation back to Lestrade's question-everybody strategy. Kilbain provides the major red herring of Segments VIII through X, as Holmes links him and Moran to mathematics and then skulks about spying on Kilbain.

After the attack on him in Segment XI, Holmes abandons Kilbain for good and again decides to examine the coffin. He remarks to Watson, "If you remember, I was interrupted the last time" (a remark which bares the device to some extent, but which is largely motivated by his frequent taunting of Watson). That "last time" was way back in Segment VII, and the action in between has been one elaborate "landing" in the film's stairstep construction. Because Watson's inquiries occupy a large early portion of the narrative's development section, any real progress in Holmes's investigation is retarded until over halfway through the film. As we have seen, that investigation provides only skimpy narrative material, hence the elaborate delaying patterns of the first half.

Terror By Night's delaying material, as structured around the three interwoven investigations, creates a narrative with a considerably lengthened stairstep structure. In a famous analysis, Shklovsky described the extremely elaborate stairstep construction in a far less conventional narrative, that of Laurence Sterne's *Tristram Shandy*. There the description of the hero's birth is delayed over and over by interruptions and inserted material of different types. In the novel, the narration constantly calls attention to these delays and how they are accomplished; such barings of the device become its dominant. Shklovsky ends his essay with the provocative remark, "*Tristram Shandy* is the most typical novel in world literature."[10] As I take it, he means by this not that *Tristram Shandy* is an ordinary novel, resembling many others closely and hence representative of them. Rather, he means that novels typically use stairstep construction to expand their material to create such a long narrative form. *Tristram Shandy*, which privileges and openly displays its delaying structures more than any other novel Shklovsky ever discussed, would be the most obvious and hence most comprehensible example of an extremely typical device. Shklovsky's essay was a pioneering study in the establishment of the concept of stairstep construction as such. Now, in looking at a conventional classical narrative work—one which in many ways stands opposite to *Tristram Shandy*—we can still find a great many delays occurring. The difference between these two types of narratives lies largely in the classical film's provision of numerous motivational devices, from the largest scale to the smallest, to camouflage from the perceiver the underlying workings of delay.

Thus we have seen that even an ordinary Hollywood film contains complex structures that challenge the analyst. By digging under the motivational materials, we can ourselves lay bare its inner workings, however much the Hollywood practitioner would wish these to remain hidden. The results, as Tynjanov suggested, are in fact as complex as

[10] Victor Shklovsky, "Sterne's *Tristram Shandy*: Stylistic Commentary," in *Russian Formalist Criticism: Four Essays*, trans. and ed. Lee T. Lemon and Marion J. Reis (Lincoln: University of Nebraska Press, 1965), p. 57.

in other types of art works. (They possess formal complexity, though their thematic material may not be as complex.) But an analysis of the motivation of narrative events does not exhaust the camouflaging structures of the Hollywood film. Stylistic patterns, which might in nonclassical works call attention to themselves, get the same treatment of thorough motivation.

STYLE AND MOTIVATION

One reason why the classical Hollywood narrative may give the impression of linearity is because the huge mass of a film's stylistic devices seems constantly to be providing us with new information. As we have seen, very little of that information may actually be leading us directly toward the conclusion of the fabula material; much of it, in fact, may be deflecting us into digressions. The stylistic devices of cutting, framing, mise-en-scene, and sound relate to all of the action in a similar way, whether the syuzhet material at any given time is a bound or a free motif. The style smooths over such distinctions and gives us a sense of watching one steady flow of events constantly progressing toward a conclusion.

Stylistic functions remain almost continually subordinated to the narrative, promoting this sense of flow; hence the term "continuity" system to describe the various guidelines Hollywood established early in its history to insure that the narrative would not be interrupted by gaps or repetitions of time or space. Most properly, the continuity system refers to a set of editing rules for joining shots smoothly and creating the impression of continuous time and space within scenes. But other techniques work along with editing to support the action and avoid distractions or lack of clarity. Again, *Terror By Night* is not representative of the usage of *all* Hollywood movies, for there is great variety of techniques even within such a clear-cut and stable system. But the film certainly adheres to Hollywood's guidelines and provides a good example of how narrative motivates style, which in turn functions to guide our understanding of narrative action and to conceal the film's formal workings.

As with the narrative, compositional motivation remains far and away the most important type. A single device may have multiple motivations, but realistic and artistic nearly always remain subordinate to compositional and transtextual in *Terror By Night*. For example, many Hollywood films contain cuts in which the characters' positions at the end of one shot are abruptly shifted at the beginning of the next (known as a "cheat" cut). This should, we would think, violate our notions of realism: people do not instantaneously move about in space. In an early scene in *Terror By Night* such a shift occurs, not once, but several times. As Vedders talks with Mr. Mock, the coffin-maker, a series of shot/reverse shots shows us each person in turn, generally favoring the one who is speaking; the cuts come between speeches or at pauses within one person's lines. This will be a frequent pattern throughout the film's dialogue scenes in train compartments, and it seems conventional enough. Yet with each cut, the position of Mock's son shifts distinctly. At the end of the opening crane shot down toward the shop, he is between the two and slightly to their rear (Fig. 2.1). The first cut shifts our view about 45° to favor Vedders; now young Mock is further forward and closer to Vedders's shoulder (Fig. 2.2). Were he not so shifted, Mr. Mock would now block our view of his son. Moreover, when the angle reverses to favor Mock, his son now appears behind *his* shoulder, to prevent his disappearance off to the right (Fig. 2.3). These spatial changes, so flagrant when laid out as illustrations, are not particularly noticeable in the film itself.

The cheat cut is possible in Hollywood because dialogue and action continue over the shot-change and guarantee a sense of continuous time and space. Here we are concentrating on Vedders and Mock: her instructions to him give us crucial information about the Edinburgh train; his sincere sympathy for her drains away as he sees how unconcerned she is about her mother's death. Why then put the son in at all? He does not speak and mostly stands gaping at Vedders, except for two brief actions: picking up her handkerchief and opening the door for her as the scene ends. Yet he serves to help characterize Vedders. She is, we begin to suspect in the course of this scene, a fake. On the surface she is elegantly dressed and has a vaguely upper-class British accent; hence the naive boy's awe at seeing her in a working-class area. But her speech contains traces of Cockney; as she drawls, "Rather a nuisance traveling by train—," she pauses and smiles at Mock, adding, "—ain't it?" in what we suspect is her own voice. Mock gradually sees through her and becomes annoyed as the scene ends. The emphasis in this scene has been primarily on the exposition of facts, but also on the increasingly apparent contrast between Vedders's appearance and real self. The boy thus helps define Vedders's disguise and, while not central to the scene, is important. We must be aware of his presence, yet not concentrate on it. Hence young Mock remains only peripherally in our minds and is the easiest of the three figures to cheat from shot to shot. Here compositional motivation takes precedence over realistic. (Note also that the walls with different tools hanging on them appear in the background of each shot, out of focus.

This is a redundant spatial cue that shows us we are still in the coffin-maker's shop, but it also keeps that visual information from distracting us from the main action.)

This is not to say that realistic motivation plays no part at all in the style of *Terror By Night*. It creeps in occasionally, just as it does in the narrative chain. Neill tends to film some shots with cluttered compositions, jamming a number of actors together, often in depth. The film has a decidedly post-*Kane* visual style, and to some degree the motivation is transtextual; mysteries, thrillers, films noirs, and similar genres tended to pick up deep staging, cluttered frames, wide-angle shooting—all of which had become conventional by the mid-1940s. *Terror By Night* takes advantage of its train setting to cluster characters together in somewhat lengthy takes, used as an occasional alternative to a shot/reverse shot decoupage of the scene. (In this realm, *The Adventures of Sherlock Holmes* [20th Century–Fox, 1939] provides an interesting contrast. Although it anticipates *Kane* in its stark lighting, its large, ceilinged sets, and its dramatic camera angles, *Adventures* usually isolates figures within the sets and breaks up most scenes into conventional cut-ins and shot/reverse shots.) Thus in the scene in which Lady Carstairs enters her compartment and is informed of her son's death, a whole group of men clusters around her and faces her (Fig. 2.4). A cut-in to Lady Carstairs emphasizes her reaction, but the scene returns to the general shot of the group rather than cutting to a reverse shot of Holmes (which would have been a more likely alternative in the 1930s). Then, after Holmes escorts Lady Carstairs out, the other men move about; Bleek ends with his back to the camera (Fig. 2.5). The staging of a scene with one major character in the foreground facing away from the camera was also a 1940s trait in Hollywood, and it is a device that appeals to realistic motivation (in life, people do stand facing different directions, and we do see people's backs). Yet compositional motivation retains its dominance. The scene's action motivates the characters' rearrangement: they move to watch Holmes escort Lady Carstairs away along the corridor. We know that the man in the foreground is Bleek, and we know he speaks the next line because Watson's and Lestrade's lips are visible and do not move. We also can recognize Bleek's voice asking, "Poor chap's mother, I presume?" This example may seem trivial, but it represents a change from earlier Hollywood practice, in which the idea was to keep everyone facing at least partially toward the front as much as possible during a scene. Indeed, *Terror By Night* contains a great many two- and three-shot framings in which characters speak to each other but angle their bodies toward the camera (e.g., Fig. 2.6). This is another Hollywood convention, involving compositional motivation on a small but pervasive scale. (As we shall see in upcoming chapters, clarity of staging need not take precedence over other motivations. In *Rules of the Game*, realistic motivation also justifies shot/reverse shot with characters turned away, but there some lack of clarity results, since we miss important facial reactions; compositional motivation in those scenes gets pushed to a subsidiary place. In *Tout va bien*, shot/reverse shot set-ups do not always permit us to see who is speaking; artistic motivation calls our attention to the deliberate lack of clarity.)

Artistic motivation may also appear in the Hollywood film, but again it is incidental to the necessities of the story. There are a few striking compositions in *Terror By Night*. As Professor Kilbain turns Watson's attempt at questioning him around and suggests that Watson himself might have committed the murder, Watson sinks down into a seat and Kilbain leans threateningly over him (Fig. 2.7). The medium close-up of the pair is distinctive, in that it is one of the few compositions in the film done with a diagonal orientation within a single foreground plane. We might be tempted to linger over it *as* a composition. Yet the framing serves at least two other functions, both relating to the narrative: it gives a rather conventional visualization of Kilbain as a threat to Watson, and it prepares for the moment when Holmes will appear, two shots later, in the background of this composition (with a rack focus transferring attention to him; see Fig. 2.8). In *Terror By Night* there are only a few such moments in which the style stands out as interesting in its own right, and certainly no instance in which a device is included solely for its own sake or to draw attention to itself; everything has *some* compositional function.

Most of *Terror By Night*'s stylistic devices have little or no realistic or artistic justification. They serve the narrative, giving us a sense of unbroken progress. Style serves to cue us about narrative information: it suggests the time and space within which the action is occurring, and it does so as unambiguously as possible; style places us in a favorable vantage point for seeing and hearing everything that the narration presents us with to use in reconstructing the fabula.

The continuity editing system is one central set of devices for constructing a clear understanding of narrative information. Since *Terror By Night* takes place almost entirely aboard a train, its most basic axis of action, or screen direction, is set up by the motion of the train itself. As the overhead view of the set shows (see diagram on p. 64), the dining car is at the front, the luggage car at the rear. The film sets up the train as moving from right background to left foreground in Segment III, where we initially see it from the platform. In every shot in

Segment III, it faces left. That becomes the standard screen direction for the train's progress throughout the film; almost invariably it moves from right to left. The film includes, at intervals, long shots of the train from outside; in virtually all these shots, screen direction is obeyed. Such cutaways to the train exterior involve stock footage and model shots; one stock shot which is cut in three times shows the cabin of the locomotive facing screen right, but this is a rare exception. On the whole, the train device does not cause problems in terms of screen direction. Within the train, shots in the corridor usually face the row of compartment doors obliquely, either toward the front or rear, and the dining car is inevitably off left—again, correct in terms of screen direction. Within the individual compartments, the eyelines and characters' screen positions set up the axes of action; these situations remain fairly simple, since each compartment has two long seats on opposite walls. The few violations of screen direction come as characters move from the corridor to a compartment, as when Watson enters Kilbain's compartment to question him (Figs. 2.9 and 2.10). Later, when Holmes returns to his compartment after the attack on his life, the eyelines between him and Watson are inconsistent. But on the whole the film keeps continuity as well as do most Hollywood films of the post-1917 period. This concern with continuity is crucial, since the characters in their series of compartments are arranged like beads on a string. To follow the action's progression, we must be able to grasp at all times whether the characters are moving toward the front or the rear of the carriage.

Given this simple maintenance of clear space as a foundation, the film employs three principal variations in the stylistic treatment of different types of scenes: compartment scenes, corridor action, and cutaways to the train exterior. Most of the questioning and actual investigation goes on in compartments and is handled in either shot/reverse shot or somewhat lengthy takes. The camera moves little within these confined spaces, except for frequent small reframings. One distinctive but almost unnoticeable exception comes in the scene in which Holmes mentions Moran to Lestrade for the first time. An extremely slow track-in occurs during their conversation, emphasizing this crucial step in solving the mystery. In the compartment scenes, characters tend to enter and exit abruptly through the onscreen doors, breaking the action into distinct subsegments.

In contrast to these conversation scenes, the portions of the action that take place in corridors generally avoid shot/reverse shot, substituting a mobile camera. We have seen how the delaying patterns depend on the narration's unobtrusively shifting our attention among the three interwoven lines of investigation. Sometimes, of course, straight cuts achieve these shifts, as when two brief scenes of Watson questioning Professor Kilbain alternate with Holmes and Lestrade interviewing Vedders. But for movements between the compartments, the film often uses a more subtle shifting device based on camera movement. As I have said, the framing shows us oblique views of the compartment doors. Frequently characters walk along the corridor in various groups, with the camera tracking along with them. Sometimes they come toward the camera, which moves more slowly than they, pans to follow them as they pass close to it, then tracks slowly after them. At other times the camera keeps up with the characters, then pauses with them as they stop at a compartment door. This camera mobility sets the corridor scenes off from the more static conversations in the compartments.

Sometimes these camera movements overtly draw our attention to things; a number of times a camera moving with a character along the corridor will pause at Vedders's compartment to reveal her staring out, spying on what is happening. Here the narration tries to center suspicion on her, even though she plays only a minor role in the actual crimes. Such moments are transtextually as well as compositionally motivated: in crime films, the framing often emphasizes clues or suspicious behavior.

But the framing also acts at other times as a far more covert form of narration. The easy mobility of the corridor shots seems at most points simply to allow us to "keep up with" the characters' movements. Yet often it will shift our attention smoothly from one set of characters to another. When Lestrade, Holmes, and Watson have finished conferring after the murder (Segment v), Lestrade decides to question Vedders. At the beginning of a shot of his compartment door (Compartment D), Lestrade comes forward into medium shot, looking off left along the corridor and consulting his list: "Vedders, Compartment C" (Fig. 2.11). As he sets out, the camera pans left with him and tracks to follow him from a three-quarters rear vantage (Fig. 2.12), with the conductor occasionally visible at the right frame line, following him. As Lestrade stops at the door of Compartment C, the camera also stops, and Holmes moves in at the right, with Watson's shadow falling on him from off right (Fig. 2.13). Lestrade goes into the empty compartment, followed by the conductor, but Watson moves in from the right and detains Holmes. They are now in a conventional two-shot framing (Fig. 2.14), and Watson makes his complaint, with Holmes urging him to investigate on his own. Holmes then enters the compartment, and there is a reframing to center on Watson, who moves along the corridor toward the rear of the car, with the framing following him and pausing at each door as he looks for someone to question (Fig. 2.15). Finally, the camera allows him to get a bit ahead, and he is seen obliquely from behind as he reaches Compartment F and knocks (Fig. 2.16). This view reverses and balances the earlier rear view of Lestrade (Fig. 2.12).

This extended take, typical of the film's corridor shots, shifts us neatly from the Lestrade line of inquiry to that of Watson. A similar ploy occurs later, at a more crucial moment in this comic digression. After his failure with Kilbain, Watson rejoins Holmes in the corridor; the latter is on his way to make his first attempt at entering the luggage car to examine the coffin. At first the two are seen in another medium two-shot, favoring Holmes past Watson's shoulder (Fig. 2.17). After some sarcastic remarks at Watson's expense, Holmes turns away and moves toward the rear right, toward the luggage car (Fig. 2.18); the camera tracks obliquely forward to follow, and Watson goes after Holmes. But rather than going on directly to the luggage car, Holmes pauses by Compartment G (the Shelcrosses) and suggests that Watson try again. The camera also pauses. Watson knocks on the door as Holmes exists to the right rear, again toward the luggage car (Fig. 2.19); rather than following him, the camera holds on Watson. Here camerawork functions along with other devices to keep the Watson digression going, focusing our attention on a minor action when the potentially informative investigation is going on offscreen. Again, the frame, which seems to move so conveniently to show us things, leads us away from the most "linear" series of events; hence the framing's motivation is once again compositional, since the mobile camera helps create the film's stairstep construction.

The third variation in stylistic treatment comes in a series of cutaways from the compartments and corridor to views of the train's exterior as it passes through the countryside. Some of these views are extreme long shots of the train as a whole, and some show only parts, such as the wheels or whistle. Such shots are conventional in a train film (e.g., *North by Northwest*), but *Terror By Night* is quite insistent in their use: they constitute approximately 41 of the film's 410 shots (splices in the print examined may make these figures slightly inaccurate), or about one-tenth.

These cutaways fulfill some predictable compositional functions: they give a sense of the journey continuing toward Scotland by showing progressively hillier landscapes, and they help show when the train is starting and stopping, as when the fake Inspector MacDonald comes aboard. A series of train parts picking up speed creates suspense as Watson and Bleek nearly miss the train in Segment III; this subsegment is transtextually motivated. But there are more of the shots than the film needs to give information or create suspense. Other cutaways serve to break the film up into scenes; almost every transition from one sequence to another involves one or more shots of the train's exterior. These little pauses help the spectator grasp the film's progression, since the temporal intervals between the scenes are sometimes brief or even nonexistent. At a few points cutaways cover shifts of locales within a single scene; in this sense they substitute for the moving camera as a device for smoothing over small-scale transitions. For example, when Holmes, in the dining car, reveals that Bleek is really Moran, the subsegment ends with Watson's protests; there follows a long shot of the train going past the camera, then a shot of a policeman entering Bleek's compartment and summoning him for questioning. As he agrees and gets up to go to the dining car, there is a cut to an extreme long shot of the train, then another to the dining car, with Bleek and the policeman entering after a few seconds. These cutaways cover the briefest of ellipses.

At times, the cutaways do not even cover such small temporal gaps. In Segment XI, when Holmes finally decides to try again to inspect the coffin, he and Watson exit from their compartment, which is the last one, just in front of the luggage car. A cut follows to a long shot of the train, then another returns us to Holmes and Watson approaching the luggage-car door. Here the action of their walk along a few feet of corridor conceivably would take *less* time than the cutaway occupies, but without the cutaway the two shots would not fit together properly in terms of the axis of action: the two men exit and turn toward the left in the first shot, but are moving to the right rear in the corridor shot.

Thus the shots of the train exterior have a great variety of functions, yet they give the impression of being the same each time. We are not likely to be aware of their different functions, and therefore their occasional use to cover mistakes or ellipses is hardly noticeable to the spectator. Few of the cutaways give us additional narrative information. We always know, for example, when the train is moving, because the sound track contains a continuous low clack of wheels at such times. But this relative lack of a direct causal function does not mean that the cutaways are included simply for their own sake. Aside from the specific functions I have suggested, in general they punctuate the action at fairly regular, almost rhythmic intervals; as a result, they may convey a sense that the narrative is moving forward steadily and in a linear fashion. Thus they serve as another compositionally motivating

77

device to mask the considerable digressions that deflect the syuzhet from its forward progression.

As this analysis suggests, the camera works in conjunction with the set design. Another glance at the overhead sketch of the relationships among the three carriages shows a schematically balanced spatial layout of narrative elements. The murder occurs about midway along the day-coach, in Compartment E, with the murderer hiding in the luggage car at the rear and the majority of the characters eating in the dining car at the front during the crime. (The victim, Kilbain, and Lestrade are the only exceptions.) Holmes and Watson occupy the compartment nearest the rear. The villian is in the one closest to the front. Thus the first half of the film, during which Holmes makes little actual progress toward solving the case, consists mainly of a gradual movement of the action toward the rear of the train—the luggage car—and away from Bleek. The first compartment we see in Segment III, once the characters have entered the train, is Bleek's; he pauses in front of it as Watson introduces him to Holmes (Fig. 2.20). Then, as Holmes and Watson move toward the rear, they pass Compartment B, which is empty (and hence de-emphasized) and Compartment C, where Vedders is snooping (Fig. 2.21). They skip D and enter E to consult with Carstairs and his mother. But as they do, the camera picks up the attendant passing in the hall and pans right with him (Fig. 2.22); he exits right, but the camera pauses on Professor Kilbain (Fig. 2.23), visible in Compartment F. He also seems to be spying suspiciously on Holmes and Watson. A cutaway to the train exterior covers a move into the Carstairs's compartment, and the scene continues. After the conversation about the diamond, Carstairs gives Holmes the registration slip for Compartment H, which he is to share with Watson. But instead of going there, the pair encounters Lestrade outside his compartment, D (Fig. 2.24). As they chat with Lestrade, a woman passes in the foreground going right, and the camera picks up her movement and tracks behind her to Compartment G (Fig. 2.25), which she enters. A cut takes us inside, where we observe Shelcross's nervous reaction to his wife's announcement that police are aboard the train. This ends Segment III, with its lengthy exposition. The second half of this segment, after the characters have boarded the train, uses the row of compartments along with fluid shifts of the viewer's attention, accomplished via the tracking camera, to introduce us quickly to the entire set of travelers (all of whom except the Shelcrosses and Lady Carstairs we have seen on the platform already). During the initial platform portion of the segment, we (along with Holmes and Carstairs) watch the coffin being loaded into the luggage car; directly after this,

Carstairs specifically tells Holmes that his compartment is "in this coach here, just ahead of the luggage van." But in fact the only compartment we do *not* see during Segment III is Holmes and Watson's.

The withholding of this area of the carriage helps mark off the stages of progression toward solving the mystery involved with the coffin. The early parts of the narrative make us suspicious of the coffin: it takes up much of Segment II and the early portions of Segment III. But now, to prevent our becoming *too* interested in it, the camera largely avoids the rear area of the day-coach. We see it only at three moments before the actual examination of the coffin. In Segment V, as Lestrade tries to enter the locked Compartment E, where Carstairs lies dead, we first see the full length of the row of doors, with Compartment H at the right foreground (Fig. 2.26). This framing calls attention to the whole lineup of suspects and also draws us nearer to where the killer is now lurking—though we are not likely to pick up on such a subtle hint. When Lestrade and Holmes are interrupted as they try to enter the luggage car in Segment VII (Fig. 2.27), we see its door for the first time; but we only get a brief view, while our attention is focused on Watson's revelation. Finally, at the beginning of Segment X, we again see a view of the corridor with Compartment H in the foreground. Holmes is actually in Compartment D chatting with Lestrade and introducing his suspicious about Moran; later he moves to Compartment H, looking back as he does so to catch Vedders snooping once again. This scene marks off, in a rather literal fashion, Holmes's move to the rear of the car. In the next segment he will finally examine the coffin. (The luggage car scenes use the fluid camera movement characteristic of the corridor scenes, while the dining car is treated as a series of smaller compartments—that is, the individual tables—with mostly shot/reverse shot.)

Once the clue of the coffin's false bottom is discovered, the whole spatial orientation of the film reverses, and Holmes's investigation becomes a move from the rear of the train toward Moran in Compartment A. Indeed, the final action takes place even further forward, with the fight in the dining car; we last see Holmes and Watson seated at a table there, waiting to hand the manacled Moran over to the Edinburgh police.

CONCLUSIONS: IDEOLOGICAL IMPLICATIONS

Of course, this schematic layout is not readily apparent upon a first viewing of the film. The action moves quickly, and there are too many characters and similar compartments for the spectator to assimilate them thoroughly. All that is apparent is that the set design and framing of space are helping in some way to organize the narrative action in a more comprehensible fashion. Yet the narration can use these same stylistic devices to conceal information as well. As I suggested at the beginning of the last section, the apparent homogeneity of the film's style, and its apparent continuity, makes the information-revealing and concealing functions of the individual devices difficult to differentiate. Occasionally we may notice a flagrant withholding of crucial matter, as in the scenes where we glimpse the killer—kicking Holmes out of the train or slipping out of the luggage car—but we cannot see his face. But as with the scenes where the camera points out suspicious actions to us, such manipulation is transtextually motivated by genre, and not seen as "unfair" on the part of the narration. On the whole, however, the constant motivation of the stylistic devices de-emphasizes their manipulative functions. Classical style seems largely informative, straightforward, "helpful." In this way it succeeds in creating a sort of veneer which conceals the underlying plot manipulations from the spectator.

Indeed, this veneer of motivation seems even to conceal considerable disparities and gaps in the plot. Some of these, such as Holmes's lack of evidence for his various conclusions and the general lack of concern over Carstairs's murder, have emerged in this analysis; yet they may be hidden during regular viewing. One fan-oriented book on the series, for example, finds *Terror By Night* "one of the most effective of the Holmes series, but it is also one of the most original murder-on-the-train movies ever made."[11] The author notices none of the problems that have emerged here. Possibly many average Hollywood films have gaps in logic similar to those of *Terror By Night*, but the overall construction gives the impression of the "tight" unity for which the classical script has become famous. The bound and free motifs that form the syuzhet's stairstep construction are motivated so that they all seem to move us forward in a linear fashion toward closure. At most, Watson's comic investigation will be noticed as a slowdown in the main action, but it will be accepted as transtextually motivated.

This analysis has concentrated on how devices function to delay narrative progression, and hence it does not begin to exhaust the ways in which the stylistic devices of *Terror By Night* are motivated: how every cut helps to shift the balance of the dialogue in terms of speeches and reactions, how tiny glances and gestures by the actors are nuances of their characters' relationships to others present in a

[11] Davies, *Holmes of the Movies*, p. 95.

scene, how depth of field emphasizes some characters and keeps others peripherally present, and so on. But it does give a general indication of how motivation confines the style of a classical film almost exclusively to functioning in the creation of the narrative.

The camouflaging motivations of the syuzhet tend to mask the ideological implications as well. Since the film appears to be entirely in the detective genre, we presume that Holmes is solving the crime in a logical, linear fashion—though, as we have seen, this is not actually the case. The thriller elements intrude and considerably roughen the form of his investigation. But Holmes is depicted as superior to the official representatives of societal law, and hence he is able to name the criminal, not through logic, but simply because of his superiority.

Though the film contains little explicit social subject matter, there are a number of implicit and symptomatic meanings that constitute the film's ideological level. It is a convention of detective novels that the detective, whether official or private, usually upholds the existing laws. Some, like Lord Peter Wimsey, may suffer guilt pangs at having brought criminals to punishment, but they seldom question the laws they uphold. In this sense, the detective genre fosters works that support the status quo and hence are weighted toward a conservative ideology. As Julian Symons put it: "The values put forward by the detective story from the time of Holmes to the beginning of World War II, and by the thriller and the spy story up to the advent of Eric Ambler are those of a class that felt it had everything to lose by social change."[12] (More recently, some authors have tried to avoid this pattern by playing with narration, as when Ruth Rendell concentrates on the points of view of victim and criminal.) The privileging of the detective as more intelligent and insightful than the other characters helps to naturalize this ideology.[13]

[12] Quoted in Dennis Porter, *The Pursuit of Crime: Art and Ideology in Detective Fiction* (New Haven: Yale University Press, 1981), p. 161.

[13] For a detailed historical analysis of the ideology of detective fiction, see Porter's *The Pursuit of Crime*. Porter's use of Russian Formalism and structuralist concepts leads to some revealing analyses of the works of Doyle, Christie, Hammett, Chandler, and others. His attempt to use Barthes's psychoanalytic concept of *le plaisir du texte* in relation to the genre is less successful. He argues that the popular detective story is a readable text, and that the consumption of it brings a pleasure comparable to that of the sexual act, with closure equaling orgasm. But, because he also wants to argue that the detective story has historically been conservative, he ends by suggesting that modernist, "writerly" versions of the detective story, such as works by Robbe-Grillet and Borges, are ideologically more progressive and are also the equivalents of *coitus interruptus* or of some sort of perpetual striptease with no payoff. While a detective story without closure, or with some sort of radical, formal distancing device, might be an ideologically desirable thing, it is going to be difficult to win converts to that view by suggesting that *coitus interruptus* is also a good thing. Nevertheless, Porter's overall historical ground-

In *Terror By Night*, the ideological implications of the narrative are strikingly conservative. The characters who are relevant to the crime are divided between the upper and lower classes. On the one hand, the victims, Lady Carstairs and young Carstairs, are extremely wealthy and in high society: the Star of Rhodesia is worth £50,000, and its owner attends functions at Buckingham Palace. Similarly, the "mastermind" of the crime is at least of the upper-middle class: Moran was an officer in India, played cricket, belongs to clubs, and is, in short, a gentleman. His motive for indulging in jewel theft is suggested to be some sort of sporting instinct; he steals perhaps for the thrill of it rather than through necessity. On the other hand, his assistants are both defined by their accents as being of working-class origins, and both are motivated solely by a cynical desire for money. In the social system of this film, lower-class characters simply carry through commands but are not capable of planning the crime. Note in this regard also the emphasis placed upon Lestrade's working-class accent and his ignorance about trout and salmon fishing, for which Holmes and Watson mock him. The middle classes provide the film's red-herring characters, in the form of the petty bourgeois Shelcross couple and the intellectual Professor Kilbain. Similarly, we can assume that Holmes and Watson are themselves middle-class. The middle classes are the bulwark of respectability and stability in society; the most obvious manifestation of this is that Holmes solves the case. But in addition, the red-herring characters are basically honest, in spite of the comic byplay with the stolen teapot. Mrs. Shelcross is highly indignant over her husband's little theft, and he confesses instantly to Watson when confronted, nervously assuring Lestrade that it is his first offense. Kilbain quite rightly points out that Watson has no right to question him and moreover is just as logical a suspect in the case. The professor also scoffs at Holmes's predilection for guarding fabulous jewels.

Indeed, the nature of Holmes's job in this case underlines the highly conservative meanings of the film—especially if we contrast it with the behavior of Doyle's original character. In the novellas and

---

ing of his analysis is impressive and convincing. Other interesting ideological analyses of the genre can be found in Stephen Knight's *Form & Ideology in Crime Fiction* (Bloomington: Indiana University Press, 1980), which has a chapter on Holmes, and Ernest Mandel's *Delightful Murder: A Social History of the Crime Story* (London: Pluto Press, 1984). The former is flawed by its naive interpretation of clichéd Freudian imagery and its persistent attempts to read effects of Doyle's personality into the stories; the latter takes an overly simple Marxist template of social history, then fits the history of the genre into it, occasionally oversimplifying or omitting data to make the case more neatly.

stories, as Dennis Porter has suggested, Holmes embodies "the heroic qualities of the ascendant middle classes" of Victorian and Edwardian England.[14] We know that Holmes takes on or refuses cases on the basis of how intriguing he finds them. At the beginning of "The Adventure of Black Peter" (*The Return of Sherlock Holmes*), Watson states:

I should be guilty of an indiscretion if I were even to hint at the identity of some of the illustrious clients who crossed our humble threshold in Baker Street. Holmes, however, like all great artists, lived for his art's sake, and, save in the case of the Duke of Holdernesse, I have seldom known him claim any large reward for his inestimable services. So unworldly was he—or so capricious—that he frequently refused his help to the powerful and wealthy where the problem made no appeal to his sympathies, while he would devote weeks of most intense application to the affairs of some humble client whose case presented those strange and dramatic qualities which appealed to his imagination and challenged his ingenuity.

Here Watson is forgetting such incidents as the £1,000 for "present expenses" that Holmes takes from the king at the beginning of "A Scandal in Bohemia," the gold snuffbox he later receives from the same source, the ring from the "reigning family of Holland" ("A Case of Identity"), and so on. One must assume for plausibility's sake that Holmes is a sort of legally respectable Robin Hood, making his rich clients' fees underwrite his less lucrative cases.

The Holmes of *Terror By Night* behaves quite differently. He takes on the comparatively mundane job of guarding a rich woman's jewel, because he suspects another attempt will be made to steal it. Yet Lestrade is already on this case, and there is no reason for Holmes to anticipate that the thieves present any intriguing challenge. The scriptwriters could have motivated all this by suggesting from the start that Holmes believes his old enemy, Colonel Moran, is lurking about. (Doyle, in fact, frequently used supercriminals like Moriarty and Moran to arouse interest at the beginning of a seemingly unimportant case.)

Since the film provides no such hint, however, we are left with the situation of Holmes as a paid watchdog. Moreover, though his client, Lady Carstairs behaves rudely to Holmes in their initial interview, the latter does not take offense. Rather, he continues to be deferential and friendly throughout the scene—very different from Doyle's cynical, ironic Holmes. Given the matter-of-fact, even insolent way the original Holmes treats his wealthy clients (e.g., in "The Adventure of the Noble Bachelor" and "A Scandal in Bohemia"), it is difficult to imagine

[14] Porter, *The Pursuit of Crime*, p. 157.

him putting up with Lady Carstair's behavior; he would have stalked out or humbled her through verbal sparring. The film's portrayal of Holmes's docility makes him the unquestioning defender of a system of laws designed to uphold upper-class values; that is, the upper classes have certain privileges, which the middle classes support by remaining moral and respectable. Those values are threatened by lower-class rebellion and occasional renegade action in the ranks of the more privileged classes, but the law's justice eventually sets all to rights once more.

Thus the film is weighted more toward the ascendency of wealth and privilege than were the books, which favored a notion that the middle classes were the source of social strength. This is not to imply that Doyle's works were particularly liberal or progressive, but they were certainly less conservative than *Terror By Night*. Holmes's habit of occasionally letting the criminals go free in the original Doyle stories at least hints that social justice is not always actual justice. When otherwise decent people commit crimes, Holmes makes himself the judge (and, in "The Adventure of the Abbey Grange," appoints Watson the jury) and takes it upon himself to thwart the official law. He can do so to the reader's satisfaction only because he has been created as a character superior to the law, and that in itself has conservative ideological connotations. While the Holmes of *Terror By Night* is equally above the law, he never questions it.

The upper-class characters with whom he deals in the film have subtle links to colonialism which help define the class relations more specifically. For example, it is stated at the beginning that the Star of Rhodesia was found by a Kaffir. Like so many spoils of colonialist rule as portrayed in British literature, it has a deadly stigma of bad fortune (not here defined explicitly as a curse). Similarly, Watson hints that the strange poison that Moran uses in his darts is probably from South America or India. Thus, although military service in India is presented as respectable (accounting in part for the fact that so little suspicion falls on Moran at first), that country can also be the source of exotic dangers. Even a trivial joke like the one made in the dining-car scene suggests a similar point: Bleek and Watson debate at length the virtues of curry, which Holmes dismisses as "horrible stuff," preferring a solidly respectable British steak-and-kidney pudding. Yet, though the outward signs of colonialism are treated negatively, there is never any question that the most obvious symbol of exploitation, the Star, belongs rightly to Lady Carstairs, or that the efforts of Holmes and Scotland Yard to preserve it for her are justified. This uneasiness in the depiction of colonialism, and the general de-emphasis of this motif, suggest an ideological problem that the film does not confront. These factors also suggest why the murder of Carstairs—not to mention two other "unimportant" characters—can seem less important than the preservation of the jewel itself. Carstairs may be lost to his mother, but his death can be avenged by the law. The loss of the jewel, however, can only be balanced by its return; as long as its owner does not possess it, its potential use by someone, especially by one of the criminals, makes any punishment of the thieves hollow. By further implication, the system of traditional laws, including those which permit colonialism, can only be upheld through the return of the Star of Rhodesia.[15]

As part of its conservatism, the film avoids the type of cynicism concerning law enforcement that was being introduced into the American cinema by the *film noir* and hard-boiled detective wings of the genre. In *Terror By Night* police officials may be slow-witted, but they are not corrupt; Holmes may twit Lestrade, but he does not oppose him. Here the casting of Rathbone in the lead becomes interesting. Although he had frequently played the caddish seducer or the other man in melodramas, his most prestigious roles had been in a series of "all-star" literary adaptations at MGM—*David Copperfield, Anna Karenina, A Tale of Two Cities, Romeo and Juliet*—just before he became typed as Holmes in the late 1930s. In effect, Universal's B unit could produce its own detective-genre equivalents of these expensive films by using largely British or pseudo-British casts in modernized adaptations of more popularly oriented classics. In this sense *Terror By Night* can be seen as using class relations to aim at a sort of lowbrow snob appeal, following the ideological patterns of the old-fashioned British school of detective fiction.

WE HAVE NOW found a number of underlying patterns in *Terror By Night* that are quite complex—particularly the differing spatial orien-

[15] The film's ambivalence in its treatment of colonialism is actually quite close to that of some Victorian-Edwardian authors. Doyle's adventure novel, *The Lost World*, and H. Rider Haggard's *King Solomon's Mines* contain remarkably parallel narratives in which small groups of British explorers discover ancient communities that have survived in isolated regions. After helping the "progressive" portions of the population to defeat a more barbaric group militarily, the explorers return to civilization, bearing a small number of diamonds and resolving to keep the location of the region a secret in order to prevent outside exploitation. The ambivalence is clear: small numbers of conscientious British visitors can aid a primitive civilization and in turn profit from it with moral impunity, but large-scale exploitation would be repugnant.

In such cases, ambivalent attitudes toward colonialism are explicit meanings. *Terror By Night*, however, deals with a type of colonialism that was largely out-of-date by 1946, and the film's audiences would not be likely to have strong attitudes about the subject. Hence colonialism remains a convenient symbol of the upper-class values that the film sets up as being threatened.

tations of the first and second halves of the film. The discovery of such complexities might lead us at first to conclude that the film is a good one. Yet in light of the many narrative problems and conventional devices we have also found, it seems unlikely that anyone would claim it is much better than average. I think we must conclude rather that the classical Hollywood system is in itself complex. Its standardized guidelines would allow a wide range of choices that would create a unique artwork. Yet every work could also borrow some of the complexity of the whole system. Many of the types of motivation we have seen at work in *Terror By Night* would have been virtually automatic to Hollywood filmmakers.

A film need not, however, adhere to established conventions so thoroughly as does *Terror By Night*. The remainder of this book will examine a variety of other films, all of them offering some type of alternative to the classical Hollywood model. Some will privilege realistic motivation, others artistic, and the resulting formal dominants will vary considerably. In examining *Late Spring*, for example, we shall see how a filmmaker can use cutaways in a train sequence to confuse in a playful way the spectator's sense of temporal flow and character position, and how primarily artistic motivation can be used to organize the editing.

These other films were all chosen because they are original and unconventional in striking ways. They differ in quality, but in comparison with the average classical film, all are "outstanding" in some way. In this sense, these other films will seem closer to the kind of subject the critic traditionally chooses. Yet they will all share with an average film like *Terror By Night* certain aesthetic problems: the arbitrariness of the syuzhet duration in relation to the fabula, the consequent need to combine digression and progression, the urge to create some degree of unity through motivation, and so on. But their individual solutions to such problems will differ greatly from those of *Terror By Night*, and hence their individual dominant structures will suggest a variety of analytic methods. Since finding the dominant is an important step in analyzing any film, the next section will deal with this basic concept.

PART THREE

Analyzing the
Dominant

3

Boredom on the Beach: Triviality and Humor in *Les Vacances de Monsieur Hulot*

He is capable of filming a beach scene simply to show that the children building a sandcastle drown the sound of the wave with their cries. He will also shoot a scene because just at that moment a window is opening in a house away in the background, and a window opening—well, that's funny. That is what interests Tati. Everything and nothing. Blades of grass, a kite, children, a little old man, anything, everything which is at once real, bizarre, and charming. Jacques Tati has a feeling for comedy because he has a feeling for strangeness.

—Jean-Luc Godard, *Godard on Godard*, 1972

THE DOMINANT

IN CHAPTER 1, I suggested that the dominant is one of the neoformalist critic's most important tools. The basic definition of the term is simple enough: the dominant is a formal principle that controls the work at every level, from the local to the global, foregrounding some devices and subordinating others. As Tynjanov put it, "A system does not mean coexistence of components on the basis of equality; it presupposes the preeminence of one group of elements and the resulting deformation of other elements."[1] In practice, however, the dominant can be a difficult concept to apply; using various statements on the subject by the Russian Formalists and later commentators, I shall attempt in this chapter to provide a more clear-cut view of how the analyst can go about formulating a dominant for a work.

At first, the dominant would seem to be simply another word for unity, for a structure that pulls together all the devices of a work into an organic whole. But, except in its earliest formulation, this was not, in fact, its meaning. According to both Victor Erlich and Peter Steiner,

[1] Quoted in Victor Erlich, *Russian Formalism: History—Doctrine*, 3d ed. (The Hague: Mouton, 1969), p. 199.

Eikhenbaum first borrowed the idea from Broder Christiansen's *Philosophie der Kunst*; wrote Eikhenbaum:

It happens only rarely that the motive factors of an esthetic object participate equally in the effects of the whole. On the contrary, normally, a single factor or a configuration of them comes to the fore and assumes a leading role. All the others accompany the dominant, intensify it through their harmony, heighten it through contrast, and surround it with a play of variations. The dominant is the same as the structure of bones in an organic body: it contains the theme of the whole, supports this whole, enters into relation with it.[2]

Steiner argues that although Eikhenbaum occasionally used the term this way, and it was picked up by Soviet scholars studying morphology, Eikenbaum soon departed from this organicist usage. His later conception was the one employed by the Russian Formalists.

He saw the work not as a harmonious correlation of parts and wholes but as dialectic tension among them. "The work of art," Eikhenbaum argued, "is always the result of a complex struggle among various form-creating elements; it is always a kind of compromise. These elements do not simply co-exist and 'correlate.' Depending upon the general character of the style, this or that element acquires the role of the organizing *dominant* governing all the others and subordinating them to its needs."[3]

This view, formulated as early as 1922, is an attractive one, for it suggests that the work of art is dynamic, and that its form challenges the spectator into an active viewing—not into a contemplation of a unified, static whole.

Other Formalists elaborated this idea. Roman Jakobson's discussions are perhaps the best known, though his definition retains a touch of the initial, relatively static, organicist concept; he considers the dominant to be "the focusing component of a work of art: it rules, determines, and transforms the remaining components."[4] A more dynamic version was worked out by Tynjanov; writing in 1923, he declared (the translators substituted the term "constructive principle" for "dominant"):

This dynamism [of form] reveals itself in the concept of the constructive principle. Not all factors of a work are equivalent. Dynamic form is not generated by means of combination or merger (the often-used concept of "correspond-

---

[2] Erlich, *Russian Formalism*, p. 178n; Peter Steiner, "Three Metaphors of Russian Formalism," *Poetics Today* 2, no. 1b (Winter 1980/81): 93.

[3] Steiner, "Three Metaphors," p. 93.

[4] Roman Jakobson, "The Dominant," trans. Herbert Eagle, in *Readings in Russian Poetics*, ed. Ladislav Matejka and Krystyna Pomorska (Cambridge, Mass.: MIT Press, 1971), p. 82.

ence"), but by means of interaction, and, consequently, the pushing forward of one group of factors at the expense of another. In doing so, the advanced factor deforms the subordinate ones. The sensation of form is always the sensation of the flow (and, consequently, of the alteration) or correlations between the subordinating, constructive factor and the subordinated factors. It is not obligatory to introduce a *temporal* nuance into this concept of flow, or "unfolding." Flow and dynamics may be taken as such, outside of time, as pure movement. Art lives by means of this interaction and struggle. Without this sensation of subordination and deformation of all factors by the one factor playing the constructive role, there is no fact of art. ("The co-ordination of factors is a type of negative characterization of the constructive principle." V. Shklovsky) If this sensation of the *interaction* of factors disappears (which assumes the compulsory presence of *two* features: the subordinating and the subordinated), the fact of art is obliterated. It becomes automatized.[5]

This passage suggests that the dominant is bound up with the defamiliarizing properties of the work. Ann Jefferson's commentary on the Russian Formalists argues that this was indeed Tynjanov's view.

A given work will include passive or automatized elements which are subservient to the defamiliarizing or "foregrounded" elements. The term "foregrounding" was developed (chiefly by Tynjanov) as a necessary consequence of the view of the literary text as a system composed of interrelated and interating elements, in order to distinguish between *dominant* and automatized factors. . . . Both sets of elements are formal, but the work's interest for the Formalist (or rather, the specifier) will lie in the interrelationship between the foregrounded and subservient elements. In other words, the active components of a work are now differentiated not only from practical language but also from other formal components which have become automatized.[6]

The dominant, then, has come to mean the concrete structures within the work of foregrounded, defamiliarized devices and functions, interacting with subordinated, automatized ones. From the spectator's perspective, we might say that the dominant governs the perceptual-cognitive "angle" that we are cued to adopt in viewing a film against its backgrounds.

The dominant is thus crucial in relating an artwork to history. According to Tynjanov:

A work enters into literature and takes on its own literary function through this dominant. Thus we correlate poems with the verse category, not with the

---

[5] Yuri Tynianov, *The Problem of Verse Language*, trans. and ed. Michael Sosa and Brent Harvey (Ann Arbor: Ardis, 1981), p. 33.

[6] Ann Jefferson, "Russian Formalism," in *Modern Literary Theory: A Comparative Introduction*, ed. Ann Jefferson and David Robey (London: Batsford Academic and Educational, 1982), p. 22.

prose category, not on the basis of all their characteristics, but only of some of them. The same is true concerning genres. We relate a novel to "the novel" on the basis of its size and the nature of its plot development, while at one time it was distinguished by the presence of a love intrigue.[7]

Put another way, the dominant is a guide to determining saliency, both within the work and in the work's relation to history. By noticing which devices and functions are foregrounded, we gain a means of deciding which structures are the most important to discuss. Similarly, in comparing the work to its context, we can determine through the dominant its most salient relationships to other works. Without some such notion, we would be condemned to study every device in a film with equal attention, for we would have no way of deciding which were the more relevant. Of course, most critics *do* make the intuitive assumption that some elements or structures are more important in a work than others. But the dominant as a tool allows us to examine such relations explicitly and systematically. As we have seen, it also enables us to perceive a dynamic rather than a static interaction between the subordinating and subordinated devices.

As this Tynjanov passage suggests, the dominant as a concept can be applied to individual works, to authors, and even to general artistic modes, such as poetry or the novel. The foregoing discussion of the dominant has been abstract, and it would be helpful now to look at some actual examples of dominant structures discussed by the Russian Formalists.

Shklovsky analyzes Dickens's *Little Dorrit* as a mystery story, even though the one line of action in the novel that we usually would consider to be a conventional mystery constitutes only one subplot among several. Yet, according to Shklovsky:

> It is interesting to note that in *Little Dorrit* Dickens extends the device of mystery to all the parts of the novel.
>
> Even the facts which are placed before our eyes at the beginning are presented as mysteries. The device is extended to them.

He mentions specifically the love of Little Dorrit for Clennam and of Clennam for Pet—especially the latter, with the novel's persistent presentation of Clennam as *not* being in love with her, primarily through the expedient of referring to him as "Nobody" (e.g., in Book

[7] Yuri Tynjanov, "On Literary Evolution," trans. C. A. Luplow, in *Readings in Russian Poetics*, pp. 72–73.

the First, Chapter XXVI, "Nobody's State of Mind").[8] One might add that this dominant governs the remarkable first chapter of Book the Second, the narration of which describes a large group of travelers gathered in an Alpine convent as if they are all being introduced for the first time, even though it is perfectly apparent to the reader that the group is made up of many of the main characters from the first half of *Little Dorrit* (e.g., Mr. Dorrit is referred to as "the Chief" and Little Dorrit as "the young lady"). At the end of the chapter, one minor character glances into the register book and reads all the names, an elaborate motivation for the clearing up of a "mystery" which has really not been a mystery at all. Thus in *Little Dorrit* the structure of mystery in one syuzhet line subordinates the non-mystery syuzhet lines, and in doing so provides the means for considerable defamiliarization in those other lines.

Eikhenbaum's essay on Gogol's "The Overcoat" finds the device of *skaz* governing the whole. (There is no equivalent term for *skaz* in English; it means any writing that imitates speech patterns—the most obvious example being dialects.) By concentrating on spoken language, he argues, Gogol minimizes syuzhet complexity. The devices foregrounded by *skaz* construction include puns, imitations of sound effects, and ultimately the entire grotesque tone of the novella, including its puzzling lapse into fantasy at the end.[9]

In the previous chapter, our examination of stairstep construction in *Terror By Night* centered around a dominant structure composed of a mixture of genre conventions. We saw how the mystery elements which seemed to govern the narrative were actually deformed by the hidden operations of the film in order to generate suspense. As a result, all the devices in the film—comic subplots, set design, camera movement, and so on—organized themselves around the need to delay progress in the rather simple hermeneutic line. In *Terror By Night*, a set of narrative inconsistencies resulted from inadequate motivation of these deformations. Most, if not all, of the other films I will be analyzing exploit the tension between dominant and subordinated structures for more systematic aesthetic ends.

Since an artist frequently uses similar dominants from one work to the next, we often can generalize about the dominant of his or her

[8] Victor Chklovski, *Sur la théorie de la prose*, trans. Guy Verret (Lausanne: Editions l'Age d'homme, 1973), pp. 190–191.

[9] Boris Eikenbaum, "How Gogol's 'Overcoat' Is Made," trans. Beth Paul and Muriel Nesbitt, in *Dostoevsky and Gogol*, ed. Priscilla Mayer and Stephen Rudy (Ann Arbor: Ardis, 1979), pp. 119–135.

overall output as well (though there will always be some differences among works, and we may usefully find variant dominants differentiating periods within a career, or other subcategories within an artist's output). Eikhenbaum characterizes Tolstoy's early dominant as "the destruction of psychological proportions, the concentration on minuteness."[10] Here, as with the theoretical discussion of the dominant, we see Eikhenbaum treating it not as a placid unifying factor, but as the suppression of the familiar structures in favor of a new and defamiliarizing one. Eikhenbaum's historical-critical essay on O. Henry investigates the dominant of the surprise ending. By concentrating on such endings, he claims, O. Henry's works are pushed toward irony and parody. Eikhenbaum analyzes the characters' lack of psychological depth—how they act purely in accordance with the mechanics of the action. He looks also at the author's use of language: "O. Henry's basic stylistic device (shown both in his dialogues and in the plot construction itself) is the confrontation of very remote, seemingly unrelated and, for that reason, surprising words, ideas, subjects or feelings. Surprise, as a device of parody, thus serves as the organizing principle of the sentence itself."[11] Thus surprise governs form—from the overall shape of the plot down to the level of the individual sentence.

Finally, groupings larger than a single artist's works are often made around dominants, and the basic features of those dominants tend to be widely recognized elements. For example, the dominant of verse was for a long time bound up with rhyme, though the blank and free verse forms have challenged that traditional view. Dominants provide the means of studying historical changes in large-scale modes. Shklovsky's *Theory of Prose* deals extensively with the introduction of the novel form and with the evolving attempts by authors to deal with the difficult organizational demands of the long prose form. He traces the shift in the novel from the early form, composed of a frame situation and a series of embedded stories (e.g., *The Decameron*), to the picaresque novel, unified as a continuing protagonist's adventures (e.g., *Don Quixote*), and finally to the nineteenth-century–style novel, with its interweaving of simultaneous plot lines (e.g., *Little Dorrit*). I have tried to do a similar kind of history of early film, comparing the narrative structures of very short primitive films, of the longer one-reel-

---

[10] Boris Eikhenbaum, *The Young Tolstoi*, trans. David Boucher et al.; ed. Gary Kern (Ann Arbor: Ardis, 1972), p. 63.

[11] B. M. Èjxenbaum, *O. Henry and the Theory of the Short Story*, trans. I. R. Titunik (Ann Arbor: Michigan Slavic Contributions, 1968), pp. 15–16.

ers, and of the feature-length film standardized in Hollywood by the mid-1910s.[12]

THE DOMINANT IN *LES VACANCES DE MONSIEUR HULOT*

How do we go about constructing a dominant for a film like Jacques Tati's *Les Vacances de Monsieur Hulot*? On first viewing, *Les Vacances* may appear to consist simply of a series of individual comic incidents loosely strung together. It does not strike one as a typical, tightly constructed narrative comedy of the Buster Keaton or Harold Lloyd variety (though as a mime Tati is often compared to these performers). By specifying the distinctive traits of *Les Vacances*, we can tease out a notion of a dominant.

The film's small comic scenes involve a succession of different characters, take place in different locales, and often follow each other with unspecified time lapses in between. Indeed, most are not causally connected in linear fashion, so that many could be rearranged considerably without affecting the basic minimal proairetic line. Perhaps equally striking, however, is the film's insertion of moments when nothing—humorous or otherwise—seems to be happening. Shots of nearly empty beaches, streets, and seascapes punctuate the humorous action, and sometimes when we do see characters, they are performing habitual, unfunny actions. We might dismiss these moments as subsidiary to the real business at hand—the jokes. Perhaps they create a "low-key" type of humor, or perhaps they are there to make the action more realistic. These are undoubtedly among their functions. But given that such moments often come at the beginnings and endings of segments of the film, they would seem to perform a more important structural function across the whole.

Nöel Burch's brief but perceptive analysis of *Les Vacances* in *Theory of Film Practice* singles out these nearly actionless moments as very important to the film's form.

Here the contrast between sequences, simultaneously involving duration, tempo, tone, and setting (interiors or exteriors, night or day) is under constant, meticulous control, determining the whole progression of the film and constituting its principal source of beauty. Aside from the broken rhythms of the gags, so perverse and yet so perfect, the principal rhythmic factor is an alternation between strong and weak moments, between deliberately action-

[12] David Bordwell, Janet Staiger, and Kristin Thompson, *The Classical Hollywood Cinema: Film Style and Mode of Production to 1960* (New York: Columbia University Press, 1985), chaps. 14 and 15.

packed, screamingly funny passages and others just as deliberately empty, boring, and flat. When the pretty girl's companion shows her an absolutely empty seascape, visible from the window of her room, and says, "Sometimes people fish down there, but there's nobody there today," boredom is being put to good use. Similar scenes aimed at creating a feeling of real boredom go on for quite some time, but it is created in such carefully controlled "doses" that it plays a special rhythmic role in the film's over-all structure. There comes to mind (among many other possibilities) the empty beach accompanied by the off-screen sounds of the restaurant dining room, the episodes of the child with his ice cream, the couple looking for seashells, etc.

In the whole history of cinema, this film, along with *Zéro de conduite*, has perhaps best succeeded in fulfilling the structural possibilities inherent in taking each sequence as a cellular unit, as an irreducible entity independent of any over-all spatial or temporal dialectic.[13]

This view of the scenes as cellular units explains the lack of causal connection I have mentioned and the possibility for rearranging scenes.

Indeed, Tati *did* redo *Les Vacances*; apparently the current release print is the product of a revival in 1961 for which Tati revised both this film and *Jour de fête*.[14] The shot Burch mentions of the heroine commenting to her aunt (not the other way round) about the empty beach has been cut from the original version. The revised print, which has circulated in France, England, and the United States for over a decade now, and upon which I based the initial version of this essay, has been trimmed from the original considerably. Many individual gags have been shortened or eliminated within scenes, and a tennis game which Hulot lost badly is entirely gone. In this revised analysis of the film I will be referring to the original French version at times, noting when a scene is not in the current release version. (In some sense, each is a "real" version of *Les Vacances*—and the longer one contains some very amusing extra gags.)

Burch's characterization of *Les Vacances* suggests that the film's dominant involves the deformation of a traditional humorous narrative by the insertion of boring moments and trivial actions. Most comics

[13] Noël Burch, *Theory of Film Practice*, trans. Helen R. Lane (Princeton: Princeton University Press, 1981), p. 64. One of the few films which *Les Vacances* seems to have influenced directly is *Local Hero*, though there the comparable routines of meals in the hotel dining room and walks along the beach are enlivened with more humor and scenic beauty, respectively. But touches like the repeated passing through the town of a motorcycle rider recall Tati strongly, and the film apparently cites *Les Vacances* specifically when the young oil-company employee tosses away the seashell the woman oceanographer hands him.

[14] James Harding, *Jacques Tati: Frame by Frame* (London: Secker and Warburg, 1984), p. 120.

would try to eliminate all traces of automatized everyday reality from their films, but Tati insists on using moments of such automatization as the material of portions of his film. In the process he paradoxically manages to focus our attention on everyday, trivial events to the extent that he succeeds in defamiliarizing them, primarily through his parallel defamiliarization of traditional gag structures.

I have suggested that the dominant structure runs through the film from the most general to the most local level: it informs style, narrative, and theme. In this chapter I will examine these three structural levels of *Les Vacances*, looking in particular at how each is controlled by the juxtaposition of boring and trivial material with more traditional gag structures.

THE STYLISTIC SYSTEM

On the level of characteristic techniques, Tati's main formal principle is *overlap*. The diverse small incidents and gags of his films may tend toward discontinuity, but he overlaps them through a complex stitching process. Using deep stagings, deep focus, offscreen sound, and multiple points of interest within a frame, he makes virtually every moment—funny or not—in *Les Vacances* dependent on an interaction between two initially separate actions and spaces. And very often one of these actions and spaces involves a trivial event or even a "dead" moment with nothing going on at all. Thus a residue of boredom affects the style of the humor; Tati often uses incomplete, subtle, or downright weird jokes. He finds humor in things no other comedian would use, and he sets up that humor within a distinctive spatial and temporal layout.

The camerawork emphasizes overlapping actions by frequently including several elements within the frame. Tati has virtually eliminated the close-up from his style even at this early stage of his career, and his subsequent films use long shots almost exclusively. There are few shots in *Les Vacances* with only one focus of attention. One gag may be played out in the foreground, while another minor action is occurring in one part of the background and the next gag is being set up in another. Typically, this setup for the next scene is almost unnoticeable, so that when Tati cuts closer to transform the background action into the central joke of the next subsegment, the continuity through overlap is extremely subtle. Since initially the two actions were in the same space, the cut is not startling enough to disrupt the flow of action. However, as we shall see when examining Tati's editing, he further minimizes the continuity between the two actions by frequently making 90° and 180° cuts, thus insuring that the background for each successive action will be different. A clear example of this process comes when Hulot and Martine are going horseback riding. As Martine begins to ride away toward the right of the frame, a car in the background begins backing toward the pony shed (Fig. 3.1). (Tati calls further attention to it with several honks on the sound track.) In the next shot, the camera is placed at an angle approximately 90° from its previous setup; here the car backs into the frame from the right (Fig. 3.2), becoming the foreground element and preparing the next gag in which the horse kicks down the rumble seat. Tati can also reverse the procedure by cutting away from an action which then appears in the background of the next shot; at one point two bathers greet each other, shaking hands just as Hulot's discarded wash water comes out of a pipe at their feet to splash them. As they move awkwardly to avoid the spray (Fig. 3.3), Tati cuts to a longer shot of the same action, this time with the henpecked tourist Henry in the foreground watching and glancing up to Hulot's offscreen window (Fig. 3.4). Thus, although the action is often discontinuous, Tati provides a sense that these incidents are linked to each other through his camerawork, which includes multiple overlapping actions within the frame. Moreover, each of these actions is in itself utterly trivial—a man emptying a wash basin, two men shaking hands, another strolling by—and the humor emerges only in their accidental interaction.

A related device involves characters who watch nearby actions. Henry is characterized not only by his silence, but also by the fact that he is often seen in the foreground or background of a shot, watching the main joke. After the winch has given way and allowed the unfinished boat to slide into the water, the camera moves from its focus on the boat's owner to reveal Henry nearby, watching the scene as his wife waits for him to follow her. This device often depends on deep focus. Although characters are not in Wellesian close-up, they may be in medium shot with other actions occurring in the depth of the frame. For example, in the funeral scene, one of the guests watches the deflation of the tire "wreath" (Fig. 3.5), then moves forward, with the camera panning right, to stare at Hulot beside his broken-down car in deep focus (Fig. 3.6). A similar deep space appears in a number of high-angle shots down onto the beach; these shots are taken from the general area of the windows of the hotel and boardinghouse. Several times Martine is seen to the left or right of one of these shots, glancing down toward the beach; then, instead of following her actions, the scene shifts to the numerous beach activities that previously were glimpsed and heard in the distance. Figure 3.7 shows her, in the shot cut from the later *Les Vacances* print, pointing out to her aunt where people usually fish; this little moment of "flat" action originally led into the amusing stretch of action involving the first tennis game, in which Hulot plays ineptly and loses.

I have already mentioned how editing is used to get closer to events that may be visible in the distance, and conversely to pull back from actions to reveal reactions. Another method of cutting links actions in a different way: cutting several times within the immediate vicinity of one action to discover other simultaneous actions. Sometimes these other actions are related to the first incident, sometimes not. After the moment when the boat slides into the sea as a result of the winch's giving way, Tati cuts to various views of the beach as the boat's owner looks around for the culprit who tampered with the winch. The winch is the point around which the sequence is built, appearing in most of the shots. It and the man standing beside it orient the viewer as the backgrounds change from shot to shot (Figs. 3.8 to 3.17). The main joke is performed quickly; the boat slides into the water. The series of shots after this simply explores the multitude of other actions. Figure 3.13 shows a shot from the original version, in which the French mother discovers that her son has been helping another woman wind yarn, and thus could not have slipped the winch's gear; a sort of "negative" joke emphasizes the point that this scene never does result in any answer as to who was the culprit. Again the emphasis is on overlap rather than on linear development.

As noted previously, Tati employs an unusual kind of cut—one which moves the camera to a new position 90° or sometimes 180° from its former setup. In close-up this would not be particularly disorienting, since the same object would be clearly present throughout. But in long shot this type of cut can completely alter the view, since the entire surroundings change and the object, while still present, appears against a different background. In this and other Tati films, the viewer may have to scan the screen for clues to the new spatial orientation. (We shall see 90° and 180° cutting again in *Late Spring* and a similar device, 90° pans and arcing tracks, in *Rules of the Game*.) In the opening travel sequence, for example, two men dash out in front of Hulot's car, forcing him to stop, as they run out to the right of the frame (Fig. 3.18). Instead of staying with Hulot, the next shot frames a bus, presumably across the street, since the two men run into the frame from the left (Fig. 3.19). Here is an approximately 90° cut in which the only clue to the bus's spatial and temporal relationship to Hulot's car is the action of the running men.

Editing of this sort abounds in *Les Vacances*. An example of a less disorienting kind of 90° cut occurs at the beginning of the hiking-party episode. Tati introduces the scene with a medium-long shot of a disconsolate woman, placed center screen, filling her backpack (Fig. 3.20); a 90° cut reveals Hulot and the hiking leader, who enters through the door, while the young woman is now to the right of the frame (Fig. 3.21). In addition, however, another man becomes partially visible frame left in the second shot; he is the victim of a previous gag in which Hulot had removed the bookmark from his book. Now we see him still searching for his place; the overlapping principle is carried through to create a visual overtone for this scene—a quiet little gag for us to notice or not. A 90° cut of this kind, used consistently, allows multiple actions to exfoliate from a single one. The numerous 180° cuts (in the sense that the camera is moved to the opposite side of the subject) perform similar functions; they shift attention to different areas of action around the main area, emphasizing the overlap among these actions.

The relations of sound to image often create or enhance the overlapping effect. (Tati foregrounds the device of the sound right at the beginning of the film by calling attention to it with the garbled railway speaker.) The famous scene of Hulot painting the kayak depends to a large degree on offscreen sound. As Hulot paints, he is distracted by a discussion of an outing by some people who are not shown onscreen at any point in the scene. (As usual, the conversation itself is trivial.) The distraction makes it possible for the paint can to float away unnoticed; thus the gag is accomplished by the interaction of two unrelated events in different spaces, and the interaction is created by sound offscreen.

Overlap is emphasized time and again through the use of beach noises over scenes inside the boardinghouse or hotel, or the opposite device of hotel noises over shots of the beach. When Hulot waits in the parlor to take Martine horseback riding, voices from the beach drift in from offscreen to provide the main sound for his pantomime inspection of the room. During the lunch scene on the second day, there is a cut to the empty beach outside, while the sound of clinking tableware and the argument between the waiter and the proprietor can still be heard, coming from offscreen. A similar scene shows some children heading for the beach while a radio ad blares from offscreen.

Hulot's first contact with his fellow guests at the hotel depends upon this type of sound device. A medium shot of the waiter introduces the arrival of Hulot; the former is standing in the lounge listening to the backfires of Hulot's car offscreen. This is the first of many times Hulot will disturb the guests by being noisy. The sound off links Hulot's space with that of the waiter and guests even before he enters the room. Note also the use of depth and sound as Hulot drives up for the tennis game, with the courts in the background and Hulot's hand in the lower right foreground; as he switches off the engine a series of backfires results, causing the players in the depth of the shot to look front and freeze.

A sonic motif that emphasizes overlap is the repeated shot of the exterior of the hotel at night while various loud sounds created by Hulot are causing the guests to turn their lights on. On the second day, the hiking party Hulot joins makes the noise; later on, it is Hulot's noisy car coming home late. This motif culminates in the attack on the hotel with the fireworks, which succeeds not only in waking the guests, but in assembling them in the lounge as well.

This last example suggests how techniques that employ overlapping may develop into a major device helping to organize the second formal level, the narrative.

THE NARRATIVE SYSTEM

A summary of the characters may be helpful, since it is difficult to distinguish them all on one viewing. A group of disparate people come together at a small resort town on the coast of France. Hulot stays at the Hôtel de la Plage, which is run by a proprietor and a waiter. His fellow guests include a retired military gentleman; an Englishwoman who referees Hulot's game(s) of tennis; a young Communist man; a businessman with his wife and son; and a couple, Henry and his wife, who spend their time walking about.

The heroine of the film is Martine, who stays at a boardinghouse down the street from the Hôtel de la Plage; she is soon joined there by her aunt, Madame Dubois. Martine and Hulot meet several times and go out together, but this comes to nothing by the end of the film. The action consists simply of a series of comic incidents in which these people are thrown together in various ways. At the end they all leave the town, and the beach is deserted until the next vacation season.

Because of the elimination of all but the barest minimum of plotting, *Les Vacances* has an overall structure that differs considerably from the typical narrative strategy. A typical Hollywood-style film would have a clear-cut pattern of narrative development; this pattern might involve a changing relationship among characters, as in a love story, or a search, as in *Terror By Night*, or a struggle, as in a Western—or more than one such element. In each case, the completion of the pattern marks the end of the film. Moreover, a classical film's protagonist would be likely to have a definite goal in mind, often one that comes into conflict with the opposing desires of other characters. Had Hulot been the protagonist in such a film, he might well have decided at the start that his fellow vacationers were a bunch of bores and set out to shake them out of their accustomed patterns; instead, Hulot seems to try to conform and simply cannot manage it. Similarly, he would have seen Martine right away and set out to win her, but in fact their relationship is intermittent, with no specification of Hulot's attitude toward her.

So *Les Vacances* lacks a linear pattern of narrative development. A vacation does not involve a logical progression of events, as the narrative types mentioned above do. A detective finds what he is looking for only at the end of the story. Hulot's tennis game, however, could come logically at any point during his vacation. (This is indicated by the fact that, as noted previously, one whole tennis game was cut from the original version without affecting the narrative. Even after his big loss at tennis in this first version, there is no indication that Hulot has conceived the goal of winning a game.) The vacation's structure is limited only by the length of time the characters can be away from their normal pursuits and by the kinds of activities available to them at the locale chosen. Thus Tati is able to be fairly arbitrary in his structuring of *Les Vacances*; instead of basing it on a progression of a set of actions, he creates his narrative on a fixed time scheme. The film in fact covers seven days at the beach.

Les Vacances is framed by introductory and final sections involving the actions of traveling to and traveling away from the beach town. The opening immediately sets up the device of overlapping activities and an interest in the characters as part of a larger group. Within the seven-day time scheme, Tati rigorously develops a pattern which will repeat across the individual days. The first day is differentiated by being primarily occupied in traveling, and the arrival itself is a comparatively extended sequence. Nevertheless, several motifs are quickly set up: the mealtime bell ringing, the dining room, Henry and his wife as a transitionary device, and the exterior of the hotel at night (here with no disruption from Hulot). But it is the second day that establishes the entire pattern of a typical resort day. I have divided the day into five sections, shown in the accompanying diagram: a.) morning, b.) lunch, c.) afternoon, d.) dinner, and e.) evening. Hulot participates in all the standard activities on Day II. He gets into minor scrapes, but his first real disturbance of the other guests comes when he leaves the dull community of the evening gathering in the lounge to join the hiking party. This is one of the main scenes of Day II, along

LES VACANCES DE MONSIEUR HULOT

	DAY I	DAY II	DAY III	DAY IV	DAY V	DAY VI	DAY VII
a. morning	X	*curtain opening* incidents on beach, including winch scene*	*sailboat* incidents on beach	*hanging net* incidents on beach tennis game*	*shutter of stand down* horse scene*	*fade-in* picnic expedition*	*fade-in* farewells* [Martine's photos] *fade-out on empty beach*
b. lunch	X	*bell* lunch at hotel scenes in street	*bell* lunch at hotel & boardinghouse	*bell* date made to go riding	X	X	X
c. afternoon	travel & arrival*	Hulot meets Martine series of short gags [First tennis game*]	cemetery*	X	X	X	X
d. dinner	*dinner bell* Hulot & other guests in dining room	shown indirectly-- Henry & wife go upstairs to dining room	X	X	X	X	X
e. evening	*Henry & wife go out* *fade-out--exterior of boardinghouse*	*fade-in* hiking party* *fade-out--exterior of lighted hotel*	*Henry & wife go out* *fade-out--exterior of lighted hotel*	*Henry & wife go out* ping-pong game* *fade-out--exterior of lighted hotel*	*fade-in* masked ball* *fade-out-- moonlit beach*	*fade-in* fireworks* *fade-out--dark hut*	X

Key: X indicates a time of day not presented in the film.
  Phrases in italics indicate transitionary devices which lead from one time of day to another or from one day to another.
  Asterisks indicate extended sequences.
  Brackets indicate scenes cut from the original version of the film.

with the winch sequence in the morning. (I have marked the extended sequences of each day with an asterisk in the diagram; originally a third extended sequence, the first tennis game, occurred on Day II.)

The overall structure of the rest of the film involves the other hotel guests' continuing to follow the schedule set up on Day II, while Hulot begins increasingly to disrupt the schedule for himself and others. The stylistic devices of overlap are important because Tati constantly sets up interactions among members of the group of vacationers. For the most part the vacationers are united in their conformity; Hulot is set up against them in his activities. The overlap of his actions with theirs creates disruption and eventually mild chaos when all patterns are reversed in the fireworks scene.

The growing disruption of routine is reflected on the chart by the number of normal activities that are not shown. On Day III Hulot blunders into the funeral in the cemetery (the one extended sequence of the day), makes friends there, and as a consequence not only misses dinner at the hotel, but again wakes the other guests with his car as he returns. On Day IV, two sections of the day are missing; neither the afternoon nor the dinner is shown. Here there are two extended sequences: the tennis scene in the morning and the complementary ping-pong scene in the evening. In the first, Hulot disturbs the group not so much by the fact that he beats them all at tennis, but by the unorthodox means he uses. In the evening lounge scene, Hulot again breaks up the habitual activities of the group by coming in twice to search for the ball. His accidental interference with the two card games reduces the guests to a more chaotic state than they had been in up to this point. The day ends with their confusion.

On Day V, more sections of the day are missing; only morning and evening are shown. Again two extended sequences take up most of the time: the struggle with the horse on the beach and the masked ball. As Hulot had disrupted the hotel the night before, so he reduces the beach to confusion in the morning. The interaction between his activities (annoying the horse until it kicks the rumble seat and traps a man inside) and those of people in the vicinity (who come to rescue the trapped man) causes the disruption. The masked ball again sets Hulot against the hotel community. By this time, however, Hulot has assembled about himself a small number of "supporters" who join him outside the circle of conformity: Martine, the businessman's son, and even Henry, who does not dare to attend the party but peers in happily through a window. The opposition of the two groups is carried through by the conflict of the sounds penetrating into one space from the other. The sound of the lounge's radio comes into the dining room each time the door is opened, while the group below is disturbed when Hulot turns the phonograph up loud.

Day VI also has two extended sequences which constitute virtually all the action. Lunch, afternoon, and dinner are not shown. The picnic expedition takes up the morning. This is elaborately prepared for by the guests, all working up toward a luncheon in the countryside. But again Hulot's actions cause him to miss the meal; he also keeps two other guests, the Englishwoman and Madame Dubois, from the picnic. Moreover, the breakdown of Hulot's car separates him for the rest of the film from Martine, who had been scheduled to go in his car; she ends up riding with the young Communist man in another. Hulot is presumably plagued all day by the dogs that chase him out of the estate, for they are still with him that evening. At that point he accidentally begins the attack on the resort with the fireworks; the sound track of explosions and machine-gun–like reports makes this into a figurative battle. It is the logical culmination of all the other assaults on conformity that Hulot has perpetrated throughout the film.

And it succeeds. The guests turn on their lights, but they also straggle out to gather in the lounge. A record, which Hulot had not been permitted to play before, is accidentally set playing by the proprietor himself. The businessman, too busy up to this point to participate in any real vacation activities, groggily puts on his boy's paper hat as he joins what has by this point become a party of sorts. His son and the Englishwoman begin cheerfully dancing to the music. In this scene overlapping, separate actions are absent. Instead of sitting about the lounge in small groups oblivious to each other, the guests are forced to interact.

Day VII marks the end of the vacation. The group, restored to order, snubs the battle-scarred Hulot; he is not even able to see Martine again. But two characters do greet him. Both the Englishwoman and, more surprisingly, Henry say goodbye to him in terms that hint that much of their enjoyment of their vacations has been due to Hulot himself. The last day balances the first. Just as the first day had shown only afternoon arrivals, followed by dinner and evening, the last day shows only morning departures. (In the original version, there is a brief scene of Martine receiving her vacation photos just as she boards the bus [Fig. 3.22]; a cut to the train shows both her and Madame Dubois examining them. The latter gets annoyed by a picture of Hulot, but Martine smiles over it [Fig. 3.23]. Presumably, Tati later found this indication of Martine's continuing affection for Hulot too obvious and sentimental, and so he cut it out.)

The smaller divisions within days are usually clearly marked by formal devices. Most days open with shots of the beach, often revealed by something being pulled aside: Martine opens her curtain to begin Day II, the sail of a boat glides by to reveal the beach on Day III, and the shutter of a souvenir stand is taken down on Day V. Similarly, every day in which lunchtime is shown, the meal is introduced by the ringing of the hotel's bell. Several evening scenes end with the hotel's lighted exterior. The regularity of the guests' routines is emphasized by the device of the radio, which recurs several times; the radio sign-off signals the general decision to go to bed. Hulot, on the other hand, *leaves* the hotel when the radio signs off on the night of the hiking party. Similarly, some moments within scenes contain almost no action. Several shots of the guests sitting around the lounge, each occupied in private activities, contain no interesting focus of attention until Hulot breaks up these activities in some way—for example, when he first arrives and lets the wind into the lounge, and later when his loud music disrupts the group. In such scenes we see the formal use of boredom in the way Burch described.

Tati also introduces a large number of characters, only a few of whom we get to know much about. Hulot is the only developed character, but he is not present in all the comic scenes. The emphasis is on the individuals in the group and on Hulot as a disruptive factor. Indeed, this narrative opposition is perhaps the film's most explicit surfacing of the dominant conflict between boredom and humor. Most of the characters are seen as isolated within the strict conformity of the group. They bounce off each other in the overlapping of their actions but generally resist any disruption of their activities. The implications of this narrative bring us in turn to an examination of Tati's use of the third level of general filmic structure, the thematic system.

THE THEMATIC SYSTEM

Many of the characters in *Les Vacances* are shown as not changing their behavior or activities when they go on vacation. The businessman keeps spoiling his family's outings by conducting business on the phone; the Communist does not put his propaganda sheets aside for a single moment. Henry is completely cowed by his wife and unable to do anything but follow her; he wears a suit and hat throughout the film. The retired military man spends his time describing his battle exploits. Hulot, and to some degree Martine and the Englishwoman, are the major exceptions to this pattern.

The characters are also isolated from each other. Our first view of the hotel guests shows them at separate tables in the lounge; a tracking shot follows the waiter as he moves among them, eliciting slightly annoyed reactions from some as he attempts to dust the tables. Finally they are shown to be individual units. (An ironic underscoring of this isolation comes—in the English-dubbed version—in a line barely audible on the sound track; as Hulot is registering, one woman comments to another that she loves the beach because one gets to know other people there.) The guests are united in this and other scenes by the sound of the radio, but it, as we have seen, tends to regiment their activities. Basically their days are scheduled for them by outside influences—the meal bell, the radio, the polite conventions of resort life. Even the picnic they go on near the end is organized in a strict fashion and led by the military man as if it were an attack mission. The characters use little imagination in thinking up activities that would be interesting to them. The guests and their routines thus motivate the presence of the banality that pervades the film.

Hulot behaves in the opposite fashion, introducing the disruptive elements that contrast with this banality. He misses meals, invents his own activities, and throws the staid life of the resort off course. When the others buy American newspapers to keep up on current events, he buys one to make into a hat for playing tennis; the contrast is made clear in a characteristic deep-space composition with the Communist reading in the foreground (Fig. 3.24). Hulot's perception of objects and activities is, unlike that of most of the other guests, not conventional. Likewise, the objects associated with Hulot are strange and humorous. Hulot's car, particularly, does not function as cars are intended to. Its breakdowns delay the regimented picnic, wake the hotel guests, and, as with his other activities, may work against him; by failing to go on the picnic he misses his last chance to see Martine. On the other hand, the earlier breakdown at the cemetery had brought him together with some new acquaintances. Hulot's actions often turn into mishaps, but they are always motivated by the spontaneity of his character. Only certain other characters who are capable of perceiving in a less rigid way recognize and appreciate this spontaneity.

By continually disrupting the group, Hulot becomes an object of contempt for most of the vacationers, but he gradually wins the friendship of some. Throughout the film Henry is seen, often with a little smile, watching Hulot's activities. At the end he reveals that he has enjoyed himself vicariously through Hulot, who has dared to do things Henry cannot. After the tennis game(s), which she referees, the Englishwoman also comes to enjoy Hulot's mishaps. She even begins to like Hulot's loud music. By the end she, Henry, and the businessman's little boy are Hulot's friends.

Hulot breaks up the gatherings at the separate tables several times during the film: when he first arrives and when he mixes up the card games. At the point of the cards sequence, the guests cannot cope with such disruption, and a fight ensues. Later the hotel's organized attempt to get them to socialize at a costume dance fails; they resist wearing silly costumes, preferring their card games. But on the next evening, Hulot's fireworks display finally forces them to mingle spontaneously in the lounge, in a party atmosphere. This spontaneity is what the characters have lacked throughout the film. Thematically, spontaneity is the result of the conflict between banality and humor, just as overlap is on the stylistic level and the "cellular" scene construction is on the narrative level.

The story is not created by placing the characters in some strange situation to generate humor; the circumstances of the vacation are extremely mundane. As always, however, Tati transforms our perception of the everyday. Most of the guests consider themselves above the absurdity of this everyday existence, but their behavior shows that they are not. For example, the evening of Day v opens with a woman reading the poster for the masked ball and turning up her nose at it (Fig. 3.25); she joins the group that refuses to go. Yet Tati juxtaposes her with another woman who is dressed in a party hat, making it clear that the clothes the sneering woman is wearing are just as silly-looking as a costume (Fig. 3.26). Similarly, at lunch on Day ii, Hulot sits beside a man and accidentally wipes the latter's mouth with his sleeve while reaching for the salt; the man betrays his annoyance with Hulot. If he had a perception of life similar to that of the characters who befriend Hulot, he would simply laugh it off. Thus the thematic material Tati is working with involves the ability of people to break away from routine and conformity. He deals, in effect, with the overlap of people's actions, and with the breakdown of social barriers set up by convention.

CONCLUSIONS

This analysis of *Les Vacances de Monsieur Hulot* has demonstrated how those devices that initially strike us as unusual in a highly original film can be distinguished and used to construct a dominant, which can then organize an overall argument. As with other neoformalist concepts, the dominant is neither wholly within the work nor wholly a product of the spectator. Once again it consists of a series of cues to which we respond as we construct our overall view of how parts relate to each other in the film at hand. Different analysts will find dominants that are at least slightly different, especially in the sense that analysts are likely to express even similar ideas in different ways. But this does not imply that the dominant is arbitrary for a film; the argument an analyst makes about it will be more or less successful, in that it will account for more or fewer of the film's devices and their patterning.

Films relate to their historical contexts through their dominants; hence standardized kinds of films will tend to share similar dominants with large groups of other films, and, as we have seen, a dominant can be used to group films by a single filmmaker. We shall see that Tati's *Play Time* uses many of the same devices and functions as *Les Vacances*. Both stand out in relation to the classical norm of comedy-film construction.

Indeed, one of the most distinctive aspects of *Les Vacances* is that the concept of a pared-down, banal environment is a convention usually associated with modern dramatic and tragic films. The art film in particular has adopted the device of the sterile environment and banal routine to create symbolic commentary on modern life. Tati is in a sense the flip side of Antonioni, whose trilogy in particular did exactly this sort of thing. Instead of asking us to interpret the banality, Tati makes it funny. As we have seen, those elements that are juxtaposed to create humor often consist of one boring action and one bizarre action—and the traditional one is the bizarre one (e.g., Hulot leaving wet footprints, Hulot's car breaking down, Hulot's kayak splitting and swallowing him as a shark would). The defamiliarizing events are, oddly enough, the banal ones. Sometimes the humorous elements take precedence, as with the fireworks assault on the sleeping guests. But at other times the comic payoff never really comes, as in the winch scene; here conventional handling would have dictated either that we follow the comic antics of the man on the boat as he gets doused or that we concentrate on the man onshore as he tracks down the culprit. Instead, we mostly watch the owner stare morosely at possible suspects. (Hulot's discomfiture under his stare leads to a bit of comedy, but it does not climax the whole gag, since we later see the owner through the dining-room window, still trying to figure out who did it.)

Eikhenbaum suggested that the dominant structure will subordinate other—primarily automatized—ones. We have seen how the usual devices that go into creating a continually funny film and a tight, linear narrative have been minimized. Tati eschews the continuity system in favor of a decoupage that offers us multiple simultaneous centers of attention. Perhaps most important, *Les Vacances* devotes much of its time to creating abstract formal patterns that are neither funny nor narratively relevant—both the gaps between the "cellular units," to which Burch referred, and the careful, consistent uses of framing and sound. Even someone who found *Les Vacances* wholly unfunny should be able to enjoy it for its formal complexity. It is no surprise that Tati once expressed interest in working with Robert Bresson.[15]

[15] Roy Armes, *French Cinema Since 1946: Volume One, The Great Tradition* (New Jersey: A. S. Barnes, 1970), p. 152.

4

Sawing Through the Bough: *Tout va bien* as a Brechtian Film

THE SEPARATION OF ELEMENTS AS A DOMINANT

THE USEFULNESS of Brechtian concepts in analyzing the films of Jean-Luc Godard is no new idea. But *Tout va bien*, with its framing device of speculating on its own production, seems particularly to represent a step toward the realization of a Brechtian film.

This essay is not the first to examine the reference, by a character in *Tout va bien*, to Brecht's program notes to *The Rise and Fall of the City of Mahagonny*, and to discuss the film in the light of Brecht's discussion in that essay of the "separation of elements." Colin MacCabe points out the appropriateness of such an approach in his article "The Politics of Separation."[1] While I am indebted to MacCabe for taking this step, I use the concept of separation differently; I shall briefly summarize the problems I find with MacCabe's approach, then outline my own.

MacCabe assumes Brecht's general categories of opera—words, music, and setting—to be parallel to Christian Metz's five matters of expression in cinema (moving images, written material, voice, noise, and music).[2] This brings up the usual problems with Metz's classification, since the categories are not parallel to each other (does a track past a billboard constitute written material or moving images?), and it privileges sound by breaking it down into subcategories while not doing the same for the image. But more important, MacCabe assumes that applying Brecht's separation of elements to the cinema involves *only* these Metzian categories. This assumption boxes MacCabe into a

A NUMBER of basic concepts in this chapter were suggested by a lecture given by David Bordwell at the University of Wisconsin-Madison. I am grateful to him for encouraging me to do this study. My thanks also to the members of his 1983 seminar on Godard, who read the original version of the article and offered some helpful criticisms which I have tried to take into account in this revision. Edward Branigan also offered his usual thorough reading; I have adopted a number of his suggestions.

[1] Colin MacCabe, "The Politics of Separation," *Screen* 16, no. 4 (Winter 1975/76).
[2] Ibid., p. 46.

critical approach in which he can only list examples of physical separation of channels. Because his scheme does not include narrative,
causality, or any other *functional* categories, it gives him no way of
showing how this separation leads to the political results Brecht speaks
of. (MacCabe himself declares the process he has embarked upon to
be "formalistic"—though this word has nothing to do with Russian
Formalism or the approach I am using in this volume.)

He solves his problem by linking the separation of the matters of
expression to the Freudian view of separation of conscious/uncon-
scious, belief/knowledge, and pleasure/desire: "The political question
becomes then one of locating an identity which must be separated out
so that it can become an object of knowledge."[3] MacCabe does not
demonstrate how the "formalistic" separation of writing from image,
image from music, and so forth will lead to the Freudian process he
describes. His conclusions assume that separation will automatically
produce a disunity disturbing to the audience, and that that disturbance is itself a process of psychological "separation" conducive to
learning.

What is important, therefore, is that in the separation of the elements the
spectator gets separated out of this unity and homogeneity—this passivity—in
order to enter into an active appropriation of the scenes presented to him.
This active appropriation is the aim of epic theatre—it is the production of
knowledge. Rather than a text compact with its own meaning, a text which
confers a unity and gives a position to the subject, we want a text whose fis-
sures and differences constantly demand an activity of articulation from the
subject—which articulation in its constant changes and contradictions makes
known—shows—the contradictions of the reader's positions within and without the cinema.[4]

But "separation" of elements and the "separation" of the spectator
from a sense of unity and homogeneity are linked here by only a se-
mantic play; MacCabe does not demonstrate any real causal connection. After all, plenty of films have separated their elements; are all
silent films more Brechtian than sound films because they separate
words from images by means of written titles? Indeed, MacCabe implies that *Tout va bien* is a retrogression in this respect from *Two or
Three Things I Know About Her* because it has fewer titles. This quan-
titative approach presumably results from an equation of technical
separation with Brechtian (and Freudian) perceptions by the spectator: the more separation, the more Brechtian a film is. But after all, a

[3] Ibid., p. 49.
[4] Ibid., p. 48.

film like *Le Million* has considerable separation of sound and image (as in the scene in the opera where one couple sings of love while the other really *is* in love), yet we would hardly want to call it a Brechtian film. I am, then, grateful to MacCabe for pointing out the applicability of the "separation" principle to *Tout va bien*. But because of the reservations expressed above, I shall take a different approach to analyzing Brechtian structures as the dominant of the film. I shall be distinguishing three types of separation: *interruption*, the insertion of material that breaks up a smooth, logical chain of narrative causes and effects; *contradiction*, the joining of stylistic techniques in a discontinuous manner, which breaks down classical norms; and *refraction*, the use of mediations between the events depicted and the spectator's perception of those events.

First of all, I propose to look not simply at the physical separation of one technique from another in *Tout va bien*, but also at the principles of the three types of separation. How are these structures of separation achieved, and how do they function in the film? Second, the "elements" the film separates cannot be seen as simple techniques with no context. Rather, I shall examine how the film works upon techniques as they have become conventionalized in traditional usage—specifically, the backgrounds of the classical cinema and the modern European art cinema. In the *Mahagonny* notes, Brecht was not speaking of all words, all music, all settings, but of those elements specifically as they existed in the opera of his day. I shall be looking, therefore, at the separation of filmic elements, not as a juxtaposition of techniques that do not happen to mesh, but rather as a construction of techniques in ways that are not culturally acceptable in the modern commercial narrative cinema. In a specific historical context, the separation of conventional structures can create the circumstances that prompt the viewer to reexamine his or her traditional viewing habits in relation to the cinema. *Tout va bien* fits into the pattern described by Stephen Heath: "Against vision, a materialist practice of film thus proposes and opposes analysis, 'analysis by means of image and sound' (to quote Godard on *Deux ou trois Choses*) in which sound is not some supplement to the cinematic essence of the image, but, on the contrary, its essential despectacularisation."[5] I shall try to show how the separation of elements leads not simply to a disunity or disturbance of the spectator's viewing habits, but to analysis of them. It is this func-

[5] Stephen Heath, "From Brecht to Film: Theses, Problems," *Screen* 16, no. 4 (Winter 1975/76): 38.

tion of the separation, rather than just separation on a technical level, that makes *Tout va bien* a Brechtian film.

PRINCIPLES OF SEPARATION OF ELEMENTS

Jacques's reference to the *Mahagonny* preface bares the device that governs the film's form. Brecht's argument in that essay rests on the assumption that each art form is an apparatus controlled not by the artist but by society. In capitalist societies, artists may think they are using art forms for personal creation, but they are in fact producers of artistic merchandise. Artists are not free to invent outside the apparatus; yet this, according to Brecht, is not the problem.

> To restrict the individual's freedom of invention is in itself a progressive act. The individual becomes increasingly drawn into enormous events that are going to change the world. No longer can he simply "express himself." He is brought up short and put into a position where he can fulfil more general tasks. The trouble, however, is that at present the apparati do not work for the general good; the means of production do not belong to the producer; and as a result his work amounts to so much merchandise. . . . An opera can only be written for the opera.[6]

Since artists can only work within the forms that already exist in their historical situations, the point for Brecht is not to create a wholly new form; this would be impossible: "*Mahagonny* is nothing more or less than an opera—WITH INNOVATIONS!"[7] These innovations were the famous characteristics of the epic theater, which included the "radical *separation of the elements.*"[8] In opposition to the fusion of elements in the *Gesamtkunstwerk*, Brecht proposed that words, music, and production be separated.

Brecht's description of opera as "culinary" (pleasurable, entertaining) applies equally to the two major filmic backgrounds against which we can examine *Tout va bien*, the classical commercial fiction film (exemplified by the Hollywood cinema) and the modern commercial art cinema. In the classical Hollywood cinema, the emphasis is on entertainment, with the stylistic elements fused to the narrative by a thoroughgoing compositional motivation, and with the continuity system rendering spatial and temporal relations clear; unambiguous characters provide the wellspring for the narrative events. The art cinema

---

[6] Bertolt Brecht, "The Modern Theater is the Epic Theatre (Notes to the opera *Aufsteig und Fall der Stadt Mahagonny*)," in *Brecht on Theatre*, trans. and ed. John Willett (New York: Hill and Wang, 1964), p. 35.

[7] Ibid., p. 37. Emphasis in original.

[8] Ibid. Emphasis in original.

reacts against this tradition by emphasizing realism over entertainment, by depending upon characters and causality that are frequently ambiguous (thus substituting a comparative lack of closure for the Hollywood "happy ending"), and by bringing forward the individual authorial voice as a prime motivator of stylistic quirks.[9] The Hollywood-style film aims itself at a mass audience. The art cinema appeals to a smaller, elite audience and is shown in specific theaters ("art houses") set aside for this type of film. It is, of course, no less a commercial cinema than the Hollywood cinema; it is a parallel, sometimes overlapping mode. *Tout va bien* defines itself primarily against the mainstream Hollywood film, and I shall use that as my main background here. But we shall return to *Tout va bien*'s relation to the art film as well.

Tout va bien bears a relationship to traditional modes of filmmaking somewhat like that which Brecht describes as existing between his own opera and more traditional opera. Yet film is not opera, and *Tout va bien* bears little resemblance to *The Rise and Fall of the City of Mahagonny*. A comparison of the two works would be an idle exercise. Instead, an analysis of the principles that Godard and Jean-Pierre Gorin have used to create a separation of elements can enable us to better understand how they have made a film at once culinary and—"with innovations"—epic.

Since an inventory of examples of sound/image separation is of little use, the critic must ask how these patterns of separation function in the construction of a set of cues for audience perception. One simple pattern of separation in *Tout va bien* involves interruption. The classical narrative film depends on a continuous flow of the causal chain. Such a clear linkage of cause and effect is ideal for the naturalization of story events, since events seem to occur inevitably and logically. Each event is thoroughly, even redundantly, motivated by a string of other events. Classical conventions of causality do not permit interruptions of a type likely to loosen the motivational links. Such interruptions should cue the spectator to examine the occurrences as constructed events rather than as natural ones.

A pattern of interruption begins early in the film, as the writing of the checks (Fig. 4.1) and the discussion over a black screen of the making of the film alternate with shots of Montand's and Fonda's

[9] For discussions of these two modes of filmmaking, see David Bordwell, Janet Staiger, and Kristin Thompson, *The Classical Hollywood Cinema: Film Style and Mode of Production to 1960* (New York: Columbia University Press, 1985), and David Bordwell, *Narration in the Fiction Film* (Madison: University of Wisconsin Press, 1985), chap. 10.

names (Fig. 4.2) and sample shots from the proposed film. Later, as the narrative begins to unfold, the interruptions become more systematic. The scene in which the factory worker Georgette explains women's working conditions to Susan begins with the camera facing the back of one of the women workers (Fig. 4.3). Twice this situation is interrupted by cuts to shots of a woman worker facing the camera and reciting a radical song (Fig. 4.4). The return to the interview takes up where it was interrupted: the two actions are alternatives cut in together, not different stages of a scene shuffled. Rather than simply showing an interview between a woman reporter and a woman factory worker, the film inserts an alternative which criticizes the interview; it reveals the contrast between the women's capacity for defiance and their complaints to Susan, which can only arouse sympathy.

A slightly later scene presents a similar pattern when a group of the radical strikers again attempt to describe to Susan the conditions in the factory. Each shot of a worker is followed by a shot in the factory, with Susan or Jacques performing the actions described (Fig. 4.5). The result is a complex set of implications. The very ludicrousness of showing stars Fonda and Montand in the actual factory setting underlines the workers' point that it is impossible to convey a sense of the worker's real situation to a nonworker. In addition, the traditional documentary style of these factory shots (with their floodlighting and lack of color contrasts) supports one young worker's complaint that the workers' explanation is exactly what the official union, the CGT, would show reporters on a tour of the factory. Again, the interruptions give a different perspective on the central action of the scene.

A number of major interruptions occur during Susan and Jacques's argument. After they have listed the activities that supposedly constitute their life together—the private activities of eating, sex, and so on—Susan declares, "If you want to talk about what we do together, about what's OK and what's not OK, you've got to say more." At this point there is a cut to a long shot, similar to one we saw earlier, of Jacques at work shooting a commercial. The next shot repeats an earlier action of Susan tearing up her copy. Further interruptions in the conversation occur when Susan mentions Jacques's image of her (the black-and-white photo of a woman's hand holding a penis) and her need for an image of him at work as well (shots of them in their respective studios). In combination with Susan's switch to direct address to the audience during this scene, these inserted images concentrate the spectator's attention on the line of argument she is setting forth; the device de-emphasizes the emotional conflict between characters. The elimination of the shot/reverse shot pattern in the dialogue aids this avoidance of empathy cues, since we barely see Jacques during Susan's laying-out of the issues.

Examples of interruption occur in scenes in which characters confront each other with explanations or arguments. The interrupting elements serve in some way as a critique or illustration of the position put forth in the scene. Godard and Gorin substitute a pattern of argumentative editing for the editing normally used in narrative films; ordinarily, cutting follows the causal chain of the story and is restricted to the narrative space of the scene.

By way of contrast, we might imagine the scene between Susan and Jacques staged in a more traditional way. Although it is difficult to conceive of an older Hollywood film's including a situation in which a couple sits down to analyze their relationship logically, the recent trend toward realistic social cinema—exemplified by films like *Ordinary People, Kramer vs. Kramer, The China Syndrome*, and *Coming Home*—might well foster such discussions. Yet it would assuredly be done in shot/reverse shot (these recent films seem sometimes to be 95 percent shot/reverse shot), with glamor lighting, soft-colored sets, and the ever-present diffusion filters. More important, the conversation would constitute a dramatic emotional event in the characters' lives; any logical line of argument involved would be subsidiary to its effects on the characters. In *Tout va bien*, we have seen so little of the couple's relationship that this scene hardly seems the result of a dramatically established set of causes.

Another form of interruption involves the use of printed material. MacCabe speaks of Godardian titles as Brechtian devices: "the punctuation of representation with formulation." (I will assume here that "formulation" means the brief summation of issues implied by the narrative action.) MacCabe criticizes *Tout va bien* for the fact that it has fewer titles than earlier Godard films: "To give up this weapon in the heterogeneisation of the cinema is to risk a lapse into a plentitude of the image—a fall into belief and away from knowledge."[10] He deplores "the diegetic motivation" given to the other writing in the film. Yet the film provides various types of motivation for its graphs, posters, signs, and the like. Some of these motivations may come from the diegesis but still cause the spectator to question the relation of the writing to the story events. The strike banner, when seen on the outside of the factory, has an unambiguous spatial and temporal status, no doubt. But what are we to assume when it hangs on the side of the cutaway set (Fig. 4.6)? Is it still part of the story, or a sort of title

[10] MacCabe, "Politics of Separation," pp. 46, 55.

grafted onto the mise-en-scene? Similarly, the writing of the checks occupies a dubious space in relation to the story. (The original production of *Mahagonny* used a variety of written and graphic devices, as designed by Caspar Neher. Projections onto the sets juxtaposed business charts and paintings with the action, and characters carried signs with slogans.)

The formulations given by the inserted titles are clear enough; most of them emphasize the relationship between the present ("Mai, 1972"; "Aujourd'hui 1-3") and the events of May 1968. But other written and graphic devices serve functions beyond formulation. In the office settings, pictures and charts on the walls create a montage effect by repeatedly juxtaposing the official management images of the factory with the statements of the workers—note the graph on the wall behind the young radical worker and the meat poster behind the shop steward as he is being interviewed.

As the young radical speaks to Susan and Jacques about how the usual reporter covers a story on the workers' plight, we see them against the freshly painted blue wall with a factory photo on it: "It's all detail, as if the guy never knew there was such a thing as a factory. He gets all sentimental, he almost cries, but he never shows the struggle, or how things change." The photo on the wall shows another side of that view: the bourgeois, management view of the factory as an idealized thing, unchanging (Fig. 4.7). One worker paints the walls in the course of the strike; while a discussion of the bargainers' negotiations goes on in the foreground, he paints the framed photos as well as the wall. Again, the inclusion of the photo juxtaposes the same management view of the factory with the worker's: the factory is a real wall to be painted, a changeable object. The paint does alter the real factory, while it simply obliterates the idealized view. Another interruption within a shot occurs when the door to the boss's office closes to reveal a scrawled caption. The coherent narrative playing space we are accustomed to in classical cinema is subverted in this way; not only events but also statements and arguments appear in this space. Action may cease while we read or notice these graphic devices. Thus while the number of titles may be reduced in *Tout va bien*, other forms of writing act effectively as functional equivalents to Godard's titles in earlier films.

These various types of interruption help make the film a presentation of events as individual situations to be watched and understood. Once the smooth flow of narrative disappears, the spectator cannot as easily take the events on the screen as pure spectacle. This idea of understanding as opposed to absorption is one of the central distinctions Brecht makes between epic and dramatic approaches to opera.

A second, related principle of separation of elements is contradiction. Numerous small-scale spatial and temporal contradictions arise from one of *Tout va bien*'s major stylistic devices—its strong discontinuities of editing. Such discontinuities are contrary to accepted Hollywood practice, in which breaks in the smooth flow of action are viewed as undesirable distractions. The elaborate "rules" of continuity editing have become the pervasive standard. *Tout va bien*'s "mismatches," repetitions of action, and other "impossible" juxtapositions set up an alternative system to that of Hollywood. Again, the viewer can see these actions only as constructs rather than as "natural" occurrences. Simple examples are to be found in many scenes. Susan sits down twice at the beginning of her conversation with Jacques. In one shot she is buttoning her blouse; in the next, her hands are suddenly under her chin (Figs. 4.8 and 4.9). The same kind of mismatching occurs at the beginning and end of the manager's interview; he is pacing, suddenly seated, then pacing again in three successive shots. Other moments that disregard continuity do not involve action, as when the manager breaks his window in order to urinate, and it is not broken two shots later.

Godard had used these devices before. From early in his career, editing discontinuities were a part of his style—the jump cuts in *Breathless*, the systematic mismatches in *Made in USA* and in the "Mao, Mao" scene in *La Chinoise*. In the early films, like *Breathless*, discontinuities represented some of the stylistic devices of the New Wave (with political implications only in that they helped the filmmakers defy the French cinema establishment). But in the middle period of Godard's career, discontinuities became somewhat Brechtian, in that they were associated with more explicitly political themes in such films as *Made in USA*, *Two or Three Things I Know About Her*, and *Le Gai Savoir*. With *Tout va bien*, the discontinuities gain a new edge, partly through the presence of the stars and partly through the discussion of this as a commercial narrative film. Seeing Anna Karina mismatched had virtually become a convention in itself by the mid-1960s. Seeing Jane Fonda in similar scenes defamiliarizes the device, making it slightly shocking once more.

Other contradictions involve sound and image relationships. Although much of the film uses simple onscreen and offscreen sound, there are moments when the source of certain sounds is unclear. When Georgette tells her story to Susan, one of the other women present narrates the events over; yet because the voice is speaking at a time other than that of the event, we never know which woman it is (Figs. 4.3 and 4.4; we also have no sense of which man it is whose voice announces "Radical Song"). One of the scenes of the group of radical workers giving their opinions involves a voice that seems not to come from any of the men visible in the frame. A slightly different sound/image relationship occurs in the scene of Susan sitting in medium shot by the factory office window; we can clearly see that her lips are not moving, yet we hear her voice-over joining in the (offscreen? non-simultaneous?) discussion (Fig. 4.10).

The female worker's song embodies another kind of sonic separation. Although the voice clearly labels it a "song," she does not sing, but only recites the words. The musical part of the song is hummed by a different voice, but words and tune do not join together into a true song.

This separation of word and image becomes emblematic of a third principle of separation: refraction. By this, I mean that the film inserts mediations between event and spectator perception. This works both in terms of the film itself, which we are led to see as an arbitrary construct arising from a specific situation, and in terms of the moments of communication within the film.

The two central characters represent the split between word and image in their jobs: She a radio broadcaster and He a filmmaker doing commercials. This split is emphasized by the placement of a camera to the left of the frame during his "interview" and a microphone in a comparable position during hers. More explicitly, Godard and Gorin follow each interview with a lengthy shot of each character at work, making clear the mediating nature of their respective jobs. The shot of the viewfinder of Jacques's camera and the dancing legs of the models bares the devices of the camera—framing, focus, distance, and so on—while the hand reaching in from offscreen manipulates the controls. A parallel shot occurs after Susan's interview, showing her attempting to record a broadcast on tape; the camera frames her from a distance, with the recording booth in the foreground. As she falters and has to go back and start again, we see the technician's hand reach off and we hear the garbled sound of the tape rewinding. Here sound transmission and its mediating qualities are emphasized. These two shots are perhaps the structural center of the entire film—the display in miniature of the principles of separation operating at every other level of the film.

The interview with Susan also contains a unique instance of refraction: the voice-over translation. As Susan speaks, her words are put into French; then, in English-language prints, subtitles translate the

French back into English (Fig. 4.11). This is perhaps the only case in which the original effect of a scene is considerably enhanced by the presence of subtitles, for here a double mediation appears. We can hear some of Susan's monologue in English and see that the subtitles are never exactly what she had originally said. Whether subtitled or not, this scene allows a spectator who understands French and English to detect the disparities between Susan's words and those of the voice-over translator. Thus Susan's monologue demonstrates the mediating nature of language.

But refraction also occurs in scenes that do not take sound, images, or filmmaking as their explicit subject. Susan's interview with Georgette is presented through an intermediary, the voice-over narrating the scene in the past tense. A broadcast announcer's voice reports the end of the strike over the last exterior shot of the factory; the announcement describes the effect of the strike on the manager and the couple held hostage, but it ignores the workers' descriptions of the situation.

Godard and Gorin create images within images, as we have seen. One shot consists entirely of a black-and-white photo of a woman's hand on a penis; the photo then becomes an element within a shot as Susan holds it up before her face (Fig. 4.12). As in earlier films, Godard's tendency to shoot perpendicularly to walls flattens space by eliminating such usual perspective cues as overlap and shadow. Near the end, the shot of Susan sitting in the café waiting for Jacques bares this device as she reaches up and puts her hand on the glass in front of his face (Fig. 4.13).

Another structure of refraction foregrounds production. Factory production is central to the narrative, but film production is also a subject of the film, in the narrative and outside of it. The opening and closing sections set up the conditions of production and establish the arbitrary nature of the narrative construct. These portions of the film present alternatives: the narrative begins with two different takes showing the couple walking by the river; at the end, Jacques waits for Susan at the café, then another take shows her waiting for him.

As a result of these three principles of separation—interruption, contradiction, refraction—the film denies spectators the possibility of plugging into traditional methods of viewing. They cannot watch the film in a familiar way and so must either reject it as "obscure" (a common complaint, of course) or seek to discover its principles of working; the latter course must involve a rethinking of traditional cinematic conventions.

GENERAL STRUCTURES OF SEPARATION

The pattern of separation works as a dominant in *Tout va bien*, going beyond the local levels of stylistic devices and individual narrative moments. The breakdown of the traditional formal pattern works in the narrative of the film on two levels: the "vertical" structure of narrative conventions and the "horizontal" structure of narrative causality.

For the purposes of this analysis, I shall divide *Tout va bien* into five major parts.

I. The discussion of making the film (everything before the first establishing shot of the factory exterior).

II. The strike at the factory (ends with the radio announcement that the strike is over).

III. Interviews with Jacques and Susan at work; their argument (ends as she threatens to leave him).

IV. Rethinking of positions (Aujourd'hui 1-3, ends with a long tracking shot in a department store).

V. The discussion of ending the film; song.

If *Tout va bien* remains within the realm of the standard narrative film, but "with innovations," the opening discussion in the film clearly cites the conventions of this narrative tradition that the director will use. Hence the framing device works to extend the principle of refraction to the entire form of the film (as a subdominant within the general category of separation). The man's voice announces that he wishes to make a film; the subsequent dialogue reveals certain necessary steps he must take: the making of a film leads to expenditure, which leads to a need for stars to bring in money at the box office. But the woman says, "An actor won't accept a part without a story-line . . . usually a love story." Thus a number of the traits that will characterize *Tout va bien* are labeled as conventional, things a filmmaker must do to make a film in a certain societal situation.

The film also cites the norm of narrative structure in the traditional cinema—conflict. The man describes his film: "There'll be him and there'll be her, and . . . obstacles between them." (Romance and conflict.) She objects that this is too vague, and they introduce social classes. But the farmers, workers (Fig. 4.14), and bourgeois groups only stand in typical portrait-poses; there is still no conflict. The man's voice goes on: "You need something more. . . . For example, 'But the calm is only apparent. . . . Beneath the surface, things are cooking.' " The farmers burn potatoes; students clash with police; union members demonstrate (Fig. 4.15).

121

Of course, *Tout va bien* never becomes a straight Hollywood romance; the context-less love scene by the river that introduces Jacques and Susan never returns. But neither do Godard and Gorin simply place the two central characters in a unified narrative with workers and bourgeois as minor characters. Instead, they mix several separate conventional generic approaches to filmmaking, interweaving their conventions without fusing the genres. First, there are traits of a popular story, the obligatory love story promised at the beginning; this involves such elements as stars, romance, and bourgeois situations. When the characters are introduced in the first section, Fonda and Montand differ conspicuously from the peasants and farmers. They pose in a studio rather than on location; the flat sunlight of the group shots gives way to a backlighting on the two stars so lush it becomes a parody of Hollywood studio lighting (Fig. 4.16). (This device of studio lighting is bared at the end of Jacques's interview, when he steps out of the frame and reveals the source of the strong backlight that has picked his body out against the darkness of this scene [Fig. 4.17].)

In many later scenes in the film, the framing does treat the stars as figures in the mise-en-scene indistinguishable from the other characters, so that the romance plot is forced into the background. The tracking shots of the factory set place Fonda and Montand in the same lighting style and relative scale as the workers in the other rooms. In several group scenes, the stars get lost behind clusters of workers in the foreground.

In contrast to the way they treat the romance, Godard and Gorin shoot much of the film using devices traditionally associated with various documentary modes; we may call this structure of the film "quasi-documentary." For example, the film uses one of the central conventions of the documentary, the interview; the CGT shop steward and the manager of the factory respond to unheard questions in long takes filmed in frontal medium shots. Yet the status of the interview is unclear—by whom are these questions asked? Unlike these long takes, the workers' interviews exhibit considerable discontinuity. Later, in the third segment, two other interviews occur: Jacques and Susan tell about their backgrounds, he to an unheard questioner. Susan's speech draws also upon another set of conventions—those of the broadcast; she sits by a microphone and a voice-over translator speaks along with her. Yet this is not a broadcast, as the next shot makes clear when she begins her actual taping session.

These interviews all take place within a clearly fictional situation. The manager's interview precedes and follows long shots of the cutaway office set, emphasizing the staged quality of the shot. Similarly, the steward's interview is abruptly juxtaposed with the clash between the CGT supporters and more radical strikers on the stairways of the same set. The interviews with Susan and Jacques fit into fictional scenes of their work.

The interviews further undermine their own documentary qualities by the variety of acting styles they contain. The actor plays the manager's speech in a highly caricatured, broad fashion (Fig. 4.18); the shop steward also gives an exaggerated performance, but not to the same extent. In contrast, Fonda and Montand give quiet, casual deliveries of their lines—closer to what is currently considered "naturalistic" in "quality" cinema acting. They simulate the hesitating, groping manner of persons actually being interviewed, but here a contradiction enters due to the fact that they are stars—we know them to belong to the romance plot, not to a documentary.

In addition to mixing elements of quasi-documentary and romance narrative, Godard and Gorin also use devices that are traditional to neither, devices associated with alternative aesthetic systems. Many of the discontinuities of editing pointed out earlier derive from the theory and practice of Eisenstein. The placards, pictures, and titles are Brechtian. Finally, Godard and Gorin use techniques that are recognizable as "Godardian": lateral tracking shots, inaudible offscreen questioners, red-white-and-blue titles, and so on. Godard also cites his own past as a point of reference in *Tout va bien*: not only does Jacques describe himself as a former New Wave filmmaker, but the opening love scene (which is rejected as not specific enough) recalls the opening of *Le Mépris*. Thus the film condemns certain aspects of Godard's career as too uncritically derivative of the Hollywood cinema. The specifically Godardian techniques, along with the use of Brechtian and Eisensteinian concepts, become components of the new system Godard and Gorin set up as an alternative.

Earlier Godard films undoubtedly derived aspects of their narratives from some of these same traditional modes. *Une Femme est une femme* combined the Hollywood musical with New Wave techniques; *Pierrot le fou* included elements of a gangster story. This pattern is common until approximately the period of *La Chinoise*. A number of the films between *La Chinoise* and *Tout va bien* were dominated by a mixture of quasi-documentary and "Godardian" techniques. *Tout va bien* marks a major stage in Godard's career because he and Gorin at last blend the essayistic mode of the Dziga-Vertov Group films with the narrative, art-cinema pattern of the pre-*Gai savoir* period. (*Letter to Jane*, which was shown after *Tout va bien* in early festival showings and during Godard and Gorin's 1973 American tour, in a sense takes over part of the essayistic function that would have dominated in the Dziga-Vertov Group films.) With this mixture of techniques Godard and Gorin are at last able to critique each mode by interweaving them, and by including the "frame" device of the discussion of filmmaking. The frame situates the romance for the spectator. What we are watching is no longer a fond playing with conventions, as in *Une Femme est une femme*, but a clear acknowledgment of a convention—romance—as a narrative construct, economically essential to the filmmaker.

Perhaps inevitably, some scenes in the film receive less critique or analysis through structures of separation. Specifically, the flashbacks to May 1968 participate the least in the pattern of interweaving conventions I have been describing. The sequence does contain interruptions and contradictions in the form of mismatches, repetitions, and the uncertain source of the sound in the "Gilles" tribute. But by and large the quasi-documentary mode used for these scenes receives relatively little critique; there is no moment in them that really places the mode of filmic presentation itself in context.

The parallel scene to the May 1968 flashbacks is Susan's period of rethinking—the department store shot. Here the narration is different. The cues for documentary are more consistently undercut, partly by the tracking shot and partly by the sound track, both of which remove the style from that of a documentary in several ways. The camera seems to be following Fonda in a real, candidly observed locale. Yet we hear her voice-over meditating on her situation. The camera behaves in a contradictory fashion. Though it seems to be following Fonda, and later the student demonstrators, it also refuses to accommodate its trajectory to theirs, letting them lag behind or get ahead and thus go out of frame. Yet the camera just happens also to pick out key moments of action (the entry of the rioters and of the police) and even pauses to show us the argument between the students and the man selling the CP books. Thus the camera pretends to be a mere recording device at the same time that it unselfconsciously betrays the effects of careful orchestration of the tracking movement with the mise-en-scene.

For the most part the film manages to keep a balance between stylistic cues, never settling into one unified mode long enough for the spectator to become absorbed into one familiar way of viewing. We must notice the conventions of romance, documentary, and art film as constructs and learn new ways of grasping them *as* constructs. *Tout va bien*'s success as a political film derives from its ability to denaturalize most of the conventions it draws upon.

The traditional romantic narrative of Hollywood motivates its events compositionally by constructing a tight, linear chain of causality which typically leads back to a single generating cause. (For example, the Maltese Falcon was made in 1539, and we find out all its pertinent subsequent history that eventually causes Gutman to want to find it, Bridget O'Shaughnessy to call on Sam Spade, and so on. In *Citizen Kane*, the "defaulting boarder's" valuable deed is the initial cause. In the typical revenge Western, the causality leads back to the murder of a relative. In *Terror By Night*, the discovery of the Star of Rhodesia is the earliest cause.) *Tout va bien* takes a considerable step away from this model of causality. Here the initial cause is one usually avoided by Hollywood: the desire to make a film. Hollywood does not motivate the actual presence of a narrative, of stars, of a locale, and so on; instead, it assumes these things and naturalizes them by redundant devices of compositional, generic, and realistic motivation. But Godard and Gorin acknowledge that all the elements they need to begin a film are constructs dictated by convention: stars, locale, and that key source of narrative causality, conflict. (In a sense, we have a very special type of realistic motivation at work here: that is how films are made in the real world.) Here refraction helps the spectator denaturalize traditional assumptions about narrative causality.

The separation of the different modes of romance and quasi-documentary also contributes to the nontraditional use of causality. The five-part division of the film presented above shows that the story of the strike dominates the first section after the setting-up of the film, while the lovers introduced at the beginning occupy a subsidiary role. The strike runs its full course in this section. After it ends, the romance takes prominence in Segment III; finally He and She come to have "obstacles between them" in the form of their argument over the nature of their relationship. Segment IV again centers on Susan and Jacques but places them once again in a broader social context—May 1968 and the consumer "factory," the department store. Thus in Segments II through IV, interruption and contradiction (achieved through a mixture of generic conventions and through stylistic traits) largely replace refraction as the primary means of structuring the narrative's form.

Finally the discussion of filmmaking returns. As the initial cause was viewed as being the desire to make a film, so the final cause is, as the woman's voice says, that "every film has to end." Again, the film is not a natural thing, but a construct, and as such it can end in different ways. Godard and Gorin present two alternative endings—Jacques waits for Susan, She waits for Him—though even then they make it clear that these particular choices are dictated by the social need for a happy ending to the love story. But *Tout va bien* has not been simply a Hollywood romance; the couple gets back together, but the woman's voice states, "We'll simply say that He and She have begun to rethink themselves in historical terms"; meaning here becomes explicit.

Although the quasi-documentary presentation of the strike and the later problems of the couple are shown separately, they have considerable causal linkage. The experience of witnessing the strike leads to the activity of rethinking that takes place in the "romance" sections. The workers themselves begin this rethinking pattern. While the manager and CGT steward both have complete official positions which they describe unhesitatingly, the workers are more tentative in their attempts to work out their own positions. They criticize each other's ways of explaining the situation to Susan and introduce her to the activity of rethinking she is to take up later herself.

In his interview, Jacques tells his story, but in spite of finding commercial production "slightly repulsive," he proposes no concrete plan of changing his situation. He also declares that he is put off by the Party's doctrine of "re-educating intellectuals." Susan, on the other hand, faces the contradictions of her job more directly; she refuses to record her editorial to suit the network policy.

In the scene at breakfast, Susan formulates the problem of rethinking; as they discuss their activities together, she says, "Since they don't satisfy you, think your dissatisfaction through, think what's *around* those headings." This comes just before she states that she is no longer content with only their personal activities: "To think about that pleasure today, I need a picture of him at work . . . and a picture of me at work."

This specific conclusion leads directly from discussions in the factory. In his interview, the young radical worker outlines the problem: "The Union talks as if, acts as if, there was a factory with nothing outside. It's like you're in here eight hours a day, and as a worker you let the Union think for you; then outside, as a citizen, you let the Party think for you, and you say a prayer for left-wing unity." This split between work and private life (a classic pattern of alienated labor in Marxist analysis) is the same problem against which Susan rebels in her argument with Jacques. Susan had not been present to hear the young radical's speech; the causality in the two parts of the film is parallel rather than simply linear. The situation of rethinking leads to similar, but independent, conclusions; the strike leads to the rethinking itself (through the network's rejection of Susan's story) but not to the shape it takes. The parallel between factory story and romance continues in the results of the rethinking. Susan decides to write a story she knows will be rejected, then to quit; Jacques contemplates leaving his job to make his planned political film about France. They have come to see their situations as capable of being changed, just as the workers had seen the factory as something to be changed.

Again, this division of the film into a series of logical arguments differs from the Hollywood norm. The difference becomes especially apparent when *Tout va bien* is contrasted with an American film which it resembles in some respects (and which one cannot help suspecting was influenced by *Tout va bien*)—*The China Syndrome*. Here the Jane Fonda character is also a media journalist, forced by a situation upon which she is reporting to rethink her romance and her job. In this case, she is doing a neutral story on an atomic-power plant and happens to be on the scene when a near meltdown occurs. One ideological difference between the two films is readily apparent: in *The China Syndrome*, two men (the Michael Douglas and Jack Lemmon characters) force her into her rethinking, while in *Tout va bien*, she discerns the necessity for it herself. *The China Syndrome* also avoids larger political issues by attributing serious problems—the dangers of nuclear energy—to individual corruption in the building of a single power plant. Most central, *The China Syndrome* reduces its abstract, social issues to individual, emotional crises by portraying all causes as relating to the personal drama of the Jack Lemmon character; his soul-searching and courage, in essence, take the place of all the logical arguments that make up the rethinking processes in *Tout va bien*.

The presence of the quasi-documentary mode in *Tout va bien* also brings with it the possibility of non-causal construction within the narrative. This alternative to causality is *argumentative*, and it exists within several scenes of interviews or discussions. The CGT steward presents facts and statistics to support a certain political position taken by the hard-line Communist union members. The manager and workers argue other positions. Susan and Jacques's argument is basically a narrative scene, but the discussion itself takes a rhetorical structure, contrasting their positions on their relationship and proposing an alternative to their current life style. *Tout va bien* is virtually a series of such argumentative passages nested in, and partially motivated by, the "love story" of its narrative.

One significance of these rhetorical passages is a further avoidance of the naturalization of ideology offered by the classical Hollywood pattern of narrative (although perhaps at the risk of setting up a new naturalization in its place). A classical narrative's tight series of causes usually arises from the traits of individuals rather than from more general aspects of society. Thus, each conflict which arises in the course

127

of the narrative appears unique, personal, and hence limited (as in *The China Syndrome*). *Tout va bien*'s rhetorical structures seek the opposite possibility: a search for solutions to problems that appeals to more generalizable principles—a move toward social solutions rather than purely personal ones.

CONCLUSIONS

As a result of these structures of separation, rethinking becomes not just the film's subject matter, but also a necessary process in watching *Tout va bien*. The spectator rethinks the situations of the workers and the lovers. But beyond this, the spectator must rethink the process of watching a film; he or she may come to see how filmic conventions have been used in the past, and how they may be used in new ways which seek to avoid and expose the naturalization of conventionalized cinematic devices.

This is not to say, however, that the process of separation I have been examining *guarantees* this response—or any other—in the spectator. The most a filmmaker can do is to create a set of cues for perception. But the spectator may be incapable of taking up those cues, for the ideology of viewing lies to a large extent in learned skills for understanding art works. The vast majority of film-goers have learned no way of viewing other than that needed to approach the classical narrative film.

In his article, MacCabe criticizes *Two or Three Things* because he claims that "the formal nature of the separation is exactly that which enables the spectator to remain untouched by it—to remain mixed in *Deux ou trois choses* still offers an aesthetic position to the viewer from which the formal operations can still be read as the tics of an original genius."[11] But *any* work can be read in this way; any unfamiliar or radical device of a work can easily be recuperated as the personal expression of the artist. Indeed, the modern art cinema and its American offshoot, auteurism applied to Hollywood films, work specifically on the viewing tactic of searching for such personal expression. No doubt some works (those of Bergman and Fellini, for example) encourage such readings, while others fight against them, seeking to create devices so radical they cannot be recuperated (the framing discussion of filmmaking in *Tout va bien*, for one). But a spectator bent on recuperating the radical work into a safe, romantic view of the artist as visionary will always be able to succeed (if only by calling the film a

[11] Ibid., p. 53.

128

failure). After all, *The Rise and Fall of the City of Mahagonny*, as we learned in 1979, can play to $50-a-seat Metropolitan Opera audiences and become part of the Met's repertory without offending its Rockefeller-based patronage. Hence the need for films and teaching and criticism that try to analyze and change the viewing abilities of the spectator, rather than simply offering new readings. *Tout va bien* presents its devices as culturally necessary, rather than as a personal vision; indeed, the filmmaker within the film seems to accept the stars, story, and other traits reluctantly. If, however, *Tout va bien* cues us against taking it as a personal vision, it has no way of controlling the way we as spectators will take these cues.

In writing this essay, I have not failed to notice that similar patterns of separation occur in other types of works. The Monty Python movies and television series, for example, take the separation of conventional elements to an even greater extreme, mixing interviews, broadcasts, and parodies of all sorts of genres from popular narrative media. (Indeed, the television series shows that it is markedly influenced by Godard; one program cites him by including a parody of *One Plus One*.)

Would we want to say that Monty Python is Brechtian? Probably not in any strict sense, and that reason can be found in a passage in an article by Ben Brewster in an issue of *Screen* devoted to Brecht. There Brewster discusses Brecht's difference from the avant-garde movements of the 1910s and 1920s.

Brecht talked of a "return from alienation" to distinguish his own position from that of the historical avant-gardes: "Dadaism and surrealism use alienation effects of the most extreme kind. Their objects do not return from alienation" (xv, 364). Their use of the A-effect was primitive "because the function of this art is paralysed from the social point of view, so that here art no longer functions. As far as its effect is concerned, it ends in an amusement" (xvi, 612).[12]

Thus amusement and a failure to return from alienation may mark a non-Brechtian separation of elements. Monty Python and other works expose and parody social conventions but stop at the level of amusement. (The main objection to *Life of Brian*, for example, related to its sacrilege; yet the film itself, like its companions, was quite popular.) *Tout va bien*, on the other hand, whatever humorous devices it may contain, is not ultimately comic or simply a satire of existing conventions of Hollywood romances.

The return from alienation marks a rejection of a simply absurdist view. To see the world as absurd is also to see it as incapable of

---

[12] Ben Brewster, "From Shklovsky to Brecht: A Reply," *Screen* 15, no. 2 (Summer 1974): 96.

change, as hopeless. The filmmaker accepts political responsibility by returning from alienation. Godard and Gorin's separation of elements criticizes, but it is not an absurdist condemnation.

No doubt *Tout va bien* remains situated in the tradition of the narrative film, even of the romance. But when Jacques refers to the *Mahagonny* preface, he also describes the type of film he hopes someday to make: "I've been trying to think things out, figure out what kind of film they'd let me do. I've been thinking about what kind of film to make. A political film on France, maybe." These lines describe an attitude similar to that in the *Mahagonny* preface: "Art is merchandise, only to be manufactured by the means of production (apparati). An opera can only be written for the opera."[13] The writer of opera and the filmmaker cannot do their work with a means of production that does not exist during their historical epoch.

Tout va bien was not made within the commercial Hollywood tradition, though it cites that tradition extensively and uses stars from it. Rather, the film draws upon the institution of the art cinema. Having left that tradition for the Dziga-Vertov films, beginning in 1968, Godard attempted to create a new kind of cinema for political purposes. Sometimes shooting in 16mm, often substituting rhetorical formal strategies for narrative, he and Gorin found themselves increasingly losing the wide audience Godard's earlier films had enjoyed. However successful one might consider films like *British Sounds* aesthetically and ideologically, they presented too great a challenge to the conventional viewing habits of most audiences. In *Tout va bien*, we can see an eminently Brechtian compromise. It returned to the institution of the art cinema; the film ran in regular theaters and allowed Godard and Gorin to make the traditional artists' tour to promote their film. (For many Godard admirers, the film was virtually the comeback of an inactive artist, since the other Dziga-Vertov films had remained outside their ken; we shall see much the same thing happening with *Sauve qui peut (la vie)*.) But although *Tout va bien* utilizes many of the art film's conventions, and indeed is an art film in many ways, it also seeks to undermine that mode of filmmaking.

Brecht's conclusion was that politically progressive opera must work to expose the social function of opera itself.

Perhaps *Mahagonny* is as culinary as ever—just as culinary as an opera ought to be—but one of its functions is to change society; it brings the culinary principle under discussion, it attacks the society that needs operas of such a sort;

---

[13] Brecht, "The Modern Theatre," p. 35.

it still perches happily on the old bough, perhaps, but at least it has started (out of absent-mindedness or bad conscience) to saw it through.[14]

Brecht's description applies well to *Tout va bien*; it is a "culinary" film which attacks the situation of its own creation. Indeed, an examination of *Tout va bien* that accepts Brecht's premises can hardly quibble because Godard and Gorin have failed to jump off the bough altogether.

[14] Ibid., p. 41.

5

Duplicitous Narration
and *Stage Fright*

DUPLICITY IN CLASSICAL NARRATION

In *S/Z*, Roland Barthes discusses the measures a discourse must take in order not to reveal the truth prematurely (and hence bring the narrative to an abrupt end). The discourse, he says, tries

> to lie *as little as possible*: just what is required to ensure the interests of reading, that is, its own survival. Caught up in a civilization of enigma, truth, and decipherment, the discourse reinvents on its own level the moral terms elaborated by that civilization: there is a casuistry of discourse.[1]

This passage distinguishes between the voice of the text itself (the discourse) and the voices of the characters within the text; the characters may lie outright. But although the classical text may have to keep the truth from its reader, it does so primarily through tactics of delay, concealment, and distraction—the "dilatory morphemes" that Barthes lists in *S/Z*: the snare, the equivocation, the partial answer, the suspended answer, and jamming.[2] The "lie" is seldom acceptable in this series, according to Barthes. Even when the text has no way of avoiding a lie, it has ways of softening it. In Barthes's example, Balzac's short story "Sarrasine," La Zambinella is occasionally called a "woman" in the text. We eventually discover that this is a lie, yet we can find motivations for it. First, the text may be artificially limiting itself to Sarrasine's consciousness, even though it is theoretically omniscient; we forgive this easily for the sake of having the story continue. Second, the story of La Zambinella is a story-within-a-story, and it is really the narrator, himself a character in the outer story, who calls La Zambinella a woman. Thus the text justifies its lie and turns it aside.

Over four decades earlier, Shklovsky had analyzed similar strategies at work, specifically in mystery stories: "Sometimes the device of mys-

---

[1] Roland Barthes, *S/Z*, trans. Richard Miller (New York: Hill and Wang, 1974), p. 141.
[2] Ibid., p. 75.

tery penetrates into the very body of the novel, into the characters' modes of expression, and into the remarks which they inspire in the author."[3] His examples, from Arthur Conan Doyle's "The Adventure of the Speckled Band," show how Helen Stoner's description of her sister's death mixes facts with deception and camouflaging. Her reference to Dr. Roylott's friendship with gypsies suggests a false solution (they may have been the killers), while the mention of his fondness for exotic animals gives an inexact hint of the method of the crime (a poisonous snake). Important details of the circumstances of the murder (the shuttered windows, Roylott's cigar smoke, a whistle, and a clanking sound) are camouflaged by others that are less crucial (the gale, the sister's door swinging on its hinges). The victim's final words point again to a false solution, as Miss Stoner suggests that "the speckled band" may refer to the nearby gypsy encampment.[4] Unlike Barthes, Shklovsky does not create a typology of deceptive devices, nor does he distinguish between lies and other types of deception. In neither theorist's example does the narration lie outright.

Is the distinction between "lying" and Barthes's other types of deception and diversion a hard and fast one, and is it indeed possible to make this distinction at all? Barthes's dilatory morphemes seem, as he himself hints, to indicate varying degrees of deception or withholding of truth—though they are not parallel or even entirely mutually exclusive categories. The *snare*, which he defines as "a kind of deliberate evasion of the truth," would seem the least "honest" of the bunch. The *equivocation* involves "a mixture of truth and snare which frequently, while focusing on the enigma, helps to thicken it." The equivocation seems to differ only in emphasis from the *partial answer*, "which only exacerbates the expectation of the truth." This category would seem the least dishonest, since it provides some progress toward the solution. The *suspended answer* is "an aphasic stoppage of the disclosure"; this metaphorical definition remains unclear but would seem to imply digression or interruption. Finally, *jamming* is the "acknowledgement of insolubility," in which the narration presumably professes to be as much in the dark as the reader.

If the snare is the most extreme of these morphemes, how does it differ from a lie, which would also seem at times to involve "a deliberate evasion of the truth"? There may be a difference of degree, but the distinction is a fine one indeed. Moreover, does the classical work avoid lying to the extent Barthes claims? He treats the avoidance of

<hr />

[3] Victor Chklovski, *Sur la théorie de la prose*, trans. Guy Verret (Lausanne: Editions l'Age d'homme, 1973), p. 153.

[4] Ibid., pp. 155–157.

lying as a nearly pervasive trait of the classical text, without producing any examples beyond "Sarrasine" itself. Shklovsky, on the other hand, takes deception to be a set of historical conventions, and presumably he would find its usage grounded in such notions as genre. To be sure, Barthes's examination of enigma and deception in a text outside the mystery genre is a valuable next step. Yet it seems risky to generalize so broadly about usage over a vast set of works like "the classical text."

I would argue that the outright lie is simply another step along the series of dilatory morphemes—another, more extreme category of the kinds of deception used by many texts, and one which differs from the others only in degree. Whether a text lies or uses other, softened types of deception seems a less interesting question than how a text motivates its deception and to what degree it acknowledges it to the reader. It is not clear that classical narration does avoid the more extreme forms of deception, but perhaps it is the case that it often motivates them in a way that will make them less apparent to the reader. In most cases, a classical text's narration would deceive in order to maintain a balance between the hermeneutic and proairetic lines until the ending. This is true in Dickens's *Our Mutual Friend*. There the hero, John Harmon, has been presumed dead and goes through the bulk of the action under two different aliases; the narration treats him as three separate characters, as in this passage from the first book, Chapter xv.

Mr. Boffin drew a long breath, laid down his pen, looked at his notes as doubting whether he had the pleasure of their acquaintance, and appeared, on a second perusal of their countenances, to be confirmed in his impression that he had not, when there was announced by the hammer-headed young man:
"Mr. Rokesmith."
"Oh!" said Mr. Boffin. "Oh indeed! Our and the Wilfers' Mutual Friend, my dear. Yes. Ask him to come in."
Mr. Rokesmith appeared.[5]

Rokesmith is actually Harmon, but the narration makes no attempt to place the lie about his identity into the mouths of the characters, or to equivocate about it (e.g., "The man they knew as Mr. Rokesmith appeared"); it simply presents it as objective fact. This is not an infrequent device in Dickens's and other nineteenth-century novelists' works.

Our Mutual Friend is a mystery novel of sorts, but a text may mislead us for other purposes than to maintain its enigma and its exist-

[5] Charles Dickens, *Our Mutual Friend* (London: Oxford University Press, 1952), p. 178.

ence—and this Barthes does not allow for at all. Consider the following passage from P. G. Wodehouse's 1928 comic novel, *Money For Nothing*.

Not so eloquently, nor with such a wealth of imagery as Colonel Wyvern had employed in sketching out the details of the affair of the dynamite outrage for the benefit of Chas. Bywater, Chemist, John answered the question.
"Good heavens," said Pat.
"I—I hope . . ." said John.
"What do you hope?"
"Well, I—I hope it's not going to make any difference?"
"Difference? How do you mean?"
"Between us. Between you and me, Pat."
"What sort of difference?"
John had his cue.
"Pat, darling, in all these years we've known one another haven't you ever guessed that I've been falling more and more in love with you every minute? I can't remember a time when I didn't love you. I loved you as a kid in short skirts and a blue jersey. I loved you when you came back from that school of yours, looking like a princess. And I love you now move than I have ever loved you. I worship you, Pat darling. You're the whole world to me, just the one thing that matters the least little bit. And don't you try to start laughing at me again now, because I've made up my mind that, whatever else you laugh at, you've got to take me seriously. I may have been Poor Old Johnnie in the past, but the time has come when you've got to forget all that. I mean business. You're going to marry me, and the sooner you make up your mind to it, the better."
That was what John had intended to say. What he actually did say was something briefer and altogether less effective.
"Oh, I don't know," said John.[6]

Here the narration misleads us for comic effect; the passage functions to undercut clichéd literary language (a frequent device in Wodehouse); it also emphasizes John's timidity, which will be essential to the stairstep construction of the narrative line. Strictly speaking, there is no lie here, but the placement of John's hypothetical speech in quotation marks in the midst of a series of "real" speeches certainly misleads us into taking it to have the same status as they do (and that impression is strengthened by its length). The use of quotation marks and dialogue passages is a firmly established convention of reading, and Wodehouse's play with our expectations concerning them is not in any way necessary for the continued existence of the novel, however

6 P. G. Wodehouse, *Money For Nothing* (London: Herbert Jenkins, 1928), pp. 54–55.

effective it may be as a comic and characterizing device. (It is certainly not essential to the latter function, since we are already redundantly aware of John's timidity and inability to propose to Pat.)

Thus Barthes's distinction between lying and other forms of deceit within a text may be a misleading one, as well as inaccurate historically. Many art works with an enigma to maintain (whether or not they are mystery stories as such) will deceive the spectator to some degree; and, as the Wodehouse example shows, deception can play a defamiliarizing function apart from any compositional necessity. We need to ask not only whether narration does lie, but also to what degree it deceives, and what sort of motivation it provides to conceal or bare its deceptions.

In regard to deception in cinematic narration, the false flashback in Alfred Hitchcock's 1950 film *Stage Fright* would seem to be an extreme and revealing example. It serves as an interesting comparison with the *Money For Nothing* passage quoted above. In the novel, John's thoughts are rendered as if they are real dialogue, while in *Stage Fright*, Johnny's actual but lying speech to Eve is rendered as an apparently objective flashback. Both are cases of narrational manipulation of the conventions of classical storytelling in their respective media. For the Wodehouse reader, the likelihood is very great that a passage within quotation marks will be actual dialogue unless signaled ahead of time as something else. Similarly, in the classical film, a flashback (cued by dissolves and a character's voice-over description of past events) will lead virtually any viewer to assume that it shows events as they are actually supposed to have happened in the fabula.

Undoubtedly, in both literature and the cinema, the likelihood is that the narration will not use the techniques of the medium overtly to deceive the reader or spectator but will signal the status of any given passage. For example, in another Wodehouse novel, *The Mating Season* (1949), we understand the status of a bit of dialogue which Bertie Wooster considers speaking. Chapter Twenty begins:

"Good morning, sir," he said, "May I make a remark?"

"Certainly, Jeeves. Carry on. Make several."

"It is with reference to your appearance, sir. If I might take the liberty of suggesting—"

"Go on. Say it. I look like something the cat found in Tutankhamen's tomb, do I not?"

"I would not go so far as that, sir, but I have unquestionably seen you more *soigné*."

It crossed my mind for an instant that with a little thought one might throw together something rather clever about "Way down upon the *soigné* river," but I was too listless to follow it up."[7]

Similarly, for the most part classical films, though they frequently use false images, usually toss in some cue to let the spectator know that what he or she is seeing is not to be taken as a real fabula event. An elementary example occurs in Lev Kuleshov's *Extraordinary Adventures of Mr. West in the Land of the Bolsheviks* (1924). Here the leader of a pack of thieves steals Mr. West's briefcase in order to be able to return it and win Mr. West's confidence. After returning the briefcase, the thief tells Mr. West an elaborate fabricated tale of how he had saved the briefcase at great risk to himself; shots of the thief talking to Mr. West are intercut with shots of the thief "saving the briefcase." Here the audience is fully aware that the latter images are embodiments of the lies the thief is telling; they gain a considerable humor from the fact that the audience has this knowledge. More complexly, *The Confession* (1919, directed by Bertram Bracken) shows us a murder scene early on, then presents two flashbacks to the same event. Each shows the murder as described by the killer, first to his confessor and then in a courtroom scene. All three versions of the scene differ markedly, but because we have seen the murder committed, we know that the killer is distorting the truth as the flashbacks occur. This device of showing images that the audience knows to constitute a character's lies is not uncommon. It is a cinematic parallel of a character's lying words in a novel.

A different, more challenging approach is exemplified by Alain Resnais's *Last Year at Marienbad*. Here images are presented that are contradictory and thus cannot all be "true" events. But again there is no deception practiced on the audience; the spectators realize the contradictory nature of the images. They may struggle to discover the "true" images, to sort them out from the rest in order to discover the underlying fabula behind the syuzhet. No image, however, can be settled upon as the "right" or "wrong" one—all are equally possible and impossible. The structural principle at work in a film like *Last Year at Marienbad* is that there is no one fabula, no identifiable truth. And since there is no truth, the images cannot lie either. Again, this device of the shot whose status as truth cannot be determined is common in the art cinema. The visit of the husband in *Persona* and the end of *8 1/2* are other examples. In certain kinds of cinema, then, we

[7] P. G. Wodehouse, *The Mating Season* (London: Herbert Jenkins, 1949), p. 168.

expect the narration to mislead or confuse us, and such an approach is acceptable, even conventional.

Stage Fright undoubtedly has raised so much controversy because its lying flashback flaunted conventions in an extreme fashion and seemed to violate the expectations associated with its genre. Not only are we not told of the lie ahead of time, but its revelation comes very late in the film. Thus what has seemed to be a suspense plot turns out to be a murder mystery. Moreover, as soon as we find this out we also learn who the real murderer is. There is no chance for us to work out the solution before the detective gives it to us—a game that is one of the main conventions of the mystery genre. Indeed, the detective/ mystery genre is one of the few classical genres whose conventions specifically discourage outright deceit, since the convention of the audience's trying to guess the killer is so widely recognized and acknowledged. The narration is supposed to be "fair." Had the flashback been revealed as a lie shortly after it ended, it seems likely that audiences would have found it less frustrating, since the knowledge that Johnny had lied would have provided one more clue for spectators to use in piecing together a solution. Alternatively, the film might have used humor to motivate the lying flashback, thus placing the whole thing in the "spoof" genre. As it is, many viewers have expressed disappointment at being tricked.

Perhaps as a result of such reactions, Hitchcock, in his interview with François Truffaut, speaks of the "lying flashback" as a mistake. Truffaut's reply is strangely naive: "Yes, and the French critics were particularly critical of that." Hitchcock then turns around and contradicts his own previous statement, giving a brief defense of cinematic duplicity.

Strangely enough, in movies, people never object if a man is shown telling a lie. And it's also acceptable, when a character tells a story about the past, for the flashback to show it as if it were taking place in the present. So why is it that we can't tell a lie through a flashback?[8]

Truffaut then squelches this statement by trying to convince Hitchcock (and apparently succeeding) that the "flashback" was indeed a mistake. In the process he not only misinterprets at one point the action contained in the flashback, but also ends by offering not a single reason why the device is wrong.

Such an argument is absurd, since it takes the flashback out of con-

[8] François Truffaut, *Hitchcock* (New York: Simon and Schuster, 1967), p. 139.

text and assumes that such a device is innately against the rules of cinema. Hitchcock was perfectly right in his defense of the device. In *Stage Fright*, the flashback is not a gimmick. Had Hitchcock simply put Johnny's lie into an otherwise thoroughly conventional suspense-thriller, it might have been a gratuitous prank on the audience. But, as Shklovsky found for mysteries, the device has penetrated "into the very body of" the film; that is, a juxtaposition between deceit and truth becomes the dominant of the film, both in the hermeneutic line itself and in the pervasive imagery of theater (equated with deception) versus everyday life (or "truth").

THE TRUE AND FALSE ENIGMAS

The lying flashback initiates *State Fright*'s complex juggling act within the hermeneutic line. The whole film needs to show us events that will keep us believing Johnny's story. Yet it must also provide us with information that, while not contradicting that belief, will allow us to understand the true series of past fabula events without too much difficulty when Smith gives it to us late in the film. Thus the flashback discloses enough of the truth to get the syuzhet moving—the murder has been committed. (It would be unlikely, given Hollywood's narrative conventions, that Johnny's story would be entirely false. If the film's ending had disclosed that *no* murder had taken place, the film would have taken on a very different shape. It might have been either trivial—the simple discovery that Johnny is mad and has led Eve on a wild-goose chase—or too transgressive for Hollywood to have considered producing. Note, however, that the discovery of a lie in the narrative and the disclosure that there has been no murder *is* the basis for another strongly duplicitous film, *The Cabinet of Dr. Caligari*. There, however, the lie and its discovery constitute the entire raison d'être of the expressionistic style of the film, which also lies outside the classical tradition of Hollywood.) Other minor scraps of truth are woven throughout this remarkable sequence, as we shall see. At the same time, it keeps back the truth about who committed the murder. The method of *Stage Flight*'s hermeneutic juggling act becomes clearer if we compare its narrative with the model Barthes sets up for the classic pattern of enigma: the hermeneutic pattern.[9] Following is the hermeneutic pattern Barthes finds in "Sarrasine":

[9] In S/Z, Barthes calls this the "hermeneutic sentence," but this is rather confusing, as it is not a sentence. I have substituted "pattern" to avoid this confusion.

Question:	"This is La Zambinella." (subject, theme)	Who is she (formulation)	? (proposal)
	I will tell you: (promise of answer)	a woman (snare)	a creature outside nature (ambiguity)
Delays:	a . . . (suspended answer)	relative of the Lantys (partial answer)	
	no one knows. (jammed answer)		
Answer:	A castrato dressed as a woman. (disclosure)[10]		

The main difficulty in formulating the hermeneutic patterns of other works in terms of this schema is to determine the difference between the formulation and the proposal of the enigma. Barthes simply separates the question mark from the question "Who is she" and places it in the proposal section. But does this imply that the formulation and the proposal are simply variations of the same question?

Josué V. Harari's essay "The Maximum Narrative: An Introduction to Barthes' Recent Criticism" suggests an answer. He divides classical narratives into four types of suspense: "*identity* (the problem of the who)," "*kind* (the problem of the what)," "*resolution* (the problem of the where—toward what)," and "*deciphering* (the problem of the how)."[11] The first two types Harari calls questions of *being*, the latter two, questions of *doing*. Since "Sarrasine" confines itself in its primary enigma to the question of identity, the proposal of the enigma simply states the formulation (who is La Zambinella) as *the* question of the story.

Stage Fright, however, *assumes* the who, the what, and the where—toward what: Charlotte Inwood (who) killed her husband (what—murder) and must be exposed as the killer (toward what—the proposed resolution by the protagonist, Eve). The question becomes one of *how* Charlotte can be exposed. But the transgressive element of *Stage Fright* is that the three assumed elements upon which most of the action is based are shown to be false, and that revelation comes only near the end. Thus the film has a double hermeneutic pattern, and the point of the narrative is as much to expose the falsity of the one as to provide the resolution for the other. Because the film's main

[10] Barthes, S/Z, p. 85.
[11] Josué V. Harari, "The Maximum Narrative: An Introduction to Barthes' Recent Criticism," *Style* 8, no. 1 (Winter 1974): 65.

question revolves around the *how* of the enigma's resolution, the formulation and the proposal of *Stage Fright*'s hermeneutic pattern may be seen as distinctly separate. Using Barthes's scheme, the double pattern may be formulated in this way:

False question:	Charlotte Inwood has killed her husband; Johnny has been blamed. (subject, theme)	Will Johnny be cleared? (formulation)	How will Eve deceive and expose Charlotte Inwood? (proposal)

Delays:	Bloodstained dress (snare and partial answer) Microphone in dressing room (snare and partial answer) Johnny's threat to Charlotte (snare and partial answer) Charlotte's reaction to dress at party (snare and partial answer) etc.

Partial answer:	Original question was false.		
True question:	Johnny killed Charlotte's husband and plans to save himself by killing Eve. (subject, theme)	Will Eve be saved? (formulation)	How will Eve deceive and expose Johnny? (proposal)
Final answer:	By pretending to help him, then revealing him to the police. (disclosure)		

Several elements of *Stage Fright*'s structure become apparent here. First, the main delaying devices are all double in function; they are at once snares (since they draw the spectator further into a belief in Charlotte's guilt) and partial answers (since they all provide clues or information which, when read in terms of the true question's subject, help the spectator piece together what "really" happened). Thus the film's delaying devices also relate to the two enigmas. In addition, their relationship to the "true" subject can only be pieced together retrospectively by the spectator, since the truth is revealed only in the last few minutes.

Second, all the delaying devices, combined with the text's duplicity in the lie, distort and reshape the true question that *would* have been posed at the beginning—something like: Is Johnny guilty? Without the reassuring "evidence" of the apparent flashback, the spectator would not necessarily accept his account and might still suspect that he had been involved in the murder. But since the possibility of Johnny's guilt is raised only when that guilt is confirmed, the true question again becomes involved with Eve's immediate danger. The true question again becomes involved in the *how* of the enigma: How will Eve deceive and expose Johnny?

Why pose a double enigma of this type? It would be fashionable and easy to say that *Stage Fright*, with its theatrical imagery, is "about" the duplicity of art, and of cinema in particular. A more traditional account might see the lie as a symbol appropriate to the film's overall theme of the duplicity of humanity, or some similar "universal message," and the expression of this theme as the film's main goal. If indeed that were how we judged films, we would have to dismiss *Stage Fright* as hopelessly naive for simplistically trying to equate theatrical representation and a murderer's lies. Instead of just serving meaning, the deception–theatrical performance juxtaposition provides an effective way of structuring a film, and one which defamiliarizes the conventions of the mystery genre. Most mysteries, for example, present spectators with earlier fabula events at the end of the syuzhet, and spectators must then retrospectively fit them into their fabula order. *Stage Fright* takes one large step beyond this, demanding that its spectators fit the new fabula information back into a set of other fabula events, *which must themselves be revised* before that fitting-in process can take place. While remaining within the classical mode, *Stage Fright* provides something of a challenge to customary viewing habits.

Having looked at *Stage Fright*'s general strategies and purposes in using the lying flashback to set up a double hermeneutic, we can go on to examine how the dominant of deceit and truth pervades the action on every level of the film, and how that dominant sets up devices that help motivate the lie itself.

The brief opening of the film that leads up to the flashback is structured so as to disorient the spectator. The film opens *in medias res*, and bits of exposition are mixed with misleading statements by the characters. Eve's first line, "Looks like we're getting away with it," seemingly implicates her in whatever the two are running from. Thus the first "information" given the spectator in the dialogue is misleading. Once she asks Johnny to explain, the main thrust of the narrative begins, and expository material begins to be presented, though in a somewhat confusing fashion. Johnny's mention of Charlotte Inwood and Eve's reaction suggest relationships but do not explain them. Here also begins a series of remarks that occur through the narrative and that can be taken in several ways, according to whether the spectator knows the flashback is a lie. In attempting to justify his and Charlotte's actions to Eve, Johnny says, "I had to help her—anybody would

145

have done." The meaning here is ambiguous. Johnny's meaning is that anybody would have been willing to help Charlotte, but the ironic additional meaning, relevant to the "real" situation with Charlotte, is that she would have exploited anybody to serve her purpose.

At this point Johnny begins his story of the murder and subsequent events. As he speaks of being in his kitchen at five o'clock, a dissolve leads into a direct presentation of the situation; at the end of the dissolve, while he is speaking of the doorbell ringing, his words fade out quickly. There follows the sound of the doorbell itself. This suggests that the flashback will be a direct replacement for Johnny's words, a straightforward version of the events which will stick more or less to Johnny's vantage point. But an examination of the flashback shows that this equation of the flashback with his words is only one factor of several. In fact, the sequence goes beyond Johnny's telling in several ways; there seem to be two separate and contradictory forces contributing to the flashback. This is perhaps most obvious in the sequence's use of point of view (POV) shots, which place the camera physically in Johnny's place. These shots occur only when Johnny is alone: first in his exploration of the Inwood house, when POV shots are used as he looks into the den, looks at the photo (Fig. 5.1), and sees Nellie discover the body and look in at him (Fig. 5.2); later, when he descends the stairs to answer the door when the police arrive, there are POV tracking shots down the stairs. Numerous other shots, while not POV shots, also stay close to Johnny and still restrict the spectator fairly closely to what Johnny knows, as with the long tracking and craning shot moving with him as he enters the Inwood house and ascends the stairs.

Yet at other points in the sequence, the camera is placed opposite to Johnny in the scene, or even in another space, showing things he has no way of knowing. In the first shot back in Johnny's apartment after he has returned from the Inwood house, the setup presents Charlotte in close-up in the foreground, with her face clearly visible, while Johnny is placed deep in the frame (in fact the deep focus is achieved by process work), with his back to the camera (Fig. 5.3). Later, in the police chase, the camera pans as Johnny's car passes, then holds on a view along a side street as Johnny's car disappears and a slow dray pulls across the street to block the police car (Fig. 5.4). The point here is not that Johnny could not know what was happening behind him, but that, in terms of the action, the camera setup is exactly opposite Johnny (and any potential POV shot—say, into the rearview mirror). Additional compositions with Johnny in the background and other action in the foreground occur in the scene at the Royal

Academy of Dramatic Art (RADA): as Johnny disappears in the distance along a corridor, the police come into close-up in the foreground; Johnny's unscheduled entry onto the stage is filmed with Eve in the foreground and Johnny in the wings behind; finally, the exit of the two from the stage is framed with the drama coach in the foreground. The high-angle shot of Johnny escaping down the Inwood staircase might be seen as a variation of this device. Also note that there are shots from Eve's POV during the RADA scene (Figs. 5.5 and 5.6). Clearly the flashback is not stylistically presented as a subjective vision or memory, and the spectator cannot take it to be so, even before the lie is known.

The flashback contains other scenes about which Johnny clearly could have no knowledge. The telephone call he makes when trying to contact Eve crosscuts shots of him with shots of Mrs. Gill, even though it is made clear in subsequent action that he has never met her and could have no way of knowing what she looks like. Similarly, the scene of the police stopping outside the RADA after spotting Johnny's cracked window takes place completely in his absence. When the shots from Eve's POV occur, Johnny is looking the other way and does not see what she sees.

This ambivalent nature of the flashback is pointed up by the super-imposed shots of what Johnny imagines to be happening; although the first supered shot simply repeats the high-angle view of Johnny's escape down the stairway—and can be taken to be a memory—the images of Nellie explaining to the police what she saw and of hands flipping through a phone book seem to be Johnny's visualization of what *may* be happening (Fig. 5.7). Yet the fact that the phone rings immediately after the third supered image seems to imply that these events were in some sense actually happening as well. This is reinforced by the fact that the police show up at Johnny's door shortly thereafter. The status of these images remains ambivalent; are they simply subjective, or do they somehow simultaneously represent Johnny's fear and what is presumably happening elsewhere?

Perhaps the flashback's most important departure from Johnny's vantage point is the portrayal of Charlotte. As we learn in his later scene with her in her dressing room, he has been operating under the assumption that she will run away with him after suspicion of her has died down. So at the point where he tells Eve the story, Johnny still has faith in Charlotte. Yet the flashback's portrayal of her is not always consistent with this. At her first entrance, she appears fairly sympathetic, in that emphasis is placed upon the fact that her husband had struck her—making her killing of him seem somewhat justified as self-defense. Marlene Dietrich's wide-eyed performance suggests real fear and confusion (Fig. 5.8). This emphasis continues until Johnny's reluctant suggestion that he might go to get her a dress to change into. From this point her character undergoes a change; she becomes far too eager to push him into this dangerous action, and she finally gets him to consent by implying that their affair is ended if he does not cooperate. She goes abruptly from the victimized wife to the selfish lover. Several times the camera is placed so as to emphasize her indifferent or even callous expressions, as when Johnny kisses her neck and she continues to powder her face (Fig. 5.9). This is much closer to the Charlotte who models her widow's weeds in a later scene; there she is even more callous and cold. Thus the flashback presents Charlotte in such a way that her calculated exploitation of Johnny is apparent to the audience, even though Johnny has not himself realized it yet. This device moves the flashback another step away from being Johnny's subjective version.

Undoubtedly there are aspects of the flashback that *are* subjective. Johnny's relationship with Charlotte is idealized. He presents himself as the selfless lover, willing to protect a defenseless woman, able to make all the plans for them both ("Your job is to try to forget everything. Let *me* do the worrying"), and quick-witted in his evasion of the police. As with Charlotte, the Johnny of the flashback is a different character from that of the rest of the narrative.

One central reason for this balance between subjective and non-subjective viewpoints in the flashback is to reinforce its "truth." It is essential to the narrative structure of the rest of the film that the spectator not think to question the flashback while viewing it. If the sequence were too obviously a subjective memory, the spectator might be more inclined to take it as a questionable version. But this is not the case. As the scene is constructed, there can be no question of its being only *Johnny's* lie. The filmic narration participates quite definitely in the lie as well.

The credibility of Johnny's story is further reinforced by the inclusion of Eve in the flashback. The sequence could easily end with Johnny's initial evasion of the police. A line of dialogue to the effect that Johnny had then come to pick Eve up at her rehearsal would be enough to cover the information conveyed in the comparatively lengthy scene at the RADA (lengthy in terms of the amount of narrative information conveyed); a more conventional film might have started the action with the RADA scene, thus giving more of an introduction before the flashback began. But by placing the RADA scene at the end of the flashback, the film gives it a "full-circle" structure. The sequence ends with Eve and Johnny on their way to her car, and it is in that car that the spectator had first seen them. Thus Eve's presence at the beginning confirms at least that much of Johnny's account. The RADA scene at least is true, because Eve herself knows it to be true. And her implicit verification of this part of the sequence casts an air of credibility over the other parts as well.

Other aspects of the flashback story are confirmed as well. The bloodstained dress is seen in the car after the film returns to the present; again, its tangible existence adds more evidence that the story is true. Of course, much of what happens in the flashback *is* true. Information is planted which will be important later in figuring out the real situation. The photo Johnny finds in the desk at the Inwood house is our only piece of evidence in the entire film of how Johnny came to know Charlotte in the first place (Fig. 5.1). Similarly, Johnny's effort to make the crime look like a robbery attempt and Nellie's witnessing of his flight are both confirmed later in the film. One of the complexities of viewing set up by the film's structure is the necessity for the spectator to sort out retrospectively the bits of truth planted in this earlier scene. Ultimately it is impossible to distinguish completely between the truth and the lies in this flashback. The first part of the sequence, Charlotte's visit, is the most problematic in this sense. Johnny's later explanation to Eve in the coach, near the end of the film, seems to account for some parts of the flashback, but others remain confused.

Eve, I hated to tell you that phoney story in your car that time, but there was no other way. Charlotte did go on to my flat after I'd killed her husband. Her dress was stained a bit, so I brought her a clean one. Then, when she went to the theater, I made a big stain on it, to make you believe me. I'm telling you the truth.

But at what point did Johnny try to cover up the murder, when did Nellie spot him, and when did Johnny get the second dress? These and other questions remain unanswered.

In addition to setting up carefully the assumptions that the spectator will carry for the greater part of the subsequent action, the flashback also establishes several major thematic strands which will be important to the narrative. Lies are mentioned several times in the course of the sequence, and, as we shall see in the next section, lies permeate the film as part of its complex structure of motivation for the device of the duplicitous flashback. The first mention of deception is Charlotte's suggestion that Johnny "call the theater. I can't play tonight. Tell them I'm ill." The duplicity is marked when she adds, "Heavens, it'll be true enough." The next reference to lying comes when Johnny talks to Charlotte of their future: "Then we'll start again, won't we? You and I. No more stealth and cheating and lying." The implication here is that their entire affair has been based on deception (far more, in fact, than Johnny realizes). Charlotte avoids answering him by simply saying, "I must hurry, darling," suggesting that the lies are not over for her part.

Another central motif set up here is the theater. Both Charlotte and Eve are actresses—Charlotte a professional, Eve an aspiring student. The relation of this profession to their "real-life" actions is first made explicit in the flashback, when Johnny says to Charlotte: "You're an actress. You're playing a part. No nerves when you're on." This idea will be referred to again and again as the characters compare themselves and each other to characters in a play. Charlotte's changing out of the two dresses even sets up her constant changing of clothes in other scenes, an extension of the "quick changes" of stage costumes she makes at the theater.

The flashback provides the only time we see Eve actually performing on a stage, in the class at the RADA; all her other performances are in "real-life" situations later in the film. Here, Johnny's precipitous entrance onto the stage causes the drama coach to remark, "This cast seems to think that acting is just fun and games." This statement anticipates Commodore Gill's later bantering about Eve's love for getting into melodramatic situations. And, although sincere in their attempts to help Johnny, both Eve and Gill take pleasure in creating dramatic situations and roles for Eve to play in them. The "fun and games" image is literally worked out later in the film when Gill resorts to the target-shooting game and employs a doll in setting up a scene to try to implicate Charlotte in the murder.

As the flashback ends, the scene returns to the car we saw at the beginning, and the love interest between Eve and Johnny is made explicit (having been strongly suggested by the embrace onstage at the RADA, when Eve seems more annoyed at being embarrassed than taken aback). The bloodstained dress in close-up ends the scene. Our expectations concerning future events are set up by these devices and are diverted away from the details of the flashback; no possibility of questioning the story just shown remains. This scene provides a transition into the sequence at Gill's cottage, where the motivating structure of duplicity begins to function more systematically.

THEATRICAL IMAGERY

As we have seen, the flashback is doubly motivated. The pattern of lies in the action tends to smooth over the comparatively radical device of the flashback. More indirectly, the film motivates the characters' (and narration's) obsession with lying through the master motif of theater and performing. The theater imagery motivates the pervasive lies, and the lies in turn motivate the use of the flashback.

Yet the flashback is *not* simply an "appropriate" device rising out of the subject matter of lying. It is not really a logical extension of duplicity, but rather the determining device of the whole film's structure of motivating devices. *It* determines the lies and the theatrical metaphor. *Stage Fright* depends on the spectator's asking the false question outlined in the previous section. The flashback plants that false question, and everything in the rest of the film is at the service of keeping the deception going; the motivating devices are important, since they make the flashback seem reasonable and thus divert the spectator from the possibility of asking other questions. How are these motivating devices of lying and performance structured?

Virtually every scene in *Stage Fright* relates to deception, to theatrical performance, or to both. The title itself embodies the film's balance between theatricality and real life. Stage fright is a fear ordinarily generated by a situation that is not really threatening—yet in this case, the danger is real, and Johnny dies under the descending "safety" curtain. The images accompanying the title and credits bare the device, even before the narrative begins. In the background, a safety curtain slowly rises, revealing not a stage, but a vista of the area around St. Paul's in London (Figs. 5.10 and 5.11). This abrupt and inappropriate juxtaposition more firmly sets up the link between the stage and real life which will subsequently be developed in the characters' tendencies to lie, play roles, and at times consciously treat their lives as parts of a melodramatic plot. (The safety curtain here is also motivated compositionally, in that it "plants" the idea of a safety curtain in our minds, so that the later quick fall of the one that kills Johnny will not confuse us.) The car in which Eve and Johnny are escaping becomes visible as soon as the last credit, "Directed by Alfred Hitchcock," leaves the screen. As the car races toward the lower center of the frame, there is a cut to a closer shot of it (Figs. 5.12 and 5.13). A longer lens is used for this second shot, so that, although the car's position is matched quite closely, its distance from St. Paul's suddenly appears much less; the space of the action has been compressed by the lens. The implicit effect of the cut is to place the spectator firmly within the space established by the credits sequence as the "stage" upon which the action of the film will take place. By extension, the change in the perspective on St. Paul's caused by the different lens further carries forward the idea of the city as a metaphorical backdrop for the action; the building does not give the impression of maintaining a natural—that is, consistent—distance from the characters. Yet at the same time, location shooting places the scene indisputably "in London," thus carrying through the dominant theatricality-in-reality structure.

Eve is the center of this structure. She is presented not only as an actress, but also as a woman who approaches life as though it were as romantic as a play. The motif of theatricality and its association with deception is set forth in the scene at Commodore Gill's cottage. Eve never questions Johnny's story. When her father jokingly calls her "a murderer's moll," he characterizes her attitude accurately, for she does enter into the situation as though she were in a melodramatic adventure. The fact that Eve is convinced that she is in love with Johnny indicates her self-deception. (Not all the characters' lies are to other people.) When at the end of their conversation Gill asks Eve if Johnny can mean enough to her to go through all this, she replies, "But he does, father." Jane Wyman's acting in this and other scenes may appear inadequate and conventional, but it underlines the romantic theatricality Eve is using as a model for her life. Eve's behavior in the taxi with Smith is silly; she goes on in a later scene to describe to him how she felt: "as though I were on a great golden cloud." This image recalls the clouds of the stage setting of Charlotte's musical number, "Laziest Gal in Town." Eve continues through most of the film to fail to distinguish clearly between theater and life.

Gill points this out explicitly in the scene at his cottage. Eve tells him, "You're just dying to get into a part of this; you know you are." Gill replies:

A part in this melodramatic play, you mean. You know, that's the way you're treating it, Eve, as if it were a play you were acting in at the Academy. Everything seems a fine role when you're stagestruck, doesn't it, my dear? Here you have a plot, an interesting cast, even a costume—a little the worse for wear. Unfortunately, Eve, in this real and earnest life, we must face the situation in all its bearings.

Just as the actions are referred to as a play, certain characters are set up as performers, while others function as audiences. When Gill meets Eve backstage at Charlotte's performance, he tells her: "You're giving a good show, a very good show indeed. A pity you've no audience." She replies, "*You're* my audience. I wish you'd give me a little applause now and then." This sets up the final sequence, in the middle of which, after her confrontation with Charlotte, Gill does applaud her.

But Gill is not the only audience to a performance, though perhaps he is the character who is most conscious that what he is watching *is* a performance. Other characters are performers, audiences, or even at times directors of the action. Divided as performers/nonperformers, the major characters function as shown in the diagram below.

Eve takes her first role, that of a sick woman, after her father jokingly suggests that she simply ask the police what they are thinking. At first he serves only as the source of inspiration for the parts she plays; later Gill stages Eve's scenes with great care, specifically the garden-party scene and the blackmail scene in the bugged dressing room.

Eve plays her role as a sick woman poorly; her confidence and ability grow with each part she assumes, until at last she is capable of saving her life through performing. In the pub, however, she "botches her lines" and drops character several times. When Smith offers to leave if sitting with strange men bothers her, Eve replies, "No, I love strange men," and feebly tries to cover this gaffe by adding, "I mean, I'm very fond of them." She also almost reveals that she knows Smith is a detective and gets sidetracked talking about her acting career.

But Smith turns out to be her ideal audience, since he accepts all explanations and is ready to overlook her faux pas up until the end of the garden party. In fact, he is the only major character in the film who neither acts nor deceives anyone. He tells Eve as he gets up to escort her home from the pub: "To be quite honest, it isn't really kind-

	Performers (marked X)			Nonperformers		
	Eve	*Charlotte*	*Johnny*	*Smith*	*Gill*	*Nellie*
Innocent accused	Audience		X		Audience	
Faithful mistress		X	Audience			
Distraught widow	Audience	X		Audience		
Sick woman	X			Audience		
Reporter	X					Audience
Doris	X	Audience		Audience (later director)	Audience and director	Director

ness at all. I mean, I'm afraid I maneuvered it." The fact that Eve had maneuvered the situation herself points up Smith's naive credulity and concomitant honesty. Smith's lack of role playing is necessary to the narrative structure, since he is the character who holds the information vital to clearing up the false enigma: the fact that Johnny has killed before. Smith does not reveal this information prematurely, but neither does he lie to conceal it. Instead, it is withheld from us precisely because Eve withholds the truth from Smith; she spends most of her time with him trying unsuccessfully to cast suspicion on Charlotte. When Eve finally manages to do this, at the end of the garden party, Smith has his own brief, aural flashback—the film's "true" flashback. On the sound track, we hear phrases he remembers—"Do you think there's anything between Cooper and Miss Inwood?" "But Eve hasn't been near it for days," "Doris"—all in the voices of the characters who spoke them earlier. We know this flashback to be true, since we have witnessed the moments when all these lines were said. When Smith finally tells Gill that Johnny is guilty, his information in itself would not be enough to convince us that Johnny is the murderer. Yet because Smith is an absolutely honest character, he can name Johnny as the killer. Johnny is guilty because it is Smith who tells us so.

Eve's second role, a reporter trying to get a story on Charlotte, proves more successful. Significantly, she also resorts to more outright lies to accomplish it. She tells Nellie that she needs to use these tactics in order to compete with male reporters, that she has played character roles (her slight pause before answering suggests that this is untrue), and that she is an old friend of Smith's. Her facility at lying and acting has improved, and she temporarily fools the cynical Nellie.

Immediately after the scene with Nellie, Eve takes on the persona of Doris, which will be her main role throughout the bulk of the film. Here she plans much more carefully than she did for the other roles, donning a complete costume and even learning lines ahead of time. (Hitchcock's cameo appearance serves to foreground the real-life rehearsal as he passes her and glances back curiously.) Eve manages to juggle her identities successfully while playing Doris, so that she is several times able to escape being found out. She reveals her role to Smith only at the moment she also succeeds in implicating Charlotte. Even then she sustains Charlotte's belief in her as Doris, enabling her to play the blackmail scene later.

Eve's ultimate success comes as she is finally snapped out of her romantic visions by the revelation of Johnny's guilt. Here she begins to act once more, but the role is no longer a persona other than herself. She simply repeats earlier events ("I'll take you to my father's boat. Come along") and reveals Johnny to the police. Her final walk down the backstage corridor with Smith remains ambiguous. The hanging lamps and circular patterns of light are similar to stage spotlights (Fig. 5.14). The suggestion may be that Eve is able now to leave behind the melodramatic events she has helped to cause. Yet there is also the possible implication that she continues in her romantic visions, that even in leaving the stage her theatrical outlook accompanies her. Her relationship with Smith has been based primarily upon role playing and deception, yet she has also been brought out of her illusions about Johnny's innocence. The film's ending remains somewhat open.

Gill, although allied with Eve, is presented as maintaining some distance from the situation and as realizing that she is romanticizing it. Without this distance, Gill's involvement in the action would simply duplicate much of Eve's function. After Eve declares to him that she loves Johnny, Gill teases her by playing exaggeratedly sweet "hearts-and-flowers" music on his accordion; he also plays a standard melodrama theme when Eve calls Charlotte "an evil spirit." Yet Gill also enters into the scheme to save Johnny; his motives are partly his concern for his daughter and partly the pleasure he takes in manipulating the "melodramatic play." To an extent Gill lives in a romanticized world, fancying himself a criminal figure because he smuggles brandy now and then: "The customs people have their eye on me." He is also a musical performer, as are the other central male figures (Johnny a member of a chorus line and Smith a pianist).

This dual quality of Gill's character is crucial. His distance from the situation, conveyed primarily through his humor, tends to foreground Eve's romantic notions and provides a perspective from which the spectator can view them. Beyond this, his apparent objectivity encourages the spectator to accept unquestioningly Gill's own conclusions about the case. His lines in the cottage scene are central: "My child, I am not deceived. If there's one thing I cannot bear, it's insincerity." Since some of Gill's premises are plausible—the blood looks like it was smeared on the dress, we suspect Charlotte of being two-faced—the spectator tends to assume his explanations of the situation are correct and will believe this through much of the film. Thus Gill's character helps to sustain the double enigma.

But despite his ability to laugh at Eve's naive involvement, Gill also begins quickly to be caught up in this "melodramatic play." As he and Eve make their plans, Gill quotes a classic melodrama line, "At last we are alone and unobserved," adding, "You know, I'm beginning to enjoy this." And as Eve's skill and involvement as an actress increase,

Gill becomes more and more a determining force in the actions they have planned together and set in motion. At first he simply makes suggestions to Eve about her general strategy. Later, when Gill arrives during Smith's visit for tea, it is he who inquires as to the police's view of Johnny's innocence; Gill even enters briefly into the acting game by pretending to forget Johnny's name. When Johnny escapes from the detective at the theater, he ends up at Eve's house; again it is Gill who takes over and makes the arrangements for his stay.

But Gill comes into prominence primarily in the last scenes Eve plays. From his arrival at the garden party, he takes over the direction of the drama. Here the characters have switched functions to a large extent. At his cottage, Gill had recommended going to the police, but Eve had held back. Now she meets Gill and tells him, "I think I'll get hold of Smith and tell him the whole story." But she has not accomplished her goal of implicating Charlotte, as Gill points out. Instead, she has gotten herself into a corner where her real identity and her role as Doris conflict too much. From this point on, she acts only as Gill directs her. (It is indeed Gill's voice, heard in the distance by Eve and Johnny in the coach, that finally alerts her to Johnny's guilt. His final direction—"Come away from him"—is also his final moment in the film, and it introduces her to her last, crucial role.) As Gill and Eve stand outside the tent in which Charlotte is singing, Gill offers her a scene.

Call yourself an actress? There's your big scene, if you've the pluck to take it. You've the law on your arm. All you've to do is rush in there and shout, "Stop, that woman is a murderess." And then she'll say, "How dare you!" and you'll say, "I'll dare and dare again. What about the bloodstained dress, eh, Charlotte Inwood?" And then she'll say—

Eve interrupts with, "Please, this is serious, father," but this speech outlines the strategy Gill does use to get Charlotte to break down, as she sees the bloodstained doll's dress (though Eve's part in this is simply to persuade Smith to be present). Gill sets up the situation, the actor (the little boy), the audience (Smith), and the essential prop (the doll with Gill's blood smeared on it [Fig. 5.15]).

The final scene Gill plans is the false blackmail attempt on Charlotte. He suggests it to Smith, once again urging Eve to continue her role. Again, Gill puts his plan forward by giving hypothetical lines.

I mean, suppose she went to Miss Inwood and said, "Look here, I've got a certain dress . . ." Oh, you needn't be afraid that Doris couldn't do it, she could do it, all right, Doris could—I mean, Eve could.

This confusion of Eve with "Doris" marks the furthest stage of Gill's progression toward an obsession similar to Eve's—an inability to see the situation except in terms of the plot he has concocted. By this point, Eve and Gill have become thoroughly immersed in the process characterized by Gill in the cottage scene as "transmuting melodrama into real life." Their playacting has come to determine the shape the real events take.

Charlotte acts as a foil for Eve in that she too is an actress who plays roles off the stage in order to deceive. A major difference between them, however, is that Charlotte is continually aware of the purposes and implications of her roles; she is calculating where Eve is self-deluding and naive. When Eve first arrives at the Inwood house as Doris, Charlotte is performing her characteristic activity, trying on and changing clothes (which she uses as costumes, just as Eve does). The arrival of the police leads her to set up the little scene in which, at Charlotte's signal, Doris announces the fictitious arrival of a doctor. Charlotte's interview with the police is linked to her stage performance through the mise-en-scene. The black flowing negligee she wears and the curved divan she reclines on in the police scene are echoed by the white negligee-like costume and three divans in her number "Laziest Gal in Town" (Figs. 5.16 and 5.17). The film also uses this musical number to repeat the theatricality-in-reality motif by cutting several times from frontal, audience-oriented views of the stage to shots taken from backstage which emphasize the theatrical paraphernalia (Fig. 5.18). In fact, it is part of this stage equipment that entraps Charlotte; the microphone used by her back-up vocal group allows the police to record Charlotte's revelations about being involved in the murder.

Finally, Johnny plays the role of an innocent accused man. This is the only role that we do not recognize as such and hence are taken in by. *We* are the most important audience for his performance, since the whole filmic structure depends on our being taken in. (This is not to suggest that the film is "used up" by one viewing. Repeated viewings reveal more of the structure of duplicity, but the knowledge remains that the basic device is the deceptive function of the "flashback.") Because Johnny is the guilty person, he must not be allowed to retain the position of the central character of the film; the Hollywood narrative system could hardly tolerate a protagonist with whom the spectator is persistently led to identify and who turns out to be a mad killer. (At least it probably could not at the height of the classical system—in part because of the Production Code stipulations about punishing guilt. By 1960 Hitchcock came much closer to using such a

157

device in *Psycho*, though even there he gets away with it partly by mixing conventions of the mystery and horror genres.) Once Johnny's story is told, the narrative keeps him in the background, diverting the spectator's attention to Eve and Gill's machinations, and particularly to Charlotte's performances. Eve is the protagonist rather than Johnny, because her belief in his story structures the entire narrative. The narration largely restricts the spectator to Eve's knowledge and consciousness (and Gill's to some extent). Consequently, the spectator is led away from the possibility of questioning Johnny's story and hence recognizing his role-playing. Those few scenes in which neither Eve nor Gill is present—Charlotte's conversation with Freddy, Charlotte's dialogue with Johnny in her dressing room, Charlotte's talk with Mellish after her arrest—are carefully handled so as to sustain our belief in Johnny's story.

The preceding analysis of character functions is a fairly traditional one, yet this is precisely the point. *Stage Fright* does indeed use a set of classic techniques—character oppositions, thematic motifs, multiple motivating devices, and so on—to justify the unconventional device of the lying flashback. By creating a dense weave of these devices, the film makes its own duplicity seem simply a logical extention of its overall meanings. *Stage Fright* does not lie as little as possible, but it does strive to camouflage the mechanics of its lies from the spectator.

CONCLUSIONS: DUPLICITY IN OTHER FILMS

Although films rarely contain such extremely and overtly duplicitous structures, *Stage Fright* is not unique in this sense. A number of films present actions that appear to be "real" within the proairetic chain of the narrative, but that subsequently are revealed as false. But most films justify their use of duplicity in a more realistic, less jarring way than does *Stage Fright*, often by resorting to character subjectivity. The false events are later explained as having represented mental processes, usually of insane or overwrought characters.

Hitchcock himself, for example, used such motivation for a scene in his 1928 film *Champagne*. There the heroine sits drinking across a table from a lecherous man who warns her that "anything could happen to a girl like you, in a place like this." After a series of shot/reverse shot views of the two, a straight cut to a medium two-shot leads to the man's attempted seduction of the woman. After she flees him in hysterics, a dissolve takes us to a medium close-up of the woman's staring face. She is at the table as before and looks around, smiling; a track-back returns to the medium two-shot framing of the pair, revealing that the seduction scene had been her frightened fantasy, though no cues had signaled its beginning.

Curtis Bernhardt's 1947 film *Possessed* is another good example of a "cautious" use of duplicity.[12] The narrative tells the story of a mentally disturbed woman, Louise. In one scene, she has a confrontation with her stepdaughter; she strikes her, causing her to fall down a staircase and die. But as Louise stands staring in horror at the body, it fades away, and the stepdaughter enters again, unharmed. The entire previous scene between the pair is revealed to have been Louise's hallucination. The "real" scene that follows parallels her vision, but this time relations between the two women are cordial. *Possessed* deceives us briefly, but in a less radical way than does *Stage Fright*. First, the lie is revealed immediately through the presentation of the real scene and the revelation that the murder was Louise's mad imaginings. Second, *Possessed* is explicitly a story of a descent into madness. In a gradual and systematic way, the film's flashbacks increasingly use subjective devices to present events. Finally, the scene just before the false murder contains a series of intensely subjective effects used as "madness" cues, particularly the manipulation of volume on the sound track. This subjectivity prepares the spectator to accept the murder as a false occurrence.

Possessed uses this isolated duplicitous scene simply to motivate Louise's recognition of her growing insanity. But another film that uses insanity as a motivating device makes its duplicity a central structuring element: *The Cabinet of Dr. Caligari*. Here the "false" story forms almost the entire film; as in *Stage Fright*, the fact of the (probable) lie is disclosed only in the last minutes. In one way *Caligari* remains more conservative in its recuperation of the central story; the film justifies its lie by making it the subjective view of a mad character: the film shows things this way only because Francis imagines them thus. In *Stage Fright*, as we have seen, the narration lies without sticking to Johnny's subjective viewpoint. Yet from another point of view, *Caligari*'s use of duplicity goes beyond *Stage Fright*'s because it remains more ambiguous at the end. Is the doctor the kindly man he appears to be, or could Francis's story contain some elements of truth? *Caligari* remains open in terms of the status of its own lie.

Dreams that are not revealed as such until the dreamer awakens are a common device for camouflaging filmic duplicity. D. W. Griffith's *Avenging Conscience* (1914) provides a typical example. The hero, re-

[12] I wish to thank Serafina Bathrick for pointing out to me that *Possessed* is a film that uses narrational duplicity.

sentful of his uncle for opposing his marriage, sits down and dozes off in his office. No other "dream" cues are given, and the action continues from there. The young man apparently kills his uncle and goes mad from guilt. Near the end of the film there is a return to the hero asleep in his chair; now he awakens, revealing that the intervening action had been a dream.

An extremely silly example of this same sort of thing occurs in the 1937 Warner Bros. comedy *Sh! The Octopus*, in which the two bumbling detective heroes get into such a chaotic fix that closure is achieved through having them wake up at the end, though in this case the entire film to this point has constituted their mutual dream.

As we shall see in the next chapter, *Laura* uses a duplicitous moment—the apparent beginning of a dream by the detective Mark McPherson—to create an ambiguity in the second half of the narrative.

These examples do not by any means exhaust the list of films employing overt duplicity. They simply serve to indicate the variety of ways in which such duplicity can be used. In no case does the film simply "lie as little as possible, just what is required to ensure the interests of reading, that is, its own survival"—to return to Barthes's generalization. The lies or deceptions presented in these films do not function only to divert the viewer from the revelation of a truth that would end the narrative. In each film, there is at least one other important formal function served. Moreover, in each, a different choice of narrational strategies could have eliminated the duplicity without prematurely revealing the ending. Such films, I would argue, are only presenting in a more overt and extreme fashion the duplicity that many, perhaps most, narratives frequently employ to balance their presentation, to withhold the truth from us, to create humor, and so on.

Artworks are surely limited in what they can do at any given point in history by the norms against which the artists work. But even within classical works, as we have seen with the Dickens and Wodehouse examples, as well as within the films mentioned here, unabashed duplicity is possible. The difference between "lies" and "dilatory morphemes" may ultimately not be a significant one. Deception, on a large or small scale, motivated to seem implicit or overt, occurs in many works.[13] It will probably seem like lying to the spectator only

[13] Although he does not deal with the notion of deception, Dennis Porter finds parallel problems with Barthes's assumptions about the relations of bound and free motifs in detective fiction. See Porter's *The Pursuit of Crime: Art and Ideology in Detective Fiction* (New Haven: Yale University Press, 1981), pp. 53–81.

when the deception is more overt than is conventional at that moment in history. This may happen through the narration's refusal to use conventional types of motivation to cover over the deception, or through the more extreme measure of baring the device outright. In either case, the narration acknowledges its own workings and, as long as this approach remains fairly rare, defamiliarizes them.

6

Closure within a Dream? Point of View in *Laura*

LEVELS OF POINT OF VIEW

THE FIRST HALF of Otto Preminger's 1944 film *Laura* leads us to believe that Laura is dead. The second half leads us to believe that she is alive. As a transition between the two halves, the narration uses a device that is relatively transgressive within the tradition of the classical Hollywood cinema. This is the moment when the detective, Mark McPherson, falls asleep in Laura's apartment, and she walks in the door. The spectator might expect that the action after he nods off represents a dream (as I did on first seeing the film). Yet he never awakens, and we are left to choose between two possibilities: that Laura is indeed alive, or that the narrative ends within McPherson's dream. The film itself refuses to aid us in deciding.

As *Laura* begins, McPherson is investigating the murder of Laura Hunt, killed by a shotgun blast to the head; he goes to see Waldo Lydecker, an acid-tongued radio and newspaper commentator who knew Laura well. Together they visit Anne Treadwell, Laura's aunt, who seems inordinately interested in a likable young man, Shelby Carpenter, who claims to have been Laura's fiancé. Carpenter declares that he had been at a concert when the murder occurred, having been told by Laura that she was going to her country house. The three men visit Laura's apartment to get the house key, which McPherson realizes Carpenter has just planted. At a restaurant, Lydecker recounts to McPherson how he met Laura, aided her career in the advertising business, and succeeded in thwarting all her romances with other men—including, he claims, Carpenter. At Laura's apartment, McPherson follows up various clues and questions Laura's maid and all the other suspects again. That night, alone at the apartment,

PORTIONS of this chapter were delivered as a lecture in David Bordwell's Critical Film Analysis class at the University of Wisconsin-Madison, October 1976. I am grateful to Professor Bordwell and his students for the discussion that followed, which raised several issues that I have incorporated into my analysis. In addition, Diane Waldman suggested several points that I have used in revising my argument in the ideology section.

McPherson obsessively goes through Laura's things, then falls asleep. Laura returns, and she and McPherson discover that a model, Diane Redfern (in Laura's apartment for a tryst with Carpenter), had been killed and mistaken for Laura. Both Laura and Carpenter behave suspiciously, but McPherson eventually discovers that Lydecker had killed Redfern, mistaking her for Laura. After McPherson leaves Laura's apartment, Lydecker returns to try again to kill her, but he is shot by the police.

The crucial moments leading up to Laura's return contain classic cinematic cues for a dream sequence. McPherson has clearly fallen in love with the dead woman, through her diaries, letters, and portrait. Late at night he wanders through her apartment, looking at her things (Fig. 6.1), drinking (Fig. 6.2), and staring at the portrait (Fig. 6.3). He sits down (Fig. 6.4), and the camera tracks in as he nods off (Fig. 6.5); after a pause, it tracks away again (Fig. 6.6). We hear the sound of a door offscreen, and a cut reveals Laura at the door. The use of an otherwise unmotivated camera movement of this type in combination with a character falling asleep could be a cue for a dream sequence; this is all the more probable since the events that follow seem so clearly a fantasy fulfillment of the detective's desires. Later I shall examine these cues in more detail against the historical background of mid-1940s American films. In the meantime, we need to examine two questions: first, do people take this sequence as the beginning of a dream, and second, what conventional cinematic cues in the scene might seem to signal this as a dream?

In relation to the first question, I have asked various friends and students, both within the field of film and outside of it, how they understood this scene. Some took it to be a dream, and some did not—which suggests that the "dream" cues are ambiguous. There is some evidence that at the time of the film's production and release, it was associated with dream imagery. The major popular reviewers are not much use in this regard, as they tried not to give away the gimmick of Laura's false death and so avoided discussing the scene of her return. Yet one contemporary reference seems significant in this context; an article on Fritz Lang's *The Woman in the Window*, a film that involves a definite trick dream structure, remarked, "The professor, Edward G. Robinson, committed one murder, was accessory to another (attempted), took poison—and woke up to find that, like Laura, it was only a dream."[1]

Some of those more closely connected with the film seem to have

---

[1] "Fritz Lang Gets Wise to Box Office," *Los Angeles Times*, 21 October 1945, pt. 3, p. 2. My thanks to Mary Beth Haralovich for this reference.

associated the role of Laura with dreams. In her autobiography, Gene Tierney refers to her character as "the dreamlike Laura."[2] Moreover, the lyrics of the theme song "Laura," written, several months after the film's release, by Johnny Mercer to David Raksin's already-popular tune, explicitly suggest that the character is a fantasy figure. The song begins:

> You know the feeling
> Of something half remembered,
> Of *something that never happened,*
> Yet you recall it well.

After describing fleeting glimpses of Laura, "the face in the misty light," it concludes:

> That was Laura,
> *But she's only a dream.*[3]

The song was commissioned by 20th Century–Fox to promote a film that was already a surprise success, and the song itself went to the top of the hit parade, with the Woody Herman record selling over one million copies.[4] The lyrics may have been written in response to an existing perception of the film among studio personnel and the public, or it may have been intended by the studio to promote such a response. In either case, at least some audiences going to *Laura* would have known the song before seeing the film and hence would have had an extra-filmic cue to watch for dream structures. Both the song and the film have achieved the status of "classics," so we can assume that this cue has persisted historically. There is, then, evidence to suggest that some audience members, both now and in the past, have linked the character of Laura to a dream, whether a literal or a figurative one.

Our second question, then, is why the track-in-and-out seems to signal a dream. To find the answer, we might look at the cinematic cues in this scene against the background of Hollywood's general conventions of this period.

Laura (released in November 1944) was made in the context of two growing trends in Hollywood: toward more convoluted temporal structuring of films via flashbacks, and toward the serious exploration of psychologically troubled characters. Though some films made during the pre-1940 period, notably *The Power and the Glory* (1933), had

---

[2] Gene Tierney, *Self-Portrait* (Wyden Books, 1979), p. 136.

[3] Bob Bach and Ginger Mercer, eds., *Our Huckleberry Friend: The Life, Times and Lyrics of Johnny Mercer* (Secaucus: Lyle Stuart, 1982), p. 136. Emphases added.

[4] David Ewen, ed., *American Popular Songs From the Revolutionary War to the Present* (New York: Random House, 1966), p. 219.

used elaborate flashbacks, it was *Citizen Kane* that popularized the use of an investigation of a complex figure as the basis for a flashback-centered narrative. Similarly, the increasingly serious treatment of psychoanalytic concepts in Hollywood led both to the idea of exploring characters' pasts for the sources of their problems and to the idea of using cinematic techniques to convey characters' impressions and mental states.

By 1944, films with such structures were becoming more common. A narrative might be told in a string of chronologically successive flashbacks around a frame story of an investigation, as in *The Mask of Dimitrios* (released 1 July 1944), or in a set of flashbacks nested within flashbacks, with multiple tellers, as in *Passage to Marseille* (released 11 March 1944). Flashbacks could be either visual or sonic, as in *Experiment Perilous* (released December 1944), which uses both types. Similarly, a film like *The Woman in the Window* (released 11 October 1944—and trade shown only three days after *Laura*) could make the bulk of its narrative a trick dream; here the explicit suggestion at the beginning of the film is that the middle-aged protagonist is feeling rebellious about his repressed, unexciting existence. Other films revolve around explorations of "troubled" characters. The hero of *Experiment Perilous* is a psychologist who investigates why the villain is trying to drive his wife and son mad; the answer turns out to stem from a childhood trauma and the man's subsequent impotence. *Curse of the Cat People* (released March 1944) deals with a lonely little girl's fantasy life; for much, if not all, of the film, we are left uncertain as to whether the friend she conjures up on a "wishing ring" is a ghost or stems from her own imagination. Stylistically, *Curse* uses much visual and aural POV to confine us to the girl's perceptions, even during the objective sequences.

Some of the cues for flashbacks and subjectivity used by these films were highly conventionalized by this point. The most common cue for a flashback was a track-in or track-out on a person telling about events in the past, combined with music (often starting exactly as the camera begins to move) and a dissolve. In *The Mask of Dimitrios*, all the flashbacks begin and end in this way, and, in addition, the dissolves have the "wavy" effect commonly associated with dreams and flashbacks. The flashbacks in *Passage to Marseille* are similar, but the dissolves are plain instead of rippling. *Laura's* scene in which Lydecker tells McPherson about Laura's past uses these same cues in a straightforward way.

Experiment Perilous is more varied and original in its treatment of flashbacks, but the cues are clear nonetheless. Rather than hearing stories of the Debereauxes' past, the hero reads them in a manuscript and diary. Here the camera tracks forward over his shoulder toward the pages, with music starting up, a dissolve to his POV of the page, and the writer's voice coming up, reading the text; a slow dissolve to the scenes of the past keeps the writing momentarily superimposed at the edges of the frame, like an iris. (The effect is somewhat similar to the Thatcher-Library flashback in *Citizen Kane*, done by the same effects department.) Other flashbacks involve the hero recalling snatches of dialogue he has heard; these scenes consist of cut-ins to him as he stares abstractedly, with additional shots of him from various angles as the flashback continues. Throughout the sonic flashback, "strange" music accompanies the voices he recalls. In one such scene, a phone rings and snaps him out of his reverie; an additional cue, a change in the lighting on his face, unmotivated by any source within the scene, reinforces the idea of his "coming back to the present" mentally. These techniques suggest that, although the most basic cues for flashbacks were highly conventionalized, other, functionally equivalent cues could be used as well. Moreover, music almost invariably played a central role in signaling changes in the status of the scene.

Significantly, some of these same cues were conventionally used to suggest dreams. Dreams are less common than flashbacks in the Hollywood cinema, but when they do occur they draw upon track-ins, music, and the like. In *Curse of the Cat People*, we see the little girl tossing in her bed, having a nightmare. The camera tracks in, and we hear her dream, a repetition of the scary "headless horseman" tale an old woman had told her, accompanied by hoofbeats. The sound is in one sense a flashback, since we heard the woman's story and the girl's fantasy of hoofbeats in an earlier scene; yet the addition of a person asleep in the scene cues us to take it as a nightmare.

More directly relevant for us, however, are the cues used in *The Woman in the Window*, which presents some remarkable parallels and contrasts to *Laura*'s treatment of its apparent dream. The films were released at almost exactly the same time and thus could not have influenced each other. (Neither could the original novels be the source of the coincidence, as the dream is not part of *Once Off Guard*, the basis for the Lang film.) Yet *The Woman in the Window* takes a similar premise—a man becoming captivated by the portrait of a woman he does not know—and turns it around by having a series of apparently real events turn out to be a dream.

Lang does not signal the beginning of Professor Wandley's dream as such. There is only one reference to dreaming early on, when Wandley first sees the portrait and his friends tease him—"We've decided she's our dream girl, just from that picture." Later that evening, Wandley sits reading and drinking at his club (it has been stated that he has had more than his usual two-drink limit); he tells the waiter to remind him when it is 10:30. As he says this, a slow track-in begins, accompanied by the low, calm music that had started earlier. After a pause for the waiter's exit, the track-in resumes as Wandley reads. A dissolve leads to a close view of a clock, showing 10:30; it chimes, a voice says, "10:30, Professor Wandley," and there is a cut to Wandley, reading. As he looks up, the camera tracks back. The dissolve to the clock begins the dream, but Lang capitalizes on the fact that tracking shots, music, and dissolves can, together and in combination, have a large variety of narrative functions. Here they seem to suggest only a brief ellipsis; we assume that this is not a flashback, because no cues suggest the past. Quite the contrary, the clock seems to indicate that a little over an hour has passed, and that Wandley's request to the waiter is a dialogue hook to cover an ellipsis. The music, drinking, and reading seem to hint that Wandley is in a mood receptive to the sort of sexually tinged adventure that follows; instead we learn much later that this mood led only as far as a dream of adventure. Only additional information could tell us that this moment is the beginning of a dream; such information is not provided until the last scene. Most important, we do not see Wandley fall asleep.

The moment of Wandley's awakening is more spectacular and more similar to *Laura*'s central sequence. We see Wandley, within the dream, sitting in his study after having taken a fatal overdose of his medicine. The phone is ringing, but he is too weak to answer, and the camera tracks in to a tight close-up as he nears death. The phone stops ringing. He lowers his head and closes his eyes. After a pause a hand comes into the frame and touches his shoulder; the clock chimes and the waiter's voice says, "It's 10:30, Professor Wandley." A track-back frames the pair in medium-long shot, revealing that Wandley is waking up back in his club (a set change having been accomplished during the tight, close framing of the hero's face). Here the move from dream to waking takes place within one shot, and it involves a track-in to a character who lowers his head and closes his eyes, then a track-back from the same character waking up.

Such classical background films suggest that Hollywood had a repertory of cueing devices which its practitioners could call upon to create a number of different situations: ellipses, flashbacks, dreams, and fantasies. These devices included dissolves (wavy or plain), tracking movements, dialogue, gestures, and especially music. A great burst of such devices all at once could create a montage sequence (often with additional special effects). A quick dissolve would just signify time passing. But in between, there was a wide latitude from which to choose, and filmmakers could combine cues to create ambiguity. Lang does so early on in *The Woman in the Window*, deliberately.

Laura's use of such cues is also, I would argue, ambiguous. Looking at *Stage Fright*, we saw that even classical films can occasionally flaunt narrative conventions by presenting us with false information. Because of its ambiguous dream device (for we never learn whether the dream is real in terms of the story events), *Laura* also seems to fit into the category of duplicitous films. Its failure to recuperate and place its duplicity gives it a more daring narrative in some ways than that of *Stage Fright*. As with *Stage Fright*, however, we can see in *Laura* an example of a film in which one daring device dictates and deforms the overall structures of the film. The "dream" is a device of subjectivity, which hints that we might expect to find other patterns related to point of view (POV) to be important in an analysis of how the dream is motivated and how it functions. Even without intensive scrutiny, it is apparent that *Laura* centers around two major POVs: initially that of Waldo Lydecker and subsequently that of Mark McPherson. The dividing point comes after the restaurant scene in which Lydecker relates the long series of flashbacks to McPherson. At the end of the syuzhet, the last scene apparently departs from both these POVs for the solution of the enigma. Already we can expect that the film's dominant involves shifting POV structures.

To be able to determine how the "dream" and shifting POVs organize the form of *Laura*, we need a method for analyzing POV. Fortunately, interest is increasingly focusing on this question. Edward Branigan's article "Formal Permutations of the Point-of-view Shot"[5] is an excellent theoretical analysis of optical POV. Yet *Laura*, despite its considerable use of characters as filters of information for the audience, uses relatively little optical POV. We need other categories to demonstrate how *Laura* seeks to guide our perception by linking it to the perceptions of certain of the characters.

I have chosen to use certain concepts loosely derived from the work of the Russian structuralist, Boris Uspensky, in his book on POV, *A Poetics of Composition*.[6] Uspensky proposes to divide POV into *levels* so that it may be analyzed; he finds four levels in literature: ideologi-

[5] Edward Branigan, "Formal Permutations of the Point-of-view Shot," *Screen* 16, no. 3 (Autumn 1975): 54–64; reprinted in revised form in his *Point of View in the Cinema* (Berlin: Mouton, 1984), chap. 5.

[6] Boris Uspensky, *A Poetics of Composition*, trans. Valentina Zavarin and Susan Wittig (Berkeley: University of California Press, 1973).

cal, phraseological, spatio-temporal, and psychological. Since his system relates primarily to literature, I have adapted it to the cinema by
finding more useful replacements for and additions to Uspensky's four
levels. The *phraseological* level is largely irrelevant for film, since it
relates solely to the language of the literary text. On the other hand,
the spatio-temporal level seems appropriate but inadequate for film,
since these two dimensions are so important and equally balanced in
a film. (Uspensky himself points out that time is predominant in literature, since spatial aspects of a work can only be presented in a temporal flow of reading. A film, however, can present all parts of a space
simultaneously.) Therefore I have separated this level into two, the
spatial and *temporal* levels. The *ideological* level clearly applies to
films as well as to literature, and I have retained it. The *psychological*
level (which, as Uspensky uses it, refers only to character psychology)
seems to me not to cover all the aspects of narrative that affect and are
affected by POV. Therefore I have broadened this level to a general
category encompassing *causal* elements. "Causal" here refers to the
motivation of story events by character traits and the motivation of
character traits by story events. Finally, as we have seen, films can
draw upon conventions established by other films to justify their use
of various devices. Some, though not all, films will have a level of POV
structures based upon *genre* conventions. *Laura* does draw upon conventions of the detective genre for some of its POV devices. The five
levels of POV I will be examining in *Laura*, then, are generic, causal,
spatial, temporal, and ideological.

These categories provide a good example of how a neoformalist
critic works out a method in response to a problem posed by a specific
film. This is not to say that these five categories could not be applied
to films other than *Laura*; they probably could. Yet I should hope that
no one would bother to apply them *in the same way* to another similar
film. The categories themselves do not dictate how POV in a film would
be analyzed, but they would probably be worth using again only in
relation to a different type of film, to challenge and test the typology—
perhaps to confirm, perhaps to revise it.

GENERIC LEVEL: THE DETECTIVE STORY

Laura is first and most obviously a film of the detective genre. As
such, it creates a gap in our knowledge; the syuzhet withholds some
fabula information. This gap is the set of events the detective must
reconstruct in order to solve the mystery. Closure often comes with
the filling of the gap, and therefore the detective must not find the

missing information until the narrative is ready to end. Much of the material in the film works not to reveal this information, but to delay and distract us from the discovery of it (as we saw in *Terror By Night*). In *Laura*, as in some other detective films, the causal gap is closed by the discovery of the criminal's identity, but the film continues. Then the narrative becomes based on suspense rather than curiosity, usually because the criminal has not yet been captured and may strike again. Still, the closing of the causal gap comes fairly late in such films, or the suspense portion would minimize the interest in the detective's building of a case.

As a result, manipulation of POV has been one of the central conventions of the detective or mystery genre. The multiple POVs in Wilkie Collins's *The Moonstone*, and the alternating first- and third-person narrators of *Bleak House* (one of whose lines of action involves the mystery surrounding Mr. Tulkinghorn's murder) were early examples. Many detective stories filter information through the detective's less insightful partner (e.g., Nero Wolfe and Archie Goodwin, Sherlock Holmes and John Watson), while third-person narration concerning a detective's and suspects' activities can skillfully move among them to conceal vital information (e.g., the novels of Julian Symons and P. D. James). The least likely type of narration in a mystery would be by a killer who withholds the fact of his or her guilt until forced into a confession at the end. But even this type remains a possibility, as Agatha Christie's *The Murder of Roger Ackroyd* shows. And to a limited extent, *Laura* draws upon this last, unlikely alternative.

Because the detective film involves a traditional assumption of a sort of game between its makers and the audience, the audience will be likely to accept a fair amount of playing with its expectations. Yet there is also a complementary expectation that the narration will not "cheat" and give us outright false information. As I noted in Chapter 5, viewers frequently express a sense of disappointment with *Stage Fright*, and my own initial, naive reaction upon seeing *Laura* was that it had played unfairly by including the dream cues. Yet one can always turn back to generic motivation and point out that there is no logical reason why a detective story, in its search to defamiliarize genre conventions, should not resort to such devices. Similarly, the very beginning of *Laura* initiates the process of distracting us from the truth by introducing the story through Lydecker's POV. Although the *Roger Ackroyd*–style narration is not unknown, convention still weighs against our suspicion falling on the narrator. At the beginning, we may well take Lydecker as the protagonist of the film, or at least as a rather acerbic Watson-type figure following McPherson about. But because

Lydecker's POV is dropped long before the revelation of his guilt, we are not likely to feel any sense that the narration had "cheated" by beginning with his voice-over commentary.

The two central characters whose POVs are not used are Shelby Carpenter and Laura herself. The basic reason is simple: they both know that Laura is alive, a fact that must be concealed. Carpenter also serves as another suspect (there must be another suspect or our attention would turn too easily to Lydecker and the immediate motivation of Lydecker's crime), but he is not important enough to warrant a POV structure even after Laura returns.

The use of POV to limit audience knowledge continues through much of the film. When at last the narrative reveals its secret—that Lydecker is the murderer—it also drops the sustained use of individual characters' POVs (although the case is ambiguous; it *could* still be McPherson's dream, and Lydecker's guilt could be part of his wish fulfillment). The final scene appears to be an "objective" or "omniscient" presentation of events; by that point, the aim is no longer the sustaining of a mystery. Rather, the narrative seeks to generate suspense, and thus it must let us know as much of the situation as possible (that Laura is alone and unaware of Lydecker's presence, that McPherson is similarly ignorant and not on the scene, that Lydecker is in the apartment). For this purpose, limited POV would be a liability.

CAUSAL LEVEL: THE DREAM

The apparent dream which begins about midway through *Laura* is the film's structural center. It is also so ambiguous and misleading as to be potentially disruptive to the narrative; it requires considerable motivation by means of a network of other devices.

The film does not try to conceal the "dream" as such; that is, it does not attempt to make it seem like some sort of other device that only appears to be a dream (e.g., it could have been presented as a trick Laura or one of the other characters pulls on McPherson to throw him off the scent). Rather, the film provides artistic and realistic motivation by making the "dream" opening part of a general pattern of dream imagery that runs through the narrative. Since the dream itself and the references to dreams are unnecessary to the narrative causality, they seem to be present for their own sakes, to add a poetic ambiance to the film. To be sure, the dream imagery tends to place an emphasis on the ethereal, idealized qualities of Laura herself, yet in a sense it goes too far, ending by suggesting that she really *is* part of a dream, and thus preventing the film from achieving complete closure.

The four major mentions of dreams in the film create considerable complexity. On the one hand, they would seem to bare the device of McPherson's apparent dream by referring to it so overtly. Yet two of them occur before the "dream" begins, and hence we can pick up on their connotations only on subsequent viewings of the film. Moreover, Lydecker says three of the four lines, and they are motivated realistically as his characteristic way of talking. An educated, sarcastic writer like Lydecker would, conventionally, be likely to use poetic imagery in his speech. Thus we might consider these references to dreams as "weak" barings of the device, though the last one is perhaps explicit enough and occurs late enough to be more noticeable. Following are the four references to dreams.

1. In Laura's apartment, Carpenter claims that he had told McPherson the wrong program for a concert he had attended because he had fallen asleep at the concert. Lydecker moves into the frame at this point and says, "Next he'll produce photographic evidence of his dreams." This remark calls attention to the nature of the cinematic representation of McPherson's "dream."

2. Shortly before McPherson falls asleep in Laura's apartment, Lydecker stops by the apartment and speaks with McPherson. In accusing McPherson of being in love with the dead woman, Lydecker asks, "Have you ever dreamed of Laura as your wife?"

3. As McPherson is about to leave Laura alone in her apartment in the last scene, he tells her: "Get some sleep. Forget the whole thing like a bad dream." Their first kiss follows this line. This is the only line about dreams that does not bare the device. Instead, McPherson speaks of the earlier portions of the narrative as being like a dream, thereby reversing the contextual cues of the film (the track-in-and-out) which tell us that the *second* portion of the film is a dream. This expansion of the notion of dreaming over the whole film gives a slight motivation to the specific dream device.

4. The poem Lydecker is heard reading on the radio as he enters Laura's bedroom contains an explicit declaration of the narrative's strategies: "Out of a misty dream, our path emerges for awhile, then closes within a dream." The transgressive property of *Laura*'s structure is precisely that it achieves closure without ever coming out of the "dream" signaled when McPherson falls asleep by the portrait.

(Laura also refers to "my dreams of a career" at one point, though this does not seem to be part of the imagery relating implicitly to McPherson's false dream.)

172

These references to dreaming do not recuperate the ambiguous dream device of Laura's return. If we notice them as baring the device, they will help point up its unconventional and playful nature. If we do not, they have little effect on how we will perceive the part of the film after Laura returns. Lydecker's remark about McPherson having dreamed of Laura as his wife, coming shortly before the "dream" cues occur, would seem to encourage us to notice those cues and take them provisionally as the beginning of a dream. However we interpret these lines, the causal structures of the narrative do not necessitate the inclusion of the dream imagery, nor do they provide a motivation for it. Yet the film's causal structures *do* provide another type of motivation that might encourage us to take the second half of the film to be a dream.

That motivation comes from McPherson's implied mental imbalance. His frequent manipulation of the pocket baseball game suggests nerves held in check ("It keeps me calm"). He does crack slightly at the party, punching Carpenter in the stomach. He has a brusque and arbitrary manner with witnesses and suspects, culminating in his questioning of Laura under the glaring lights at the police station; there he leans over her aggressively (and with definite sexual connotations) to demand, "Now did you *really* decide to call it off, or did you just *tell* me that, because you know I wanted to hear it?" (Fig. 6.7). More obliquely, the reference to a gun battle in the past in which McPherson was so badly injured that he was left with a "silver shinbone," combined with his pocket baseball game, hints at experiences that have left scars on his mind.

But most of the setup for McPherson's susceptibility to a wish-fulfillment dream comes in the scene just before he falls asleep. A relatively long stretch of time passes with little straightforward causal progress. McPherson's drinking (the length and amount of which are suggested by a dissolve partway through the scene) plays a large part in cueing us toward a dream. The track-in to McPherson as he falls asleep places the liquor bottle in prominent close-up (Fig. 6.5). In addition, McPherson wanders through Laura's bedroom, looking at her bed, handkerchief, perfume, and clothes; this already strongly suggests that the character is entertaining a sexual fantasy.

In causal terms, Lydecker's visit in this scene is motivated primarily as another attempt to get his clock and other possessions back. But this visit is actually unnecessary. He has already asked for them in an earlier scene, and nothing ever comes of this new request. (The reference to the clock does set up the final revelation of its secret compartment, but, again, the clock has already been stressed more than once.) The primary reason for his presence is the other portion of his talk with McPherson, which sets up for the spectator an awareness of McPherson's obsession with Laura. Lydecker reveals that McPherson has put in a bid for the portrait; he taunts the detective about his fantasies of life with Laura. His parting words make all the hints explicit: "You'd better watch out, McPherson, or you'll end up in a psychiatric ward. I don't think they've ever had a patient who fell in love with a corpse."

Interestingly, the film uses none of the conventional "expressionistic" devices to indicate McPherson's mental state. Dana Andrews's performance is restrained, making McPherson appear as a tough, phlegmatic cop; only an occasional bit of emotion breaks through, for example, the two times when McPherson is unable to restrain a tiny, triumphant smile when Laura declares she will not marry and does not love Carpenter. The film introduces expressionistic shadows (Fig. 6.8) and strange angles only at the moment when it also departs from the POV of both characters (McPherson and Lydecker), in the scene of Lydecker's final entry into Laura's apartment. Here we discover that he is the real madman; the expressionistic devices are appropriate (generically) to him. Clifton Webb's performance changes abruptly, as he stares wide-eyed, starts nervously, and moves like a sleepwalker into Laura's bedroom. In general, the film uses mild subjectivity to motivate the "dream," but it reserves the stronger stylistic indicators of madness for the moments that seem to lie outside the POV of either character.

SPATIAL LEVEL: ATTACHMENT TO CHARACTERS

As I have mentioned, *Laura* contains relatively few optical POV shots, in contrast to the films of, say, Hitchcock. Yet the narrative does guide itself via the presence of certain individual characters within the action. Uspensky introduces a term that may help us to look at how *Laura* creates POV spatially; he terms a general close following of a character "spatial attachment."[7]

Theoretically the filmmaker is free to cut to any locale or angle at any time. But in practice, Hollywood has mapped out a range of spatial possibilities (the 180° rule, the shot/reverse shot, establishing shots, signals like fades and dissolves for changes of locale, etc.); most films in the classical Hollywood tradition motivate the framing and editing

[7] Ibid., p. 58.

through the presence of narratively significant action. Characters provide much of this action.

Not every scene in *Laura* sticks to Lydecker or McPherson exactly, but we are generally "with" Lydecker in the first half and McPherson in the second. The beginning uses Lydecker's voice-over to assign the POV to him, even though we see McPherson on the screen before we see Lydecker. Lydecker says: "Another of those detectives came to see me. I had him wait. I could watch him through the half-open door." Here the film uses the most obvious cue—a verbal desciption in the first person of a character's visual attention—to place the POV with Lydecker. The camera is not in fact looking from Lydecker's POV, or anywhere close to it; the bathroom door he mentions is off to the left of the initial and final framings of the first shot. But the spectator discovers this only later; during the lengthy first shot, the use of the voice-over strongly suggests that we are in some sense looking at the detective along with Lydecker. The door has allowed Lydecker's voice-over to glide smoothly from the undefined time and space of his first line ("I shall never forget the weekend Laura died . . .") into the actual time and space of the plot's initial events.

From the point of the first interview between Lydecker and Mc-Pherson, the narrative arranges for Lydecker to accompany the detective on his visits to other witnesses and to Laura's apartment. Lydecker's presence in these scenes violates any notion of realistic motivation; a detective would be unlikely to allow one suspect to be present while others were being interrogated. Yet, because Lydecker's continuous presence is necessary to the narrative's use of his POV, he goes along. Here, as in *Terror by Night*, we can see how frequently the classical Hollywood film allows compositional motivation to take precedence over the realistic type.

In later scenes, Lydecker continues to provide verbal cues for POV. When he and McPherson inspect Laura's apartment, Lydecker objects to the detective's use of the term "dame" in relation to Laura; he says, "Look around—is this the home of a 'dame'?" as they move to a position in front of the portrait. This is the first time we have seen the portrait since the credits sequence, and Lydecker turns McPherson's (and our) attention to it by saying, "Look at her" (Fig. 6.9). This command leads to a cut to a medium shot of the portrait from approximately Lydecker's POV (Fig. 6.10). Significantly, this is the same framing of the portrait that had appeared under the credits. The camera aligns itself exactly with Laura's glance within the scenographic space of the picture; her body and head are both turned to her left to face the implicit viewer. The slight low angle and placement of the camera

slightly to the right of the picture pick up this direction of body orientation and emphasize it (although one crucial aspect of the painting
is obviously that the woman's eyes "seem to follow you" and can be
seen as looking at the viewer from any point in the room). The next
shot is a medium two-shot which concentrates on Lydecker's fixed
gaze; he is closer to the camera, and his face is picked out clearly by
the light while McPherson's eyes are hidden by the shadow of his hat
brim (Fig. 6.11).

The flashbacks allow the narrative to dispense with McPherson's
physical presence for long stretches of time. His role as listener motivates the telling of Laura's story, but the POV is Lydecker's, both
through voice-over and through spatial attachment to him within the
flashbacks. Again, aside from the many shots that present space in a
way that was conventional in the mid-1940s Hollywood film (fairly long
takes mixing with shot/reverse shot, a mobile camera unobtrusively
following action and reframing, etc.), the style continues to emphasize
Lydecker as looker. Consider, for example, the scene in which he
walks to Laura's apartment after she has broken her regular date with
him for the second time. Over a long shot of Lydecker on a sidewalk
(Fig. 6.12) we hear his voice saying, "Then I found myself before her
apartment building." At this point there is a fast track forward to a
medium close-up as Lydecker turns and looks up and off left (Fig.
6.13). A street light in the background of the shot motivates the careful
picking out with light of the upturned face. Once again this marking
of Lydecker's gaze leads to one of the film's relatively few optical POV
shots, a low-angle medium shot of the window as Laura's and a man's
shadows move onto it (Fig. 6.14). The voice-over says, "It pleased me
to know she was home till I saw she was not alone." Precisely at the
word "till," the second silhouette passes onto the window; here we are
exactly restricted to Lydecker's viewpoint, both spatially and soni-
cally.

Another device that comes in during the flashbacks and elsewhere
is the placement of the character in the foreground of a shot looking at
something placed prominently in the frame; this is a classic form of
spatial attachment (often noted in the treatment of the reporter
Thompson in *Citizen Kane*, for example). The dissolve to Laura reading Lydecker's disparaging column on the artist Jacoby reveals Lydecker sitting in the left foreground, lit so dimly as to be almost a
silhouette; he is looking away from the camera at Laura as she sits in
bed reading (Fig. 6.15). The camera follows his gaze by tracking in to
a medium shot of her as Lydecker's voice-over describes the article.

The framing scenes before and after the flashbacks also motivate them visually as Lydecker's memories. Before each flashback, Lydecker glances away from McPherson and assumes an abstracted stare as he speaks. The returns to the present always find Lydecker still staring. For example, after the medium close-up of Laura sitting and smoking while listening to Lydecker read his column to her, there is a dissolve back to the restaurant table. Lydecker sits in medium close-up, staring abstractedly (Fig. 6.16), and says, "Then one Tuesday she phoned and said she couldn't come." After this line, the camera tracks back to bring McPherson's shoulder into the left foreground of the shot (the classic shot/reverse shot framing), and at the same time Lydecker stops staring and glances left at McPherson to deliver his next line, "It didn't matter, really" (Fig. 6.17). Then he turns away immediately and begins to stare again as he continues his story, while a dissolve leads to the next flashback (Fig. 6.18). This careful exclusion of McPherson in order to follow Lydecker's attention is typical of the entire string of flashbacks. (The placement of McPherson in the foreground corner of the shot does not function to signal his POV, as the shot of Lydecker looking at Laura [Fig. 6.15] does. In both cases, Lydecker's voice and the general context of his storytelling cue us that this is his POV rather than McPherson's.)

The relatively unimportant role McPherson has played throughout Lydecker's telling of Laura's story prepares the way for the extreme shift that takes place as the two men leave the restaurant. They talk briefly before parting; at this transitional point, the spatial configuration favors neither man (Fig. 6.19). As Lydecker turns and walks right, away down the sidewalk, the camera executes a complex movement which, combined with McPherson's actions, serves to mark forcefully the moment of passage from Lydecker's POV to McPherson's. As Lydecker begins to leave, the camera cranes slightly up and moves in toward McPherson, also panning right to keep Lydecker in the frame; the composition is now in deep space, with McPherson in the foreground as he says, "Thanks for the wine" (Fig. 6.20). Lydecker leaves the frame, and the camera tracks left with McPherson (Fig. 6.21); he turns toward the camera, looking down and right in tight close-up (the closest shot of anyone in the film to this point), then turns to look off right, in profile, after Lydecker (Fig. 6.22). An automobile horn also serves to mark the moment as the image fades out. (This fade is a strong dividing marker; it is only the second in the film, the first having introduced the sequence in the restaurant.) No significant causal action follows the men's parting; the pause and complex camera ma-

177

neuvers function to transfer the narrative POV from Lydecker to the character whose gaze forms the only action at the scene's end.[8]

From this moment to the apparent end of McPherson's POV with the revelation of Lydecker as the murderer, most scenes begin either with McPherson's arriving at a locale or with his being already present as others arrive to talk with him. In the first scene after the shift in POV, we discover McPherson in Laura's room pursuing his investigation. First Bessie's arrival and then the arrival of Lydecker, Treadwell, and Carpenter lead to conversation scenes. The scene in the street when Laura meets Carpenter in his car starts as an apparent departure from McPherson's vicinity; a pan and track left as Carpenter drives away reveals that McPherson has, in fact, been present watching the scene. Indeed, the restriction to his POV has motivated the fact that we could not hear what Laura and Carpenter talked about—a conversation that would "give away" too much about both the romance and mystery lines of action. In this case, restricted POV promotes retardation.

In the next scene, McPherson follows Carpenter's car to Laura's country home. The action inside the house begins with only Carpenter present, looking around stealthily and beginning to take down the gun to hide it; at this point McPherson enters and starts questioning Carpenter. But even here the narration attempts to motivate the events as spatially attached to the detective; when he asks Carpenter, "You hadn't borrowed it [the gun] lately, even just bring it back tonight?" the reply is, "You followed me here, you saw me come in—you ought to know." At times the narrative cannot avoid leaving McPherson's vicinity, as with the conversations between Anne Treadwell and Carpenter at the bar during the party at Laura's or the subsequent conversation in the bedroom between Treadwell and Laura. Here the POV structure favors Treadwell, but only on the causal level; Carpenter's rather undesirable semes, combined with McPherson's obvious attraction to Laura, should prompt us to sympathize with Treadwell's arguments against a match between Laura and Carpenter. For a brief moment, as Laura realizes that Carpenter believes she committed the murder and she leaves him to enter the bedroom, the narrative tends

---

[8] In the original script, McPherson was to begin a voice-over description of his reactions to Lydecker's stories; his commentary in this and other scenes would have served to mark the shift in POV more decisively. In general the lines originally written for McPherson made explicit some meanings that are implicitly conveyed in the finished film's action. See *"Laura," L'Avant scène cinéma* no. 211/212 (July-September 1978): 35 passim.

toward her POV on the causal and spatial levels. But for the most part, the POV sticks with the detective as much as possible.

The spatial structures of McPherson's POV come to a head in the scene of Laura's return. After inspecting the bedroom, he returns to look at the picture; although there is no optical POV shot, he stands in approximately the position from which the original view of the painting under the credits must have been filmed, and from which Lydecker first pointed it out to him (compare Figs. 6.23 and 6.10). There then follow the drinking, the contemplation of the portrait, and McPherson's falling asleep. The whole lengthy sequence leading up to Laura's return is necessary to motivate both McPherson's growing love for her and the "dream" aspect of the track-in-and-out and subsequent action. We have had indications of McPherson's "nerves" before this, but the exploration of the room allows us to concentrate wholly upon his state of mind, which we might then construe as highly susceptible to the kind of wish-fulfillment "dream" that apparently follows.

Up to this point in the film not a single device has been used whose motivation was not in some way linked to the characters' actions and attentions. If we take the camera movements to be similarly linked to McPherson's attention, then we almost have to understand them as a dream cue, with the camera timed to reach him just as he nods off, and then pulling back as if we have entered into the fantasy world in his mind. (This notion of getting physically closer to characters in order to "enter their minds" is a metaphor worked out in rather literal-minded fashion in Hollywood's repertory of camera devices, though a fade or dissolve would frequently be added to suggest the moment of actually penetrating into the mental state. See, for example, the track-in and dissolve on the heroine of *The Locket* as she finally remembers the crucial childhood trauma that caused her mental illness. In a less obvious fashion, the convention I have already noted of having flash-backs begin with a tracking movement toward the teller implies that we are "with" that character's memories.) A dissolve at this point would make no difference, as it might be either a dream or ellipsis cue; a "wavy" dissolve would be explicit enough to establish the following action as a dream. The lack of such a subjective-style dissolve leaves the dream ambiguous. Raksin's musical score for this scene, though not specifically a dream cue, underlines the romantic-fantasy element of McPherson's exploration of the apartment.

If we posit for a moment that the camera movements do not cue a dream, what function *do* they perform? Most likely they could be taken as a narrational comment on the remaining action: McPherson, obsessed as he is with Laura, treats her as a dream object rather than as a real woman. Yet there is no conventional cue available to the film-maker to signal to us whether this will be a metaphorical dream (i.e., part of the film's overall dream imagery) or a real one. Since the latter possibility seems the more likely, we will probably choose it unless given contrary evidence. (Some viewers might take the lack of an awakening at the end of the film as a retrospective cue that the suggestion of a dream was just a metaphorical touch.)

The apparent end of the use of character POV occurs at the moment of the revelation of the mystery's solution. After Laura's argument with and dismissal of Lydecker, he exits, and there is a cut to him pausing outside the apartment door. A sudden change in filmic style signals a departure from McPherson's POV which is *not* a return to Lydecker's (although, as I have mentioned, the "dream" aspect of the narrative makes this departure problematic). The low camera angle of the shot combines with the tense, quiet music and sudden appearance of large expressionistic shadows on the walls to mark the change; Lydecker's expression becomes tense and crafty as he pauses on the staircase (Fig. 6.8). After a brief return to the conversation between Laura and McPherson, the latter finds the gun and leaves. From here on the characters scatter, and the film proceeds by intercutting among them, building up a quick suspense involving a last-minute-rescue situation. The parallel editing precludes any sustained use of spatial attachment, although our attention briefly links up with that of Lydecker, since we know what Laura and McPherson do not—that Lydecker is stalking her. But for the most part, character POV is dropped as a sustained device; indeed, the very end of the film involves a move away from the action altogether. Laura and McPherson walk off right toward the dying Lydecker, but the camera does not follow their action; instead it tracks over to the shattered clock as we hear Lydecker's final words, "Good-bye, my love." The ending briefly recapitulates in reverse the opening, in which a track past the twin clock and other artifacts had been accompanied by Lydecker's past-tense narration. David Bordwell has suggested that these final words may be a return to Lydecker's original voice-over narration, rather than simply sound from off-screen.[9] It seems to me that the "true" status of the voice could be either type. This ambiguity further complicates the generally transgressive devices of Lydecker's narration and the "dream."

Excepting the possibility that the track-in-and-out that began the "dream" was a cue for a metaphor, this final tracking movement is the only overt authorial comment in the film. Here a symbolic interpre-

[9] In class discussion, October 1976.

tation of the shattered clock seems called for. In one sense, the main object that suggested Laura's constricting links to Lydecker has now been destroyed, and she is free of him. In another sense, Lydecker has tried to kill the one woman he loved and ends by shattering the emblem of their strictly intellectual relationship. The clock also parallels and stands in for the murder of Diane Redfern; there have been several references to how the shotgun blast mutilated her beyond recognition, and clearly the film could not present a literal representation of her corpse. Whatever meaning the spectator attributes to the moment, it marks a move away from the diegetic world to a meaning or meanings imposed from a more omniscient narration. This extradiegetic force creates closure for the narrative without resolving the questionable status of the dream. A scene with McPherson waking to realize that Laura was really still dead would not in itself create closure; he would still have his case to solve, and the dream would have been just another red herring. For this reason, the narration ends up painting itself into a corner. It must close the narrative within the dream or risk trivializing the dream device by having McPherson wake up. By moving away from the characters at the end, the narration seems to leave them in the dream, while it imposes a sense of finality on the film as a whole.

TEMPORAL LEVEL: THE PAST

The syuzhet of the film starts well into the fabula events. This elimination of the early portion of the fabula is typical of the detective genre, of course, but *Laura* leaves out the murder *plus* the beginning of the investigation. Not only is the murderer's identity a mystery, but we do not know who the victim is—and we are not aware that we do not know for the first half of the film. One of the reasons the film is so talky is that the characters need to spend a great deal of time filling us in on earlier fabula events.

To present some of these past events, the narrative introduces the long series of flashbacks narrated by Lydecker. This seems to set *Laura* up as a *Citizen Kane*–style narrative, with the character of the title already dead as the syuzhet opens. The question "Who was Laura?" temporarily becomes a device similar to the central question in *Kane*, "What was Rosebud?" Because the flashbacks occupy such a long stretch of the syuzhet time, they bolster the idea that we will never see Laura in the "present" sections. The flashbacks provide the spectator with as much of Laura's presence as the star billing of Gene Tierney would seem to warrant. Moreover, once the shift to Mc-

Pherson's POV comes, we might expect that his reading of Laura's diary might lead to a parallel set of flashbacks for the second half of the film. Thus the possibility of her return is camouflaged by the temporal structure of the syuzhet.

At the opening of the film, Lydecker begins a past-tense voice-over narration; even before the first fade-in, he says, "I shall never forget the weekend Laura died." This statement suggests that the narration is placed somewhere in the future in relation to the images that immediately appear. But what is the temporal status of the voice? At a later point in the opening shot, Lydecker says, "I had just begun to write Laura's story when another of those detectives came to see me." Are we to take the voice-over as a part of that written story? Is the voice speaking after the entire series of fabula events, or at some point between the syuzhet's opening and the discovery that Laura is not dead? Of course there is no "real" time in which Lydecker's voice speaks. But the failure of the narrative to assign the voice-over a clear temporal relation to the images serves its own ends; for now, it must keep from us the fact that Laura is not dead. Here, even though the POV is ostensibly Lydecker's, the necessities of the text show through. Lydecker has no reason to lie in telling the story to us, but the narrative demands that he say she is dead. By making unclear the temporal relation of his words to the fabula events, the narration is able to cover over its misleading claim that Laura is dead.

The use of the voice-over at the beginning also helps set up Lydecker's apparent innocence. By placing McPherson's investigation in the first half of the film and his discovery that Laura is alive in the second, the narrative allows Lydecker to dominate the first half by means of his recounting of the flashbacks. (Clearly if McPherson had heard Lydecker's story while aware that Laura was alive, both he and we would have a very different view of the flashbacks than we do when they are told with only Lydecker's POV to guide us.) Lydecker seems to be the protagonist, and hence an unlikely suspect. McPherson's rather unpleasant character seems to do little to contradict this suggestion of Lydecker's innocence and central importance. Nevertheless, *Laura* does not seem to violate traditional conventions of "fair play" in the detective genre, though it and the novel it was based on may have played with and stretched them a bit. The manipulation of POV has been a traditional device for withholding information from the reader; the important factor here is that the narration does not present it with any patently false material. Lydecker's tales of Laura's past are apparently the literal truth, and his voice-over narration does not lie either.

IDEOLOGICAL LEVEL: THE PORTRAIT AND THE
TWO KINDS OF MEN

Laura contains a painting of its title character which derives from a specific tradition of portraying women in Western art. John Berger has described this tradition in *Ways of Seeing*: "Almost all post-Renaissance European sexual imagery is frontal—either literally or metaphorically—because the sexual protagonist is the spectator-owner looking at it."[10] Berger is speaking of the genre of female nudes, but he generalizes his argument to other forms of depiction as well.

Today the attitudes and values which informed that tradition are expressed through other more widely diffused media—advertising, journalism, television.

But the essential way of seeing woman, the essential use to which their images are put, has not changed. Women are depicted in a quite different way from men—not because the feminine is different from the masculine—but because the "ideal" spectator is always assumed to be male and the image of the woman is designed to flatter him.[11]

The portrait in *Laura* is not a nude, but the positioning of the woman within it follows the pattern Berger points out. She sits facing left but turns her body and head to gaze out at the spectator, offering herself for examination. This treatment of the woman as a submissive object to be visually possessed by a male spectator is a common feature of the classical Hollywood cinema, and *Laura* raises this feature to the level of the subject matter itself. *Laura*, a film about a man who falls in love with a portrait (not "with a corpse," as Lydecker says), also offers Gene Tierney as an object of contemplation for the cinema spectator. This is not to imply that I favor the current critical procedure, mentioned in Chapter 1, of mechanistically sorting out characters in every film as powerful or weak according to which "has the gaze." In *Laura* such a pattern is a systematic part of explicit and implicit meanings.

This pattern begins in the credits sequence, when we see the portrait for the first time (Fig. 6.23). I have described how framing slightly to the right and below the portrait is the apparent direction of the woman's gaze in terms of her posture within the scenographic space of the picture; this is where the camera places us in this opening (and, as we have seen, it links our initial view of the portrait with those of Lydecker and McPherson). The portrait returns in scene after

[10] John Berger, *Ways of Seeing* (New York: Viking Press, 1973), p. 56.
[11] Ibid., pp. 63–64.

scene, lit glowingly no matter what the lighting conditions are in the rest of the room.

The equation of the ability to gaze at the portrait with the possession of the woman it depicts becomes quite evident in the scene just before the "dream" begins, as Lydecker asks for his clock and other things back: "You want the portrait? Perfectly understandable. I want my possessions—my vase, my clock, and my screen. Also perfectly understandable." The painting is simultaneously an artwork to be owned and a woman to be possessed. (Recall Lydecker's "Look at her," as he faces the portrait in the first scene in which it appears.)

The film goes even further and includes the portrait's painter within the story, as Laura's lover. For Lydecker, the portrait arouses jealousy of Jacoby because he reads the position of the woman within it as a record of the creation of the painting ("Jacoby was in love with her when he painted it"). Her turned body and outward glance are, in Lydecker's view, directed at Jacoby. McPherson, on the other hand, takes the gaze much more simply to be directed at him as he stands or sits before it. If indeed the second half of the film has elements of a wish-fulfillment dream, it is partly because the Laura who returns is the idealized object from the painting, beautiful and submissive to the character whose POV we as spectators adopt—McPherson.

The character Laura is indeed filmed in such a way as to keep her the beautiful visual object of the painting (for us as well as for McPherson). Time and again a scene will favor our view of her by turning her out away from the person she is conversing with, toward the camera. She is lit far more attractively than any other character, with glowing three-point glamor lighting. (The portrait itself contains a depiction of such lighting, with a "halo" effect around the body.) In the second shot of Laura and Carpenter on the balcony during Treadwell's party, for example, both camera positioning and lighting emphasize her and make him fade into the darkness at the edge of the frame (Fig. 6.24).

This kind of framing and lighting of the female lead is fairly typical of Hollywood films, however. *Laura*'s difference lies not only in its bringing these strategies to the surface through the use of the painting, but also in its emphatic depiction of the obsessive and fetishistic treatment of the heroine. McPherson not only falls in love with the portrait, but also explores Laura's bedroom. In the process he gazes at her bed and a dainty handkerchief (Fig. 6.25; it acts as a substitute for a piece of underclothing), sniffs a bottle of her perfume, and opens the closet to look at Laura's dresses. This fetishistic behavior continues after her return, in the remarkable scene in which McPherson takes her to the police station. There he turns the glaring "third degree" lights on her and hovers very close to her (Fig. 6.7) as he finally extracts her admission that she remained engaged to Carpenter only so she would not seem to believe him guilty.

Laura fits perfectly into the tendency described by Laura Mulvey in her article "Visual Pleasure and Narrative Cinema," wherein she develops ideas on the treatment of women that are similar to Berger's. Mulvey argues:

An active/passive heterosexual division of labour has similarly controlled narrative structure. According to the principles of the ruling ideology and the psychical structures that back it up, the male figure cannot bear the burden of sexual objectification. . . . Hence the split between spectacle and narrative supports the man's role as the active one of forwarding the story, making things happen. The man controls the film phantasy and also emerges as the representative of power in a further sense: as the bearer of the look of the spectator, transferring it behind the screen to neutralise the extradiegetic tendencies represented by woman as spectacle. This is made possible through the processes set in motion by structuring the film around a main controlling figure with whom the spectator can identify.[12]

My purpose here is not to test Mulvey's argument in full, with respect to either its applicability to *all* films of the classical period or its Freudian underpinnings.[13] Certainly the use of the woman as a visual object and the assumption of a male spectator is a common phenomenon in the classical narrative cinema, and it is a central factor in *Laura*.

The POV structures we have already examined serve to motivate this use of the heroine. We do not simply look at Laura; we look at her as

[12] Laura Mulvey, "Visual Pleasure and Narrative Cinema," *Screen* 16, no. 3 (Autumn 1975): 12.

[13] Indeed, I would argue that the pattern Mulvey finds is common but not universal in the Hollywood cinema. In "Visual Pleasure and the Narrative Cinema," she says that "the male figure cannot bear the burden of sexual objectification." Yet historically there have been a number of male stars treated visually and narratively in the way she claims is reserved for women; these would include, in at least some of their films, Rod La Roque, Rudolph Valentino, Richard Barthelmess, John Barrymore (see especially *The Tempest*, in which he gets a far glitzier visual treatment than costar Camilla Horn), Victor Mature, Cornel Wilde, and Howard Keel (compare his first entrance in *Showboat* to that of Ava Gardner—they are treated virtually identically). Mulvey explains male stars' glamorous characteristics as "not those of the erotic object of the gaze, but those of the more perfect, more complete, more powerful ego conceived in the original moment of recognition in front of the mirror." This claim is impossible to prove or disprove, but it might work for Barrymore, Douglas Fairbanks, and others. Yet I think there are also "weak" male stars who sometimes play heroes who need to be goaded (often by active women) into activity: La Roque, Valentino, Barthelmess, Charles Ray, and so on. Miriam Hansen discusses this issue, in greater detail and dealing specifically with Valentino, in her "Pleasure, Ambivalence, Identification: Valentino and Female Spectatorship," *Cinema Journal* 25, no. 4 (Summer 1986): pp. 6–32.

others do. In this case there are two "main controlling figures"; we do not necessarily "identify" with them in any straightforward way, but their presence and POVs manipulate our own view of much of the action. Certainly the apparent dream constitutes a device that allows us to look at Laura and enjoy her submission to McPherson's gaze and our own; that is, the film cues us to enjoy it. After all, *Laura* is ultimately more concerned with the romance than with the mystery. (Note the lack of attention paid to such tasks as motivating clearly McPherson's discovery of the hidden chamber in Lydecker's clock.) Once McPherson is finally identified as the protagonist, Laura must submit to him in order to bring closure to the romance. We may actually find her submission to him unpleasant, but probably only if we are aware of the film's strategies of exploitation of her.

The character Laura is perfectly designed to fit the role of the passive visual object. She is beautiful but has almost no semic material assigned to her. (Other characters *tell* us she is "sweet," "talented," and "imaginative," but we see little evidence of any of these in Laura herself.) She conforms as a character to Mulvey's description of the typical function of women in the classical cinema; that is, she does not generally initiate action on her own. (The only exception is her attempt to approach Lydecker for the pen endorsement; her lecture to him on his bad manners intrigues him at that point, but he soon becomes a sort of Svengali to her.) Rather, she is all things to all the men of the narrative, responding to them submissively; her apparent defiance of some of the men occurs only when she is prompted into it by another man. This makes her the perfect object of McPherson's fantasy "dream" of the second half. Suddenly the seemingly promiscuous, sophisticated Laura of Lydecker's flashbacks becomes the potentially faithful and loving wife of the detective. Her behavior toward McPherson is so submissive at times as to support the pattern of a wish-fulfillment dream. When he questions her about her relationship to Carpenter—had she decided to marry him? is she in love with him?— she responds in the negative, exactly matching McPherson's desired image of her.

Indeed, I would argue that the reason Mulvey's article applies so thoroughly to the character of Laura is that she is unusually passive in terms of Hollywood conventions. Such passivity may, however, be a convention of the 1940s mini-genre of the "portrait" film. *The Woman in the Window* and *Experiment Perilous* also center around paintings of beautiful women; in these films as well, the hero falls in love with the heroine without ever having seen her, and in each his fantasy vision of her comes true (though only as a dream in the former). *Portrait of Jenny* (1948) combines this idea with the ghost genre also popular during this period. The equation of the woman with a painting prompts her portrayal as a beautiful, passive creature.

Laura's passivity is enhanced by the failure of the film to include her POV. Had we been shown a section of the narrative from her standpoint, the "dream" would have been considerably weakened; the novel, which does not use the "dream" device, does include a portion told in the first person by Laura. As we shall see, the original ending of the film, as conceived and filmed by Preminger, did shift to Laura's POV; the change in the ending in the final version leaves the "dream" far more ambiguous than it would have been otherwise.

Aside from this passivity, several devices contribute to the film's rendering of Laura and other women in the film as images oriented toward an implicit male spectator. For example, Laura's is not the only picture in the film. Lydecker has an antique portrait of a woman in a three-quarters frontal pose over his fireplace; there is a similar painting in Laura's apartment above the desk. Several times McPherson inspects groups of artworks arranged on walls: the masks in the first scene and some small, oval silhouette portraits in Laura's country home. These are not pictures of women, but they create a general pattern of artworks and "aesthetic contemplation" that realistically motivates the presence of the central portrait.

The implicit opposite of the portrait within the narrative is the police photo of the dead woman's body. The film cannot go so far as to show the photo, of course, but it does make reference to it. Lydecker asks, "McPherson, tell me, why did they have to photograph her in that horrible condition?" Lydecker has decided to kill Laura specifically so that others cannot possess her, and he chooses a method that will also obliterate her appearance—a shotgun blast in the face. Lydecker's obsessive act holds some rather unsavory implications about the whole idea of the visual representation/possession of beauty (e.g., that for Lydecker the mutilation of "Laura" has substituted for the sexual possession of her, and hence he is still "jealous" of having others see her body), and the film leaves the whole reference to the police photo on the periphery of the narrative.

Berger points out that traditional paintings of nudes often contained mirrors.

The mirror was often used as a symbol of the vanity of women. The moralizing, however, was mostly hypocritical. You painted a naked woman because you enjoyed looking at her, you put a mirror in her hand and you called the painting *Vanity*, thus morally condemning the woman whose nakedness you had depicted for your own pleasure.

The real function of the mirror was otherwise. It was to make the woman connive in treating herself as, first and foremost, a sight.[14]

The narrative does not assign a specific seme of vanity to Laura, but a number of scenes depict the female characters primping in mirrors. Laura pulls out a little mirror from her purse and is checking her appearance as she meets Carpenter at Treadwell's party. Treadwell applies makeup in a mirror as she talks to Laura in the bedroom later in the film. The tacit assumption here is that the women look so good in the film because they are just naturally concerned with being glamorous. Laura's apartment is full of mirrors: there is one on either side of the front door, one in the bar, and at least six in her bedroom (including the three panels of the closet doors). Several times we see her reflection in mirrors as she is ostensibly looking in them to put on her hat (Fig. 6.26) or brushing her hair (at her dressing table in the last scene). Interestingly, the film makes little attempt to suggest that she is actually looking at herself at these points; she barely glances in the mirrors in either scene and is positioned so that we are the ones who can see her reflection most clearly.

But the film goes beyond the simple use of mirrors to force the woman to connive in the display of her own body to the cinema spectator. Laura is a designer of advertisements, and almost all the examples we see of her work follow the same pattern as Berger has described, with the female models in the ads turning their bodies and gazes out toward the spectator. (The only exception is the barely visible pen advertisement which Lydecker endorses; it contains only a small photo of him, since his name, rather than his appearance, is the selling point.) When Carpenter enters Laura's office, the easel in the background holds an ad portraying a blonde woman looking out seductively. Carpenter's design featuring Diane Redfern shows her from the back but still turning to gaze out over her shoulder. Finally, the photograph of Diane Redfern that Laura shows McPherson shortly after her return is posed very similarly to Laura's own portrait, but with Redfern facing right and turning body and face to look out at the spectator (Fig. 6.27). This photo is seen in another of the rare optical POV shots—this time motivated by McPherson's glance.

Mulvey describes two common patterns of displaying women in Hollywood-style narratives: first, the control of women through the ascertainment of guilt, and their punishment, which takes the form of

[14] Berger, *Ways of Seeing*, p. 51.

voyeurism; second, the creation of satisfaction purely through the viewing of the beautiful object or a representation of it, which is fetishism.[15] Again, the general applicability of this argument is not the issue here; nevertheless, *Laura* specifically contains a surprisingly direct working out of these patterns in the two characters whose POV the narrative presents.

This voyeur/fetishist split between Lydecker and McPherson, respectively, reflects a general set of opposing semes in their characters. They represent two stereotypes that are traditional opposites in the ideology of Hollywood: the intellectual versus what we might call the "man of action." Hollywood usually cannot cope with the intellectual, who serves as the villain in *Laura*. (There are a few Hollywood films that place intellectuals, or odd versions thereof, in protagonist roles, but these tend to be comedies—e.g., *Ball of Fire, Horse Feathers.*)

The first part of the film, in which we perceive the events in relation to Lydecker's POV, strongly marks his voyeuristic tendencies. Aside from such details as his observation of McPherson in the first scene, there is a later scene in which he listens in on a conversation between Carpenter and Laura as they dance in a restaurant. Eventually he is driven by jealousy to watch her window from the street when she and Jacoby are together, and to wait in the snow to determine the identity of Laura's lover. His line "There were others, of course" suggests that he kept close tabs on Laura's life (to the point of hiring detectives to spy on her lovers). His excuse for visiting McPherson in the scene just before the "dream" starts is "I happened to see the lights on," as if he has continued to lurk outside in the street as we had previously seen him doing.

McPherson takes the opposite tack. To be sure, he does engage in certain voyeuristic activities by reading Laura's diary and letters, and by arranging little confrontations in order to watch the participants' reactions. But he becomes obsessed with Laura, as we have seen, through gazing at her portrait, through examining her intimate possessions, and finally through submitting Laura herself to intense scrutiny under the guise of an official questioning. Both men are alike in that they use their respective activities to gain knowledge about Laura and hence control over her.

The parallel voyeur/fetishist and intellectual/man of action splits acquire other implications in the course of the film. Lydecker is associated with art and the (parasitic) activity of the critic, while McPherson is concerned with the practical. (He uses the antique clocks to check

---

[15] Mulvey, "Visual Pleasure and Narrative Cinema," pp. 13–14.

his watch, and his initial impulse is to handle and inspect delicate objects d'art; he several times uses the artistic activities of others as clues.) Similarly, Lydecker is scrawny, while McPherson (like Laura's other male friends) has a "lean, strong body," in Lydecker's words. (Note in Fig. 6.28 McPherson's tiny smirk as he looks off at Lydecker getting up out of the bath in the first scene.)

These distinctions have class implications as well. Lydecker loves art because he is of a leisured class that is depicted as the only group capable of appreciating it. Carpenter's genteel southern background makes him a dilettante; in him, a superficial appreciation of culture indicates an accompanying lack of ability to do real work. But aesthetic understanding is again something with which the Hollywood film cannot really cope. McPherson, the man of action, is also a man of the people; his artistic sensibility is minimal. He falls asleep at concerts (he says) and smashes an antique clock. His pocket baseball game, along with Lydecker's talk of "the policeman's ball" and "the bleachers," creates a set of values in opposition to those ascribed to the artworks that pervade the wealthy world he enters.

The film sets Laura up as a character with a "working girl" background. Lydecker grooms her into accepting a more sophisticated, luxurious life, but her origins motivate her eventual ability to love McPherson. Although she is able to appreciate the aesthetic sphere of Lydecker, she also retains many associations that permit her to escape its taint; she works in the practical world of advertising, she gardens and goes for walks in the woods, and she loves virile men.

The film takes the traits of the two main male characters so far as to suggest obliquely that Lydecker is impotent. The censorship code would prevent any overt characterization of this nature, and whether Lydecker is "really" impotent is not the issue. The narrative assigns him semes conventionally associated with impotency, in order to support its general ideological view of the intellectual male. Lydecker makes several slighting references to the virile-looking men Laura is attracted to: Carpenter is "a male beauty in distress" and Jacoby "was so obviously conscious of looking more like an athlete than an artist." (Here the film acknowledges its own split: there are people who look like artists and those who look like athletes. Jacoby would seem to offer a possible compromise, but the fact that the film ultimately seems incapable of admitting such a combination of traits may explain why Jacoby does not appear more prominently in the narrative—even though he would be a logical suspect in the crime.) In the final scene Lydecker tells Laura, "You have one tragic weakness. With you, a lean, strong body is the measure of a man, and you always get hurt."

190

At other points the narrative marks Lydecker as old (Carpenter's joke about Lydecker still dancing the polka, Lydecker's reference to himself as "Old Mother Hubbard") and ill (his epileptic seizure). Lydecker also betrays a distaste for sex in his line about Laura's future "disgustingly earthy relationship" with McPherson. And we cannot overlook (in a Hollywood film) the fact that Lydecker spends his romantic evenings with Laura reading his columns to her. Lydecker acts more as a protector of Laura than as her lover, and she finally admits that her ties to him are primarily those of gratitude. These hints at impotency are a hidden explanation of the otherwise admirable Laura's promiscuity during her relationship with Lydecker. A 1944 audience might well have picked up on these signals readily. *Experiment Perilous* contains a similar pattern, with the villainous husband obsessively suspecting his wife of having a lover; at one point he remarks, "Mentality never quite makes up for the physical, does it, my dear?"

In the fantasy-fulfillment of desire during the second part of the film, Laura turns to McPherson as a new lover. His pursuit of her culminates in the questioning at the police station, where he gets her to admit she does not love Carpenter. Laura is at first annoyed by his false arrest of her. But at his reply, "I had reached a point where I needed official surroundings," she suddenly realizes he is in love with her; she smiles and tells him, "Then it was worth it, Mark." Her first use of his given name foregrounds the moment of her sexual surrender. This surrender is brought about by the very characteristics that set McPherson apart from Lydecker—his strength, his roughness, and his physical dominance over her. The scene carries a definite suggestion that Laura not only submits to McPherson's domination, but enjoys the surrender precisely because it has been forced from her.

Thus the use of the two men's opposing POVs indirectly supports the implication that women are naturally drawn to certain qualities in men and not to others. The film suggests that men have qualities either like those of Lydecker or like those of McPherson, that intellectualism and physicality are mutually exclusive traits. Women clearly wish to submit themselves to "disgustingly earthy relationships." Such connotations suggest that gender roles in many Hollywood films are unfair not only to women.

CONCLUSIONS

Were the Hollywood mode of production the uniformly conservative institution described by most historians, we would have to consider *Stage Fright* and *Laura* to be inexplicable aberrations. Yet, as David

Bordwell, Janet Staiger, and I have argued elsewhere, Hollywood encouraged limited technical and formal experimentation in the interest of novelty.[16] The problem with *Laura*, however, remains that the relatively transgressive device of the false dream remains ambiguous and unresolved. In *Stage Fright*, the lying flashback was obviously a deliberate device—a decision that created consistent and far-reaching formal consequences throughout the film. But in *Laura*, we can never be sure what effects the dream imagery and the shifts of POV create over the whole film.

Part of this problematic quality seems to have crept into the film because of certain events and conflicting decisions during the production process. Preminger, who had recently returned to 20th Century–Fox after a period away due to a feud with Darryl F. Zanuck, originally proposed making a film of Vera Caspary's recent bestseller, *Laura*. In spite of Preminger's successful completion of *In the Meantime, Darling* in December 1943, Zanuck refused to let him direct again, assigning him to *Laura* as producer only, and specifying that the film be budgeted at the B level. The first scenario draft contained three different POVs, including Laura's—thus following the novel. (Caspary's novel is a rather clumsy application of multiple POVs, derived, as she admits, from *The Moonstone*.) Zanuck liked the script enough to boost the film, after some revisions, to A status. Rouben Mamoulian took the directing post and shot part of the film. Early rushes, however, did not impress anyone, including Zanuck, who finally gave in and reassigned the direction to Preminger.

Until recently, most historians have based their accounts of *Laura*'s production on Preminger's version of how the film's ending was shot. According to him, Zanuck insisted on having a new ending shot after the first version of the film was complete. In the second version, an added stretch of dialogue in an earlier scene had Laura tell McPherson that Lydecker's account of their meeting was a lie, and that his behavior to her had been far more generous and sentimental than Lydecker had indicated. This would have set up the final scene, in which Laura would hide the shotgun and try to persuade Lydecker to flee; instead, he would visit her apartment in an attempt to kill her. There McPherson and the other police would capture (not kill) him. Preminger recalls having shot this as a second ending, which Walter Winchell persuaded Zanuck not to use after all.

More recent accounts based on the original script and Fox company

---

[16] David Bordwell, Janet Staiger, and Kristin Thompson, *The Classical Hollywood Cinema: Film Style and Mode of Production to 1960* (New York: Columbia University Press, 1985), chaps. 7, 9, and 19.

memoranda indicate that this version, with Laura trying to help Lydecker escape, was in fact the original ending shot by Preminger, and that it was replaced by the current ending of the final film. Similarly, Laura's claim that Lydecker had lied about their early relationship was cut, as were her and McPherson's voice-over narrations.[17]

The new accounts do not necessarily clear up all the questions surrounding *Laura*'s production. But they seem to suggest that the inconsistencies concerning the dream device may have gradually crept into the film, in part as a result of personnel shifts; of the numerous rewrites by different authors, each trying to solve the problems perceived by Zanuck; and of the general disagreements between Preminger and his production superiors at Fox. Zanuck's main concern was that *Laura* utilize as extensively as possible his potential star, Gene Tierney, the only lead actor chosen by Zanuck rather than Preminger; Zanuck was reportedly skeptical about Clifton Webb and Dana Andrews, both relative unknowns in the film world. He also insisted that the story line be made as clear as possible, hence the initial plan to use McPherson's voice-over to make explicit things that are implicit in the images and music of the final film. According to David Raksin, the composer, Zanuck wanted to trim the scene in which McPherson falls asleep, but Raksin persuaded him to leave it intact by promising to provide a romantic score to suggest the detective's frame of mind.

The film was a great success, making stars of the three principals, who continued as long-term Fox players. Preminger also stayed there before going independent in the 1950s. Thus the issue of clarity, which had plagued the production, died down as *Laura* became one of Fox's most prestigious releases of the year (as evidenced by the reviews and by Clifton Webb's Oscar nomination).

When examining *Terror By Night*, we saw that an ordinary film is likely to draw upon automatized conventions to the extent that its defamiliarizing power is minimal and lies mostly in the area of reality rather than in its deviation from other artworks. Yet there is a great deal of leeway in Hollywood for defamiliarization, and it can take many shapes. Indeed, the classical system could hardly have lasted as long and been as successful as it has if it did not permit such defamiliarization. In Chapter 2, I suggested that the classical cinema has a built-in complexity upon which any film, even an undistinguished one, can draw. Similarly, we can now see that Hollywood's system of motiva-

---

[17] Recent information on *Laura*'s production is from Rudy Behlmer, *America's Favorite Movies: Behind the Scenes* (New York: Frederick Ungar, 1982), pp. 177–199, and from Jacques Lourcelles, "*Laura*: Scénario d'un scénario," *L'Avant scène cinéma* no. 211/212 (July-September 1978): 5–11.

tion can be brought to bear upon anomalous devices, such as *Stage Fright*'s lying flashback and *Laura*'s ambiguous dream cues, and can weave these devices through the texture of the film's dominant. Defamiliarization is thus controlled in classical films, and hence it is often less extreme than in the other types of films we are examining in this book.

PART FIVE

A Formal Look
at Realism

7

Realism in the Cinema:
Bicycle Thieves

REALISM AS A HISTORICAL PHENOMENON

LET US JETTISON at the outset two common assumptions about realism: first, that realism depends on a natural relationship of the artwork to the world; second, that realism is an unchanging, permanent set of traits shared by all works perceived as realistic.

By now, few film analysts would hold to the first assumption. It is widely recognized that realism is an effect created by the artwork through the use of conventional devices. As Shklovsky argued, representational artworks use the principles of their respective media to create form out of the raw material provided by nature; they do not simply seek to create a duplicate of nature itself: "To try to imitate nature in the representational arts would amount to wanting to attain an inadequate goal with inadequate means." He gives an example, from Helmholtz, of how the actual difference between the light of the open sky and that in a forest shadow is about 20,000:1, while in a painting of trees against a sky, the contrast is closer to 16:1. Shklovsky concludes, "A painting is something constructed according to laws proper to it, and not some imitative thing."[1]

We can see the absence of a natural relationship between the artwork and the world in the fact that so many different styles have been historically justified to their publics as "realistic." Indeed, any artwork can be said to be realistic on the grounds of some criterion or other. The Surrealists presented their highly stylized creations as following the logic of dreams; Pop Art elevated mundane objects to the status of museum pieces; abstract art can be seen as capturing a spiritual reality; the most grotesque political caricatures take actual social occurrences as their subjects. In this very broad sense, all art has natural links to reality, for no one could create perceptual objects wholly apart from some aspect of one's experience of the world. (Even abstract art

---

[1] Victor Chklovski, *La Marche du cheval*, trans. Michel Pétris (Paris: Editions Champ Libre, 1973), pp. 87–88.

draws upon familiar colors, shapes, and other perceptual qualities of reality.) But such a broad sense of the term "realism" is not useful. We might therefore be tempted to try to define a set of traits constituting a more specific realist style.

Yet this second assumption, as I suggested at the outset, is also unacceptable. No one set of traits can define realism for all time. (This is not to say that films within individual, temporally limited realist movements cannot be defined as sharing traits.) If realism is indeed a formal effect of the work, then what we perceive as realistic should change over time, as norms and viewing skills change. For neoformalists, the concept of types of motivation is the main tool for distinguishing realism—realistic motivation is one of the four types (the others being compositional, artistic, and transtextual). Motivations are sets of cues within the work that allow us to understand the justification for the presence of any given device. If the cues ask us to appeal to our knowledge of the real world (however mediated that knowledge may be by cultural learning), we can say that the work is using realistic motivation. And if realistic motivation becomes one of the main ways of justifying the work's overall structures, then we generalize and perceive the work as a whole as realistic.

Realistic motivation can never be a natural, unchanging trait of works, however. We always perceive the work against shifting norms. Realism, as a set of formal cues, changes over time, as does any style. It has the ability to be radical and defamiliarizing if the main artistic styles of the time are highly abstract and have become automatized. Jan van Eyck's extraordinarily detailed, textured pictures using the newly developed technique of oil painting are realistic art by virtually any criteria; yet their defamiliarizing qualities must have been profound for a public used to the more conventional fresco, mosaic, and enamel techniques of the period. Similarly, early programmatic symphonies, like Beethoven's Sixth ("Pastorale") and Berlioz's Symphonie Fantastique, which use the depiction of narrative-like scenes as a form of realistic motivation, departed in a startling way from the familiar Haydn/Mozart sonata-form symphony (though the tendency for composers or listeners to bestow descriptive titles on such symphonies— e.g., "The Hen," "The Clock"—testifies to an existing impulse toward realistic motivation in music). In our own century, Duchamp's found objects and the Superrealist art movement provide examples of realism as the basis of avant-garde innovations. (Duane Hansen's sculptures, made by casting from living people and using real clothes and objects, are surely no less disturbing than is the extreme stylization of de Kooning's violent abstract-expressionist images of women.) Realisms, then, come and go in the same sorts of cycles that characterize the history of other styles. After a period of defamiliarization, the traits originally perceived as realistic will become automatized by repetition, and other, less realistic traits will take their places. Eventually other devices will be justified in quite a different way as relating to reality, and a new sort of realism will appear, with its own defamiliarizing abilities.

Because of its defamiliarizing power, realism is not alien to neoformalism—even though many would probably think of "formalism" and "realism" as opposite things. But realism *is* a formal trait that we attribute to art works, and realism was in fact important to the Russian Formalist theorists, for at least three reasons. First, everyday reality is part of what art defamiliarizes (along with other aspects of life such as ideology and other art works). Shklovsky, in fact, has said that the concept of defamiliarization itself came from his work on Tolstoy's realistic writing. He quotes from Tolstoy's diary a passage about being unable to remember whether he had dusted his room already; a habitual act had become so automatic as to go unnoticed: "Tolstoi restored the perception of everyday reality by describing it in newly found words as though destroying the habitual logic of associations he distrusted." Shklovsky concludes, "Thus 'eccentric' art can be realistic art."[2]

A second reason why neoformalism is concerned with realism is because reality forms part of the material of which the work is constructed—though it is, of course, transformed by the traits of the medium into something quite different from what it was originally. This happens quite obviously in a case presented by Shklovsky: the novelist Rozanov (pen name, Nikoláy Ognyóv) has created a new genre by inserting into his books whole articles on literary polemics, photographs, and so on.

The laws which lead new forms to be created and which necessitate resorting to new materials have, at the death of forms, left a void. The soul of the writer has searched for new subjects.

Rozanov has found a subject. A whole category of subjects, subjects of everyday life and the family.

Shklovsky declares that when grand language is the norm, the use of common language becomes a revolt.[3] Thus the choice of subject mat-

---

[2] Viktor Shklovsky, *Mayakovsky and His Circle*, trans. and ed. Lily Feiler (New York: Dodd, Mead and Co., 1972), pp. 114, 118.

[3] Victor Chklovski, *Sur la théorie de la prose*, trans. Guy Verret (Lausanne: Editions l'Age d'homme, 1973), p. 279.

ter from reality can create defamiliarization, depending on the norms of the period.

Third, and finally, realism as a style can be defamiliarizing, quite apart from its subject matter. Eikhenbaum found this to be the case with Lermontov.

After Marlinsky, Veltman, Odoevsky, and Gogol, where everything was still so labored, so heterogeneous, so unmotivated, and therefore so "unnatural," *A Hero of Our Times* looks like the first "light" book; a book in which formal problems are concealed beneath a careful motivation and which, therefore, was able to create the illusion of "naturalness" and to arouse an interest in pure reading. Attention to motivation becomes the basic formal slogan of Russian literature from the 40s through the 60s ("realism").[4]

For neoformalism, realism is neither a natural nor an inevitably conservative trait of artworks. It is a style which, like any other, needs to be studied in its historical context.

This is not the place to deal extensively with the history of cinematic realism. But a thumbnail sketch of important moments when realism has come to the fore may indicate how its defamiliarizing power has waxed and waned over time. Directly after the invention of cinema, its power to reproduce moving photographic images of the real world was enough to astonish viewers (not because they were naive, but because the new art form stood apart so distinctly from any possible background). Indeed, it is difficult to imagine a more purely Bazinian realism than that of the Lumière films. The primitive cinema quickly adopted conventions of narrative representation from the existing arts and developed its own as well. The next period when realism became a major issue was probably in the early teens, with the introduction of naturalism in both narrative (e.g., Feuillade's melodramas of the 1911–1914 period) and acting (e.g., Griffith's work with the Gish sisters, Blanche Sweet, and others). After the formulation of the classical studio cinema in the teens, location shooting in postwar Swedish and French films seemed to many a radical break, as did the documentary feature film in the United States (e.g., *Nanook of the North, Chang*) and the Soviet montage movement. Since then we have had Poetic Realism in 1930s France (primarily perceived as such only retrospectively), Italian Neorealism (seen immediately as a radical break with past traditions), and the many variants on the modern art cinema, which often appeal to realism (particularly psychological depth).

As this sketch indicates, realism has often been perceived as a de-

---

[4] Boris Eikhenbaum, *Lermontov*, trans. Ray Parrott and Harry Weber (Ann Arbor: Ardis, 1981), p. 170.

parture from the norm of popular, classical, familiar cinema. In spite of the recent tendency in film studies to assert that Hollywood-style cinema creates classical realist films,[5] Hollywood has usually been equated with fantasy and escapism. Claims that this or that film is realistic often involve contrasting it with the classical cinema, for example, "The war movies you'll see aboard the Intrepid weren't made in Hollywood" (New York City subway advertisement for the Intrepid Museum, June 1985), or "You won't regret having taken the time to follow this narrative, for it is neither a tale of adventure nor an extravagant fantasy that you will hear, but a true story in all its purity" (English-dubbed voice-over at the beginning of *The Return of Martin Guerre*). The departure from popular "entertainment" cinema can take a variety of directions, all of which could be motivated realistically. The Intrepid Museum ad copy points to actual rather than staged events occurring before the camera, while *Martin Guerre*, a period piece, stresses its own authenticity of detail in historical reconstruction. The opposite of abundant detail can also be perceived as realistic; Carl Dreyer removed most of the paraphernalia of a real farmhouse in *Ordet*, yet the resulting simplicity functions to suggest the spartan existence of the Danish farm family; Robert Bresson's films achieve an intense concentration on textures by focusing in on a very few objects. Depth of psychology in characterization may be one index of realism, as in the films of Ingmar Bergman and Michelangelo Antonioni. On the other hand, a refusal to reveal characters' inner states (as in late Bresson films) can seem like objectivity on the part of the narration. Ambiguous or unhappy endings are generally treated as more realistic than are the ubiquitous happy endings of the Hollywood-style film. Yet this is merely a convention, since in everyday life we must assume that events can turn out either well or ill for the parties involved. Thus many of the traits that have come conventionally to represent realism over the course of film history have done so primarily because they were departures from the prevailing classical norms.

Such departures often seem most radical at the beginning of a new

[5] This assertion has been closely associated with the theoretical work of *Screen*, and particularly with that of Colin MacCabe. See his "Realism and the Cinema: Notes on Some Brechtian Theses," *Screen* 15, no. 2 (Summer 1974): 7–27, and "Theory and Film: Principles of Realism and Pleasure," *Screen* 17, no. 3 (Autumn 1976): 7–27. The notion of the classical realist cinema is prominent in the latter article, particularly on pp. 8 and 17–21. MacCabe adopts the strategy of defining realism ahistorically, as involving, in all eras and places, a homogeneity of discourses that places the viewer in a fixed, noncontradictory position in relation to a represented "truth" (this in spite of the claim on p. 25 that MacCabe favors "analysing a film within a determinate social moment").

trend, with the effect of realism diminishing as more extreme uses of the same approach appear in other films. For example, when Vittorio De Sica's *Bicycle Thieves* first appeared, in 1948, André Bazin hailed it as the finest example of the Italian Neorealist trend, and he emphasized the elements of chance in its narrative. With the appearance four years later of *Umberto D*, Bazin lost none of his admiration for the earlier film, but he declared, "It took *Umberto D* to make us understand what it was in the realism of *Ladri di Biciclette* that was still a concession to classical dramaturgy."[6] The background had shifted over the intervening four years, and Bazin noticed changes in his notions of the Italian movement's realism. Moreover, the repetition of the same realistic traits gradually makes their conventional nature apparent, and the early films that seemed strikingly realistic appear mannered upon re-viewing (as has happened with *On the Waterfront*, for example). In other, probably much rarer, cases, the passage of time may make audiences perceive a film as *more* realistic. This was the case with *The Rules of the Game*. This chapter and the next will examine *Bicycle Thieves* and *The Rules of the Game*, each widely recognized as an example of realism in the cinema. The first was immediately perceived by audiences as realistic, and it became a success in many countries precisely because of the novel quality of its realism. *Rules*, on the other hand, met with much incomprehension upon its initial release, and it was only after years had passed, and such films as *Bicycle Thieves* had taught audiences new viewing skills, that *Rules* also won widespread acclaim as a realist film. The contrast in the receptions of each film should indicate strongly the historical nature of perceptions of realism.

The critical esteem in which these and other realist films are held today results in large part from the writings of Bazin, the leading proponent of realism in cinema. Currently Bazin is rather out of fashion, since the widespread recognition of the conventional nature of representation makes his belief in an ontological link between the film image and reality seem naive. Yet Bazin's view of realism was grounded in skillful formal analysis, and his concentration on the multiple functions of camera movement, depth, offscreen space, acting, and mise-en-scene resulted in some fine essays on the individual Italian Neorealist films in particular. His chief mistake, it seems to me, was his treatment of the whole history of the cinema as a teleological quest for total cinema—that is, for total reproduction of the phenomenal world.

[6] André Bazin, "*Umberto D*: A Great Work," in Bazin, *What is Cinema?* vol. 2, trans. Hugh Gray (Berkeley: University of California Press, 1971), p. 80.

But if we eliminate this element and treat cinematic realism as a non-teleological historical phenomenon, Bazin becomes very useful indeed.

WHY DO WE PERCEIVE *BICYCLE THIEVES* AS REALISTIC?

One of the most striking things about *Bicycle Thieves* for us today is that, although it is in many ways far more realistic in its effect than are Hollywood-style films, it uses skillful continuity editing techniques throughout. The sort of shot/reverse shot that appears in the opening scene between Ricci and the employment-agency boss (Figs. 7.1 and 7.2) recurs throughout the film; eyeline matches, points of view (POVs) (Ricci watching the pawnshop man climb the giant racks of sheets), chases (the flight of the thief with the bike), montages (Ricci and Bruno cycling to work in the early morning)—all are used "correctly" in terms of classical convention, with only a very few violations of screen direction. Bazin's essay on the film admits that its decoupage does not distinguish it from an ordinary film. But, he adds, the shots were chosen to keep the events paramount, with the style refracting them as little as possible. A naturalness results from the "ever-present although invisible system of aesthetics."[7]

Is Bazin suggesting, then, that the classical continuity system is somehow more natural, more transparent than others, and hence in itself more suited to realism? How would we square this with his other claims about deep focus and the long take (neither of which *Bicycle Thieves* uses to any extent) as developments within Hollywood away from editing and toward the preservation of real space and time? In "An Aesthetic of Reality: Neorealism," Bazin pointed to Orson Welles as having "restored to cinematographic illusion a fundamental quality of reality—its continuity." (Here Bazin refers to temporal continuity as such, not to the term "continuity" as it refers to editing.) "In contrast, classical editing breaks space up by logical sequence or subjectivity." He characterizes such editing as conventionalized: "The construction thus introduces an obviously abstract element into reality. Because we are no longer used to such abstractions, we no longer sense them."[8] In neoformalist terms, Bazin is talking here about the automatization of classical decoupage. Continuity editing is unnoticeable in *Bicycle Thieves* because its basic techniques are so familiar. But Bazin is also arguing that this automatized set of techniques serves

[7] Bazin, "*Bicycle Thief*," in *What is Cinema?* vol. 2, pp. 47–58.
[8] Bazin, "An Aesthetic of Reality: Neorealism," in *What is Cinema?* vol. 2, p. 28.

new functions in Italian Neorealist films, and hence the style is not simply identical to that of Hollywood films.

Elsewhere, Bazin distinguished between classical editing, which uses the logic of the narrative action to guide the breakdown into shots, and Neorealism, in which a temporal continuum guides that breakdown (hence the respect for chance incidents and "dead" intervals, even in the course of a coherent ongoing syuzhet). For our purposes here, what Bazin's claims imply is that *Bicycle Thieves* downplays originality in editing in order to foreground the defamiliarizing powers of other aspects of the film. As we shall see, the film's structure does depend to a great degree on emphasizing temporal flow. On the one hand, chance and peripheral events constitute a disproportionate amount of the film. On the other, deadlines and appointments, so central to the classical narrative, take on a great importance here as well— but now they perform the crucial additional function of guiding our understanding of the central syuzhet threads over the course of the numerous small digressions.

I should note that Bazin does not take the temporal basis of Neorealist editing as a direct capturing of reality; for him, scenes are structured "to give the succession of events the appearance of an accidental and as it were anecdotal chronology."[9] Elsewhere, he refers to the elaborate planning used to give *Bicycle Thieves* "the illusion of chance."[10] Thus, in spite of Bazin's mystical tone in certain passages, such as those on De Sica's love for his characters, or on Neorealism's concern with immanence,[11] we should not dismiss the remainder of his analysis as naive.

Similarly, although Bazin does not discuss it, the sound in *Bicycle Thieves* contributes relatively little to the film's impression of realism. In contrasting *Farrebique* and *Citizen Kane*, Bazin pointed out that a gain in realism in one technological area seemed to mean a corresponding sacrifice of realism in another. *Kane*'s deep focus and long takes depended on a stylized studio mise-en-scène, while *Farrebique*'s technical sloppiness resulted from the decision to shoot entirely within real locations. The Neorealist directors were unable to record sound directly, and they had to rely on post-synchronization; yet silent shooting allowed for a great camera mobility which Bazin praised. "Some measure of reality must always be sacrificed in the effort of achieving it."[12] The sound in *Bicycle Thieves* is in fact quite conventional, with

[9] Bazin, *"Bicycle Thief,"* p. 52.
[10] Bazin, "De Sica: Metteur en Scène," in *What is Cinema?* vol. 2, p. 68.
[11] Ibid., pp. 69-73, 64-65.
[12] Bazin, "An Aesthetic of Reality: Neorealism," pp. 29–30.

nondiegetic music underscoring dramatic moments (as when Ricci first spots the thief in the rained-out flea market) and ambient crowd noise giving a sense of bustle to locations. Sound and editing are both areas which *Bicycle Thieves* tones down to emphasize its formal departures from other conventions.

Bicycle Thieves's realism lies in those areas where it departs most extremely from classical usage. Its subject matter draws upon an historically recurring notion that a concentration on the working and peasant classes makes for more realistic action. The narrative based on this subject matter then introduces a considerable number of peripheral events and coincidences; it must also introduce careful temporal cues to unify these chance events into a tight series within a brief time span. The use of non-actors and location shooting makes the style of the mise-en-scene and cinematography obviously realistic. The resulting appearance of objectivity in the presentation of the various problems that confront Ricci also affects the ideology, making it seem balanced and compassionately humanistic. Finally, *Bicycle Thieves* systematically cites the norms of entertainment filmmaking from which it departs. The dominant suggested by this list can be formulated as consisting of selective departures from the conventions of the classical Hollywood cinema, motivated as realistic. Other conventions of that cinema which *Bicycle Thieves* retains are deformed by being forced into new, heightened motivating functions, since they must help to justify, display, and contain the film's original, realistic aspects. Overall, this dominant creates a film that both differs from the classical Hollywood cinema and makes us conscious of that difference. The motif of the citation of Hollywood films is particularly important here, as it bares the device of this dominant.

Let us examine each of these areas of realistic motivation in turn, and the specific nature of this film's dominant should become more apparent.

SUBJECT MATTER

An art work that deals with working-class or peasant characters is not automatically realistic, of course. In Shakespeare's plays, such characters were often confined to the comic subplot, and the Baroque era was full of poetry and oratorios on the picturesque, imaginary, nymphs-and-shepherds vision of the countryside (e.g., Handel's *Acis and Galatea*). But at intervals over the past few centuries, a notion has surfaced that the life of lower-class figures presented with the appearance of objectivity is more realistic than that of middle- or upper-class subjects. In certain historical circumstances, the introduction of such new subject matter stands out against the prevailing background. For example, after a lengthy tradition in European painting in which peasants were treated as comic or allegorical figures (e.g., Brueghel), the genre paintings of Mathieu, Louis, and Antoine Le Nain of the 1630s and after broke ground by rendering the artists' provincial family members and acquaintances in quiet, dignified poses (e.g., Louis's 1640 "Peasant Family," in the Louvre). Their work was quickly forgotten, overshadowed by the dominant classicism of painters like Nicolas Poussin; his flamboyant mythical and Biblical subjects, like "The Rape of the Sabine Women" (Metropolitan Museum of Art), were far more fashionable. (By now, tastes have probably changed to the extent that the relative appeal of Poussin and the Le Nain frères has been reversed.) In the nineteenth century Gustave Courbet revived this approach (in contrast with the sentimentalization of the peasantry by his contemporary, Millet). The school of Naturalism in literature also treated the lower classes with an attempt at scientific objectivity, as in George Moore's *Esther Waters* and Emile Zola's *Les Rougons-Macquart* cycle.

The effects of this latter tradition have lingered into our own century and have, I suspect, shaped what we think of as realistic subject matter in cinema. Hollywood has in general avoided subject matter of a naturalist variety, considering it too sordid and depressing for a mass audience. Those few Hollywood films that have attempted to deal with the lives of ordinary people have been seen as daring, relatively uncommercial projects: for example, Erich von Stroheim's *Greed*, Josef von Sternberg's *The Salvation Hunters*, King Vidor's *The Crowd* and *Our Daily Bread*. Even in these films the narratives deal with highly dramatic incidents. *Greed*'s romantic triangle, combined with Trina's mad obsession with wealth, culminates in two murders and in McTeague's hopeless situation at the end, stranded in Death Valley; in *The Salvation Hunters*—usually described as containing no action— the hero and heroine get mixed up with petty criminals and prostitution; *The Crowd* involves the hero's courtship, his child's death, his near suicide, and his reconciliation with his wife; *Our Daily Bread* shows the efforts of a group of unemployed people to create a cooperative farm in the face of local opposition. While the subject matter of these films does stand out within the Hollywood norm, *Bicycle Thieves* goes further yet. Bazin points out: "Plainly there is not enough material here even for a news item: the whole story would not deserve two lines in a stray-dog column. . . . It takes on meaning only because of the social (and not psychological or aesthetic) position of the victim."[13] I shall be arguing, and indeed Bazin also acknowledges, that the psychological drama between father and son ultimately over-shadows the issue of the lost bike. But the use of a stolen bike as the basis for the search that precipitates this family drama is certainly non-Hollywood,[14] and the social issues do remain important to the film's overall effect.

NARRATIVE STRUCTURE

"The illusion of chance" that Bazin pointed to is perhaps the most im-mediately apparent aspect of *Bicycle Thieves*'s narrative structure. Chance here involves two kinds of relationships among events: inter-polated events incidental to the action and coincidences that further the action.

The incidental events help give *Bicycle Thieves* its rich, detailed texture. Rather than the condensed, dramatic time of the classical nar-rative, in which all moments must contain significant action (or mu-sical numbers, or comic relief, or some other generically motivated material), *Bicycle Thieves* seems to recreate the rhythm of real events, with trivial and important happenings alternating. These events can serve a variety of functions—creating detail for verisimilitude, plant-ing seemingly trivial material that will later be drawn into the central action, or suggesting symbolic or social meanings. Early on, as Ricci helps his wife carry water and they discuss how to redeem the pawned bike, a group of children passes in the background (Fig. 7.3). This group seems to be just part of the authentic background detail, yet the children are playing at bride-and-groom, with the pair in the lead wearing a veil and hat. Since Maria is about to pawn her trousseau sheets to get the bike back, the moment provides a bit of symbolic irony, but one which is barely stressed. Similarly, the boys playing a game in the street outside the fortune-teller's house seem merely to provide verisimilitude, until Ricci turns and asks one to watch his bike while he goes in search of Maria (Fig. 7.4); this moment sets up bike theft as a possibility. (The title itself, seemingly so neutral and objec-tive, not only cues us to expect the thefts, but ironically contrasts them with each other in order to point up Ricci's hopelessness at the end—as an honest man driven to steal.) A more noticeable departure from

[13] Bazin, "*Bicycle Thief*," p. 50.
[14] *Pee-Wee's Big Adventure* (1986) might seem to belie this claim, but I think it in fact bolsters it. Generic motivation traditionally permits farces to center around trivial or strange subject matter; a Hollywood drama or "high" comedy still would not be likely to depend on such an event. Note also that Pee-Wee Herman is represented as a sort of bizarre child figure and is the subject of antiestablishment cult interest.

the central action comes as Ricci is learning to put up movie posters. In the establishing long shot, we see him and his supervisor, as well as an accordion-playing boy and his beggar companion (Fig. 7.5). As a wealthy-looking man passes and the boys unsuccessfully ask him for money, the camera pans to keep this action centered, even though Ricci and his supervisor are out of the frame by the end (Fig. 7.6). A cut to a new long shot returns us to a concentration on them. The pan functions to generalize the contrast between rich and poor to the society as a whole, but the begging boys play no role in the narrative action. Other scenes function in similarly tangential ways, mostly filling out the film's generally oppressive depiction of Italian society: the homosexual who approaches Bruno at the bike market, the group of chattering German seminarians who shelter near Ricci and Bruno during the rain, Bruno's interrupted attempt to urinate during the chase, Bruno being slapped by a priest when he accidentally invades the confessional, the truck with team supporters that passes the tired pair, the details of the wealthy family's meal in the restaurant, and other such moments.

Coincidence plays a large role in linking the major section of the syuzhet together. Ricci's first glimpse of the thief at the bike mart is not too unlikely, since the man would come to such a place to deal in stolen bikes. But the second encounter, outside the fortune-teller's place, is sheer chance. Again, it is coincidental that another boy should be drowning just after Ricci has left Bruno by a bridge, or that when Ricci steals a bike, its owner should run out the door only a second or two later. (As he is wearing a hat, we must infer that he was on his way out anyway.) A Hollywood film would make some attempt to motivate these events compositionally by planting earlier references that would make them seem less startling. As we saw with *Terror by Night*, classical films rely more heavily on compositional than on realistic motivation, and hence they create a sense of causal unity. Neorealist films like *Bicycle Thieves* appeal to notions of the randomness of reality when they fail to provide other motivation for incidental or coincidental events.

But in spite of these systematic chance events, the overall narrative of *Bicycle Thieves* is quite carefully constructed. Indeed, to compensate for a certain loosening of causal connections, other unifying factors have been heightened. Specifically, the film provides a very clear-cut series of deadlines, appointments, and dialogue hooks that keep us oriented at all times, no matter how far the action digresses or how abruptly it shifts. Such priming devices make us anticipate that a certain action will occur at a certain later point; hence we recognize it when it does occur, and our understanding of the ongoing events is reinforced. Deadlines, appointments, and dialogue hooks are very common in the classical film, but here the introduction of chance has forced them to serve a set of functions slightly different from the norm. Rather than creating the redundant unity characteristic of the Hollywood script, priming devices in the Neorealist film hold chance events in check.

The film's action takes place over a relatively short span of time, from Friday when Ricci gets his job and redeems his bike, to Sunday afternoon, when his search fails and he is caught trying to steal another bike. The overall action breaks into two major parts, characterized by different narrative strategies. Up to the point where Ricci and Bruno come out of the church and realize that they have lost track of the thief's old accomplice, we are constantly being cued to anticipate future events. The exposition has revealed almost nothing of the characters' pasts—only that Ricci has been out of work for two years and that he has pawned his bicycle. From the very start, a series of deadlines focuses on whether Ricci will succeed in his various goals.

1. In the opening scene, on Friday, the employment-agency boss says that Ricci must have a bike by the next day to get the job (deadline).
2. Later that day, now with his bike, Ricci visits the poster office and is told to report at 6:45 the next morning (appointment).
3. Early Saturday morning he drops Bruno off at his job and says he will return at 7:00 that night (appointment).
4. After the theft of the bike, Ricci tells his friend Biaocco that he must have it back by Monday (deadline). They agree to search on Sunday (appointment). This functions as a dialogue hook into the next scene.

The Sunday search occupies the remaining action, with the final Monday deadline hanging over Ricci the whole time. During the first two-thirds or so of the film, these deadlines and appointments give a sense of constant progression and of unity.

Then, after the argument with the old accomplice in the church, the means of progression from scene to scene change considerably, and the change functions to shift our primary concentration from the search for the bicycle to the relationship between father and son. Were the film to continue its original approach, the street name that the old man gives Ricci would have served as a dialogue hook into a scene of the pair searching in that street. But Ricci does not follow up on this clue. (This is ostensibly because the man could not give him the exact number, yet one would assume Ricci would go there anyway. As it is, the old man becomes irrelevant, since Ricci spots the thief by chance.) Instead, Bruno chides Ricci for bungling the situation in the church, and Ricci slaps him. This in turn leads to the lengthy digression of their argument, the scene of the other boy's near-drowning, and their visit to the restaurant. Throughout these scenes, their changing moods are the only threads that guide the action; no progress is made in the search itself. (Indeed, during the restaurant scene, Ricci's description of what a good job he had found makes the search for the bike seem already a lost cause.)

These scenes reach Bazin's ideal of decoupage constructed around a temporal continuum rather than around the logic of a tight narrative. The argument in the road and Ricci's subsequent assumption that Bruno is drowning occupy one stretch of uninterrupted time; then, after a dissolve covers the brief time of their crossing the bridge, the reconciliation scene and visit to the restaurant also occur without ellipsis. Thus for a few scenes *Bicycle Thieves* abandons the abstract construction of time through verbal foreshadowing cues and presents an illusion of the rhythm of events occurring in actual time.

Ricci's decision at the end of the restaurant scene to visit the fortune-teller moves the narrative back to the search line of action, but only through the film's most notable coincidence, his sighting of the thief in the street. The dramatic action with the bike progresses continually to the point when the owner of the one Ricci has stolen decides not to charge him. At that point the spectator once again switches from being interested in what will happen in the future to being concerned with the changes from moment to moment in the characters' emotions; the relatively lengthy series of shots of the pair walking hand in hand and in tears stands apart from the search plot in the same way that the argument/restaurant portion of the action had.

Thus, although *Bicycle Thieves*'s careful script construction superficially resembles that of the classical film, its abrupt changes in tactics help to undermine the conventional hermeneutic line. The question through the first portion of the film, up to the end of the church scene, is whether Ricci will find the bicycle in time to keep his job. Yet for a lengthy section of the film from that point, we are led to downplay that question and wonder rather what effect the loss of the bike will have on the family. Finally, though we do learn the answer to the original question, the ending seems open and ambiguous, since the theft of the bike has clearly become a secondary issue, and our main concern at the end is the impact of the day's events on the father-son relationship. In one sense, the fact that Bruno takes Ricci's hand seems to suggest some sort of forgiveness or acceptance on the part of the boy. Yet we are still left in doubt, I think, as to whether the pair links hands because they are resilient and can rise above their difficulties or because they are simply now united in their resigned disillusionment. Certainly we are not left with any fear that Bruno will reject his father, but there is a definite hint that the idyllic optimism of the family group seen early on in the film may be gone forever. Again, by now the open and unhappy ending has become a cliché of the modern art cinema, but we should bear in mind that *Bicycle Thieves* was one of the first widely seen films that used it, and it undoubtedly seemed quite original then. Subsequent usage has pointed up the conventional nature of a device that must have conveyed a strong sense of realism to postwar audiences.

MISE-EN-SCENE AND CINEMATOGRAPHY

Perhaps the most obvious cues for realistic motivation come in the film's mise-en-scene, with its use of non-actors and location shooting. Bazin has suggested that De Sica's style is difficult to analyze because it is so purely realistic; his style "has as its paradoxical intention not to produce a spectacle which appears real, but rather to turn reality into a spectacle."[15] That is, De Sica shoots the real streets and tenements of postwar Rome in such a way as to make them interesting in their own right—to defamiliarize them through the very novelty of realism in the face of the dominant studio-bound system. (The height of studio filming in major Western producing nations like France, Italy, Germany, and the United States had been in the 1920s, 1930s, and early 1940s. By 1948, extensive location filming was still a relative novelty, though it was soon to become more common.)

In spite of Bazin's claim that every shot in *Bicycle Thieves* was done on location, this is clearly not the case. The entire scene of the drive with the street cleaner was done with back projection. Some interiors—the various apartments and probably the brothel—were done in studio sets and are lit quite skillfully in the standard Hollywood three-point system (Fig. 7.7). Indeed, De Sica occasionally uses artificial light as well as reflectors in location scenes, rendering three-point lighting in the street (Fig. 7.8). Similarly, the extensive camera movements are technically impressive. The opening scene includes a crane shot that moves from an extreme-long view of the crowd by the employment agency down to reveal Ricci sitting in the foreground.

[15] Bazin, "De Sica: Metteur en Scène," p. 67.

The tracks with Ricci and Maria over the barren hills near their apartment, or those with Bruno and Ricci during their argument, or those with Ricci as he walks on the slope by the river are smooth, without the jouncing typical of much early location filming. Indeed, *Bicycle Thieves* had one of the highest budgets of any of the Neorealist films, and its very careful planning and execution show in the slickness of the finished film's style.

One could argue, of course, that this slickness of style works against realism, rather than rendering the purity and invisibility that Bazin claimed for it. After all, sunlight does not come from three directions out in the street, and a craning movement is normally one of the least self-effacing of camera techniques. For some critics, technical crudeness is associated with realism, since it conveys a sense of the filmmaker's lack of control over shooting conditions in documentary modes. Indeed, Bazin's praise for *Farrebique* and *Kon-Tiki* is based on that very notion. Yet realism is such an arbitrary concept, and we can appeal to so many different aspects of reality in order to motivate artistic devices, that there is no reason why technical crudeness should be the only possibility for realism. *Bicycle Thieves* seems to borrow techniques so familiar from classical studio filmmaking that they would seem invisible to most viewers: three-point lighting, the laying of tracks for smooth exterior camera movement, and so on. The viewer then would be led to concentrate upon the obvious authenticity suggested by the unglamorous faces and clothes of the characters, the vistas of tenements and streets, and so on. The same would hold true for the fact that a professional actor dubbed Ricci's voice, thereby eliminating possible distractions that the unskilled voice of non-actor Lamberto Maggiorani might have produced.

IDEOLOGY

Bazin takes *Bicycle Thieves* to be a Communist film, and he praises it as such.

Its social message is not detached, it remains immanent in the event, but it is so clear that nobody can overlook it, still less take exception to it, since it is never explicitly made a message. The thesis implied is wondrously and outrageously simple: in the world where this workman lives, the poor must steal from each other in order to survive.[16]

But it is not clear that this notion adds up to a pro-Communist stance. Indeed, given the film's objective approach and ambiguous ending, it

[16] Bazin, *"Bicycle Thief,"* p. 67.

is difficult to conclude that the film is advocating any particular approach to a solution. All directions seem equally closed to Ricci. After the police have informed him that they can help only if he finds the bike himself, he goes looking for his friend Biaocco; he first interrupts a Communist Party cell meeting (the nature of this group is not made clear in the English titles) to ask about Biaocco, but he is shushed by the speaker. Biaocco and his fellow street cleaners help in the search through the bike markets, but this comes to nothing. Finally, the charity of the wealthy volunteers in the church scene is shown to be condescending and superficial; they, too, have no inclination to help with an individual problem. This charity is the main alternative social institution which the film contrasts with the Communist Party, and neither is made to look particularly attractive. De Sica parallels the two scenes involving these institutions by having the rich lawyer who is leading the prayers glance around in annoyance when Ricci speaks too loudly—recalling the Communist speaker's shushing of Ricci in the earlier scene. Historian Ken Friedman suggests that this skeptical depiction of the Party resulted from changes in contemporary Italian society.

After the war, the groups [various leftist organizations] had formed a coalition and rather than seek a revolution, the Communist-dominated coalition sought election to political offices. At the time of the filming of *Bicycle Thieves* the economic condition of Italy was approaching a critical stage. . . . Thus, in 1947, the political transition from an anti-fascist unified front to political-social programs resulted from a break-down of the Communist-dominated coalition. *Bicycle Thieves*, then, finished turning the cinematic movement from one depicting the struggle and unification of postwar Italy to one of social criticism.[17]

De Sica chose to focus on an incident relating to unemployment, one of the most important problems of postwar Italy. Rejecting bureaucracy, the Communist Party, and upper-class charity as possible solutions, De Sica also portrays individual human action as offering little more in the way of hope.

Precisely because chance and coincidence are so prominent in the narrative's causal chain, the characters' situations seem to depend mostly on luck—and luck in this society seems usually to be bad. The film's ideology appears to be less Communist-oriented than a liberal, humanist view which refrains from placing the blame for the situation anywhere, but which also finds all potential solutions equally problem-

---

[17] Ken Friedman, "A History of Italian Cinema: 1945–1951," in *Literary and Socio-Economic Trends in Italian Cinema* (Los Angeles: Center for Italian Studies, Dept. of Italian, UCLA, 1973), p. 115.

atic. This notion of a balanced, rational, humanist outlook ultimately contributes to the film's impression of realism. It is not simply escapist fare which ignores the realities of the world by avoiding serious political subject matter; after all, De Sica faces up to the grim side of life. But neither is it propaganda, which promotes one view and hence is assumed to lack objectivity. The film's ambiguous ending reflects its "balanced" ideology.

Bicycle Thieves can end without adopting a definite ideological stance in part because the political implications of the story become submerged at the end in the drama between the father and son. Bruno's presence in the narrative thus serves, among many other functions, to create a compassionate tone that counterbalances the film's objective treatment of politics. This compassion and the emotional relationship between Ricci and Bruno probably have been a major reason why *Bicycle Thieves* has been one of the most popular of Neorealist films up to the present day.

CITATIONS OF THE CLASSICAL CINEMA

De Sica and scriptwriter Cesare Zavattini were consciously creating a realist alternative to the classical entertainment film. To underscore and make clear the nature of their departure from the norm, the filmmakers inserted into *Bicycle Thieves* a motif of ironic citations of the classical cinema, especially Hollywood films. Most obvious among these are the first two: as Ricci enters the poster office to receive his instructions, he passes a wall covered with posters for such films (Fig. 7.9); his first assignment the next day is to put up posters showing Rita Hayworth in a conventional glamor pose. The contrast between the types of characters portrayed in such films and those in *Bicycle Thieves* is clear enough. (Ricci's utter indifference to the subject matter of the poster also suggests how alien the glamor depicted is to his everyday life.) Later, more subtly, other movie references appear in the backgrounds of scenes: among the stalls Ricci and the street cleaners pass at the market is one covered with movie fan magazines. (Anna Magnani, by this point a famous star partly as a result of her role in *Open City*, is recognizable on the cover of a magazine in the very center of the stall; see Fig. 7.10.) In the brothel, we can catch a glimpse of a Clark Gable photograph on the wall behind the thief.

The implication of these references becomes quite clear during the drive in the street cleaner's truck as he takes Ricci and Bruno to the second flea market. Chatting about how rain spoils his Sunday off, the man remarks that he does not go to movies because he finds them boring. We must infer from this that he means ordinary popular films, and that he does not like them because they are so irrelevant to his life. Such a remark reflects the views of De Sica and especially of Zavattini, who wanted to make realistic films which they hoped would be of interest to working people. Ironically, they ended up making films treasured by the elite art-house audiences of foreign countries.

CONCLUSIONS: THE POPULARITY OF *BICYCLE THIEVES* IN THE UNITED STATES

As with other films of the Neorealist movement, *Bicycle Thieves* was more popular abroad than in Italy. The conservative Venice Film Festival ignored it, giving its 1948 award to Olivier's *Hamlet*. (The Venice prizes never went to Neorealist films and seldom to Italian ones; conventional quality British, French, and American films figured prominently in the top awards during the 1940s and 1950s.) But *Bicycle Thieves* won honors in other European countries, and by the time it was finally released in the United States in late 1949, it already had a high reputation. Critics praised it; it did well in the art cinemas and garnered the foreign-language awards of both the New York Film Critics and the Academy of Motion Picture Arts and Sciences. After the success of *Open City* and other films, American critics were well aware of the realist movement in postwar Italy. De Sica was widely compared with Rossellini, and the term "Neorealism" cropped up occasionally in these discussions.

Bicycle Thieves was perfectly calculated for the fast-growing art-cinema market in the United States, or, as *Variety* put it: "Commercially, the pic is a cinch to clean up in the art houses. It should also find limited bookings in some standard theatres."[18] The film provided a skillful blend of classical technique and realism. For American audiences, who were not personally concerned with the problems of postwar Italy, the film was entertainment in a new and defamiliarizing guise. While from our current perspective the film may seem more slick and conventional than realistic, we should remember that in 1949 it seemed in the forefront of a mildly avant-garde trend that set it apart from ordinary commercial cinema.

The contemporary reviews tend to suggest that the various aspects of the illusion of realism that I have been analyzing here were indeed perceived as realistic at the time. In relation to plot construction, for example, *Variety* found that the "picture moves along at an unaccus-

---

[18] "The Bicycle Thief," *Variety Film Reviews* (New York: Garland Publishing, 1983), vol. 8, 7 December 1949.

tomedly good pace for a foreign-made, except for one slack spot midway."[19] Unfortunately the reviewer did not specify which scene, but I suspect he meant the restaurant sequence, part of that section I described as dropping the tightly constructed search temporarily to concentrate on the father-son relationship.

Reviewers certainly considered the film to be realistic. *Variety* said De Sica was among those "who found in postwar Italy the raw materials for a new brand of naturalistic drama"; Bosley Crowther wrote that "the natural and the real are emphasized, with the film largely shot in actual settings and played by a non-professional cast." *Variety* even found the cinematography realistic: "Photography throughout is first rate in the hard manner of the U.S. documentary-type product." Critics noticed the lack of closure at the end as well. Crowther said, "it comes to a close with a fade-out as inconclusive as a passing nod," and *Newsweek*'s reviewer saw the ending as "the kind of restrained, dramatically inconclusive climax that is more usual in the well-written short story than on film."[20] Reviewers were well aware that the actors were nonprofessionals, and they praised their performances, especially that of Enzo Staiola as Bruno.

Perhaps most important, American reviewers were able to perceive the narrative, in spite of its basis in current Italian society, as universal in its thematic range. *Variety* considered that *Bicycle Thieves* had "a story incredible in its simplicity as the basis for a 90-minute film"; yet "while the story appears so narrow, it could hardly be broader. In its telling is the whole cosmic concept of right and wrong and of man's desperate need of security." Similarly, Crowther found that it had "a major—indeed, a fundamental and universal—dramatic theme. It is the isolation and loneliness of the little man in this complex social world that is ironically blessed with institutions to comfort and protect mankind. . . . De Sica is concerned here with something which is not confined to Rome nor solely originated by post-war disorder and distress." *Newsweek* also found that it "has a warm, human significance that avoids the well-trodden issues of class struggle and depravity born of chaos."

Such remarks are to a considerable extent appropriate to *Bicycle Thieves*, which manages to have things both ways: it criticizes contemporary Italian society, yet also creates a psychological drama that ultimately becomes the main concern and makes the film seem "univer-

---

[19] Ibid.
[20] Ibid.; Bosley Crowther, "The Bicycle Thief," *The New York Times Film Reviews* (New York: *New York Times* and Arno, 1970), vol. 4, p. 2380; "New Films," *Newsweek* (26 December 1949): 56.

sal" in a way that the issue of Italian unemployment never could. Surely, however, the American reviewers generalized *Bicycle Thieves* more than the film deserved. Its realism may have been a small change from the cinematic norms of its time, but it was a change nevertheless. *Bicycle Thieves* fit, in effect, into a growing conception of realism that, in the United States and Britain at least, was becoming a new norm—a realism dependent on the sort of psychological drama, unhappy ending, and ambiguous causality that characterized *Bicycle Thieves*; a realism that is a central trait of the institution of the art cinema. As we shall see in the next chapter, this new conception of realism helped create an interest in *Rules of the Game* which had not been aroused upon that film's first appearance.

8

An Aesthetic of Discrepancy:
The Rules of the Game

RULES'S DOMINANT

IF WE ASSUME, as I did in the previous chapter, that realism is a formal, historical trait of films, informing the levels of subject matter and narrative as well as of style, then wherein lies the realism of *Rules of the Game*? Its high-society subject matter and elaborate parallelisms immediately set it apart from *Bicycle Thieves*. André Bazin also had great insight into this film, however, and perhaps he, more than any other writer, has been responsible for the respect that the film community has for it today. This passage exemplifies both the strengths and weaknesses of Bazin's analysis.

One of the most paradoxically appealing aspects of Jean Renoir's work is that everything in it is so casual. He is the only film maker in the world who can afford to treat the cinema with such apparent offhandedness. It took Renoir to muster the audacity to film Gorki on the banks of the Marne or to handle the casting of *The Rules of the Game*, in which almost all the actors, except the servants, are so marvelously out of their usual characters. If one had to describe the art of Renoir in a word, one would define it as an aesthetic of discrepancy.[1]

Whether Renoir achieves his effects as effortlessly as Bazin seems to think is another matter altogether (he does call it "apparent offhandedness"). Bazin assumes, in a rather mystical fashion, that Renoir simply respects the nature of the settings, the actors, and the objects he films, allowing their reality to shine through his fiction and transform it. With formal analysis, we may be able to specify what devices Renoir uses to achieve this apparently effortless, casual effect. Yet Bazin's notion of discrepancy seems a valuable one, characterizing *Rules* more aptly perhaps than any other Renoir film. In neoformalist terms, Bazin is describing something about the film's dominant.

[1] André Bazin, *Jean Renoir*, trans. W. W. Halsey II and William H. Simon (New York: Simon and Schuster, 1973), p. 30.

I would suggest that *Rules* does achieve an effect of realism by creating discrepancies—but not simply between a constructed fiction and an essential reality which Renoir preserves intact. Rather, *Rules* contains within itself extensive structures based on classical filmmaking principles, and it uses these in large part as a background against which to place other structures that differ considerably from that tradition. The discrepancy between conventional classicism and these other elements pushes us to comprehend the latter as realistically motivated. Thus *Rules* does not assume a background of the classical film and depart entirely from it (as Bresson's or Tati's films do). Nor does it cite that background briefly in order to point up its own difference (as Ozu's films frequently do). Instead, the classical tradition remains extensively present in *Rules*, bound up inextricably, but also at odds with, the distinctively "Renoirian" traits that help make the film so intriguing. This juxtaposition of classical and nonclassical devices exists on all levels of the film: in the narrative line, in the spatial and temporal layout of the whole, and even in the formal structures of the thematic material. (In this it differs from *Bicycle Thieves*, in which certain techniques are made "invisible" by conforming them to classical usage—editing, sound—while other techniques depart from classicism in the direction of realism.) In terms of the latter, *Rules* deals with the contrast between conventional and social appearances and nonconventional departures from them. Thus the device of discrepancy between conventions and departures from the norm acts as a dominant in the same way as overlap does in *Les Vacances de Monsieur Hulot* and separation does in *Tout va bien*.

NARRATIVE: PARALLELISM VERSUS AMBIGUITY

One of the film's most noticeable features involves the extensive, systematic, and explicit use of parallelism. Critics invariably point to the comparison drawn between the classes of servant and master as a whole, between the hunt and the fête, and between various specific characters. André and Marceau are both poachers—Marceau literally and metaphorically—and their simultaneous attempts to seduce other men's wives eventually merge to cause André's death. Robert and Schumacher are the outraged husbands, both fighting their rivals in the course of the fête. Octave resembles Marceau in some ways, Christine seems inclined to emulate some traits of Lisette. *Rules* makes these parallels very explicit indeed, as when Marceau remarks that André was killed like an animal in a hunt, or when Corneille, ordered by Robert to "Stop this farce," inquires, "Which one?" Virtually any viewer notices most of these parallels on first seeing the film, yet critics often spend an inordinate proportion of their analyses dealing with them. This is one example of how an insistence on interpretation as the primary critical tool renders films banal: critics, using interpretation of already explicit meanings, simply automatize the basic structures of *Rules*, while downplaying the systematically challenging structures that lend it much of its interest.

Parallelism gives the film an appearance of tight narrative construction. Characters and actions have been carefully laid out to match or contrast with each other, and since there are many characters and events, a dense weave of interrelationships results. Partly because of the parallels, we are able to keep track of the basic story line easily. There may be many characters, but they are all concerned with conventional appearances, with fickle versus faithful love, with honesty, and so forth. Indeed, parallelisms become so important that they play almost as great a role in unifying the film as does causality.

The parallelisms are part of a general application of certain principles of eighteenth-century French drama. *Rules* cites this tradition, primarily in its opening titles, which include a quotation from Beaumarchais's *The Marriage of Figaro*. (This quotation returns in the fête sequence, where the first shot begins on a close-up of sheet music on the piano that has sketches of cupids aiming arrows—echoing the end of the Beaumarchais text, "If love has wings/ Is it not to fly?") Canons of classical French drama had gone to extremes in demanding perfect motivation of the causal chain, accompanied by a unity of time and space. Common conventions of comedy involved mistaken identity, disguise, the frequent switching of romantic partners, and parallels between masters and servants. *Rules* adopts some of these devices, but in a selective, self-conscious way.

Against such careful structuring, however, the film places its unconventional narrative aspects. Tight parallelism and traditional genre conventions are important, but because the film withholds a few crucial events and character motives, parts of the film remain unexplained or ambiguous. The unclarity arises primarily because the narration refuses to provide information about Christine and André's relationship in the period before his flight across the Atlantic. Yet we are apt at first not to notice the omission of this part of the fabula events. The narration of *Rules* seems to be particularly objective, with a wide range and depth of knowledge that it imparts to us in a communicative fashion. From the very first scene, the narration establishes its ability to move from character to character at important moments in the action: when André mentions Christine to the radio interviewer, we move at once to Christine's bedroom. Using crosscutting, the narration provides us with an introduction to the woman under discussion (though her expression as she turns off the radio does not indicate her reaction). Similarly, we soon see Octave's and Robert's responses. When Robert phones his mistress, we also see her immediately, and the appointment that they then set up soon leads to a meeting in which they discuss their relationship. In short, we are given the impression that the narration will take us to the most causally salient space and time, freely presenting us with information. Moreover, the narration seems completely knowledgeable: we do not form any spatial attachment to a single character or group that would limit what we find out about the others. The narration knows all the characters equally well. Hence we may consider the film's narrative particularly dense; we get a great deal of information in quick succession (sometimes simultaneously) about a large number of characters. (By way of contrast, Bresson's films quickly flaunt their own narrations' refusal to give us much access to fabula information.) Yet, arbitrarily, *Rules*'s narration withholds information about Christine's past and present reactions—information that we would need to construct a fabula line without ambiguities.

As part of its apparent communicativeness, the narration fills us in on some past fabula events—those events that occurred before André's airplane lands in the opening scene. Here is the basic information we learn about previous events, virtually all of which is given to us in early scenes, or when we first meet the relevant character.

1. Octave and Christine grew up together in Vienna, where Octave was studying under her father, a famous conductor, now dead. Octave has failed to become a conductor.
2. Marceau lost his job as an upholsterer as a result of the Depression.
3. Robert and Geneviève have been lovers for over three years.
4. Christine and Robert married about three years ago.
5. Lisette and Schumacher married about two years ago.
6. Lisette and Octave have carried on a flirtation or affair for some time.
7. Saint-Aubin has admired Christine for some time.
8. Christine has known André for some months, inspiring him to prove his love for her by flying the Atlantic.
9. Recently, Robert and Christine have planned a hunting party at their chateau.
10. Recently, Schumacher has written a letter asking for Lisette to be transferred to the chateau.

Most of this information involves characters' situations and relationships, rather than specific events that immediately cause the effects seen in early scenes. André's comments over the radio form the precipitating cause that affects all the other relationships in some way during the course of the film. (The hunting party constitutes another isolated event, serving as a motivation for gathering all the characters together so that their interactions can be presented in a compressed fashion.)

But the apparently communicative narration actually holds back a few bits of crucial fabula information that would allow us to understand the cause of André's outburst and also the various results it brings. Specifically, we never learn what happened during those few months of friendship between André and Christine. Did they have an affair? Was she in love with André but faithful to her husband? Did she consider André simply as a friend? Was she unsure of her own feelings? What did she do to lead him to expect her to love him? In spite of the fact that there is considerable talk about their relationship, we find out very little about it. (The same sorts of ambiguities arise, more obliquely, concerning Saint-Aubin's admiration for Christine. Has she encouraged him in some way? Her question to Lisette about friendship with a man could apply to him as well, as we learn when Christine unexpectedly turns to him first during the fête.)

One conventional way of giving us information about Christine and André's relationship would be the inclusion of a flashback to scenes of them together before his flight. They might also speak of the relationship, to each other or to someone else. Strangely, they never discuss it together and say little about it to their friends. We might expect to be filled in by André in the dialogue between him and Octave after the car crash, but rather than telling his friend about Christine, he simply denounces Robert and says once again that he flew the Atlantic for Christine's sake. Later, Octave assures Robert that nothing has happened between André and Christine—but how does he know? Is he right?

Essentially, we know only the effect of the relationship on André. He is in love with Christine. We need to know little more about him, since his main function is to precipitate changes in the existing relationships. Around Christine, however, the rest of the narrative action pivots, and we know little of her motives and feelings.

Much of what we find out about her comes through the remarks of other characters. Virtually everyone summarizes her character at one or more points. This is a standard way for narration to convey information about characters, but, again, we have difficulty judging which characters have a basis for what they say. Geneviève considers her an unsophisticated foreigner, but this may be her Parisian chauvinism. More than once Octave suggests that Christine is still like a child and needs protection—yet she handles the speech about friendship very well on her own and at least acts the sophisticate in her conversation with Geneviève the morning after the hunt. (Christine seems to believe Octave is the one in need of protection; her declaration of love for Octave includes her statement that she will take care of him: "Je vais m'occuper de toi"; it recalls the words used by Lisette in the scene in which the two women discuss having children: "Seulement ça occupe beaucoup.") Jackie tells André he is wasting his time with Christine, but she may say this out of jealousy. Almost any character's view of Christine may be suspect in a film that emphasizes the keeping up of appearances.

The narration creates no comparable suppression of motivations or past actions with respect to other characters. On the simplest level, there is a cluster of minor figures who are characterized in the fashion of classical theatrical comedy, with one trait apiece. Among the upper-class characters, there is Charlotte, with her passion for card playing; Madame La Bruyère, who is a hypochondriac; the homosexual, about whom we learn only that he *is* a homosexual; the general, with his devotion to traditional aristocratic values; and so on. Serving as a sort of chorus and cross section of high society (the people for whom Christine must keep up appearances), they add an ironic touch to most scenes—most importantly, serving to focus the final scene primarily on Robert's and Christine's behavior rather than on André's death. *Rules* becomes a bitter satire rather than a tragedy largely as a result of these characters, but they need not in themselves be complex to perform their functions. Similarly, most of the servants either are made up of one trait apiece (Corneille's Jeeves-like competence, the chauffeur's anti-Semitism, the cook's pragmatism) or receive no individual characterization at all. In general, these minor figures provide the norm of straightforward characterization against which Christine's ambiguous behavior stands out.

The other major characters fall midway between these two extremes. Each consists of a cluster of fairly clear-cut traits to which the narration gives us access, since they frequently express their attitudes and their opinions of each other. They may be insincere or changeable, but we usually realize this as well. On the whole, they remain consistent and behave as we might expect them to—*except* when they are dealing with Christine. Since none of them seems to understand her thoroughly, their responses to her make their own actions take on a degree of the ambiguity that characterizes her. Octave, for example, usually behaves in a reasonably consistent fashion, but his reaction to Christine's declaration of love is difficult to interpret. We begin to ask the same questions about him that we have asked primarily about her. Does he really suddenly realize that he loves Christine romantically, or is he simply saying what he feels she wants him to say (that is, is he protecting her again)? On the whole, however, the characters are not obscure. For example, Robert continues to act as we would expect from his declarations of love for Christine and his self-confessed weakness, which permits other characters to manipulate him. Geneviève declares her desire to stay with Robert early on, and although she later professes to be willing to break with him, the scene hints that she actually wishes to continue their relationship; her behavior at the fête confirms these hints. Marceau, Schumacher, and Lisette all behave as their statements and actions would lead us to expect (e.g., Marceau's obvious immediate attraction to Lisette, Schumacher's threat to shoot Marceau, Lisette's opinions about flirtation).

Christine remains the source of most of the narrative ambiguity, and this brings up the issue of acting in *Rules*. Since the film's initial release, critics have commented universally on the acting in certain roles. Bazin argued that all the upper-class roles were cast against type, and that the resulting incongruities were exploited by Renoir for realistic purposes. Other writers have pointed to Renoir's own performance as Octave, occasionally to Dalio's supposed physical inappropriateness as a French aristocrat, and, inevitably, to Nora Gregor's physical and histrionic "problems" as Christine. Alexander Sesonske, in his generally useful analysis, found Gregor "cold and stiff," but he saw this as thematically appropriate to her position as the foreigner unable to fit into French society. Raymond Durgnat remarked on her "lack of dramatic experience" and claimed that her addition to the cast altered Christine's characterization (with the implication that she was inadequate to the demands of the original script). Christopher Faulkner found her performance inadequate, posing a "critical enigma." Gerald Mast considered her physically unattractive and generally miscast, but he followed Bazin in finding in this miscasting the advantages of added ambiguity and mystery.[2] Some of these writers convey the impression that Gregor was inexperienced, and that Renoir cast her

---

[2] Alexander Sesonske, *Jean Renoir: The French Films 1924–1939* (Cambridge: Harvard University Press, 1980), p. 418; Raymond Durgnat, *Jean Renoir* (Berkeley: University of California Press, 1974), p. 186; Christopher Faulkner, *Jean Renoir: A Guide to References and Resources* (Boston: G. K. Hall, 1979), p. 120; Gerald Mast, *Filmguide to The Rules of the Game* (Bloomington: Indiana University Press, 1973), p. 22.

simply because he saw certain qualities in her that he felt fitted the role. In reality, Gregor had been a silent film actress (most notably in Dreyer's 1924 *Michael* at UFA) and had gone to Hollywood to star in a few German versions of MGM films during the short-lived period of multiple-language productions around 1930. She had apparently been away from films since the early 1930s, but she was hardly an inexperienced amateur. In looking at her performance, we should ask whether its oddnesses are due to inadequacy or to some other reason, and whether Christine's ambiguities result from Gregor's performance. I would argue that, in fact, her performance, like Renoir's, Dalio's, and Roland Toutain's, is adequate for her role. As we have seen, the narration systematically treats Christine differently from the other characters, omitting her key past actions and providing her with few moments when she expresses her feelings and opinions in the open way the other characters do.

In general the casting follows the overall strategy of the film by including a considerable number of actors whose looks and behavior are consistent with classical conventions of film acting; against these portrayals, the main performances of the non-servant roles stand out as more realistic. Carette was known for his comic servant roles; similarly, Paulette Dubost had played maids in earlier French films; and Gaston Modot had been in films for decades, playing everything from comic roles to brooding villains. All three play exactly as one might expect, slightly broadly, as cuckold (Modot) or clown (Carette). Marceau's little gesture as he leads Robert off to see his rabbit snares (Fig. 8.1) is one example of the exaggerations conventional to such a role. The actors in minor roles play in even broader fashion. For example, after Madame La Bruyère's request for coarse salt, the assistant cook rolls his eyes heavenward (Fig. 8.2). The homosexual's behavior is not far from the Franklin Pangborn school of acting, and in general the bit players could all transfer directly into a Hollywood society comedy with no questions asked.

Against these extensive examples of standard acting of the period, the actors in the main upper-class roles stand out to varying degrees. Mila Parely, as Geneviève, is perhaps closest to the norm. Yet interestingly, because we know her to be the affected, sophisticated Parisian, we are led to see her performance *as* a performance, and to seek to determine the "real" feelings behind her affectations. The central moment here comes after her statement to Robert in the marsh that she is also bored with him and willing to break off. A sudden close-up of her, turning away from Robert, privileges the moment when she asks for an adieu that will take her back three years, to when Christine

225

did not yet exist (Fig. 8.3). The intensity behind her words is revealed to us rather than to Robert (out of focus, not looking at her), suggesting that her feelings belie her words. Dalio, as Robert, probably seems to most modern audiences perfectly suited to his role; the incongruity apparently sensed by some 1939 viewers of a Jewish actor playing a French aristocrat has presumably been lost for most modern spectators. Indeed, his appearance now seems completely suitable, his gestures and expressions skillful—as in his sudden lapse from elegant to frantic movements when Robert drops a screw, in his sweeping snap of the fingers to signal to Marceau that the coast is clear, and in his famous series of triumphant but embarrassed glances at the audience and his new limonaire during its presentation at the fête.

Modern audiences probably have more trouble with Toutain's alternation of wild outbursts and stolid silences as André—yet, at the time, he was a star of action B pictures in France and known to be a sports car driver in private life. He would seem to have been cast to type, at least for 1939 audiences. But even today his performance seems functional, given that we are not supposed to concentrate on André's own reactions, but on the effects his actions have on those around him. Certainly he shares with Renoir and Gregor a physical awkwardness which tends to undercut him as a conventional romantic hero—yet, again, that is not what he is supposed to be. Renoir's performance goes one step further from the classical norm contained within the film. He speaks far more rapidly than is usual and uses very broad gestures, especially in the dialogue after the car crash.

Even more problematically, Gregor certainly does not fit the conventional role of the romantic heroine, especially the *femme fatale* to whom so many of the men in the film are drawn. She is not particularly beautiful, is a bit old to play a naive bride of three years, and is somewhat clumsy (note her awkward gestures backstage early in the fête scene, as she reacts to Geneviève's embracing Robert); she tends to gaze with little change of expression at the other actors as they speak. Yet this and all the other unconventional performances in the film suggest a realistic motivation. If we do not want to reject these performances, we can justify them by appealing to notions such as (1) not all people behave in the same way (some do gesture broadly, others are inexpressive); (2) people who are less than gorgeous fall in love (indeed, couples who are as glamorous as movie stars are exceptional in reality); and (3) we do not always understand why people act as they do. Indeed, a couple of critics have pointed out that the fight between André and Saint-Aubin may look silly, but that it is probably closer to a real fight than are the choreographed fisticuffs of the Hollywood western.[3] This, I take it, is exactly the sort of justification *Rules* invites us to make for certain of its performances.

Looked at in this way, Gregor's acting probably conveys to us everything that the script provided in the way of character traits and reactions for Christine. When she jokes with Octave on her bed, her speech, "I don't wish to be the ruin of a great hero . . . ," gives us quite a bit of insight into her attitude. Gregor delivers it mockingly, affecting the pompous tones of an oration, and Octave smiles in response. This moment—reflected in both the lines themselves and the delivery—reveals Christine to be less naive than some other characters (and, following them, some critics) assume her to be. She clearly knows the conventions required to face the public and disguise one's feelings. This little moment with Octave motivates her later ability to give the slick speech that covers the awkward situation of André's arrival at the chateau; there she represents herself not as his "ruin" but as the friendly inspirer of the "great hero." Gregor is not inadequate in this speech, nor in the other moments that hint at Christine's feelings. Her half-amused, half-bored reaction when Madame La Bruyère begins telling her about diphtheria vaccine suggests that Christine may be tired of her upper-class hostess role; this helps explain why she would turn to as many as three potential lovers during the fête. Her lines in the hunting scene about having lost her taste for shooting tend to confirm this indication. (The point here is *not* that she is a sensitive soul because only she fails to enjoy the slaughter of the animals.) Her desire for children leads us in the same direction. Note that the reason she wants them (not conveyed in the subtitles) is because they fill one's time. When Lisette says, "It's necessary to spend all one's time with them, or else there's no point in having them," Christine replies, "That's what is wonderful. I don't think of anything else anymore." (This response seems to contradict Lisette's earlier claim to Octave that thinking about André is what keeps Christine awake at night—yet another case of a character's judgment of Christine seeming questionable.) Similarly, in her other scenes with Octave, Gregor is as expressive as the role allows. It is the narration, rather than the acting, that renders Christine ambiguous, and her ambivalence ripples out at times into the other characters and their actions.

If the tight structure of the classical French drama, particularly its parallelisms, provides the narrative background contained in *Rules*, then the film's mixture of tones and its ambiguities form the main departures from tradition. For a film that cites classical drama, *Rules*

---

[3] Mast, *Filmguide*, p. 54; Sesonske, *Jean Renoir*, p. 402.

seems reluctant to fall into a recognized genre; it remains an uneasy blend of comic and tragic conventions. The various switches of romantic partners and cases of mistaken identity lead to death rather than to a neat set of happy couples. Yet André's death comes as the result of an accident in the midst of his dishonorable action of stealing his host's wife—hardly the heroic death of the great French tragedies (e.g., Hippolytus's dispatch by a sea monster, described in such exalted terms in Racine's *Phedre*). As with the acting, the sudden switches of tone and the ambiguities in the narrative can most easily be justified by an appeal to realistic motivation. Reality is not structured, and therefore it admits of incongruities and ambiguities. We do not always understand people; therefore we may not understand their actions. Gaps in the story information provided by the narration suggest incompleteness. While in the classical film we usually know everything we need to know, we acknowledge that in reality we can never know anything completely. Ambiguity thus becomes one way of cueing us to take the film's narrative as realistic.

From the late 1940s on, as a result of the success of the international art cinema, ambiguity as a cue for realism became a familiar convention. Italian Neorealist films like *Bicycle Thieves*, with their open endings and chance events, were among the first films to draw on this notion extensively. Later, when New Wave films rebelled against the current classical French norm, the "Cinema of Quality," they did so in part through an appeal to realism. Location shooting and other stylistic traits were important, but these films also used loose plotting and causal gaps and suspension (as in the freeze-frame ending of *The 400 Blows*) to create ambiguities. Antonioni's psychological dramas, Bergman's increasingly enigmatic symbolism, and similar qualities that served to endear the European art film to American intellectuals all solidified the association of ambiguity with realism—a realism invariably contrasted with the too-neat, too-obvious Hollywood film.

Unfortunately for Renoir, ambiguity was *not* a convention so readily graspable as realistic for those few viewers who saw *Rules* in 1939. Certainly some European films with pretentions to high art had utilized it in the 1920s. *The Cabinet of Dr. Caligari*, for example, has an ambiguous ending (is that doctor really a kindly fellow, or is he as sinister as Caligari himself?). Epstein's *La Glace à trois faces* is structured entirely around our inability to determine which, if any, of the three very different accounts of a man given by his three lovers is accurate. (Here the title and other strong contextual cues warn us that ambiguity is the dominant.) These and other 1920s films like them were explicitly marked as radical departures from Hollywood film canons, and, like the later generation of "art movies," they appealed mostly to intellectual viewers interested in complex filmic forms and in challenges to interpretive strategies. The major nonclassical stylistic movements had gone out of existence by the early 1930s; by then, challenges to classicism often made more direct appeals to realism. Early forerunners of Neorealism appeared in a number of countries: Walter Ruttmann's *Accaio* (1933) in Italy, Renoir's *Toni* (1935) in France, Ozu's *An Inn in Tokyo* (1935) in Japan. These films, however, did not depend on ambiguity as a cue for realism, but on more obvious choices, such as location shooting, working class milieus, and Depression-oriented subject matter (in contrast with the studio glamor of the classical cinema).

Given this situation, Renoir's strange mélange of classical narrative norms and ambiguous causality and characterization would be likely to present too great a challenge to 1939 audiences. Whether the adverse reactions of viewers were due, as Renoir seemed to believe, to their resentment of the film's social commentary is difficult to determine now. Given that they seem frequently to have found the character of Octave incomprehensible (Renoir's subsequent cuts mainly involved this role), I suspect that at least part of the problem resulted from a simple lack of appropriate viewing skills—not surprising in the late 1930s. Claude Gauteur's invaluable article "*La Règle du jeu* et la critique en 1939" points out that the critical reception of *Rules* was not unanimously adverse. But, as Gauteur suggests, the unqualifiedly hostile reviews tended to appear in the large-circulation journals like *Le Matin, Le Figaro, Paris-Midi*, and others that would have had considerable impact. Those reviewers who gave favorable notices often did have reservations, usually about the performances of Gregor and Renoir. The most positive discussions came in small, specialized film and art journals, such as Maurice Bessy's review in *Cinémonde*.[4]

Gauteur classifies the reviews. A few attacked Renoir as a left-wing filmmaker. More frequently they simply could not comprehend the mixture of genres, as in this typical reaction:

What does Mr. Jean Renoir want to do? That is a question which I asked myself at length in leaving this strange performance. A satiric comedy in the genre that made Frank Capra's fortune? But this laborious fantasy, rendered in heavy dialogue, is exactly the opposite of the ironic spirit. A comedy of manners? Whose manners, since the characters don't belong to any known

---

[4] Quoted in Claude Gauteur, "*La Règle du jeu* et la critique en 1939," *La Revue du cinéma image et son* no. 282 (March 1974): 56.

social type? A drama? The intrigue is carried on in such a puerile way that one cannot linger over this hypothesis. (James de Coquet, *Le Figaro*)[5]

Other reviewers expressed basically the same opinion.

The characterization also came in for criticism; speaking of the fête scene, one reviewer declared:

All this confusion amuses us, then begins to disturb us. We realize that we are now two-thirds through the film, and that we know basically nothing about the main characters. Mr. Renoir has seized upon their tics and their appearances marvelously. But beyond that, we can't distinguish anything. If the director wanted to show us the emptiness of their heads and their hearts, he has gone too far. Even with people who are like comic butterflies, there remains in spite of everything a certain consistency in their desires or their tastes. One doesn't describe a rich man just through his mania for collecting musical boxes. (François Vinnueil, *L'Action Francaise*)[6]

Thus, though some recognized the intriguing qualities of *Rules* immediately (and, interestingly, they were mostly film historians), the overall response was incomprehension.

However, the revival of the reconstructed film at the 1959 Venice Film Festival and the gradual rediscovery of it throughout the 1960s propitiously coincided with the period of greatest interest in the art cinema, when the ambiguity/reality convention had been firmly established. As we saw in the previous chapter, ambiguity is far from being the only way to cue realistic motivation, and that is not its invariable use. Indeed, the different circumstances surrounding *Rules*'s initial appearance and its revival evidence the historically specific nature of realistic motivation.

SPACE AND TIME

The filmic techniques that create space in *Rules* follow a dominant strategy similar to that of the narrative level. For example, the film contains many segments handled with Hollywood-style sets, lighting, framing, and editing. Some conversations are rendered through shot/reverse shot and other continuity devices of decoupage, with each actor lit with a three-point setup. Yet other scenes contain considerable departures from classical Hollywood usage: the careful matching of location work and studio settings goes beyond what Hollywood typically did, and the huge, multi-roomed chateau set and narrow, four-walled corridor are unusual. The increased camera movement permitted by

[5] Quoted ibid., p. 60.
[6] Quoted ibid., p. 61.

such sets is thought of as specifically "Renoirian." Many scenes also avoid shot/reverse shot, keeping more characters onscreen at once than is typical in the classical film.

Bazin's concentration on offscreen space and depth as traits of realism in this film was undoubtedly correct. Though, as I have suggested, no filmic trait is innately realistic, in the context of this film, these techniques combine to suggest a realistic space. The narrative, with its subject matter of contemporary social mores and its systematic mixture of tones and use of ambiguities, would cue us in that direction. Beyond this, all the sonic and visual devices combine to suggest a space that extends consistently in all directions. The offscreen space is not undermined by inconsistent or impossible cues, as in *Vampyr*,[7] or kept fairly neutral, as in *Siegfried*. Through frequent revelation or concealment of offscreen space via figure movement, camera movement, set design, and offscreen sound, *Rules* appeals to our schemata of space in the real world. Real space has no limits; there is always something behind what we look at, behind us, and on every side. Only a limited stretch of space becomes part of the diegetic world of any film's story, but the filmmaker can choose techniques that emphasize or de-emphasize offscreen space as a consistent extension of seen space.

In *Rules*, set design is crucial to creating our sense of an unusually extensive and consistent space. A few sets respect the classical norm: the design of Christine's bedroom in the Paris house resembles that of a bedroom in a Hollywood film. But the ground floor of the chateau was built as a unit, which would not ordinarily be done in Hollywood-style filming. There had been multi-roomed sets built in the United States since at least the early 1910s, but a unit including more than two or three rooms would be unusual. Eugene Lourie, Renoir's set designer, built the chateau interior to fit the exterior appearance of the real chateau used for the location work; he conceived the large entry hallway as a hub for the rest of the rooms.

I wanted to build all the rooms of this floor on the same set to clarify the visual connections between rooms and allow Jean more fluidity in staging the continuous chase of Modot after the elusive Carette. It would offer a more elegant way of shooting, without obliging the camera to cut from one set to another. By combining the two stages, I would have a useful area of about 150 by 60 feet.[8]

[7] David Bordwell, *The Films of Carl-Theodor Dreyer* (Berkeley: University of California Press, 1981), pp. 103–109.
[8] Eugene Lourie, *My Work in Films* (New York: Harcourt Brace Jovanovich, 1985), p. 62.

Lourie went for historical authenticity as well as for continuous space; he bought a real seventeenth-century oak staircase and built the hallway around it. He also avoided the normal French production practice of using painted paper on the floors, substituting real parquet and simulating marble with concrete slabs. The rooms were decorated in different period styles to give a sense of successive owners' changes; the mirrors in the Paris house were designed to suggest an actual fashion in rich interiors of the late 1930s. The lengthy corridor on the upper floor, so flashily shown off in its entirety when the camera pans with Robert (Figs. 8.4, 8.5, and 8.6), would have been unusual for a classical film. Its extreme length and nearly complete set of four walls (with only a small gap behind the camera to accommodate the crew and equipment) indicate a consistent attempt at verisimilitude in the settings. (Other examples of such interiors include the servants' dining hall and kitchen—another extremely deep set—and the large hallway with central staircase in the Paris house.)

Few critics have spent much time examining the set design of *Rules*, even though it involves perhaps the most obviously realistic group of devices in the entire film. Bazin dwells on the framing used to show the space, yet the extensive camera movements and depth would have been impossible without sets that could accommodate them. Perhaps Bazin assumed, as many viewers seem to, that even the interiors were shot on location, and certainly Lourie's sets manage to suggest a real chateau's interior with remarkable success. (One indication of his skill comes at the cut from a location exterior view of Corneille holding an umbrella over Geneviève [Fig. 8.7] to a track-in toward the door as she stands inside greeting other guests in the hallway [Fig. 8.8]. It is difficult to detect that the shift to the studio setting comes here, and not at the subsequent cut to an interior view of the hall; the matching of the sets is virtually perfect.)

The sets in *Rules* furnish a good example of how realism can be created through elaborate formal manipulation. Lourie has recalled: "From the outset of our scouting we were determined to shoot the interior scenes on sound stages. Renoir, as usual, preferred the controlled conditions of a set to the haphazard accommodations of location shooting."[9] Indeed, the careful lighting of the sets, and of the narrow upstairs corridor in particular, would have been impossible to achieve in comparable location interiors. Through careful planning and the coordination of stylistic devices, the filmmakers achieve the effect of realistic space.

[9] Ibid., p. 57.

Renoir did not work with Lourie on the designs, nor did he have them done with specific framings in mind. According to Lourie, delays in the location shooting prevented Renoir from familiarizing himself with the sets until shortly before he began to work in the studio. Indeed, "the ballroom set, with the adjoining corridor at the back, gave Jean definite ideas on how to stage the ball sequence and the beginning of the Schumacher chase."[10] Lourie, who had worked on earlier Renoir films, seems to have planned ahead to allow Renoir maximum flexibility for his characteristic deep staging and camera movements. In doing so, Lourie may have even exaggerated his previous design principles in a way that allowed Renoir to push those techniques further than in his earlier films.

With this possibility of suggesting extensive continuous space within the chateau, Renoir creates an intricate weave of stylistic devices that once again place cues for realistic time, space, and action against the background of more conventional usage. Most of the stylistic devices are coordinated around the suggestion of a high degree of bustling activity and interaction among the characters. This is not surprising, since *Rules* is a social satire, geared toward generalizing from the actions of a representative set of characters. In this sense, realism in *Rules* could be seen as having an ideological purpose: to enable us to see the film's fairly broad and obvious thematic material as applicable to contemporary French society, *Rules* asks us to perceive the central characters as realistic, and as part of a dense pattern of action.

The sense of bustle and interaction infuses the spatial and temporal levels alike. While in the Hollywood cinema we have a sense that one major action takes place after another (hence the linearity attributed to that mode), in *Rules* the rhythm of actions seems quicker because of simultaneity. Space seems constantly shifting and extensive, with frequent changes and dense staging.

The staging of action forms the basis for the camera movements, for the activation of offscreen space, and for other realistic techniques. To a greater degree than in most classical films, *Rules*'s characters are often in frenetic movement. There are relatively static conversations, of course, especially in the first few scenes, but even some of the main expository scenes take place with the characters moving restlessly about, sometimes turning their backs on us (a device not common in Hollywood until *Citizen Kane* became influential). For example, in Christine's conversation with Robert just after the radio broadcast in the first sequence, the shot/reverse shot and reframing pans are famil-

---

[10] Ibid., pp. 66, 69.

iar enough from Hollywood films; but Robert moves away from Christine while they talk (his movement being motivated by his action of putting the mechanical doll on a table). For part of his important speech asking her why she did not go to the airport, his back is turned. Christine spins about as she expresses her relief. In general characters in the film seldom stay still for long. In comparable American films of the same period, for example, *Holiday* and *Ninotchka*, the characters sit for lengthy conversations. (Note how often Hollywood characters sit or lean casually against things so that they are kept in fixed spots for shot/reverse shot.) In *Rules*, the only lengthy scene of shot/reverse shot among seated figures comes with the servants' dinner, and there the brief introductions of new characters, the large number of characters who speak (often from offscreen), and the comings and goings in the background prevent the scene from creating any sense of static positions.

Other scenes again place the character so that he or she is facing away from the camera. We first see Geneviève seated with her back to us, on the phone with Robert. In her conversation with Christine at the chateau, both women turn away from the camera at one point, this time motivated by Geneviève's packing and crossing to the dresser. In all such cases, we can appeal to notions of realism to explain any lack of narrative clarity that might result from our being unable to see appearances or reactions.

The bustling staging returns frequently. Octave and Robert seem to settle down on the sofa, to discuss André's invitation to the chateau, with a standard shot/reverse shot handling (Figs. 8.9 and 8.10). Yet Octave stands up almost immediately, and shot/reverse shot becomes mixed with camera movement until finally they both move into an extreme-long shot framing; this distant view continues as they move around the central table, with Octave giving his important lines about people all having their reasons. The layout of this scene is typical of the film, with the characters refusing to light anywhere; the decoupage uses, then drifts away from, a classical scene breakdown.

The arrival at the chateau intensifies the use of bustling movement, since here all the characters come together. Geneviève's entrance triggers the first of the many framings in which minor characters move quickly in and out of the frame. A whole series of characters greets her, creating a breathless pace. At first, such moments are fairly simple; the basic action here is just the greeting of Geneviève, and we have no need to be able to distinguish the various characters and gestures. The greeting is a "landing" in the staircase construction of the entire scene. As this business ends, the camera moves in for a balanced two-shot of Robert welcoming Geneviève, and the film thus avoids any risk of our missing their reactions.

This scene does prepare us for the arrival of André, however, which is handled in a similar but more complex fashion. Robert hastens forward to shake hands with André, and immediately other guests cluster about (though note the careful clearing away of characters so that we can concentrate on the general's speech to André about being of a dying race—the beginning of an important motif). During Christine's speech about being André's friend, the shot is dense with movement and multiple centers of interest. It begins with a simple close-up of her, with André in the background (Fig. 8.11); the camera then pulls back to a balanced two-shot framing (Fig. 8.12), into the background of which walk Octave and Robert, frowning nervously (Fig. 8.13). As Christine continues, they begin to smirk, and the framing pulls back (Fig. 8.14) to a *plan américain* of the group as they congratulate Christine and Robert proposes the fête (Fig. 8.15). The camera follows him to Charlotte (Fig. 8.16), then back as Christine sets the date (Fig. 8.17). The shot ends after a pan with Octave to the stairs (Fig. 8.18); he remains there with Geneviève after the other characters exit right. This shot demonstrates how *Rules* creates the sense of almost constant movement, of both figure and frame, but also takes care to make sure we notice important actions, even when they occur simultaneously.

Unless we are willing to notice and scan these overlapping actions, we will miss a great deal, and the film cues us as to this device's importance. It is bared in the scene between André and Octave in their bedroom, just after the busy corridor actions, when André asks, "T'as fini de gesticuler comme ça?" as Octave moves restlessly about. Similarly, the shot that lingers over Robert's rapid glances at his limonaire, the crowd, and the floor (Fig. 8.19) stresses the ceaseless activity of the actor. (Such shifting glances, comic and touching at this point, return in a more sinister fashion as Robert behaves much the same way when giving his guests his speech about André's death—see Fig. 8.29).

As with most of the film's other stylistic devices, the busy movements intensify in the fête scene. (Indeed, like many highly original films, *Rules* gradually increases the complexity of all its devices, cueing the spectator as to the viewing skills needed to perceive them.) Backstage (shot 229),[11] Christine reacts to Geneviève's embracing Robert, then grabs Saint-Aubin and exits with him as André watches;

---

[11] All shot numbers are from the decoupage in *L'Avant scène cinéma* no. 52 (October 1962).

this shot is so dense with action as to be nearly illegible. Quite a number of the shots that move among various characters during the subsequent searches, chases, and fights are similarly difficult to grasp in a single viewing. The fight between André and Robert, with combatants and books flying into the shot from offscreen, and the chase through the crowded dance floor exemplify the film's increasing use of frenetic and simultaneous actions.

There would be a variety of possibilities for treating such staging in the framing and decoupage. A Soviet montage film would be likely to break it down into many short shots, while a classical film might keep the action relatively shallow, with frequent reframings and perhaps relatively lengthy shots (as in the fast-paced pressroom scenes of *His Girl Friday*). Renoir combines his staging with framings that create considerable depth at certain points. This device occurs increasingly as the film continues, paralleling the growing complexity and increasing pace of the action.

Really deep stagings do not appear until the scene of Octave's visit to the La Chesnaye house (Fig. 8.21). Later in the same scene, as Lisette enters the study with Octave's breakfast (Fig. 8.22), the cut through the door keeps Robert and the servants' search for the dropped screw momentarily in the background (Fig. 8.23). Such stagings become more common in the chateau scenes, beginning with André's entrance and culminating in the fête scene. There the spectacular lateral tracking shot that shows Schumacher searching for Lisette and André watching Christine's flirtation with Saint-Aubin culminates as the latter couple leaves; the camera pans and tracks with them until they are in the depth of the shot, entering the cards room (Fig. 8.24). From this point on, very deep shots connect activities going on in a number of rooms simultaneously. In shot 242, for example, Octave speaks to Saint-Aubin in the foreground trophy room, and in the background we see through the hallway and cards room doors, all the way to the dancing ghosts onstage in the ballroom (Fig. 8.25). In the course of the shot, we glimpse Schumacher, Lisette, and André in various planes in between.

This use of depth to frame foreground characters' reactions and background tangential actions differs from classical practice. Most 1930s Hollywood films strung out their actions in linear fashion, and even the post-*Kane* deep-focus style seldom offered viewers competing actions within the same frame. (Often, depth simply moved the characters far apart for over-the-shoulder shot/reverse shot.) Generally the camera is in the optimal position to catch the main action. For Bazin, the crowded, bustling quality provided by framing in depth is ideal for suggesting realism. No doubt such framings appeal to realistic motivation, yet we should recall that the actions have been carefully staged and framed to create this effect—there is no capturing of a preexisting deep space. In this treatment, actions become less linear in their presentation; their orchestrated quality gives a sense of what we might take to be the simultaneity characteristic of real events.

Yet here again, *Rules* cuts off these very deep compositions whenever our attention needs to focus on a particular action. When, in shot 247, André enters the trophy room and confronts Saint-Aubin, Jackie comes in behind him and closes the door, creating a shallower set of planes, with fewer distractions in the rear. Octave's wandering through the chateau early in the fête scene helps set up a sense of chaos spreading through the chateau, and this sense of action continuing offscreen in a real space carries over even into scenes of more limited dramatic action. In *Rules* the use of depth is intermittent, combining moments when concerns of realism dominate with others when narrative clarity becomes paramount and depth is de-emphasized.

To achieve the orchestration of realistic and compositional motivations of space, Renoir uses a number of devices, some conventional, others less so. The most simple of these is a cut or a closing door's reducing the number of planes visible. But Renoir's camera movements employ some distinctive methods of manipulating attention to depth. One such method involves the consistent use of arcing tracking movements and 90° pans, which brings a new segment of space into view without a cut. A second technique "choreographs" tracking and panning movements around the movements of multiple characters.

The arcing movements begin in the Paris house as Christine moves from her bedroom to Robert's study (shot 17); a small camera movement reveals more of the hallway and brings additional servants into view, quickly conveying the social status of the couple. Later in this scene, a quick pan and a track forward reveal Lisette in an adjacent room as Robert tells her that Schumacher has written requesting her transfer to the chateau. Once again, the pattern becomes far more prominent at the chateau, as when the camera arcs in to frame Geneviève being greeted in the chateau hall, or as in the subsequent kitchen scene, as the camera moves 90° around the table during the conversation with the exasperated cook (compare Figs. 8.26 and 8.2, two stages of the same shot). Here the movement brings other servants into view, one of whom the camera then follows leftward in the next shot, picking up Christine and Madame La Bruyère once more as they stand chatting on the kitchen steps.

237

Another example of greater depth occurs three shots later, as we initially see the two women coming out of the kitchen door in a fairly shallow composition with the camera facing the wall perpendicularly (Fig. 8.27). As they look off toward the front door, a quick 90° track places us looking past Christine at André entering in the depth of the shot (Fig. 8.28). During the fête this kind of camera movement occurs time and again, revealing certain offscreen actions and losing others. Pans function in the same way; at one point we begin with a relatively flat two-shot of Christine and André (Fig. 8.29), and the space remains shallow as Marceau, Schumacher, and Lisette run through directly in front of the couple. But then a pan of about 90° reveals Robert standing looking on, with Corneille behind him (Fig. 8.30). Shots of the long upstairs corridor similarly can begin or end with a simple conversation in a limited space (as in shot 286, which pans from the view in Fig. 8.31 to that in Fig. 8.32). The shots leading up to the moment when Corneille trips Schumacher and ends the chase all contain such movements. In general, part of the frantic quality of the fête arises from the camera's abrupt shifts from one action to reveal a different, previously offscreen action whose progress we had lost track of during the scene's rapid changes. Similar, though less complex and abrupt, movements occur during the scenes outdoors near the end, as Schumacher and Marceau spy on the activities in and around the greenhouse.

All these devices for creating multiple points of interest within a single shot function in part to emphasize the apparent objectivity and knowledgeability of the narration. In the classical film, the narration moves to the most convenient point for a view of the central actions. *Rules*'s narrative increasingly consists of multiple actions that take place simultaneously—and so quickly that they seem to outstrip the narration's ability to keep us informed. During the fête, for example, we catch glimpses of the central hallway from the cards room. Robert and Geneviève exit down a corridor to the right rear and we see Schumacher and Lisette apparently going toward the kitchen (Fig. 8.33). Then the camera tracks left with Octave, passing the card players (Fig. 8.34); when Octave reaches the next door leading out to the hallway, we unexpectedly see Schumacher and Lisette approaching, much closer than they had been (Fig. 8.35). In such shots Renoir achieves the effect of many actions going on at once, quite independent of any narrational control. The narration seemingly can catch only bits of these actions and give us at best a partial view of any one subplot. Again, I should stress that this sense of fleeting glimpses of ongoing events is a formal effect of the work, not an actual capturing of reality.

But the easiest way for the spectator to grasp these "confusing" events as coherent would be through an appeal to realistic motivation.

The "choreographed" camera movements also aid in creating this effect of a narration that must hurry and shift constantly to keep up with the dense action. In some shots, if the characters' movements diverge, the camera seems to hesitate over which character to concentrate on. For example, after the arc into depth for André's arrival (Figs. 8.27 and 8.28), a cut to a reverse shot shows Christine greeting Octave (Fig. 8.36); he takes her arm to lead her forward as the camera arcs into a medium shot of her greeting André (Fig. 8.37). Both Octave's and Christine's movements initially motivate the camera's direction, as Octave passes through the foreground and ends at the far left and Christine moves to the other side of André. The camera does not mimic either Octave's or Christine's movement, yet it takes both their trajectories into account. In effect, Renoir often links the movements of the camera to a whole set of cues within the mise-en-scene—the characters' stances, glances, and movements—in a manner that is parallel to the way a classical film links its continuity editing to similar cues. Certainly the classical film also links camera movement to figure movement, for following or reframing. But Renoir gains complexity by taking more than one actor's movements into account, and since the different actors move in different ways, the resulting camera trajectory is a sort of compromise between them. Thus the camera does not simply mimic the actions of the characters, but rather weaves in the midst of and around them in a different, but organized, path. To use the choreography metaphor, the camera becomes another dancer, moving in relation to human dancers but with its own distinct pattern of steps.

Again, the overall effect is of a narration overwhelmed by the amount of action it must convey to us—constantly scanning, hesitating, and changing our vantage point in order to give us more information. The lengthy shot in the middle of the servants' dinner (shot 117) offers another example of this hurried and shifting effect, with the camera panning and pausing as the action proceeds. Schumacher, who has been speaking to Lisette, moves to the rear, and the camera pans left as the cook comes forward to deliver his speech about potato salad; then, as he retires, the camera once again pans left with Schumacher, only to pan right again as it frames Marceau's arrival. Moreover, because the servants' table remains in the foreground, the panning movement centers Corneille in time for his dialogue with Marceau.

This pattern, like most of the film's other devices, culminates in the fête scene, most notably in the tracking shot (shot 239) through the onlookers at the rear of the ballroom—a shot that simulates the effect

of crosscutting without using a single cut. The initial motivation for
the track right is Schumacher's parallel movement in the outer corridor (Fig. 8.38). As he moves right, out of sight behind a wall, a servant's movement in the same direction but inside the room takes over
the motivation of the track (Fig. 8.39). Letting the servant exit right,
the camera pauses as it reaches the next door just as Schumacher reappears (Fig. 8.40). As he moves right and disappears again, the camera
tracks right as if to follow but seems to catch unintentionally the exchange between Christine and Saint-Aubin about her being drunk.
The camera tracks on without stopping, but it pans back to keep them
in view (Fig. 8.41), as if the narration regrets the necessity of leaving
this action. Panning once again to the right, the camera picks up Lisette and Marceau embracing in the third doorway, and the camera
centers on the doorway just as Schumacher reaches it; in spite of the
tiny scene with Saint-Aubin and Christine, the camera has remained
linked to the initial motivating figure, Schumacher. Yet, as Marceau
and Lisette separate, the camera pans slightly right to reveal André,
staring jealously offscreen at Christine; he and Schumacher are the
only characters visible at this end of the rightward camera movement
(Fig. 8.42). A pan back to the left reveals Marceau leaving toward the
left in the corridor, with Lisette trying to follow. Schumacher, stopping her, moves leftward after Marceau, and the camera tracks, once
again paralleling his movement. Again he is lost to our view behind
the wall, and we see Saint-Aubin and Christine get up to leave, the
camera continuing to track behind them at the same rate (Fig. 8.43).
But now the camera's movement is wholly motivated by theirs, and,
as they pause to look defiantly back toward André, the track-forward
slows. Finally, a pan left as they exit sets up considerable depth in the
final composition of the shot (Fig. 8.24).

This shot, one of the most complicated in the film, demonstrates
how the camera can hesitate between actions and can modify its trajectory to accommodate new characters who suddenly appear. The
whole chase scene that follows involves many such movements,
though as the action becomes faster and more chaotic, the individual
shots increasingly lack the careful symmetry and alternation of this
one. All such camera movements appeal to the notion that offscreen
space contains ongoing actions potentially as interesting as those we
are watching at any given moment, and that all the actions, onscreen
and off, belong to a consistent, unbroken, real world.

Not all scenes are so crowded with incident. I have suggested that
the pre-chateau scenes are handled in a less unconventional way, and
that even in the busy fête sequence there are islands of calm during

which a few characters talk quietly. In conversation scenes, paradoxically, the narration's attempt to show all the characters at once results
in the *de*-emphasis of offscreen space. One of the means Renoir consistently uses to treat conversations is to set up two characters, often in
profile facing each other, in a foreground plane. Sometimes other
characters appear between them in the background. Such setups begin early on, with André and Octave's conversation at the airport. At
first they are the only significant figures present (Fig. 8.44), but precisely when Octave tells André that Christine did not come to see him,
the radio announcer appears between and beyond them, slightly out
of focus (Fig. 8.45). This kind of straight-on view into a semicircular,
shallow space recurs throughout the film. The device gives Renoir a
way to avoid the disadvantages that shot/reverse shot may create in
certain situations. Shot/reverse shot usually forces us to concentrate
on either the speaker *or* the listener by placing the other at least partially offscreen. With Renoir's shallow two-shots, we see both characters simultaneously and equally.

The shot/reverse shot technique's orchestration of our attention to
speaker and listener channels bits of narrative information into a
steady, linear flow. Shot/reverse shot minimizes simultaneity in the
presentation of action and at the same time limits character response
to the most salient moments in terms of narrative functioning. Renoir's
shallow two-shot alternative systematically holds speaker and listener
onscreen so that our attention to either is less patterned. This is not
to say that Renoir does not guide our attention within such scenes by
means of movement, sound, and figure placement, but there are definitely many moments when such cues emphasize more than one character at a time. In the conversation at the airport, Octave and André
are balanced in profile, and there is little to choose from in terms of
where to look at any given moment. They speak in rapid succession,
and each registers rapidly changing facial expressions as the other
speaks; for example, Octave abruptly stops grinning when André asks
if Christine has come. In a different way, when at the chateau Robert
thanks Christine for her handling of the awkward situation with André
(shot 123), we are likely to glance at Christine at intervals to search
her face for a reaction. She betrays no emotion and barely moves as
he speaks, but our curiosity about her character is likely to keep our
eyes shuttling back and forth in this balanced two-shot, even though
Robert does most of the talking and moving. Other examples of this
technique occur: after the car crash, between André and Octave (shot
42); when Robert pauses as Marceau tells him he has always wanted

to be a servant (shot 93); and in most of the conversations that punctuate the fête scene.

As usual, Renoir gets the best of both worlds by also using conventional Hollywood shot/reverse shot, usually for the most important statements by the characters or simply when they are too far apart for a two-shot. For example, Christine's early conversations with Lisette are done in a series of two-shots (with mirrors functioning here, as elsewhere, to get variants of the profile two-shot by allowing frontal views of the reflected characters); yet the scene goes to shot/reverse shot when Christine is leaving and turns back to ask Lisette if it is possible to have a friendship with a man. Here both spatial separation and the need to emphasize their lines motivate the switch in techniques. Shot/reverse shot appears again: between Geneviève and Robert in her apartment, as André tells Jackie he does not love her, and during the servants' dinner. (In the latter scene, shot/reverse shot takes over the usual function of camera movement by rendering the bustle of the action.) In general, more conversations are handled with the balanced, shallow-space framing than with shot/reverse shot. Of roughly twenty-eight conversations in the film, eight are filmed with shot/reverse shot, thirteen with a balanced framing, and seven with some combination of the two. Once again, to account for Renoir's use of the seemingly more static two-shot alternative, we may turn to realistic motivation. The simultaneous presentation of speech and reaction appeals to the notion of the simultaneity of events occurring in the array of the unbounded world. Shot/reverse shot's linearity, on the other hand, though it promotes narrative clarity, seems to filter and reduce that array, and hence it appeals to compositional motivation. (At least it does so in terms of the realism that *Rules* constructs; there have been attempts to justify shot/reverse shot as realistic, primarily by drawing upon the idea that it follows the natural attention of an invisible observer on the scene.)

Like these many spatial devices, the temporal structure of *Rules* follows many conventional strategies as well. The narrative action begins *in medias res*, as it does in many classical films. Within scenes there is temporal continuity, with neither elliptical nor overlapping editing. Dialogue hooks link scene to scene in a clear fashion, and frequent appointments and references to upcoming events also help us understand the temporal relations among scenes. There are no flashbacks or flash-forwards to confuse the temporal order of the fabula.

But there are also some unconventional uses of time in *Rules*. The important earlier events skipped by the *in medias res* opening are not filled in unambiguously by exposition—as we have seen with André and Christine's past relationship. The continuity within scenes often jams together multiple simultaneous events that the classical cinema would separate and handle in a more linear fashion with crosscutting or with shorter scenes. In this sense, for example, the hunt, with its crosscutting and succession of brief exchanges among small groups, cites the norm, while the fête uses the more dense Renoirian presentation. (The hunt is a brilliant scene, of course, but its very conventionality and clarity of meaning have drawn critics to concentrate on it to the exclusion of other equally interesting, but more challenging, scenes.) Similarly, while dialogue hooks and appointments do keep temporal succession clear, they fail to explain why six days, between the conversations the morning after the hunt and at the beginning of the fête, should be elided—with no apparent change in the characters' situations afterward. Finally, the avoidance of flashbacks actually makes the film's narrative *less* clear. A flashback or two to earlier events would be useful—*if* classical clarity were the goal.

CONCLUSIONS

If *Rules* mixes conventional and unconventional devices, it does not attempt to blend them imperceptibly together. The differences remain readily apparent and are often disturbing. The contrast between clarity and ambiguity, the abrupt shifts of tone, and the strange mélange of stylistic techniques have disturbed even those critics determined to impose as much unity as possible on the film. I suspect that one reason Bazin chose *Rules* as an exemplary realist film (although he certainly would not have put it this way) is because it embeds its realism firmly within the very norms that realism tends to violate. Hence *Rules* flaunts its realism not simply by appealing to notions of how life really is, but by creating abrupt and challenging juxtapositions to other norms of filmmaking. (By way of contrast, *Bicycle Thieves*'s motif of citation of the classical cinema situates its own realism as distinctly separate from the norm.)

The net result, presumably, is that the spectator cannot settle down into one set of viewing skills for very long at a time. The film itself requires that we make frequent adjustments, and in this sense it differs vastly from the classical cinema. The viewing skills required by the latter are extensive (more so than most recent critics and theorists seem to believe), but they are so familiar as to lack any real challenge for most of us. Among the vast numbers of classical films, precious few cheat or play with our expectations in really daring ways. (In *Stage*

Fright and *Laura* we saw relatively limited examples of such play within the classical mode of filmmaking; *Bicycle Thieves* provides a smooth blend of realist and classical traits.) In *Rules*, the challenges seemingly result in a sense of variety and of a relatively wide range of perceptual and cognitive experience. A sense of realism tends to emerge because the film cues us to think of this range as being similar to that which we experience in the real world, rather than being similar to the limitations we experience in conventional artworks. Realism is not reality, of course; in any given historical period, it consists of a new set of conventions that appear to depart from standard norms specifically by appealing to motivation that can be considered realistic. As we saw in the previous chapter, as time passes and such appeals become more familiar, their conventionality becomes more and more apparent, and this new set of cues loses its ability to make spectators appeal to realistic motivation. Like other styles, realism can become automatized. But after a period when realism is not a common norm, it can regain its defamiliarizing force.

It seems worth reiterating in closing this section of the book that no filmic technique or method of combining techniques is innately realistic. Similarly, just because a film demands a variety of viewing skills, as *Rules* does, it does not automatically create an effect of realism, as the systematic disunities of Godard's films show. Whole films, existing against specific historical backgrounds, create the effect of realism.

PART SIX

The Perceptual Challenges
of Parametric Form

9

Play Time: Comedy on the
Edge of Perception

PARAMETRIC FORM

THE REMAINING chapters of this book will deal with a concept that is
relatively new to film studies, and that has been formulated primarily
by practitioners of neoformalism: parametric cinema. In Chapter 1 I
referred briefly to this concept, defining parametric form as being governed by a structuring principle in which artistic motivation becomes
systematic and foregrounded across a whole film; artistic motivation
then creates patterns that are as important as or more important than
the syuzhet structures. As this is a very difficult concept, and one
which has little currency in film studies, it may be worth spending
more time on it than on the others dealt with so far. Four extended
examples should help demonstrate the nature of parametric form. Two
of these films—*Play Time* and *Sauve qui peut (la vie)*—present the
spectator with a perceptual overload, while the other two—*Lancelot
du Lac* and *Late Spring*—use a pared-down, sparse style.

In general, we may characterize as parametric those films that allow
the play of stylistic devices a significant degree of independence from
narrative functioning and motivation. This term derives from Noël
Burch's *Theory of Film Practice*, in which he calls the various possibilities of the medium—those elements that provide the potential material for variation—"parameters."[1] David Bordwell has developed
upon Burch's treatment, describing extensively the uses of parametric
variation by the narration of fiction films.[2] He has shown that the kind
of play with stylistic features usually associated with abstract and other
non-narrative filmic modes can come forward in narrative films as
well, sometimes predominating over syuzhet considerations, sometimes alternating with them in importance.

[1] Noël Burch, *Theory of Film Practice*, trans. Helen R. Lane (Princeton: Princeton
University Press, 1981).
[2] David Bordwell, *Narration in the Fiction Film* (Madison: University of Wisconsin
Press, 1985), chap. 12.

Bordwell links parametric cinema to total serialism in music, an approach that gained currency particularly in France in the 1950s, in the wake of the spread of twelve-tone serialism: "The crucial aspect of serialist doctrine is the possibility that large-scale structure may be determined by fundamental stylistic choice."[3] Cinema is not completely parallel to music, in that musical parameters are abstract and mathematically precise (e.g., pitch, rhythm). Narrative cinema, on the other hand, depends on the representation of events, and there is no logically limited, preexisting set of stylistic choices from which to choose a group of parameters. (The cinema has no scale, no whole and quarter notes, etc.)

Bordwell defines parametric play as occurring "when only artistic motivation can account for [stylistic patterning]." If a certain stylistic figure running through a work does not appeal to reality to justify its presence, if we cannot see it as necessary to the ongoing action, and if it does not refer to other artworks' conventions to allow us to grasp it, then that figure becomes what Bordwell calls an "intrinsic norm" of the parametric work, and one which exists solely to call attention to itself.

At first this may seem an odd notion. How do we perceive this parametric play if it does not relate to the syuzhet's time, space, and causality, except by proximity? Bordwell argues that E. H. Gombrich's concept of *order* explains the viewing skills that allow us to grasp abstract elements even in a narrative work. Extremely subtle and elaborate patterns would be elusive no doubt, and we shall see how Jacques Tati's *Play Time* varies its types of gags, ranging to some that are just barely perceptible. But even there, the film cues us extensively as to what to look for. Moreover, the number of discrete stylistic items thrown at us in *Play Time* creates a dense perceptual play, but the individual items are in themselves quite simple, as is the narrative line. Bordwell argues that "the most clear-cut cases of parametric narration can definitely be perceived in viewing."[4] This is partly because most such films isolate only a few parameters for extensive use, and hence the repetition can be quite redundant. Moreover, we will have schemata available that enable us to notice stylistic variation: the pattern of the syuzhet will help give a pattern to the repetitions. For example, the horse whinnies in *Lancelot du Lac* do not necessarily serve narrative functions in every case, but we may be able to remember them and notice their return because we have a sense of which

[3] Ibid., p. 276.
[4] Ibid., p. 284.

actions we have previously heard them accompany. Also, directors tend to use a consistent style across single films and among different films. Bresson's earlier films also had included parametric variation, as Bordwell demonstrates with *Pickpocket*. (This is not to say that Bresson simply repeats the same strategies identically, as his further stylistic experiments in *L'Argent* demonstrate.) We have already seen how Tati's *Les Vacances de Monsieur Hulot* develops stylistic patterns of overlap across repetitive cellular units of narrative: the seven days of the vacation. We can now see that these foregrounded, interchangeable devices constitute parameters.

Another aid to noticing parametric play is the tendency for certain types of techniques to be singled out—offscreen versus onscreen space, sound motifs, and so on; Burch lays these out systematically in *Theory of Film Practice*. Anyone familiar with the possibilities of the film medium will be able to categorize the choices made by a given film. The variations on optically slowed motion in *Sauve qui peut (la vie)* would be an example of an instantly recognizable parametric device. Finally, parametric films tend to be either unconventionally dense or unconventionally sparse. Those that are unusually dense often give the spectator frequent signals as to what to notice, or they alternate between moments that are artistically and narratively motivated. Those that are sparse encourage us to look and listen intensely for the few devices presented. In the sparse approach, the just-noticeable difference comes into play: "It is one aim of the sparse approach to explore the boundary between what is and is not recognizable."[5] We will see a particularly strong play with this boundary in *Late Spring* in Chapter 12.

Because of the difficulty in keeping track of repetition and variation across a lengthy temporal work like a feature film, we must not expect to find very precise and intricate parametric patterns in most films.

Once the intrinsic stylistic norm is in place, it must be developed. Style must create its own temporal logic. But it is unrealistic to expect parametric form to exhibit detailed intricacies. As in serial music, the more convoluted and less redundant such form is, the more imperceptible it is likely to be. Consequently, the parameters cannot all be varied at once. Several must be held constant if repetition and variation are to be apparent.[6]

Thus we are not likely to find parametric films using a mathematical set of variations as in serial music—though some films will contain such features. Rather, a simpler form, like a rondo (*ABA*) or theme

[5] Ibid., p. 286.
[6] Ibid.

and variations ($AA^1A^2A^3$, etc.), will be likely to govern repetition. Stylistic variation will tend to be additive, and it will not necessarily come to a neat resolution of a pattern, in the way that the syuzhet might achieve closure.

In a parametrically organized film, form can lure us into perceiving style for its own sake. But the result need not detract from the narrative. Quite the contrary, if we cooperate and follow these stylistic patterns as well as (not instead of) the narrative, our perception of the film as a whole can only be more complete, more intense. But we must first be willing to assume that a film's form is not limited to its narrative and our activity as viewers is not aimed simply at a constant interpretation of all elements in terms of the meaning they create. Such a viewing procedure, commonly called a "reading" in current parlance, limits both the film and our perception of it. (Such "readings" may or may not be claimed to be infinite and playful, but they are bound to be all of a single type if one limits oneself to that part of the film's formal web that we call "meaning.")

PERCEPTUAL PLAY TIME

For many years, critics and audiences were able to consider Jacques Tati a minor genius of film comedy. His first three features appeared simply to copy the pantomimic approach of the great silent comedian/directors. Based as they were upon the minute observation of everyday human behavior, Tati's comedies could apparently be relegated to an honorable position outside the mainstream of contemporary cinema. The appearance in 1968 of *Play Time*[7] challenged that view, changing forever the way we look at Tati. Perhaps only at that point did it become entirely possible to grasp all the subtleties of Tati's earlier films, all of which were enhanced by the viewing skills that *Play Time* taught us. The analysis in Chapter 3 would probably have been quite different without my having had a familiarity with *Play Time*. It was necessary to take Tati more seriously before we could realize the extent of the formal challenges he was presenting to us.

Tati's differences from Keaton, Lloyd, Chaplin, and others are probably more numerous than his similarities to them. The American silent

[7] The title is, in fact, two words, not *Playtime*, as it has usually been written. The difference is not negligible, since the separation puts more emphasis upon the implications of the two words (especially "time"), while retaining the meaning of the single term.

Any analysis of *Play Time* not based on the original 70mm version—which I have never seen—must remain tentative. At least the 1982 re-releases have restored the wonderful sequence of Hulot's visit to a friend in a glass-walled apartment complex.

comedians were working firmly within the system of the classical Hollywood cinema. Indeed, Keaton and Lloyd may not have been better comic mimes than Chaplin, but the superiority of their films resulted from their greater mastery of continuity style and classical narrative structures. Tati largely rejects this classical system. Instead, he uses the traditional comic structure of a series of "gags" to create the basis for an alternative filmic system. As with the alternative systems constructed by Robert Bresson, Yasujiro Ozu, Kenji Mizoguchi, Miklós Jancsó, and others, this system has historically had minimal influence; it remains specifically Tatian. It shares with these other filmmakers' styles, however, the use of parametric form.

Part of the classical cinema's strength lies in its ability to provide us with a comfortable set of viewing procedures. These are built up by viewings of many films, the majority of which utilize the classical approach. In most such films, we have few doubts about what we shall see or what viewing skills to apply. Indeed, most viewers see such a large percentage of Hollywood-style films that they may have few other viewing skills; hence there has been a tendency to lump together all other films, however varied, into the broad categories of "art" films or "experimental" films.

As a result, the strongly parametric film, in departing from the classical system, must create a degree of perceptual uncertainty. When we go to Godard, Bresson, or Ozu films for the first few times, we may be at a loss as to what viewing procedures are appropriate to these unfamiliar works. The value of these films rests less in their thematic material than in their ability to shift our habitual perceptions of filmic conventions through defamiliarization. Any film creates some uncertainty; in the classical film, however, this is virtually always confined to the realm of the narrative hermeneutic. We are invited to follow the syuzhet, reconstructing the chain of causally ordered fabula events.

One major point of interest arising from *Play Time* involves the implications of a film that places itself resolutely outside the classical tradition by remaining perceptually ungraspable. As we shall see, the film deflects attention outward from the simple cause-and-effect chain and the series of gags that form its most perceptually familiar level. Ultimately this concentration on perceptual difficulty has ideological implications; the perceptual skills necessary for resolving the uncertainty of viewing *Play Time* relate to social as well as to filmic practice.

What perceptual tactics does *Play Time* imply for the spectator? The multiple implications of the title help to suggest various levels upon which the film operates. Most literally, the story deals with the play

251

time (i.e., vacation time) of a group of American tourists. Their appearances interweave with the work time of Monsieur Hulot and the various businessmen in the first half of the film. The clear thematic material concerning the uniformity of modern life hardly needs detailed explication. Suffice it to say that by the latter part of the film, after the destruction of part of the Royal Garden restaurant, the concept of "play time" undergoes a change. Through the imagination and ingenuity of individuals reacting against their sterile environment, the characters transform work time into play time. The somber gray tones of the early scenes disappear in a riot of color during the bus trip to the airport; utility vehicles form a carousel and workers perform their tasks in new ways (for example, the man who carries a desk with its legs in his pockets). This development from a literal to a metaphorical application of the "play time" idea constitutes the film's thematic core.

But "play time" has at least one further implication—for ourselves, the film's audience. Any film engages spectator perception in a more or less playful way; many films, however, remain so firmly entrenched within conventional modes that their play is at a minimum. For example, the prevalent shot/reverse shot pattern of Hollywood-style films and television has become so familiar that most people never notice it. Tati's *Play Time*, perhaps as much as any film ever made, invites our perceptual engagement with the film at *every* level; so intense can this involvement become, indeed, that many people find it a tiring experience to watch the film.

Jonathan Rosenbaum has suggested one reason why *Play Time* demands so much of us perceptually; as he says, "The subject of a typical shot is *everything that appears on the screen.*"[8] That is, Tati does not always center and foreground comic gags for us; in many cases, we must seek out the potentially funny elements. As a result, everything offers itself as a possible part of the film's humor; we must scan the screen continually and pick out sounds from the jumble on the track.

Such scanning is exactly the kind of perception that parametric form seeks to foster. In some areas Tati's parameters are limited: he uses primarily long and medium-long distances in framing; camera movements are usually short, diagonal following tracks that are difficult to notice; there is no shot/reverse shot editing; and so on. He uses these restricted techniques in systematic ways. Yet these limited techniques serve to foreground the main parametric structures: the dense mise-en-scene and the disorienting cuts that result from editing several il-

[8] Jonathan Rosenbaum, "Tati's Democracy," *Film Comment* 9, no. 3 (May-June 1973): 37. Emphasis in original.

legible shots together. Thus, although some of Tati's self-imposed stylistic limits suggest a "sparse" approach, the overall effect of *Play Time*
is one of considerable perceptual overload.

This method of structuring a comedy film differs so much from the
classical norm that we need strong cues for new viewing and listening
skills. *Play Time*'s opening portion acts as a guide to the film's structures. The causal action of the narrative proper does not start until we
see the tour arrive at the customs gate; hence the lack of relevant
events in the first six shots encourages us to concentrate on the specific
ways in which the film uses sound and image to create humor.

The film begins with pre-credits music involving percussion; at a
seemingly arbitrary point in this music, the bright credits shot of
clouds fades suddenly in from the blackness. Already we encounter
the sound track as a separate level from the image track—as something
to which we should pay close attention in its own right. (Unfortunately, most of this music seems to have been edited out of the re-
release print.) The opening shot of a building against the sky introduces the film's most basic motifs—modern buildings and reflective
glass (Fig. 9.1)—outside any narrative context. Here we look without
being able to identify any apparent function of establishing a locale for
action. (Part of the point, indeed, is that such buildings are so bland
in their design as to yield no clue to their purpose. The airport/hospital
confusion of the opening depends on this quality of the building's exterior.) The film's first humorous moments occur in the second shot,
which includes one fairly traditional visual joke and one similarly traditional sound gag: the nuns' flapping headgear and squeaky shoes
(Fig. 9.2). Thus *Play Time* gradually presents us with structures that
lead us to pay equal and active attention to image and sound.

The film's third shot is more remarkable, however; it begins to introduce the multiple visual and aural focuses of attention that will
structure the rest of the film. The couple in the foreground act as our
"instructors" in this shot. As it begins, they are watching the nuns
(Fig. 9.3); throughout the lengthy shot, they alternate between talking
to each other and turning to watch various people who pass by them.
In most cases, it is the wife's attention that initially shifts, and it is
drawn by the sounds the people make: the clinking tray pushed by the
man in white, the footsteps of the military man and of the woman with
the towels. In at least one case, as the janitor enters, her attention
seems to be attracted initially by the bright colors: the blue of his uniform and the pink of his broom. The wife further directs our attention
by saying to her husband: "Look at that man. He looks very important,
doesn't he?" and "Look, there's an officer." (These lines are from the

English-dubbed version, but the French dialogue is comparable.)
Thus the shot's action does not consist of a series of gags, but rather of
a series of moments that draw our attention to potentially funny-look-
ing or -sounding people.

The scene gradually becomes more complex. After several of these
moments of attention-shifting, Tati creates a sound joke; the woman
with the towels appears to be carrying a baby, yet the sound of the
baby's cry actually comes from the carrier at the lower left of the
frame. This carrier has been almost invisible, since its color and texture blend in with the rows of chairs against which it is placed; our
initial inability to notice it creates the basis for the gag. This shot also
begins to introduce several characters at once rather than one at a
time; by the moment the cut comes, there are multiple points of attention. This complex combination of mise-en-scene and sound will
reach its climax in the restaurant sequence.

In general, we are left on our own after this beginning to search the
frame and sound track for comic material ourselves. Occasionally a
character within the scene will again embody the pointing function.
Waiters point out the faults of the Royal Garden restaurant to its har-
ried architect, ensuring that we, too, will see them. One woman indicates to her dancing partner a crown impression on a man's back
(Fig. 9.4), then turns to reveal to us that she has one on her own
back (Fig. 9.5). The women in the tour exclaim, "Oh, look!" when they
see the ultra-chic couple at the hatcheck room (Fig. 9.6). The whole
structuring of the film around a group of tourists (who come specifically to *look at* and *listen to* Paris) plays up the act of paying attention
to appearances and sound.

PERCEPTUAL DIFFICULTY

Even if we pick up on these cues and strive to perceive *Play Time* in
new ways, much of its humor remains elusive. Critics like Noël Burch
and Jonathan Rosenbaum have pointed out that the film is so complex
that one is likely to see quite different things from one viewing to
another.[9]

It does seem to be the case that one simply *cannot* see and hear
everything in the film in one or even several viewings. In addition, it
seems that, more than in most films, different people will notice different things—hence the tendency for friends to point out gags to each

[9] Burch, *Theory of Film Practice*, p. 47; Jonathan Rosenbaum, "Tati's Democracy"
and "Paris Journal," *Film Comment* 7, no. 3 (Fall 1971): 6, and 7, no. 4 (Winter 1971/
72): 2–6.

other when watching the film. I was lucky enough to see the film again in 1982—during the British re-release of the pre-*Traffic* features—in a North London family theater; the middle-class audience consisted of families and middle-aged and elderly couples. Most were obviously familiar with the Hulot character. The pattern of their laughter and the remarks I was able to hear were revealing, as they conformed closely to what one would predict from an intuitive sense of the film's difficulties. I shall refer to their responses at some points in this analysis, as evidence of a nonacademic audience's ability or inability to notice certain types of gags in *Play Time*.

How has Tati managed to structure his comedy to be at once completely enjoyable to many audiences (the London group applauded and laughed frequently throughout), yet at the same time so dense that it defeats our perception to the degree noted by Burch and Rosenbaum? *Play Time* contains a variety of types of gags, ranging along a continuum from the fairly conventional self-contained "bit" to the moment that barely suggests that one might find something potentially funny present. (Here *Play Time* develops on the contrast between banal and funny elements in *Les Vacances de Monsieur Hulot*.) In addition, the film creates scenes in which multiple comic actions compete for our attention. Hence the film uses at various times (1) denial of apparent gags, (2) completion of gags, and (3) overabundance of gags.

In the middle ground of this set of possibilities, we have the complete gags, sometimes with elaborate preparations which set us up for the laugh to come. In one such bit, we see several shots of Hulot examining, pinching, and sitting in the black vinyl chairs of a waiting room; all this leads up to the "payoff," when the back and seat of one chair collapse, then "inhale" to remove all traces of Hulot's actions (Figs. 9.7 and 9.8). The running gag of the repeated seasoning of the broiled turbot during the restaurant sequence also involves elaborate lead-in material. Such actions occur near the center of the frame, and no competing gags draw our attention from them. In these ways, the film so points up these moments that no one would be likely to miss them. (The North London audience applauded the moments when a salesman turns on his broom's headlights and when another "slams" the door silently; other big laughs went to the makeup glasses, the Greek-column wastebasket, and the door breaking at the Royal Garden.)

But a wealth of the comic material in *Play Time* is difficult to catch, in spite of the fact that it follows a relatively traditional gag structure. Many spectators do not notice that the man who locks the tourist agency door behind Hulot bends his head directly behind the door

255

handles so that he looks as if he has sprouted a pair of horns, causing Hulot's startled reaction (Fig. 9.9). (Not a single chuckle from the North Londoners greeted this gag. Silence also accompanied the moment when Tony, the doorman, pretends to the businessman that he cannot find the change from the cigar purchase; he receives permission to keep it as a tip, and then in the background of the next shot he begins counting the money, which has been in his hand all along.) The framing also refuses to emphasize the man who puts a coin in a parking meter and appears to start up the whole "carousel" in the traffic-circle scene near the end (Fig. 9.10). *Play Time* is full of such isolated moments, which we may notice or not.

Often, especially in the restaurant sequence, Tati stages several gags simultaneously, making it literally impossible to see all of them in one viewing.[10] At the same moment when the maître d' mixes the headache remedy that Hulot mistakes for champagne, Schultz is at the other end of the table, ordering his meal by pointing at the stains on the waiter's shirt (Fig. 9.11). Sound overlaps in the same way. As Barbara and her friend Genevieve have a conversation outside the tourist agency in which they mistakenly identify a modern skyscraper as the Pont Alexandre III, we also hear the offscreen voice of the sole male member of the tour: "They have green buses here." Later, in the restaurant scene, a visual gag and a sonic gag compete for our attention. While two waiters finish their comic business of setting a table in the foreground, a woman in the tourist group in the back says: "I can't stand this another minute. All those who wanna charge, say 'aye.'" We hear a chorus of "ayes," and the women move forward in the far background of the shot (Fig. 9.12).

The restaurant scene culminates in a particularly "busy" shot of multiple activities: the fussy businessman figures his check, a man performs a comic striptease to the applause of two women, the short tourist in the raincoat dances, two members of the jazz band improvise on the devastated stage, Hulot and Barbara leave, Schultz flings cigarettes to the entire group, and so on (Fig. 9.13). We can at best catch

[10] Barry Salt insists that "despite the claims made by some people that these separate actions in different parts of the frame actually involve different simultaneous comedy interests, calm viewing of the film shows that this is not so, and that there is only one point of any narrative or comedy interest going on at any one instant, in just one area of the frame" (*Film Style & Technology: History & Analysis* [London: Starword, 1983], p. 338). The "some people" are presumably Jonathan Rosenbaum, Lucy Fischer (in "Beyond Freedom and Dignity: An Analysis of Jacques Tati's *Playtime*," *Sight and Sound* 45, no. 4 [Autumn 1976]: 234–239), and/or me. I can suggest only that my analysis offers some concrete examples of simultaneous gags; any "calm viewing" of the film that falls short of soporific will confirm these and reveal other examples.

only portions of each action, while continuing to scan the screen for other gags. As it goes on, *Play Time* tends to become more dense. In part, this build-up corresponds to an acceleration in humor. Yet *Play Time* would almost certainly be an even funnier film if the less perceptible jokes were separated, centered, and developed one by one. The systematic use of imperceptibility is in itself one of the film's main structuring parameters and governs the dominant.

The comic status of some of *Play Time*'s jokes remains unclear. One long shot of Schultz's "Chez Nous" corner of the Royal Garden shows him admitting a new couple to join him. Simultaneously at the right, a waiter unwittingly carries an elaborate plate of dessert over the head of a bent-over dancer (Fig. 9.14). This latter gag suggests a further strategy by which Tati plays with our perception. *Play Time* invites us to scan the screen and listen for jokes, then provides many "incomplete" gags; our expectations, based upon viewing skills appropriate to more traditional comedies, are frustrated. In the gag with the elaborate dessert, we might expect the humorous moment to climax when the waiter lets the food drop on the dancer's head—yet no such thing happens. The humor here rests solely in the fact that he *might* have dropped it. Similarly, when Hulot kicks a sponge along the sidewalk in the morning scene, then mistakenly places it on the cheese counter, we can only see the humor of the situation by anticipating that someone will eventually buy it as cheese (Fig. 9.15). In *Play Time*, the potentially funny situation provides a great deal of the film's total comic effect (which is presumably why some people do not find Tati's films funny at all). We are forced to search for many of the gags; in the process we discover humorous situations that are hinted at but not developed.

BARING THE DEVICE

Play Time contains a small number of structures that acknowledge explicitly the film's perceptual difficulty. Foremost among these are the black-and-white, life-sized photograph cutouts in the backgrounds of scenes. Since Tati places many of his actors in stiff, static poses, even a spectator who notices the cutouts will have difficulty being sure in every case whether a figure is a real person or a cutout (especially since the same background figure may be a cutout in one shot and a live actor in the next). Tati flaunts the illegibility of his mise-en-scene, while simultaneously inviting us to play this perceptual game. As a result, on later viewings of the film, we may scan the backgrounds looking for cutouts, rather as we scan for bits of comic action.

The play with background figures begins in the third shot, with three women posed against light windows at the far rear (Fig. 9.3). Their tiny movements and returns to static poses are almost impossible to notice, unless one ignores the rest of the action. In later shots of the scene, one or two of these women are actually replaced by cutouts, and at least four cutouts appear, somewhat more conspicuously, in the long shot of the downstairs lobby (as the woman pats the valised dog). From this point on, they are seen in backgrounds of numerous shots; since they are black-and-white photos, they blend in with the black and gray costumes of the businessmen and uniformed women in the first half of the film. Tati even uses cutout cars in the background of a couple of shots, including the first interior of the travel agency (Fig. 9.16). The small car between the bottoms of the two posters at the left is a cutout. (Like the clothing, most of the cars seen in the first half of the film are black or silvery gray.)[11]

A couple of shots carry the functions of the cutouts over to real objects or people. These appear in contexts where they are perfectly visible in the frame but almost impossible to see because of the action going on elsewhere in the frame. In the restaurant scene, a single shot contains the "through-out Greek style" wastebasket, centered in the frame (Fig. 9.17); other shots of this space show it unoccupied by any object.

Earlier, in the scene in which Monsieur Giffard bangs his nose on the glass door, the film flaunts its own illegibility again. At the right side of the frame stands a businessman, unmoving and in a pose similar to those of the cutouts. He is relatively close to the camera and perfectly visible (Fig. 9.18). Only after all other action has been played out does this man suddenly "come to life" and walk across toward the left. Here an absolutely gratuitous device exists solely to point up its own perceptual difficulty.

Finally, the film's structure of denial of humor combines with this flaunting of imperceptibility, beginning in the opening airport scene, with the motif of the "false Hulots." In the background of one of the airport interiors, a man who looks like Hulot appears and drops his umbrella with a loud clatter. Nothing in the narrative at this point informs us that this is not Monsieur Hulot; the man simply leaves. He reappears only in the scene of the real Monsieur Hulot's entrance,

---

[11] The inconspicuous placement of the cutouts at the back of busy scenes may have been *too* subtle. At any rate, Tati used black-and-white cutouts again to brilliant effect in *Parade*. There he places them much closer to the camera—among the audience members in the circus hall and on the stage during one number. See Kristin Thompson, "*Parade*: A Review of an Unreleased Film," *The Velvet Light Trap* no. 22 (1986): 81–82.

when it is this first false Hulot (distinguishable by his yellow socks) who hooks umbrellas with Hulot. Here the denial of humor extends to the withholding of the film's star/hero, but again the joke is almost unnoticeable. (The audience in the North London theater applauded when the first false Hulot appeared; then, when the real Hulot turned up, one person near me assured his companion, "Yes, it is Hulot." This device seems to be perceptible, at least retrospectively, to some audience members.) Other men in raincoats and hush-puppy shoes are confused with Hulot later in the film; the short, pushy sightseer who gets Hulot into trouble at the trade show, and the man whom Giffard sees from the rear and hails as he crosses a street. These false Hulots not only create a perceptual gag motif based upon mistakes, but also serve thematically to suggest that Hulot is typical of a non-conformist group of people who still exist in this bland urban society.

CONCLUSIONS: DEFLECTION INTO EXCESS

Ultimately it is difficult to tell what is "supposed" to be part of the humor in *Play Time*: what is funny, potentially funny, or simply intriguing or neutral. As a result, we encounter a film in which we cannot fully distinguish the comic from the non-comic. Everything begins to look strange and funny, and this fosters an unusually prominent status for the film's excess. (In a previous study,[12] I defined excess as an inevitable gap in the motivation for the physical presence of a device; the physical presence retains a perceptual interest beyond its function in the work.) The film's departures from traditional gag structures in the directions of denial and overabundance tend to undermine motivation; if we are uncertain as to what we should consider funny, we must also be uncertain as to the motivation for the presence of the undefined devices. A viewing of the film that does not simply ignore its nontraditional comic strategies must inevitably notice excess.

Excess exists as a potential way of viewing any film, since no amount of narrative or other types of motivation can completely contain the materiality of the image and sound tracks. Yet a film may encourage viewing procedures that lead us to ignore excess. The classical Hollywood-style narrative cinema attempts to minimize our concentration on excess by subordinating the material aspects of the film to the narrative flow. The traditional ideology of viewing fostered by the classical cinema assumes that the film dictates the terms under which it will be watched.

[12] Kristin Thompson, *Eisenstein's Ivan the Terrible: A Neoformalist Analysis* (Princeton: Princeton University Press, 1981), chap. 9.

Other films, however, may deflect our attention from an exclusive concentration on narrative, toward style and unstructured material. The simplist, most traditional way of doing this involves the presentation of the picturesque composition. For example, the Dietrich films of Joseph von Sternberg contain a kind of "tame" excess by virtue of their artistically motivated clutter of decorative mise-en-scene. Such excess can exist primarily because it does not interfere with our understanding of the narrative to any great extent. Classical narrative films are usually highly redundant; the fact that attractive compositions draw our eye does not mean our attention drifts entirely away from the significant elements of the causal chain. The framing still concentrates upon the space containing action relevant to the narrative; compositions tend to favor narrative elements by centering or balancing them. Visual qualities in von Sternberg's and other Hollywood films may even be functioning analogous to the unobtrusive sound track music; both music and visuals are structured to blend in with and enhance the narrative action. To a limited degree, then, the Hollywood cinema can tolerate this slight departure toward the encouragement of the viewing that notes excess. (Such minimal idiosyncracies occasionally form the justification for the treatment of a director as an "auteur.")

Play Time uses a considerably different strategy for deflecting our attention toward excess. To begin with, the film's narrative causality is extremely simple—a time scheme of two days and two nights (the second night occurring only in the last shot) containing three basic situations: the tourist group's visit, Hulot's appointment with Giffard, and the opening of the Royal Garden. Tati uses virtually none of the classical hermeneutic structures to generate our interest in "what will happen next." In a conventional narrative involving *Play Time*'s tourist group line of action, the heroine Barbara would probably have a specific place in Paris she has always longed to visit, and the regimented tour would thwart her desire again and again, until the kindly Mr. Hulot stepped in to help her visit the locale at the end. The actual film, however, consists of a tiny number of narratively important moments (e.g., Hulot's chance meeting with Giffard at night, the accident with the orange), separated by long strings of narratively inconsequential gags (inconsequential in that few of them actually relate to the forward impetus of the causal chain, as with the Greek-column wastebasket jokes). A narrative with so little forward drive provides a great potential for deflection of attention outward toward excess.

Also, although the composition of *Play Time*'s mise-en-scene is striking in many complex ways, it is hardly beautiful in a conventional sense. Rather, by deflecting our attention outward from the main gags, the film forces us into new viewing procedures, which include the perception of excess. Nor do the implications of the fact that the comic and the non-comic become indistinguishable stop with the simple viewing of the film. The encouragement of the perception of excess which *Play Time* provides can successfully transform our perception in general. As we have seen in Chapter 1, this transformation is the primary function of art and is accomplished through defamiliarization. We should aim to become aware of how such perceptual shifts occur, however, for the ideological implications of the artwork lie partly in this process. Defamiliarization should be a matter of our active understanding of the work's overall effect, as well as of our response specifically to its structured, cued effects.

Play Time structures even our transference, at the end, of aesthetic perception to everyday existence, by continuing its theme music for several minutes after the images stop—so long that we are forced to get up and move about to this music. The film's sound track becomes an accompaniment for our own actions, inviting us to perceive our surroundings as we have perceived the film.[13] Indeed, those who have entered fully into the perceptual play of watching this film may well begin to see and hear the world in Tatian terms. The title *Play Time* gains one further implication—for our own everyday perception. It becomes difficult to hear a garbled loudspeaker announcement or to see a modern skyscraper without thinking of *Play Time*.

The structural strategies of excess in *Play Time* carry through absolutely its thematic ideological implications. *Play Time* does not present an analysis of the political system responsible for the uniform, sterile environment of the modern world. Rather, the unplanned destruction of that environment by a set of casual acquaintances sets up anarchic activity as the problem's solution. The imaginations of individuals are presented as spontaneously creating alternatives; the symbolic culmination of this idea comes as the American businessman Schultz takes the plans of the Royal Garden from the architect and hands them to Hulot, saying, "Partner, tonight the Royal Garden is ours." (As usual, this interaction takes place in the background of a scene.)

The imaginative perception of the modern world which these characters display is the representation within the fiction of the perceptual skills we need to develop in watching *Play Time*. In effect, the film provides us with the ability to see the humor in our own modern en-

---

[13] In the original Paris run of Tati's next film, *Traffic*, the audience, upon entering the theater, was confronted by a large mirror; the mirror reflected the passing traffic on the street outside.

vironment and hence to overcome its oppression, at least a little. Moreover, the imaginative leaps we need to make in coping with *Play Time* may well suggest how we might see the real world as potentially different. Tati's place in cinema history may be closer to Godard's than to Keaton's or Chaplin's. Like Godard, Tati is among the few filmmakers who attempt both to criticize social conditions and to create films that force us into new film-viewing skills; these skills are precisely those that offer ways of dealing with the social conditions as they exist outside the film as well. Widely different as the political stances of Godard and Tati are, their systems both offer this absolute inseparability of perceptual challenge and ideological implications.

10

Godard's Unknown Country:
Sauve qui peut (la vie)

I like to see things for the first time. Just as ordinary people like to see a world
record broken because it's for the first time; the second time they're less interested. Pictures are made to make seen the unseen. Afterward you can drop
it and go on again. It's like tourists who go into an unknown country.
—Jean-Luc Godard, quoted by Jonathan Cott, in "Godard: Born-Again Filmmaker"

NARRATIVE STRUCTURE AND GAPS

WHEN Jean-Luc Godard made *Numéro deux* in 1975, he presented it
to the world as his move into a new kind of filmmaking. Advance publicity treated it as a remake of *À bout de souffle*, with the title suggesting that *Numéro deux* was a "second first feature." The resulting
film was, of course, no remake of an earlier work. Instead, it incorporated the results of the video experiments that proved so important in
Godard's work of the second half of the 1970s. But if the presentation
of *Numéro deux* to the public was calculated to regain for Godard the
wide art-house audience of his pre-Dziga-Vertov-Group days, the attempt failed. There followed further video experiments in *Comment
ça va* and two lengthy television works, and then Godard tried a similar approach to publicizing *Sauve qui peut (la vie)* in 1980. Once again
Godard was starting anew at filmmaking. This time the American popular press bit: "Godard at the Crossroads," "Godard: Born-Again Filmmaker," "Godard: Return of the Master," "Godard Redux."[1] Journal-
ists and reviewers who had not seen a Godard work in nearly ten years
responded with great warmth, acting as though their old favorite were
returning from years of inactivity or confused wandering. His motor-

THIS ESSAY was written after I made a short presentation on *Sauve qui peut (la vie)* in
David Bordwell's Godard Seminar at the University of Wisconsin-Madison in the spring
of 1983. It has benefited from the discussion of the film on that occasion.

[1] The authors of the articles are, respectively, David Ehrenstein, *Los Angeles Exam-
iner*, 13 January 1981: C1, 3; Jonathan Cott, *Rolling Stone* (27 November 1980): 32–36;
Dan Yakir, *New York Magazine* (6 October 1980): 31–34; and David Denby, *New York
Magazine* (20 October 1980): 83–84.

cycle accident of 1971 figured prominently in reviews, as though it had taken Godard nearly ten years to recover from it and make another film. Under other circumstances, *Sauve qui peut*, basically an unpleasant and confusingly presented narrative about unlikable people, might have been dismissed as inferior to *Weekend* (the last "real" Godard film for most of these writers); in fact, the new film garnered a surprising number of compliments and some raves. The advertising became studded with plaudits signed by very familiar names.

Godard played up to and promoted this reaction in the manner of the filmmaker prostitute he repeatedly insisted he was. He obligingly dismissed the post-1968 films to interviewers during his American tour to promote *Sauve qui peut* ("He confessed that his pix of the '60s were 'at the wrong time with the wrong people at the wrong place,' and did not get through to a large audience"; "I'm a born-again filmmaker"[2]). He used the "second first film" angle and got away with it; reviewers applied it to *Sauve qui peut* without a backward glance at *Numéro deux*. The film did not exactly regain Godard his place as *the* art-house filmmaker for America (that place having been seized by the New German filmmakers, and especially Fassbinder, during the 1970s). But Godard was back in the fold.

The terms of his acceptance, however, were particularly strange. Descriptions of the film treat it as an absolute return to the "traditional" pre-1968 Godard approach. Reviews give confident (and inaccurate) plot summaries as if the film were readily graspable; mentions of the film's remarkably dense sound-image relationships and even its insistent use of slowed-down printing techniques are absent from many accounts. Yet the difficulty of sorting out a clear story line and the opacity of the style are to me the most striking aspects of the film. Godard seems to have been clever enough to make a film from which the casual viewer could pluck out a relatively clear set of events, character traits, and thematic implications; yet, at the same time, he was able to continue his formal experiments unhindered. *Sauve qui peut (la vie)* does not, I think, simply return to the previous Godard. Indeed, the film may be, as Godard claims, the beginning of a fifth period in his career.[3]

Certainly the films he has made since have, to varying degrees, carried through on similar strategies. Godard's films from *Sauve qui peut* to *Détective* seem to be aimed quite consciously at several types of audiences: art-cinema audiences, journalistic reviewers, academic

---

[2] Lawrence Cohn, "Jean-Luc Godard Enlivens New York," *Variety* (8 October 1980): 7; Cott, "Godard: Born-Again Filmmaker," p. 36.

[3] Cott, "Godard: Born-Again Filmmaker," p. 36.

critics, and that relatively small group of viewers interested in experiments with parametric form. Godard seems well aware that this last group is not large enough to sustain his work commercially, and he makes his films conform to art-cinema conventions to some extent. In some cases he even seems capable of manipulating the critics of his films. The video work *Scénario du film Passion*, for example, serves a remarkable mixture of purposes. It is, to begin with, a parody of the genre of documentaries about the production of films. While most such films concentrate on the design and production phases as being the most visually interesting, Godard talks about the scenario phase—even though the video contains almost no footage of the planning stages. Beyond this, *Scénario du film Passion* is a meditation on the process of filmmaking—one which is partly serious and partly a joke on what the critical establishment will presumably say about him and *Passion*. The enigmatic, contradictory statements he makes about film and himself feed the sorts of interpretations such critics inevitably make. And the video allows Godard to get a second work out of the same footage he used for *Passion*—one that could be shown on television as a long, free trailer for the feature (as when it was run on Channel 4 in England in 1983). In *Détective*, a number of the characters go around speculating on the motivations for various other characters' actions and on the causes behind events; their speeches seem to anticipate the kinds of things that spectators and critics might think or write when confronted with difficulties in the film. In sum, Godard's very sophisticated grasp of his own position in relation to the institutions of filmmaking and exhibition seems to have been built into the very form of his recent films. This helps explain how those determined to see them simply as conventional art cinema can ignore so many of the strange and difficult aspects of the films—their more abstract, parametric play. Of course, having a level of parametric structures that exists alongside the syuzhet, to be noticed or not, is typical of parametric films in general; one need not notice the perceptually difficult gags in *Play Time* or the unique spatio-temporal system of Ozu's works to enjoy those films. Yet Godard's films take one extra step, as if he had consciously realized this fact about parametric form and taken it into account when planning his films. Perhaps the greater complexity and difficulty of the recent films, which make it hard to construct a coherent fabula on just one viewing, serve to cue us to look for these parametric aspects. There are elements of these films that are extremely difficult, if not impossible, to account for as far as their functions in the narrative go. They are, to use a rather awkward term, almost "meta-parametric" films—films that explore the impact of parametric form on the perception of narrative. Most critics have ignored this aspect of recent Godard; they apparently assume that the narrative opacities are simply additional obscure symbols to be interpreted (often by means of comparison with the clearer meanings of Godard's earlier films). Without abandoning interpretation, let us try looking at both the difficulties and the parametric play in *Sauve qui peut (la vie)*.

What are the difficulties in perceiving *Sauve qui peut*? For many viewers, the first impression of the film is of a fairly simple story, complicated a bit by the step-printed slow-motion effects (hereafter called step-SM) and sonic tricks. But the basics are clear enough. Once more a prostitute (Isabelle) provides a metaphor for capitalist exploitation. An intellectual couple (Paul and Denise) working in the mainstream media—in this case at a television station—try to rethink their situation; Denise quits her job to live in the country. This suggests a city/country opposition, representing societal corruption and aloof purity, respectively. Further, the use of the name Paul Godard for the hero who fails in his various relationships with women suggests Jean-Luc Godard, trying to redeem himself for his earlier, notoriously sexist uses of women in his films. (Reviewers almost universally took Paul as a simple autobiographical portrait of the director—his "double," as David Denby put it.[4] The car accident is linked to Godard's cycling accident, Paul's television work to Godard's video work, and so on.) The ideological implications are similarly clear, waiting to be summarized: "modern diseases of spiritual loneliness and futility."[5]

The complexity of the film was deceiving indeed. Not only could critics interpret it simply, but they could ignore entirely its many gaps and complications. Pauline Kael, who grudgingly admired the film, complained, "This is the only time I have ever felt that the smattering of narrative in a Godard film wasn't enough; there's so little going on in 'Every Man for Himself' that you want more drama."[6] This opinion, little though it fits the actual film, does not surprise one, coming from a reviewer who probably watched the film once. (This is not to say that the film's complexities are not apparent on first viewing; I decided to write this essay while viewing the film for the first time.) But even Colin MacCabe, an academic critic who has dealt extensively with recent Godard, professes himself surprised at "the relatively straightforward use of narrative," and, astonishingly enough, he even concludes that Godard has given up his intensive work on the sound track; *Sauve qui peut*, he finds, "reluctantly and hesitatingly accepts a cer-

[4] Denby, "Godard Redux," p. 83.
[5] Ibid.
[6] Pauline Kael, "The Current Cinema," *The New Yorker* (24 November 1980): 203.

tain dominance of the image." Further evidence of academic critics' failure to notice the great degree of difficulty offered by the film can be found in three articles by the editors of *Camera Obscura*. All simply assume that Paul Godard equals Jean-Luc Godard in a straightforward way; Janet Bergstrom assumes the "conversation" between Paul and the gym instructor to be simple, offscreen diegetic sound; Constance Penley assigns clear sources to the various women's voices heard reading over at intervals; Bergstrom assumes that because we hear Marguerite Duras's voice during the car trip, she is actually in the car at that moment; and Elisabeth Lyon says that Denise is living in the city at the beginning of the film and moves to the country.[7] As we shall see, I find these and other, similar devices considerably more problematic and nuanced than these essays suggest. Yet the fact that popular reviewers and academic critics alike have distorted the film in describing it should alert us to strategies in the film that deserve a closer look.

Upon closer examination, then, *Sauve qui peut* proves to have many ambiguities, uncertainties, and unexplained events that make the reconstruction of a fabula line from its syuzhet presentation difficult. Where, for example, do the events occur? A few reviews place the action in a "nameless Swiss city."[8] In fact there are five distinct general locales, and the differences among them have a significance for the film's ideological implications. There is a city (Geneva); a town (Nyon, twenty kilometers along the coast of Lake Geneva, on a main train line from Geneva); an unidentified village near Nyon; a farm near that village; and the countryside between these points (see Fig. 10.1). The television station where Paul and Denise work, Cecile's school, Paul's hotel, the traffic scenes, Isabelle's apartment, and the hotels where she visits clients are all in Geneva. Denise and Paul have been sharing an apartment in Nyon, which she wants to give up in order to live on a farm in the mountains. Isabelle moves from Geneva to this apartment at the end. Michel Piaget's press, which Denise visits, is in the village near which she settles. We see her biking on roads around Nyon and the village. Getting these locations straight helps a great deal in understanding the story; the differences also add nuances to the simple city/country opposition. We see these locations as settings

---

[7] Colin MacCabe, " 'Slow Motion,' " *Screen* 21, no. 3 (Autumn 1980): 111, 113; *Camera Obscura* no. 8-9-10 (1982): Elisabeth Lyon, "La passion, c'est pas ça": 7–10; Constance Penley, "Pornography, Eroticism": 13–18; and Janet Bergstrom, "Violence and Enunciation": 22–30.

[8] Denby, "Godard Redux," p. 83; Kael, "The Current Cinema," p. 197.

for the various stages of the characters' attempts to change their lives; the changes are not as sudden and simple as they may at first appear.

A breakdown into scenes may help in a discussion of the story of *Sauve qui peut*. (This segmentation marks off breaks on the image track; as we shall see, a line of sound will often carry over two or more transitions between segments, so that a different division into scenes would be possible—had we the critical tools to notate sound as simply and clearly as we can the image.)

I. Credits (Shot 1). A pan over clouds, with music.

II. A hotel (Shots 2–5). Voice singing opera; Paul phones Denise at a television station, but she is not there. He leaves the room and is followed and accosted by a homosexual bellhop.

III. The Swiss countryside near Nyon (Shots 6–12). Denise biking on a country road; introduction of freeze frames and step-SM. Shot 7 is a title, numbered -1, with "Sauve qui peut." Shot 9 is a title, numbered 0, with "La vie."

IV. A village restaurant (Shots 13–16). Denise at a table; a conversation at a nearby table. She asks about the music she hears and learns that Michel Piaget is at the soccer field.

V. A village soccer field (Shots 17–24). Denise bikes to see Michel at the soccer field. They discuss his father's business and the landscape; she arranges to come to his press. Some step-SM in two shots. Shot 19 is a title, numbered 1, with "L'imaginaire."

VI. A farm (Shots 25–30). A woman shows Denise how to feed cattle.

VII. The farm and a television station in Geneva (Shots 31–34). Denise calls Paul to tell him she is moving out of their apartment; he is to pick up Duras. A woman in the farmhouse tells her which room she will have. Shot 32 shows Paul, but not on the phone; in shot 34, he talks to Denise. The scene ends with an argument, and also with the first mention of Cecile and Paul's ex-wife.

VIII. The farm (Shots 35–36). Horses in a field; Denise in her room, dressing and writing. Her reading carries over part of the next segment.

IX. Michel Piaget's press, in a village (Shots 37–43). Denise rides to Michel's press. Step-SM over a shot of hands setting type; he shows her the facilities and offers her a book commission. She bikes away.

X. Countryside near Nyon (Shots 44–48). Denise biking. Classical-style string music becomes mixed with an accordian, revealed as coming from a family standing by the road. Step-SM of Denise; then superimpositions of a tractor over her, then her over a tractor.

XI. The Nyon train station (Shots 49–59). Denise arrives at the station and sees the Marlboro racing car and Georgiana slapped for refusing to choose between two men. Step-SM on this action. The scene ends with the departure of the car, the departure of the two men with Georgiana, and Denise pacing as the train passes.

XII. An athletic field (Shots 60–70). Paul picking Cecile up. Shot 61 is a title, numbered 2, with "La peur." Step-SM in shot 65, with a conversation over about daughters' sexuality. Paul and Cecile drive away. Duras's voice begins over shot 69.

XIII. A classroom (Shots 71–75). Paul is in a classroom where students are watching a tape of *Le Camion*. Duras is next door but will not speak. Paul reads a quotation from her writings. Duras's voice comes up again over the last shot.

XIV. The television station (Shots 76–87). Duras's voice continues over the scene, joined by piano music, accompanying Paul and Cecile driving. There is a cut to Denise at the station; Duras's voice is heard, talking about women's domain and childhood, as Denise goes to meet Paul in the parking lot. After an argument about his failure to bring Duras, he drives away with Cecile.

XV. A restaurant (Shots 88–102). Paul and Cecile park the car. Cecile's reading about blackbirds begins and continues into the restaurant scene with Paul's ex-wife Colette. Paul goes to call Denise; there is a cutaway to Denise. Paul gives Colette a check; they discuss Denise's departure, over cutaways to Denise in a street. Paul gives Cecile some shirts and leaves.

XVI. A lunch counter and train station (Shots 103–106). Step-SM on a line of cars in the street. Paul and Denise at a lunch counter discuss her departure to the country. (During this conversation she mentions being fed up with Nyon.) There is a cutaway to a woman listening to a joke, puzzled by music. The scene ends with Denise and Paul fighting as they part.

XVII. Streets (Shots 107–113). Paul in a street, then in a cinema queue. He is picked up by Isabelle as a man comes out of the cinema complaining that the sound has been cut off. Step-SM in shot 110. There is an argument between a couple in the street; they decide to go to a movie. A row of cars is out of focus; Isabelle fakes orgasm, with a woman's voice-over talking about household routine.

XVIII. Paul's hotel room and streets (Shots 114–128). Shot 114 is a title, numbered 3, with "Le commerce." A voice-over continues to the end of the title. Paul pays Isabelle. She shops, walks, and is picked up by pimps; they warn her not to work independently and spank her. She parks her car.

XIX. Isabelle's apartment (Shots 129–141). Isabelle's sister waits for her. Isabelle comes in and phones about apartments. Her sister needs money and arranges to be a prostitute for a month, giving half her money to Isabelle. Isabelle mentions leaving for the country.

XX. A hotel room (Shots 142–160). Isabelle goes to Monsieur Personne's hotel room and acts out a fantasy about being his daughter; at intervals there are cutaways to traffic in the street. In the hall, Isabelle meets an old schoolmate and makes an appointment about a job. The scene ends with Isabelle's overhearing a conversation between Personne and another woman about the failure of the fantasy scene.

XXI. An editing room (Shots 161–162). Isabelle arrives at a parking lot; inside, she meets a man editing film. He offers her money to travel and stay in hotels in various cities.

XXII. Another hotel room (Shots 163–180). A line of cars. Inside the hotel, Isabelle buys Marlboros; she goes to a room where a businessman and his assistant, Thierry, direct her and another prostitute, Nicole, in various sexual situations. Isabelle calls Denise and arranges to see the apartment on Saturday. Over part of the scene, a woman's voice speaks a passage about heroes as losers.

XXIII. Road; park; Denise and Paul's apartment in Nyon (Shots 181–188). Isabelle is driving at night; in the morning, she parts from her companion in a park and goes to the apartment. She sees Paul jump on Denise, with a lengthy step-SM effect. Paul goes out.

XXIV. Nyon (Shots 189–191). Shot 189 is a title, numbered 4, with "La musique." Paul sits on a bench by the family with the accordian. Denise sits in Isabelle's car; they talk and arrange the transfer of the apartment. Isabelle tells Denise that Paul is at the station.

XXV. Nyon (Shots 192–196). Countryside. There is a cut to Isabelle in the apartment, with a client. Denise sees Paul for the last time at the station. Isabelle is by the window; Denise is on the road. Paul's voice begins over the last shot.

XXVI. Paul's hotel and a street (Shots 197–210). A line of cars; Paul is in the hotel room, calling the television station. He reserves the room for six more months and goes out to pick up a new car. He sees Colette and Cecile and tries to arrange a reconciliation. He is hit by a car and apparently lies dying; Colette and Cecile walk away, past an orchestra in an alley.

On the basis of this segmentation, we can look at the difficulties in determining the time scheme of the film. At several points in the course of the film characters refer to days or times, but piecing these together poses problems. For example, after Paul pays off Isabelle in his hotel room at the beginning of Segment XVIII, we see a shot of her shopping for soap, then one of her walking in a parking lot. Are these shots that suggest days passing in a routine way (a sort of little montage sequence), or does she do these things immediately after leaving Paul? By tracing through the references to days, as well as the alternation of day and night scenes, it is possible to rough out an approximate time scheme.

The syuzhet duration seems to be about a week. Segments II through VII (Paul's departure from the hotel in the morning, Denise's biking and visit with Michel, the scene of Denise learning to feed cattle, and her phone call to Paul) all take place on an unspecified day, probably Wednesday. She refers on the phone to having placed an ad on Wednesday (the ad for the apartment which later leads Isabelle to her). At the beginning of Segment VIII we see Denise dressing early in the day; a lengthy series of events, up to Segment XVII, all seem to take place on Thursday, presumably of the same week that the ad appeared. (This includes Denise's visit to Michel's press, her bike trip back to Nyon, the scene at the Nyon train station, Paul's picking up of Cecile and the apparent attempt to take Marguerite Duras to the television station, the argument with Denise, Paul's dinner with his ex-wife Colette and Cecile, his talk with Denise before her departure by train, and Paul's meeting with Isabelle.) Isabelle's subsequent scenes with her sister, her clients, and the people who offer her a job (Segments XVIII through XXII) occur on Friday; during this day she makes an appointment to see Denise's apartment on Saturday. The night driving shot that begins Segment XXIII provides the transition to Saturday morning; the remainder of Segment XXIII, in which Isabelle sees Paul leap upon Denise at breakfast, shows the only Saturday

271

events. From this point on the time scheme becomes choppy. We know from Paul's phone conversation in the last segment that the film ends on a Wednesday morning. Probably Segment XXIV, in which Denise sits talking with Isabelle in the car, takes place on Sunday. The next scenes show Isabelle sitting at breakfast with another client, then Denise's final parting from Paul at the station. This is probably Monday, since Denise had told Michel she would definitely return to the village on Monday, and on Wednesday Paul says he has been depressed for two days over Denise's departure.

The time scheme is not as crucial to *Sauve qui peut*'s overall structure and ideological implications as is the pattern of locales. But the difficulties in piecing it together testify to the film's pervasive strategy of impeding the audience's comprehension of details.

We learn about the characters in a similarly oblique way. Isabelle, for instance, first appears in Segment XVII in close-up. She speaks to someone standing off left: "You want to see a film?" Immediately following this line, the man with the little boy begins shouting that the sound in the theater has been cut off. This joke goes on over shots of Isabelle wandering alongside the cinema line, looking for a customer. Our thought upon first seeing her might be that she is on a date, speaking to a man we cannot see clearly (in fact, the offscreen man is Paul). Then the comic business distracts us from immediately grasping what she is doing. We soon figure out that Isabelle is a prostitute and has picked Paul up, but most likely on first viewing we will have missed most of what was going on in the cinema-line shots. Similarly, when Denise phones Paul from the farmhouse in Segment VII, she speaks several lines before she mentions his name; the implications of the scene's opening are likely to be lost on us, since we have no idea to whom she is speaking.

These are the kinds of things that additional viewings, and especially editing-table analysis, can clarify. But even the most careful analysis cannot find answers to all the questions that linger. What is Michel Piaget's relationship to Denise (ex-lover? cousin? friend?)? Who is the man with black hair and black suit seen in three shots (in the cinema line, parting from Isabelle in a park after her drive to Nyon, and finally walking by the side of the road as Denise bikes off into the countryside at the end of Segment XXV)? Perhaps he is the "ex-boyfriend," Anatole Napoli, mentioned by Isabelle in her talk with Denise. But if so, what is he doing in that cinema line or on the roadside? Why does Isabelle's sister, riding in the car that hits Paul at the end, say she recognizes him? It is possible, of course, to ignore these problematic elements and give a simple synopsis of the action. But to do so one must boil down the film considerably, skimming off the confusing elements. One must, in short, ignore a considerable portion of the film. The problem for the critic, as I take it, is to deal with the film as a whole. If a film refuses to be fully comprehended, that in itself is a formal element. In this case, as I have suggested, the difficulties may be seen as an attempt to deflect our attention toward parametric structures.

OVERALL STRATEGIES

In a sense, the principles governing narrative and style in *Sauve qui peut (la vie)* are a reversal of the ones Godard and Gorin had used in *Tout va bien*. The earlier film had dealt with the social necessity for rethinking one's life and the factors that can lead to this rethinking. Although this thematic material was worked out in a narrative with major characters, the larger structure of the film was rhetorical. As we saw in Chapter 4, the political situation was presented first as an argument, with the shots of various social classes in static poses. The voices speaking over then added conflict, characters, stars, and a love story, thus embodying these political elements in a concrete narrative context. By including the framing device of filmmaking, Godard and Gorin could also examine the social limitations on making films and how one might rethink the filmmaking process itself. *Tout va bien* ended with the characters beginning to reconsider their lives. The filmmaking frame story was perhaps the perfect Brechtian device for that project, but Godard could not simply repeat the formula in film after film.

Sauve qui peut seems to take up where *Tout va bien* left off, but with a different strategy. Again we have an intellectual couple engaged in commercial media work. The woman has been considering quitting her job for two years and finally does it; the man refuses to act, and they separate. (It is as if Jacques in *Tout va bien* had responded to Susan's demands by sullenly agreeing to drive her to the airport.) But *Sauve qui peut* eschews an abstract rhetorical structure. In *Tout va bien*, rethinking had been held up as clear-cut, almost simple (quit one's job or not, stay together or not); *Sauve qui peut* places its emphasis, not on the argument in favor of rethinking, but on the concrete implications of actually doing the rethinking of one's life in modern society. The concentration at every level is on "life," on the details of changing one's situation: the difficulty of giving up a job or a lover, the necessity of finding an apartment, the choice of modes of transportation, the resistance from one's friends, and the decision about the sort

273

of environment in which to live. In some senses, the film uses a more traditional approach as a result, but in others, it is still full of Godardian innovation. We seem to see the characters' actions presented as in a traditional art film, with psychological depth and ambiguous causality. But these traits function to embed the politics more concretely in the historical situation. In *Tout va bien*, the historical rethinking was done in terms of a contrast between France in 1968 and France in 1972. But in *Sauve qui peut* there is only the present. Godard needs barely to suggest why rethinking would be necessary. The concrete causes of rethinking in *Tout va bien*—Susan's and Jacques's captivity during the strike, their experiences in May 1968—have no direct parallel in *Sauve qui peut*. Instead, Godard can simply assume the necessity for rethinking. The signs of that necessity are pervasively present: the motifs of the Marlboro and Coke ads, the cruelty of men toward women, the emphasis on prostitution, and the separation of work and love. The film uses only one brief scene to make explicit the links between these things and the abstract argument for changing one's position in society. This comes in Segment XVI, the lunch counter scene, in which Paul and Denise talk before she leaves on the train. The dialogue here contains obvious parallels with Susan's argument with Jacques over breakfast in *Tout va bien*; Denise says: "Love should grow from work, from gestures made together, and not only at night, you said. And nights should grow out of days." Politics as such are almost absent from *Sauve qui peut*, but the results of political action on people's lives are present everywhere.

More specifically, *Sauve qui peut* fits into a pattern which MacCabe has pointed out; in discussing the film, he writes of Godard's move away from a specifically Maoist program after 1973, and his concentration on "the division of work and love effected by an ever-increasing division of labor."[9] Laura Mulvey and MacCabe discuss Godard's new interest in sexual politics in relation to *Numéro deux*, but the description fits *Sauve qui peut* as well.

It is these moments which mark a crucial shift in the terms of Godard's presentation of sexuality. For the first time the chickens have come home to roost. The problem of sexuality is not *wholly* signified by a woman; the problems of male sexuality, and the attendant undercurrents of misogyny and violence, come out into the open. Godard and Mieville [Anne-Marie Mieville, who also co-scripted *Sauve qui peut*] now explicitly investigate the nature of male sexuality that turns women into an image of its desire and, crucially, the repression of homosexuality as one of the founding moments of that sexuality.

[9] MacCabe, "Slow Motion," p. 112.

The violence against women, the emphasis on anal sex, turns around this ambiguous relation to other men.[10]

The misogyny and violence in *Sauve qui peut* are obvious, and the episode at the beginning as Paul angrily rejects the bellhop's overtures introduces the homosexual motif into the film early on. The relationship of misogyny to the repression of homosexuality becomes clear in the scene in which Isabelle and another prostitute, Nicole, obey a series of orders given them by a businessman and his male assistant, Thierry. Although the two men never touch each other, the boss arranges the women between himself and Thierry; the rhythmic sexual gestures of Thierry, directed at Isabelle or Nicole, are in turn transferred in the same rhythm to the boss—making the prostitutes a sort of conduit for sexual contact between the two men. The men also humiliate the women gratuitously in the course of the scene. Godard makes the import of the scene doubly clear by having the boss direct Isabelle to apply lipstick to him as part of the sexual chain he constructs.

Politics are by no means absent from *Sauve qui peut*, but now we have an examination of sexual politics in the context of a specific social situation. Hence it takes no extraordinary events like participating in a strike to trigger rethinking and change; the process grows logically from the circumstances of everyday existence.

Yet if the process of rethinking is more concrete in *Sauve qui peut* than in *Tout va bien*, its implications are also far bleaker. *Tout va bien* ended on a fairly optimistic note, with the couple seemingly planning to stay together, presumably to do some sort of politically correct and potentially effective work. But in *Sauve qui peut*, although the characters may rethink their positions, the options possible in modern society seem limited indeed. Denise may escape, but the film offers no suggestion that she can do much in the way of politically effective activity. Her existence becomes almost monastic as she gives away some of her possessions to Isabelle, takes up a regimen of biking in the mountains, and lives in a single room of a farmhouse. The only way to defeat the effects of society upon oneself, it would seem, is to shut society out as completely as possible.

This idea of escape comes out clearly in the settings of the film. Denise had lived in Geneva, and she has moved to Nyon to share an apartment with Paul; now she goes to a farm. Paul not only refuses to

---

[10] Laura Mulvey and Colin MacCabe, "Images of Woman, Images of Sexuality," in MacCabe's *Godard: Images, Sounds, Politics* (London: The BFI and Macmillan, 1980), pp. 99–100.

go with her, he stays in Geneva in an expensive hotel. Isabelle mentions to her sister that life is too difficult in the city, and that she may move to the country; in fact, she ends up living in Nyon. We are left in doubt as to whether she will eventually follow Denise's path or take the job she is offered, which involves traveling to a series of cities and staying in hotels. Michel Piaget, who seems to be set forth as a sort of privileged example, lives in a village and controls his own work to a large extent, running a press where much of the work is done by hand. Although the reviewers universally took Paul Godard to be a stand-in for the director, Michel comes rather closer to Jean-Luc Godard's own life style. At the time of the film's production, Godard was living in Rolle, a small town near Nyon, further away from Geneva along the lake shore (see Figure 10.1); he was running his own small film and video firm.

Sauve qui peut sets forth a few basic ideas—city versus country, commerce versus independence, sex versus work—very simply. Then it combines these with a dense stylistic weave of concrete times, spaces, and events. The fabula-syuzhet relations are confusing. Our understanding is impeded in part by a series of motifs that distract us from the main action (e.g., the exact repetition of the line "That's not what passion is" three times) and in part by the use of sound as an interference device.

These stylistic difficulties help pull us away from a concentration on the concrete circumstances of the characters' lives. Again, the strategy is the opposite of that in *Tout va bien*, which had introduced an abstract situation in the opening sequence and then put it into a narrative. Here the style frequently distances us, encouraging us to interpret implicit rhetorical meanings that might help motivate the film's formal difficulties. If we want to figure out what is going on in *Sauve qui peut*, we must struggle to cope with its bombardment of material, both narrative and stylistic. Out of a welter of details, we must strive to find a pattern. This is not necessarily the same as simply interpreting a theme. After all, the thematic material, as we have seen, is fairly simple. Rather, once again Godard is experimenting with parametric form, seeking a way of forcing his audience into developing new viewing skills; those viewing skills involve analysis of a type that could be applied to events outside the film as well.

THE DENSE STYLISTIC WEAVE

Sauve qui peut contains many difficult parametric structures that tend to break up the links between cause and effect in the narrative chain.

Two major stylistic patterns seem opposed to each other. On the one hand, the freeze frames and step-SM tend to protract certain actions— lingering over gestures far longer than their simple narrative significance would seem to warrant. On the other hand, many moments in the film contain a rapid jumble of devices, presented two or more at a time, so that our attention is split. At such moments, we may focus on one thread at the expense of missing the others, or we may try to follow all and understand any one of them imperfectly. This frequently happens, for example, when the sound of one line of action and locale plays over another action occurring elsewhere. Sound in general plays a tremendous role in rendering the film illegible—that is, difficult to grasp in the time allotted for perception.

As with many difficult films, the opening serves as a guide to what is to come. Even the credits suggest the film's formal strategies. Critics have noted that these declare *Sauve qui peut* to be a film "composed," not directed, by Jean-Luc Godard. Already our attention is drawn to music. By implication, music, and sound in general, will play an unusually prominent role in *Sauve qui peut*'s dominant. The title credit also stresses this (Fig. 10.2). Here the registration mark and the words "Copyright 1979 Sonimage" appear in the same size and style of print as the title. The film's whole title almost seems to be "Sauve qui peut (la vie) Copyright 1979 Sonimage." "Sonimage" is the name of Godard's film and video company. (This name has a double meaning: most obviously, "son" [sound] - "image," but also "son" [his or her] "image.") Thus the juxtaposition of sound and image links itself to the film's title credit. The alert viewer should already be prepared to listen hard.

The opening scene specifies the devices we can expect to notice. Immediately upon the cut from the credits to Segment II, an opera singer's voice is heard, loud, on the sound track. At first we may be uncertain about whether the voice is diegetic. Godard has been fond, we know, of using stretches of classical music in his films, non-diegetically. When Paul pounds on the wall, that issue resolves itself. But are we listening to a radio, a phonograph, or a live singer practicing? When Paul moves to the door and begins to open it, there is a cut to him in the hallway outside—an ellipsis, though the sound continues uninterrupted offscreen. After the dark hallway scene, during which the Spanish bellhop appears and first accosts Paul (again, an action we cannot grasp until the shot outside the hotel, when the bellhop approaches Paul by his car), Godard shows the hotel lobby in extreme-long shot (Fig. 10.3). The singer's voice continues with no change of volume, in spite of the fact that the source is presumably now on a

277

floor somewhere above. Paul, the bellhop, and the women whose bags the latter is carrying enter at the top right, meet in a confused group at the top of the escalator, and proceed down and out at the lower left. The shot is insistently illegible. We do not know what is going on with Paul and the bellhop, and we can barely pick out Paul and the others among the various people on the upper level of the lobby; Godard refuses to cut in to guide us. The shot is reminiscent of many in Tati's *Play Time*, both in its setting and in its playing out of the scene in extreme-long shot. Yet the shot also reverses Tati's strategy by refusing to guide the spectator even via the sound track. The dim sounds we hear coming from the space of the shot are resolutely drowned out by the singer's voice. Nevertheless, Tati's mastery of sound seems to have influenced Godard in his work, even though *Sauve qui peut* and *Play Time* are vastly different kinds of films. At any rate, the fact that the man who comes out of the cinema complaining about the sound being cut off is carrying a little boy on his shoulders almost certainly refers to the scene in *Play Time* in which a group of people—including a man carrying a small boy—watches the final stages of the Royal Garden restaurant's construction. (In fact, Godard had wanted Tati to play this small role in *Sauve qui peut*, that is, the man who comes out of the cinema complaining about the sound being cut off.[11] Unfortunately Tati refused, perhaps due to considerations of health. He had said he wished Hulot could become a minor character appearing in many films.) Moreover, the credits of *Sauve qui peut*, with their pan over clouds, can perhaps be seen as another homage to *Play Time*. Certainly Godard's recent films link him closely to parametric filmmakers like Tati.

The tidbits of narrative information included in the opening scene are difficult to catch. We see Paul in a hotel, but we have no way of knowing he is living there indefinitely; we learn this only in Segment xv, when Colette asks him if he has moved. He calls Denise at the television station and discovers she is not there. But we do not learn that they both work there, that they have been lovers for some time, or that she is planning to leave him. Most of this information is parceled out slowly across the first half of the film, only becoming clear in Segment xvi, as Paul and Denise talk at the lunch counter.

Upon first viewing, the film's stylistic distractions may seem random or arbitrary. There is, however, a pattern of parameters running

---

[11] Godard, in conversation with David Bordwell, Minneapolis, Spring, 1981. Godard has also stated: "I fall very easily into the comic. I love Tati and Jerry Lewis" (in Don Ranvaud and Alberto Farassino, "An Interview with Jean-Luc Godard," *Framework* no. 21 [Summer 1983]: 9).

through the film that governs many, though not all, of the formal repetitions. In creating this pattern, the film breaks down into larger portions, or clusters of segments, each centered around a different character or group of characters. Bordwell says of parametric films,
"Redundancy is achieved either by limiting the range of stylistic procedures or by strictly paralleling segments of the syuzhet."[12] In *Sauve
qui peut*, the numbered intertitles help mark off such segments and
hint at associations for each character. Stylistic traits vary among these
portions, though there is no cut-and-dried rule which the film sets
itself. In general, the step-SM effects, the motifs, and even sound
usage vary to differing degrees from one portion to another.

After the opening segment in the hotel has introduced Paul and
given us some idea of what to expect from the film stylistically, the
remaining segments of the film tend to fall into four large portions,
each concentrating on a different character. Segments III through XI
stay largely with Denise, cutting to Paul only when she phones him.
Then the film moves to Paul as he picks up Cecile at school in Segment XII and stays mostly with him to the end of Segment XVII. At the
end of that segment, the camera lingers in close-up on Isabelle's face
as she fakes orgasm while having sex with Paul; this marks the transfer
of attention to her, and we see her activities in Segments XVIII to
XXIII. In XXIII, the three main characters meet for the only time in
the film, and the narrative focus moves among them in Segments XXIV
and XXV. The final segment, XXVI, returns to an exclusive concentration on Paul, paralleling the opening scene.

The intertitles that occur at intervals during the film help mark
these various changes in concentration. Each has a large numeral at
the center, over which is written a phrase or word: "-1, Sauve qui
peut" (Save who can); "0, La vie" (life); "1, L'imaginaire" (the imaginary, the visionary, the fantastic); "2, La peur" (fear); "3, Le commerce"; and "4, La musique." The first two titles come in Segment III,
as Denise rides her bike, and "L'imaginaire" occurs early in Segment
V, the scene in which she meets Michel at the village soccer field. For
the rest of the scenes that concentrate on Denise, there are no further
titles. The second shot of Segment XII, after we see one shot of Paul
at a school athletic field, is the "La peur" title. "Le commerce" begins
Segment XVIII, and we see Isabelle involved in activities as a prostitute. Finally, "La musique" introduces Segment XXIV, with its more
generalized range of knowledge.

[12] David Bordwell, *Narration in the Fiction Film* (Madison: University of Wisconsin
Press, 1985), p. 285.

These portions of the film, with their attendant titles, help clarify the patterns of slowed-down printing effects in the film. Some of these are brief freeze frames, others uneven slow-motion movements achieved in the printing rather than the shooting stage. By not shooting the scenes originally in slow motion, Godard is able to avoid a smooth, merely lyrical quality to the slowness. The spasmodic nature of these moments removes them from the more conventional lovers-running-through-the-fields sort of slow motion common in the commercial cinema. The slowed effects can serve in part as emphasis, like italics; in part as a distancing device applied to the scene; and in part to create individual associations for the different characters.

All the freezes and step-SM in Denise's scenes are associated with her. They first occur in Segment iii as she rides her bike; later, in the soccer field scene (Segment v), she remarks that the landscape is "quiet as an image," and there is an immediate cut to a medium shot of an athlete, with the slowing techniques used. We next see Denise leaving, with step-SM; in each of these shots, offscreen voices continue speaking at a normal rate, underscoring the contradictory nature of the slowing devices. These moments have an ambiguous motivation. They may be suggesting Denise's subjective perceptions, or they may imply a commentary on the action imposed by the filmic narration. The rest of the examples follow this pattern: in Segment ix, slowed effects of a man's hand setting type accompany Denise's reading, over, of the text she is writing; these effects return for her reaction as she sees the family with the accordian at the side of the road; and finally the effects are used again as Denise sees a young woman, Georgiana, slapped by her male companion at the Nyon train station.

These effects are at first closely associated with the texts of the intertitles. The first slow-motion shot of Denise on her bike (shot 6) leads immediately to the "Sauve qui peut" title (shot 7), which in turn leads to another step-SM shot of her (shot 8), and then to the "La vie" title (shot 9). Similarly, the athlete shot and the next of Denise leaving (shots 22 and 23) come only a few shots after the "L'imaginaire" title (shot 19). There are no further titles in this portion of the film, but Denise's reading, which begins in Segment viii at the farm and continues into the next segment, contains the words "La vie," harking back to the title of the film. Her description of life tallies with the slow-motion devices as well: "a more rapid gesture, an arm which moves out of time [à contretemps], a slower step, a puff of irregularity, a false movement," and so on. The last two instances of the device seem linked to Denise's point of view. She reacts strangely to the accordion player, almost as if she could hear the cacophonous blend of diegetic accordion sound with the non-diegetic string music that had begun earlier. (Indeed, in Segment IV, Denise has asked about music which apparently no one but we and she can hear.) In the scene at the station (Segment XI), there is some possibility that the shots of Georgiana being slapped are Denise's subjective vision; the increased cutting rate, the close views of Denise looking, the introduction of a new, strange musical theme as the offscreen argument accelerates, Denise's glance into the camera lens (the only such glance in the film), and the return to a long shot in which events go on as if nothing has happened—all these cues could be interpreted either as real or as Denise's reaction to the threat of violence in the argument she witnesses. But, as in a number of scenes in the film, the actual status of what we see and hear remains indeterminate.

The freeze-frame and step-SM devices in Paul's portion of the film have associations quite different from those in Denise's. They all occur in scenes of his relationships with the women in his life, and they all relate pretty straightforwardly to the "fear" title that characterizes him. As he watches Cecile at play (Segment XII), a step-SM device stretches out her gestures, as the voices of Paul and another man, heard off or over, discuss their daughters' sexuality. Since the man's voice is not that of the athletic coach, we could assume that the dialogue is Paul's memory or a scene imagined by him. (Again, repeated cuts to him looking at the ground and up at Cecile or the offscreen coach reinforce this assumption.) Later, as Paul embraces Denise, we see the step-SM effects in a shot of cars that introduces the scene at the lunch counter as he is about to part from Denise, and in the scene in which Isabelle picks Paul up in the cinema line. Such moments help to specify Paul's refusal to try to change his situation; his fear originates largely in his relations with women. We can see this also in his treatment of them, of course—as in the way he tosses the shirts aggressively at Cecile or jumps on Denise or grabs Colette to prevent her from walking past him in the last scene.

In Isabelle's scenes, the device also has a fairly clear-cut set of associations. Her title is "commerce," and specifically sexual commerce. As Isabelle is manhandled by her pimps, we see the action slowed for a moment; as Monsieur Personne describes his fantasy scene to her, one of the cutaways to the street slows the action of a young woman and man meeting and kissing. Then, as Isabelle carries through the fantasy, displaying her body to Personne, the device recurs; it continues in the next shot, a lateral track past a country landscape. The narration seems to be trying, during Isabelle's portion, to generalize her position as a prostitute to the population as a whole—a sort of intellectual montage to associate the metaphor of prostitution with all sexual and commercial intercourse.

The next, and most memorable, step-SM effect comes in Segment XXIII, as Isabelle watches Paul leap upon Denise and the two roll on the floor in each other's arms. The moment brings the three together for the only time in the film, and the slowed effect blends the associations it had had for each. The obvious effect the printing has on the action is to make it look at once like an embrace and a fight. From Denise's portion of the film, the shot recalls the slowed moment when Georgiana was slapped; the music over is the same theme, returning for the first time. For Paul, the step-SM effects were associated with his relations with women, and especially with his fear of losing Denise. And the shot is an eyeline match, following a medium close-up of Isabelle standing in the doorway looking at the couple; this glance-object pattern strongly recalls the preceding segment, when two similar close shots of Isabelle had shown her watching the scene in the office with the boss and Thierry humiliating the other prostitute.

The moments of step-SM in the final scene, as Paul kisses Cecile and detains Colette, and then as he falls to the ground after being hit by a car, recapitulate the "fear" association fairly straightforwardly.

Aside from the step-SM effects, the various unusual sound-image relations are the most striking stylistic devices in *Sauve qui peut*. Often the sound does not synchronize with the action within the image: it may be non-diegetic music, offscreen sound, sound from a different space, or sound from an uncertain source. Sound overlaps from segment to segment, so that the spectator has some difficulty in telling when the scene has shifted.

There is some differentiation among the larger portions of the film as to when these sound overlaps occur. After the initial scene in the hotel (Segment II), which, as we have seen, introduces many of the devices the film will use, the sound continues into Segment III. Over the first shot of Denise riding her bike, we hear the bellhop's voice shouting, in Spanish, "Evil town" twice. But on the whole the "Sauve qui peut"/"La vie"/"L'imaginaire" portion of the film contains fewer sound overlaps between segments than do the later portions. Only about half of the shifts in scene within Denise's segments have sound overlaps. Once Paul's and Isabelle's portions begin, however, every transition from one segment to another involves a continuing sound, diegetic or non-diegetic.

The result of this is to make Denise's portion of the film somewhat easier to grasp. We can tell more readily when one scene ends and another begins. Some of the segments in this portion are relatively simple in their presentation of narrative events: Denise talking to Michel at the soccer field, learning to feed cows, or getting the book commission from Michel. The simplicity of the segments sets Denise apart somewhat. Certainly reviewers and other spectators seem to take her as the main identification figure. This makes sense in narrative terms. To be sure, all the main characters in the film are to some extent unpleasant—even Denise, who is unnecessarily abusive to Cecile during her argument with Paul. But she is still the character who has decided to change her life for the better, and her project is set forth in clear terms in these early scenes.

In contrast, the later portions are more complex and difficult. The Duras voice-over in Paul's scenes and the monologues by women's voices in Isabelle's scenes make these segments less comprehensible. These portions mark an intensification of a general structure of sound-image relations that pervades the film. Godard is creating a set of parameters on the sound track; he explores a variety of possible plays upon diegetic and non-diegetic sound sources, upon possible relations of cuts on the sound track to cuts on the image track, and upon possible temporal relations of sound to image. Because these devices keep changing, sometimes in startling and even funny ways, the spectator's perception of the film is considerably impeded at times.

We have already seen how the credits (like those of *Play Time*) introduce an emphasis on sound, and how the opening scene plays on uncertainties about sound sources and temporal consistency between sound and image. Such play on diegetic sound becomes a running gag through *Sauve qui peut*. Once in each of the three characters' portions of the film, someone asks what the music is that she hears. Each instance works as a baring of the device, and each is done in a different way. When Denise asks the waitress about music in Segment IV, there has been non-diegetic music playing sporadically since near the beginning of the preceding scene; the moment seems at first a simple joke. But as the conversation proceeds, and the waitress asks what music Denise means, the latter points outside and says, "There." Has she been hearing a different music than we have, coming from within the story space? But the waitress denies there is any music, and we are left with an enigmatic little moment in the film. In Segment XVI, within the "La peur" section devoted to Paul, a woman at the lunch counter becomes confused by hearing music. Here the music comes up only shortly before her question and could plausibly be diegetic sound, such as Muzak. Finally, in Isabelle's apartment (Segment XIX), a woman's voice offscreen (or over?) asks about music, and this time no music has played at all.

This motif works alongside the two moments in the film when apparently non-diegetic music is revealed to have a visible source: once when the non-diegetic music on the track over Denise's bike ride becomes blended with an accordion sound, and a cut reveals an accordion player beside the road; and again in the last shot, as Cecile walks down the alley and passes an orchestra playing the accompanying music. In this latter instance, the orchestration changes completely, from an electronic ensemble to strings and back as the panning camera reveals, then conceals, the orchestra.

In a few scenes, people seem to be responding to sounds we hear, when in fact they are responding to something else. During the restaurant scene (Segment IV), two women at a table are gossiping, and we continue to hear their voices over a close-up of Denise. After one of the women says, "In France?" (not subtitled in English), the conversation cuts out and Denise looks off, saying, "That's right." She is responding to an unheard question from the waitress. Segment XX, Isabelle's visit to Personne's hotel room, begins with a long shot of a street corner; Personne's voice begins over this shot, and a passerby turns and looks toward the camera. We may think at first that he is the one speaking, or that he is responding to an offscreen voice, but the cut to Personne in bed, not speaking, eliminates both these possibilities. This shot leads to another cutaway, a new shot of pedestrians; one woman turns and smiles as Personne's voice says, "Hello" (Fig. 10.4). (Personne's name suggests a pun on *son* [sound], which would bare the device of sound manipulation.)

Such devices create patterns, in that they are repeated, but usually there is some variation among them. For instance, Godard uses a series of moments when the source of a sound is uncertain. This happens very simply in the scenes of Denise's bike riding, when bells occasionally are heard on the track. In a single case, two equally plausible sources for one sound are given: an engine's sound comes over the superimposed shot with the tractor that ends Segment X, but it also carries over the cut and synchronizes with the cars that move past in the street as the train station segment begins. Yet more complex is the use of Duras's voice, which seems, when it commences late in Segment XII, to be non-diegetic narration. In Segment XIII we discover that it apparently comes from the videotape being played in the classroom; it stops when the tape is switched off. Yet the voice resumes again later in the scene, without the motivation of the tape, and it continues over into the next scene, when Paul is driving to the station. Paul's memory? Duras's actual presence in the back seat? But it continues over shots of Denise inside the station as well. Similarly, the three monologues spoken by women's voices over scenes of Isabelle engaging in sex with her clients defy complete explanation. None of the three voices, which differ from one speech to the next, belong to either Isabelle or Denise. While they sometimes seem to fit the situation at least tangentially (the description of a woman thinking about housework during sexual intercourse, the memory of an idyllic day at a beach), they could be Isabelle's fantasies to distract herself from the situation or passages of texts she recalls. Or they could have no relation to Isabelle's thoughts, functioning only as narrational commentary.

Sauve qui peut also creates a series of parametric variations on the temporal and logical status of sounds. Godard cuts among various types of sound within a single scene or shot: in Denise's first cycling scene, among music (non-diegetic), synchronized effects (diegetic), and bells (status uncertain). The cattle-feeding scene ends with a cut to silence on the sound track before the cut in the image. As Denise and Isabelle sit talking in the car in Segment XXIV, the loud train sound remains up for awhile, then cuts out abruptly, making the voices audible; by way of contrast, in the following scene, Paul's entire farewell to Denise is drowned out by a passing train's roar, which Godard refuses to eliminate. Such devices of cutting on the sound track are bared in the scene in which Isabelle visits the man who offers her a job. He is editing a film, but we do not see the images upon which he is working; the sound, however, cuts on and off as he runs the viewing machine.

Finally, Godard occasionally shuffles sounds and images together to create an impacted and overlaid temporal effect. As Segment VII begins, Denise is speaking to Paul on the phone. In the next shot, we see him at the television station talking to a colleague rather than speaking on the phone; piano music accompanies this shot, with no diegetic sound, yet Denise's voice cuts in partway through the shot, and we return to Denise, continuing the same conversation. This leads to the medium close-up of Paul that ends the segment; here he is on the phone talking with Denise. In Segment XV, Paul is seated at a table with Colette and Cecile; he gets up to make a phone call. A cut reveals Denise at a video machine, answering the phone. After this very brief shot, the scene returns to the restaurant, with Paul already reseated. Only at this point do we hear Denise say, "Hello." The temporal compression here continues as Colette and Paul discuss Denise, with cutaways to Denise, already walking in the street.

This analysis of the sound and image structures of *Sauve qui peut* may make the film seem more neat and restrained than it actually is.

The parametric variation of sound devices is fairly systematic; yet this usage still differs vastly from the muted, limited variations on small numbers of colors, sounds, and gestures that one finds in a film like *Lancelot du Lac* (Chapter 11). Godard's style remains rough and difficult. With patterns overlapping each other, the overall structure remains only partially graspable.

CONCLUSIONS

Some of the generalizations I have made so far about *Sauve qui peut (la vie)* do not distinguish it clearly from Godard's earlier films—especially the pre-*Gai savoir* work. While the film is not a complete return to Godard's familiar style of that period, its use of perceptual overload certainly recalls such films as *Two or Three Things I Know About Her* and *La Chinoise*. They had included sound-image counterpoint and, as David Bordwell has pointed out, permutational structures; *Vivre sa vie*, for example, is a virtual catalogue of alternatives to shot/reverse shot in the presentation of conversation scenes.[13]

But Bordwell and other critics have also pointed out that the early films created a heterogeneity of tone and style through a sort of collage technique, mixing traditional conventions and modes of filmmaking freely within and between scenes. *Sauve qui peut* is perhaps the first of the features largely to abandon that approach. (Bordwell discusses this technique at length, and I have analyzed it in Chapter 4 in relation to *Tout va bien*.) For the most part, the non-diegetic graphic inserts—the posters, the photographs, and the book titles—are gone. We no longer switch suddenly from a fictional narrative scene to a quasi-documentary one; the characters in *Sauve qui peut* do not face the camera at intervals to respond to questions as in an interview. Godard has also ceased to blend the art cinema with borrowings from and homages to the classical Hollywood cinema. In the early 1960s, he could still treat *Some Came Running* as a contemporary source; by 1979 Godard had abandoned the auteur theory, and the great auteurs of his *Cahiers du cinéma* days were mostly gone. The references in *Sauve qui peut* are reserved for two non–New Wave, modernist French filmmakers—Tati and Duras, whose work on the sound track seems to have influenced Godard's. Godard's move away from the New Wave and into the more recent, mainstream art cinema is signaled in *Sauve qui peut* also by the relatively muted cinematography. The familiar splashes of primary colors that used to form flat backdrops

[13] Ibid., chap. 13.

for the action are largely gone by this point. Only hints of them survive, as in the Marlboro red-and-white pattern, which returns in the hotel clerk's desk lamp and on the wall of the alley in the final shot. Another unusually conventional move for Godard is the inclusion of cut-ins and even over-the-shoulder shot/reverse shot (Figs. 10.5 and 10.6). There are few uses of flashy "Godardian" cutting in the film; perhaps only the choppy scene of the pimps' Mercedes chasing Isabelle really revives his earlier style. Here two takes of the same action are inserted, and shots of two different red cars (one irrelevant) are cut together.

The collage style of the earlier Godard has been modified in favor of a more consistent tone. But at the same time, he has intensified his use of abstract, parametric stylistic structures. Except for *Vivre sa vie*, most of his films had used formal motifs sporadically; here the play with sound-image relations becomes pervasive, and Godard insists upon it by the numerous barings of this device—to the extent that, as I suggested at the outset, the film becomes a "meta-parametric" exploration of the effects of this type of form.

All this stylistic play does not result in an enhancement of the film's basic ideological implications. As we have seen, reviewers have been able to interpret these fairly easily, even without being able to summarize the plot correctly or notice the stylistic difficulties. Denise clearly is the one able to save her life by leaving the city and capitalist society. (The title, which does not mean "Every Man For Himself," is not really translatable into English, meaning literally "Save who can (life)." The American title, aside from being sexist—there is no gender implied in the original—is misleading. Denise in fact wants to cooperate with Paul in changing their lives, but he refuses.) Paul, equally clearly, is the intellectual serving the existing political system without believing in it. The Duras line that Paul reads about her making films because she does not have courage not to has usually been read by commentators as a statement by Jean-Luc Godard; yet it applies more directly to Paul and Denise. He has not the courage to quit his job; she has, but can do little more than retreat, making notes for a project that may turn into a book.

Formal analysis may polish up these readings a bit, but to little purpose. The ideas the film uses are hardly new or startling—the dehumanization of modern society, the metaphor of prostitution for the selling of one's labor and for all sexual relations, the connection between misogyny and repressed homosexuality. But, as Godard surely recognizes, similar ideas may serve over and over again for the creation of films. The point is not simply to come up with new ideas, but to be able to work creatively with old ones; for a filmmaker, it is not to repeat fixed styles, but to explore fresh ways of leading spectators to perceive anew each time. "Pictures are made to make seen the unseen. Afterward you can drop it and go on again. It's like tourists who go into an unknown country." For some spectators, *Sauve qui peut* will seem a betrayal of Godard's intensely political work of the late 1960s and 1970s; for others, it may seem a pleasing signal of his return to earlier, and more familiar, days. But I suspect it is neither. Few, if any, filmmakers have so resolutely refused to settle into one approach; Godard's experimentation has continued throughout his career. (Indeed, his recent criticism of the New Wave makes sense, because, after his initial success, Godard's films of that period do tend to fall into a pattern. *À bout de souffle* still seems one of the most daring of his pre-1968 works.) There is no one familiar Godardian landscape, though each of us may have a favorite work; the appearance of a new Godard film consistently holds out the promise of taking us unto unknown country.

11

The Sheen of Armor, the Whinnies of Horses: Sparse Parametric Style in *Lancelot du Lac*

THE ELLIPTICAL NARRATIVE

ROBERT BRESSON's 1974 film *Lancelot du Lac* is at once a very simple and a very complex film. The narrative contains relatively few events; while it depends partially on the fact that virtually any viewer will have at least some knowledge of the Arthurian legends, it also treats some actions so elliptically as to confuse us about certain causal relations. Similarly, the film's style uses techniques sparsely, introducing, and then varying, a number of elements throughout the film. Armor, horse whinnies, birdcalls, the various locales, even the methods of staging and framing shot/reverse shot segments—all play in rhythmic ways across the film.[1] Although *Lancelot* is a narrative film, not all its stylistic repetitions serve the syuzhet action, or help us to reconstruct a fabula line. Rather, much of the interest of the film's style remains independent of narrative functions.

Once we begin to look at *Lancelot*'s parametric variations, as well as at how style serves the narrative, the underlying complexity of the film becomes apparent. Limited though the number of elements participating in these patterns may be, Bresson combines and recombines them in ways that are difficult to grasp upon one or two viewings (although they are clearly there and, once noticed, can be seen during a viewing). Hence an apparently simple surface leads us into a convoluted texture.

Stylistically, *Lancelot* is a quintessential Bressonian work. Typically, Bresson is known for the deliberately inexpressive quality of his style: the expressionless performances of his actors, the refusal to establish spaces and to emphasize certain events with long shots, and the like.

[1] In an early review, "Bresson's 'Lancelot du Lac,' " *Sight and Sound* 43, no. 3 (Summer 1974): 129–130, Jonathan Rosenbaum mentioned the basic strategy of these elements; my analysis develops similar points.

By doing a period piece, he was able to introduce armor into his panoply of devices for avoiding expressive performances. Not only do his actors deliver lines tonelessly, but often we see their faces or hands or feet sheathed in blank metal. And by equating the horses so completely with his human characters, he can show actions at one further remove by framing only the legs or bodies of the horses. Stylistic techniques similar to ones Bresson had worked with for three decades were used to perfection in this film.

Yet *Lancelot* was, after *Le Procès de Jeanne d'Arc*, only Bresson's second period piece. His early reputation had been as a great adapter of literature. *Les Dames de Bois de Boulogue* and *Le Journal d'un curé de compagne* were hailed in France in the early 1950s as perfect cinematic translations of the original texts. As Bresson remarked: "I would like the source of my films to be in me, apart from literature. Even if I make a film from Dostoevski [i.e., *Une femme douce*], I try always to take out all the literary parts."[2] Bresson seemed to internalize the original, then create the filmic equivalent.

In a sense, *Lancelot*, too, is an adaptation. And if its presentation seems elliptical, we might suspect that Bresson assumed a certain knowledge on our part of the original: the general idea of the Round Table, Lancelot and Guenevere's affair, Mordred's rebellion against Arthur, and so on. The story events themselves are simple; Bresson has eliminated many events included in what I take to be a close source among the Arthurian legends, *La Mort le Roi Artu*, which itself is quite a short book (less than two hundred pages in a recent translation).[3]

The film's action can be segmented as follows.

I. (Shots 1–13). The forest: fights, knights riding (the failure of the Grail quest).

[2] Paul Schrader, "Robert Bresson, Possibly," *Film Comment* 13, no. 5 (September-October 1977): 27.

[3] *La Mort le Roi Artu* is the last of the five volumes of the French prose Vulgate Cycle, c. 1230, author unknown. One of the longest extant versions of the Arthurian legends, its other volumes include events connected with Merlin, Lancelot's earlier life, and the quest for the Grail. The translation I have used is J. Neale Carman's *From Camelot to Joyous Guard: The Old French La Mort le Roi Artu* (Lawrence: The University Press of Kansas, 1974).

It has been stated (in Jane Sloan's *Robert Bresson: A Guide to References and Resources* [Boston: G. K. Hall, 1983], p. 88) that Bresson's film is based upon Chrétien de Troyes's "Le Chevalier de la charette" (translated by W. W. Comfort as "Lancelot" in de Troyes, *Arthurian Romances* [New York: Dutton, 1914], pp. 270–359), but I can find no events which the film and this work have in common; de Troyes's account covers an earlier period in the Arthurian legends, long before the Grail quest.

II. (Shot 14). Close-up of the Grail with crawl title explaining the situation; drum and pipe music.

III. (Shots 15–24). The forest: peasants gathering wood encounter Lancelot, lost. The credits.

IV. (Shots 25–40). The castle, night: Lancelot returns, meets Gauvin and others; the wounded arrive; Lancelot and Gauvin's meeting with Artus.

V. (Shots 41–73). The castle, day: Lancelot goes to the forest shed, meets Guenièvre for the first time since his return; he tells her their affair is over.

VI. (Shots 74–76). Castle chapel: Lancelot arrives late for mass, sees Guenièvre with Artus.

VII. (Shots 77–97). The castle: Artus says he will close off the Round Table room; introduction of Mordred.

VIII. (Shots 98–111). The tents: Lancelot and Gauvin discuss Artus's decision; Gauvin says the other men watch Guenièvre's window.

IX. (Shots 112–115). Hallway of the castle: Guenièvre and Gauvin talk; he praises Lancelot as a saint; Gauvin asks Artus for a goal, is told to pray.

X. (Shots 116–147). The forest shed: the second meeting of Lancelot and Guenièvre; she still refuses to release him from his oath to her.

XI. (Shots 148–172). The battlements and tents: Lancelot and others discuss the moon; Lancelot offers friendship to Mordred, who refuses.

XII. (Shots 173–182). Lancelot's tent: Gauvin reveals that some of the men are going over to Mordred; Lancelot gives him a jeweled bridle.

XIII. (Shot 183). Castle chapel: Lancelot prays for strength to resist temptation.

XIV. (Shots 184–191). Castle yard: knights arrive from Escalot with a challenge to a tournament; Artus, Gauvin, and Lancelot discuss it.

XV. (Shots 192–208). Castle yard: practice at tilting; training of a horse.

XVI. (Shots 209–240). The forest shed: the third meeting of Lancelot and Guenièvre; Lancelot gives in to Guenièvre; they are spied on by Mordred and others.

XVII. (Shots 241–276). The tents: Mordred and supporters argue with Gauvin and Lionel about Lancelot; Mordred sets up an assassination plot. Lancelot says he is not going to the tournament; others depart.

XVIII. (Shots 277–288). The castle: assassins lurk in the hall as Guenièvre bathes; Lancelot sets out for the tournament alone at night, disguised.

XIX. (Shots 289–304). The forest: while riding to the tournament, Mordred accuses Lancelot to Artus; the others defend him.

XX. (Shots 305–397). The tournament: Lancelot arrives without revealing his identity; he defeats knights from his own side.

XXI. (Shots 398–411). The forest: riding back from the tournament, Gauvin and others chide Mordred for his accusation of Lancelot.

XXII. (Shots 412–433). The castle: the knights arrive home; Gauvin talks with Guenièvre, who thinks Lancelot has gone forever.

XXIII. (Shots 434–444). Castle and tents: two knights set out to look for Lancelot.

XXIV. (Shots 445–452). Castle yard: the two knights return, unsuccessful; a storm begins, which keeps Guenièvre awake.

XXV. (Shots 453–460). The tents: Mordred and others see Lancelot's flag tattered; they assume he is dead.

XXVI. (Shots 461–471). Mordred's tent: Mordred and his supporters play chess at night; Gauvin confronts him.

XXVII. (Shots 472–495). The forest shed: Guenièvre admits to Gauvin that she loves Lancelot; Gauvin prevents Artus from entering, sends out the knights to search again.

XXVIII. (Shots 496–516). The forest: an old peasant woman refuses to answer the knights; she has Lancelot in her cottage; in spite of his wound and her warning, he departs.

XXIX. (Shots 517–523). The castle: Lancelot and his men break in and rescue Guenièvre from a cell.

XXX. (Shots 524–525). Deserted castle: Bors, Lionel, and Lancelot discuss the siege, decide to attack.

XXXI. (Shots 526–542). A tent at Artus's camp: as Gauvin lies dying, he praises Lancelot.

XXXII. (Shots 543–552). Deserted castle: Artus sends a message offering to take Guenièvre back.

XXXIII. (Shots 553–565). Deserted castle: Lancelot and Guenièvre have their final talk; she is resigned to going back, he resists it.

XXXIV. (Shots 566–607). Outside the deserted castle: Lancelot escorts Guenièvre to Artus's camp; he goes back and hears of Mordred's rebellion; Lancelot's men arm and leave.

XXXV. (Shots 608–644). The forest: a riderless horse; knights riding; archers shooting from the trees. Artus is dead; Lancelot, wounded, utters Guenièvre's name and falls, dying.

A detailed comparison of this outline with the events of *La Mort le Roi Artu* would be pointless, since Bresson's version bears so little resemblance to the original. A few examples should suffice to show that little of the film's elliptical narrative can be filled in even by someone completely conversant with the original French prose version; these examples should also demonstrate the direction in which Bresson moved to fashion his narrative structure.

Bresson has simply eliminated most of the original events (e.g., there were three tournaments and an additional battle with the invading Romans), while expanding a few elements greatly. Thus most of the first half of the film comes from one summary sentence in *La Mort*: "Now, though Lancelot had behaved chastely by the counsel of the holy man to whom he had confessed when he was in the quest of the Holy Grail, and though he had apparently renounced Queen Guenevere, as the tale has related before, as soon as he had come to court, not one month passed before he was smitten and inflamed as much as he had ever been at any time, so that he fell back into sin with the queen just as he had done earlier."[4] This particular passage Bresson elaborates into three separate meetings between Lancelot and Guenièvre (Segments V, X, and XVI) before Lancelot gives in to her and resumes their affair.

The elimination or compression of events in an adaptation is common enough, of course. But Bresson eliminates or compresses some things only partially, leaving bits of puzzling information which seem to hint that we have missed something along the way. In the French prose version, Gawain's brother Agravain is a central figure, the one who first tells Arthur of Lancelot and Guenevere's adultery. Mordred becomes the main villain only late in the narrative, after Agravain's death. Bresson's version combines Agravain and Mordred's functions in Mordred's character alone. Yet Agravain is present, noticeable in one scene only: the argument before the departure for the tournament (Segment XVII). There we can recognize him only because Gauvin addresses him as "brother." At other times he is simply spoken of. Bresson similarly makes fairly important supporting characters of Lionel and Bohort but gives us no clue that they are Lancelot's cousins. As a result, the factions in the infighting among the knights remain confusing. Moreover, Agravain's death at Lancelot's hands during the rescue of Guenièvre—of which we learn only when Lionel mentions it after

---

[4] Carman, *From Camelot to Joyous Guard*, p. 4.

the fact in Segment XXX—performs a major causal function in driving Gauvin to fight Lancelot and receive his fatal wound (Segment XXXI).

Perhaps the most indirectly presented segment of the film, and the one during which the spectator would benefit the most from prior knowledge, is Segment XXIX, Lancelot's rescue of Guenièvre. It begins with a shot through a barred window of knights and squires running past; a cut reveals a doorway, with Lancelot entering as Guenièvre's voice calls for help from offscreen. As Lancelot approaches Guenièvre and lifts her, we see that his sword and hands are bloody. Only in the last shot of this seven-shot segment do we see the barred window in the background and realize that the opening shot had been filmed from inside Guenièvre's cell. And finally, as Lionel follows Lancelot out at the end of this shot, we see a tent beyond the doorway and realize further that this scene has occurred within the battlements of Artus's castle; Lancelot has been attacking the castle to rescue Guenièvre. Yet the last time we had seen Guenièvre, she was in the forest shed, with Artus agreeing not to break in upon her. The events of the original version had Guenevere captured and condemned to death by fire; Lancelot and his followers actually rescued her from a pyre in an open space before the castle. (Thus even those familiar with the original will not necessarily be able to follow the action in this scene.) When the rescue occurs in the film, we have no idea that Lancelot needs to rescue Guenièvre, much less that he has attacked and defeated the troops of Artus's castle at this point. Only in the next scene, when Lionel tells Lancelot which knights the latter has killed in the battle, do we grasp what had happened.

Still more elliptically, at the end of Segment XXX Lancelot decides to attack Artus's army, which is besieging Lancelot's castle. (In the original, Lancelot takes Guenevere to his own well-staffed castle, Joyous Guard; in the film, they simply take refuge in a nearby deserted castle.) As he and his men run out to the battle, we hear several seconds of the sound of horses' hooves and armor clanking. This sound stands in for the entire battle; the cut to the next scene depicts its aftermath, with Gauvin dying.

Lancelot contains almost none of the redundancy of the classical Hollywood film. But Bresson's method of avoiding a straightforward presentation of fabula events is not to overload our perception with narrative material, as Godard might. Often he simply does not give us enough cues for us to make the relevant narrative connections. Neither is the difficulty of Bressonian narrative that of obscurity in need of interpretation (à la Bergman or Fellini); this is not a symbolic structure which we can piece together. We simply do not receive enough fabula information to assemble a complete picture.

Difficulties in grasping fabula-syuzhet relations form a pattern across the film. Segment I's action begins very late in the King Arthur story; in effect, the short scenes with anonymous combatants form a sort of sparse "montage sequence" summarizing the degeneration of the grail quest into brutality. Thereafter we might expect to get references to earlier events scattered through the rest of the film, especially in the early scenes. Instead, the narration introduces a crawl title which summarizes in the most cursory fashion a series of lengthy past actions.

After a series of adventures which were tinged with the marvelous and of which Lancelot du Lac was the hero, the knights called by King Arthur the "Knights of the Round Table" set out in quest of the Grail. The Grail, a divine relic, the goblet of the Last Supper in which Joseph of Arimathaeas caught the blood of Christ on the cross, would gain them a supernatural power. It was believed to be hidden somewhere in Britain.

The wizard Merlin, before dying, consecrated the knights to this sacred adventure. He interpreted certain signs, which named as leader of the quest, not Lancelot du Lac, the greatest knight in the world, but an extremely young knight, Perceval (Parsifal) the "Very Pure."

Hardly had they left the castle when the knights dispersed. Perceval disappeared. They never saw him again.

Two years have passed. The knights have returned to the castle of King Arthur and Queen Guenevere, having suffered heavy losses and without having found the Grail.

After the end of the crawl title, the major portion of the film—Segments III to XXVIII—involves a much more leisurely presentation of a few events. The intervals between scenes are short, though the durations of those intervals often are not specified. No significant action is left out in this portion, and we see most events directly; the only exceptions are Gauvin's reports to Lancelot involving Mordred's growing influence among the knights and the men's tendency to watch Guenièvre's window. Similarly, few past events are revealed, and most references to the past simply reiterate the failure of the quest and the loss of many knights. Here the exceptions involve Guenièvre and Lancelot, who speak of his past vow to her and of her gift of a ring (Segment V), and Gauvin, who recalls an incident in which Mordred had deliberately splashed Lancelot when crossing a stream (Segment VIII). For the most part, these scenes concentrate on the onscreen debates about Guenièvre and Lancelot's relationship, about the reasons for the failure of the quest, and about the correct future policy for the Round Table.

These scenes are balanced between Lancelot's initial return to Camelot (Segment III shows him lost in the forest on his way there) and his later return (in Segment XXVIII he leaves the peasant hut). Between his departure from the hut and the rescue in Segment XXIX comes the film's first elimination of major causal action through ellipsis—the sentencing of Guenièvre and the subsequent attack by Lancelot's troops. From this point to the end of the film, as we have seen, large ellipses continue: the transition from Segment XXIX to Segment XXX eliminates the rest of the battle and its results; we learn of the death of Agravain in Segment XXX. Another major battle occurs between Segments XXX and XXXI. Both of the next two scenes fill us in with information about it: Lancelot has fatally wounded Gauvin (Segment XXXI) and has deliberately spared Artus's life (Segment XXXII). Finally, the bulk of the final battle is not shown; we see Artus already dead and Lancelot dying. Thus the overall pattern of the film's presentation of fabula information is: severe compression of many events (Segments I–II), leisurely and direct action (Segments III–XXVIII), and highly elliptical and quick action (Segments XXIX–XXXV).

The overall narrative function of this pattern is to concentrate our attention on the characters' doubts and questions, rather than on the excitement and glamor typically associated with battles in classical historical epics. (A similar de-glamorization goes on in the elliptical treatment of the tournament scene.) But at the same time, the changing pattern of narrational presentation undermines narrative comprehension in favor of abstract patterning. The film gets us used to one type of fabula-syuzhet relations, then switches tactics near the end, confronting us with events that we suddenly find much more difficult to follow. These two results of the film's overall shape—a narrative function and an anti-narrative function—reflect on a general level the parametric patterning of specific stylistic devices.

Aside from the elliptical plot, another reason for our inability to grasp the narrative completely arises from the opacity of the characterization. We know that Bresson uses non-actors and often withholds from them any knowledge of the entire story. Their expressionless performances have become a recognizable trait of the Bressonian style. Bresson has said that he wanted to eliminate the magical happenings of the original Arthurian legends: "I am going to try to transfer this fairy tale into one realm of feelings, that is to say, show how feelings change even the air that one breathes."[5] And he has also said, "I think the only way to reach the public with historical characters is to show them as if they lived at the present with us."[6] For Bresson, this does not mean that his historical characters behave as real people might in our epoch; rather, his historical characters behave exactly as do his contemporary characters. Jeanne d'Arc behaves similarly to Mouchette, Lancelot similarly to Fontaine. In any cast, Bresson achieves through his nearly expressionless actors a ritualistic sense of acting. A steady rhythm of actions and speech contributes especially to this sense. Bresson seldom reveals psychological motivations through conventional acting; rather, he often concentrates on feet, hands, torsos, and visored faces for the gestures of his action. But he does show us faces as well, and their occasional expressions stand out all the more against the usual neutrality. In fact, Bresson contradicts Schrader when the latter claims that one seldom sees faces in *Lancelot*, that they are covered or kept out of the frame: "When he comes to pray in front of the cross, you see him entirely, you see his face. I don't see what you mean."[7] In this film, the tiniest gestures and glances become expressive. Gauvin's puzzled frown when Guenièvre tells him Lancelot has left them forever becomes a striking moment. The same is true of voice quality, as when Lancelot emphatically tells his men that he will support Artus against the rebellious Mordred. Such moments gain not only in emphasis but in intensity through their comparative rarity. Yet overall there are many moments when we cannot grasp the characters' motivations.

If Bresson has modernized the original legends' narratives by concentrating on characters' feelings, he has also given a very modern ideological bent to his story. *La Mort le Roi Artu* put much stress upon the redemptive power of the characters' penitence. Guenevere became a nun after Arthur's fatal battle with Mordred. Then, upon hearing of her death, Lancelot became a priest and died in bed a few years later. Lancelot's companion, an archbishop, has a vision of Lancelot ascending to heaven and, upon his death, comments, "Now I know well that penitence is of greater value than aught else; I shall never leave off penitence as long as I live."[8] The only hint of any penitence

---

[5] Jean-Luc Godard and Michel Delahaye, "The Question: Interview with Robert Bresson," *Cahiers du Cinéma in English* no. 8 (February 1967): 27.

[6] Ian Cameron, "Appendix—Interview," in *The Films of Robert Bresson*, ed. Amadée Ayfre et al. (New York: Praeger, 1970), p. 134.

[7] Schrader, "Robert Bresson, Possibly," p. 30.

[8] Carman, *From Camelot to Joyous Guard*, p. 172.

in the characters in the film comes in Segment XXXIII, as Guenièvre insists she must return to Artus, so that she and Lancelot may atone for the bloodshed they have caused. But Lancelot does not agree with her, and we never have any indication that he goes to his death repenting.

The original version of the downfall of the Round Table suggested strongly that Lancelot and Guenevere's adultery was the underlying moral cause, with Mordred coming in only later in the story to be the immediate cause of the deaths of Arthur and his knights. Bresson shifts the blame to a sort of social corruption creeping into the Round Table and its chivalric values. When Lancelot blames his sin for his inability to find the Grail, Guenièvre responds: "You were all relentless. You killed, plundered, burned. Then you turned on each other, like madmen, without realizing it. And you blame our love for this disaster." Bresson does not emphasize the violence more than does the original, which contains many explicit descriptions of battles and wounds. But *Lancelot* does eliminate much of what had seemed to justify the violence in the original—the chivalric code. Only a few references remain, as when Guenièvre berates Lancelot for sparing Artus's life when he had a chance to kill him. The original tale presents, at great length, a one-on-one duel between Gawain and Lancelot, with Lancelot displaying chivalry by offering to undergo a period of atonement for killing Gawain's brother, in order that he need not fight and kill his friend. In Bresson's film, Lancelot simply kills Gauvin by mistake, offscreen, in the melee of the battle.

In *La Mort*, Arthur's army meets Mordred's on Salisbury Plain (not in a forest), but Lancelot is not present to support Arthur. Mordred's side suffers huge losses but, by dint of vastly superior numbers, finally kills Arthur and the remaining Round Table knights (though Arthur kills Mordred in the process). Bresson attributes Mordred's victory to quite a different cause than does the original—his use of archers hidden in trees, picking off the clumsy knights riding below. Rather than simply going down to defeat, the Round Table becomes the victim of a new age with different technology. Its vanquisher, Mordred, is emphasized, time and again, as being cowardly—the opposite of the chivalric qualities the knights cultivate in themselves. Along with the other magical events of the narrative, Bresson completely eliminates the elements of Arthur's mystical death—the hand in the lake that grasps Excalibur, the boatful of women who transport the dying king to his tomb, and so on. Thus the implications that the values of the Round Table will endure into the future are also eliminated. All this does not imply that Bresson is being realistic or historically accurate

(he has said that the setting, costume, and prop designs were deliberately anachronistic). Rather, by taking a mystical set of events and
making them seem historically concrete to modern viewers, he has
provided a way of enabling us to see their ideological implications
without the relatively optimistic emphasis of the original. *Lancelot* adheres to the increasingly bleak outlook of Bresson's later films; rather
than finding a religious or moral grace, as in the earlier ones, the characters now lose the grace they have in the face of a corrupt society's
pressures.

But Bresson's anachronisms and modern ideology only make the
film *seem* historically concrete to us. Other changes wrought by Bresson render the whole thing impossible as well. For one thing, the
characters are far too young to have lived through all the triumphs of
the Round Table and to be now in a late period of decline. *La Mort*
specifies the characters' ages: near the end of the story Arthur is
ninety-two, Gawain seventy-six; Lancelot about fifty-five, and Guenevere about fifty. There is no way to insert Bresson's characters into
a plausible chronology extending back into the past; by eliminating
their earlier lives, Bresson suspends them in a period of decline that
holds few hints of the former glories of Camelot. (The effect is once
again to emphasize the bleakness of the society and the loss of grace.)

In such circumstances, the love of Lancelot and Guenièvre becomes
not a cause of corruption and a reason for chastisement, but the only
apparently positive force in the society. From the beginning Bresson
emphasizes the impending end of the Round Table: the old peasant
woman says all the knights who passed are doomed to death; Lancelot
remarks to Guenièvre, "Everything is finished for us here in Britain";
and Artus listlessly refuses to appoint new knights to the Round Table
or to undertake any new projects. With the chivalric code already
moribund, the lovers seem to have the only vitality in the group.

Given such a situation, the narrative's chief interest comes to lie not
primarily in physical action and in quest journeys, but in the characters. This may seem somewhat odd, in view of what I have already
said about expressionless performances. But here we come back to
Bresson's elliptical narrative. Characters do, in fact, talk a great deal
in the film, and they often discuss their feelings and beliefs. Yet there
is considerable ambiguity about them as well, especially given the lack
of exposition concerning their past actions and motivations. Gauvin is
a particularly mysterious character. At first he seems merely a friend
of Lancelot's, discontented at the inactivity of the Round Table. But
his remarks about the men watching Guenièvre's window, his own
glances up at it (three of the four shots of that window are from his

point of view), and his increasing role as Guenièvre's defender hint that he is perhaps himself in love with her. This would make him the ideal knight in the traditional terms of chivalry, since he keeps his passion on the platonic level; he also does his duty by battling Lancelot to avenge his brother's death while continuing to admire and defend his opponent. Yet all this remains only a possible set of traits for Gauvin; the narrative withholds so much information that we cannot say anything for sure. The same is true to some degree of Artus, whose reactions to learning of Guenièvre's adultery are not shown. Only Lancelot and Guenièvre's motives are known extensively, and this once again focuses attention on their love as the one positive force amid the social decay in Camelot.

NARRATIVE AND NON-NARRATIVE
FUNCTIONS OF STYLE

The indirect presentation of narrative material in *Lancelot du Lac* results in part from its stylistic systems. These sometimes function to serve the narrative; at other times the style works by a parametric logic of its own. Bresson introduces a device or pattern, then varies it, often without regard to the causal logic of the scene's action. Trying to interpret such variations symbolically in relation to the syuzhet action usually leads to frustration, or banality.

There are two major systems across the film which Bresson uses to introduce and vary his stylistic devices; I will deal with these and then describe some localized devices. The first overall system is the easier to notice: the limited number of motifs, visual and aural, that recur at intervals. But Bresson also structures whole scenes as variations of each other—to create narrative parallels, or simply to provide abstract variations that are of interest in themselves.

Motifs. Some motifs are so pervasive that they do not require extensive analysis. Armor, for example, appears in every scene of the film and is associated with all the characters except Guenièvre and the peasant and servant classes (though we can assume that the helmeted foot soldiers of the final battle come from these classes). But even within such a ubiquitous device, Bresson works numerous subtle variations. Armor can create narrative connotations; for example, Lancelot wears his armor during his meetings with Guenièvre as long as he resists her, then strips it off as he gives in to her at the third rendezvous. After the first segment, which begins with a beheading, armor carries a suggestion of dismemberment. This motif returns when the peasant child brings Lancelot his leg armor; Bresson frames this low, so that the pieces take on the appearance of legs (Fig. 11.1). And in the final scene, the armor of the dead knights irresistably suggests a junk heap, a succinct image for the end of the Round Table and the chivalric conceptions behind it.

But the use of armor goes far behind these obvious thematic implications. Much of the film's visual interest lies in reflections, and specifically in the play of light on armor. *Lancelot* is notoriously a dark film, even in 35mm prints. In many shots, the composition consists of patterns of tiny highlights against dark backgrounds. In the bright scenes, the armor changes by reflecting the bright but neutral tans, whites, and greys around it. Bresson has managed to find a costuming substance that makes the figures like chameleons, changing to fit their environment—yet in no case do the suits of armor add strong color to the scene. Rather, they help produce the muted brown, white, and grey tones that dominate the film, especially in the numerous castle scenes. Against these, the many tiny patches and flashes of bright color stand out boldly.

The tents serve a similar range of functions. In their simplest form, they are locales for straightforward narrative action. Thematically there is an opposition set up between the knights in their tents and the looming castle walls; the flimsy tents perhaps enhance the pervasive sense of the imminent end of the Round Table. The tents also, however, undergo changes similar to those in the armor. They, too, change color: white by daylight, glowing orange when lit from behind by a lantern, and utterly black in dark night scenes. This lack of strong color makes them a perfect blank background against which other elements can be seen. In particular, the various colored shields and flags over the tents' entrances stand out. For example, as the knights and their squires depart for the tournament at the end of Segment XVII, we see their horses go through the frame and exit; once they are all out we see only two white tents forming an almost solid white field, with a portion of one shield in green, red, white, and black at the upper left, and one with blue and white zigzags at the upper right (Color Plate 1). For a moment we have a Mondrian-like composition dropped into the middle of a narrative film.

These shields, along with the leggings of the knights, the embroidered reins, and the horses' saddle blankets, provide splashes of color against the otherwise somber tones of the film. More than the tents or the armor, these colored elements become part of an abstract formal pattern largely independent of any narrative function. Each tent has a different shield and flag, yet these are not used as an identification system for the knights. Indeed, we barely learn who most of the knights are—it would be difficult to draw a clear set of connections between them and their shield markings. When Lancelot's flag is shredded by the storm, we need to be told it is his. The green, red, and white shield with black dots visible in Color Plate 1 is apparently Artus's; we see it near his seat at the tournament and again over his tent as he receives Guenièvre back from Lancelot in Segment XXXIV. Yet one would have to have a good eye for pattern to be able to make the connection on the basis of two scenes—and, at any rate, the association is not confirmed until our last view of Artus alive. Occasionally we do get a color motif assigned to a specific character. Gauvin's pink leggings identify him for us in those many moments when Bresson frames the characters from the waist down. And Lancelot's orange saddle blanket helps us keep track of him during the fragmented presentation of the tournament scene; but even in this case we must be quick about noticing it, since it appears only in flashes.

Mostly, however, these colored elements participate in graphic play. The flags at the tournament tell us little; we do not even find out until the next scene that Lancelot has in fact jousted against his own comrades rather than against the Escalot knights. Similarly, the horse blankets are arranged graphically and rhythmically within shots to provide a variety of colors, rather than to let us know who is riding past. In the final shot of Segment XXIX, Lancelot's rescue of Guenièvre from Artus's castle, we see a line of knights ride into the deserted castle which Lancelot will use as his stronghold. The first knight has a bright red saddle, the second a blue, followed by orange and red; Lancelot is next, with Guenièvre behind him in a pink dress under a dark cloak. Finally, four other horses pass with green, blue, orange, and blue blankets, respectively. Again, no knight except Lancelot is identifiable; Bresson, working on abstract color variations, lines up his colors so that no two horses in a row are the same.

The film's patches of color tend to be small in the frame because they usually appear in the backgrounds of scenes. (The few exceptions, as when the camera pans or tracks up to a rack of brightly embroidered reins [Color Plate 2], become virtual explosions of color.) But the color so stands out against the prevailing tones that it draws the eye away from the more narratively salient foreground; in general, bright colors always tend to "come forward," even if they are in the background of a shot. Often the color comes in the form of the shields on the tents, which tend to slide in and out of the frame because there is a good deal of camera movement following the walking knights. But Bresson has a continuing device that also introduces color; in conversation scenes, people often pass by in the background—squires leading horses in daylight scenes, carrying lanterns in night ones. Their passages seem almost ritualistic, adding a rhythm to the scene rather than simply providing verisimilitude. They would not be particularly noticeable ordinarily, but Bresson often makes them the most colorful element in the shot.

Such movements may serve to punctuate scenes, coming at certain key moments in the action. For example, in Segment XVII, as Lancelot stands in a tent entrance, we see hanging on another tent in the background a black shield with a yellow X on it; just before he announces to the other knights that he will not be going to the tournament with them, a knight passes behind him, leading a horse with a red blanket (Color Plate 3). (Bresson's use of people passing in backgrounds somewhat resembles a device in Ozu's color films; there street or alley shots often contain rhythmic movements of people passing back and forth in the depth of the shot—most prominent are women wearing bright red sweaters. Ozu's device usually occurs between scenes, however, and serves to create graphic interest rather than to emphasize moments in the action.) This function of color as emphasis is, however, somewhat random, since other key moments go unmarked by such motifs, and, given Bresson's pared-down style, there are few gestures or lines of dialogue that are not important. Moreover, at other times, bright colors seem to call attention away from the main action rather than emphasizing it. In one of the film's most extraordinary shots, the establishing view of Artus standing before his tent waiting to receive Guenièvre back (Color Plate 4), the prevailing colors are the deep green of the forest and the white of the tents; but one horse at the left has a bright red blanket that calls attention off to that side. The horse plays no part in the action, and, indeed, the next cut back to a view of Artus's tent eliminates the horse, and hence the splash of color, from the frame. (Here Bresson's usage is much closer to that of Ozu.)

I have mentioned that some of the uses of color punctuate dialogue or action. To some extent, the same is true of the more pervasive sonic motifs. The offscreen whinny of a horse occurs in about half of the segments, as when Gauvin walks across the yard to tell Guenièvre that Lancelot has returned (Segment IV) or when Lancelot looks up at Guenièvre's window and promises he will return from the tournament the next day (Segment XVIII). The sound serves as a mild sort of marker, but, again, it is used arbitrarily; in many equally important passages, there is no such marker. Or in others, the horse whinny may give way to a note on an offscreen horn; this latter sound comes at only five moments: (1) when the other knights welcome Lancelot home, (2) when Lancelot tells Artus he has not found the Grail, (3) over the first shot of the moon, (4) over subsequent shots of men looking up at it, and (5) as the two knights set out to search for Lancelot after the tournament. There seems to be no particular pattern for this usage in terms of creating specific parallels among the types of action thus marked.

Birdcalls form a more specific motif, and there are three different types of calls. The opening scene introduces a cawing sound, as we see crows pecking at two armored skeletons hanging in the forest. Distant cawing is heard offscreen, primarily during the scenes with the peasants in Escalot, and later as Lancelot lies bleeding after leaving the tournament. This motif culminates in the final scene as we see the crows in the sky, circling above the dying knights. It quickly comes to have a close association with carrion and works in with the many forebodings of the downfall of Artus's knights.

The second type of birdcall comes from the bird perched outside the forest shed where Lancelot and Guenièvre meet. This call is harsher and more prolonged than the cawing. It marks moments in the progress of their affair: as the camera frames Guenièvre's scarf when she leaves it on the bench, and later, when she says she wanted to see Lancelot one more time and raises her eyes to his.

The third type of bird sound comes only once. After we see the knights carrying Guenièvre to Lancelot's stronghold, following the rescue (Segment XXIX), we hear a bird singing. This brief sound provides us with perhaps the only indication of joy resulting from this action; we never witness any rejoicing on the part of Lancelot or Guenièvre. This indirect use of sound to substitute for a scene not shown us would thus be parallel to the sound at the end of Segment XXX that substitutes for the battle. Although all these birdcalls have some apparent narrative function, they often distract us more from the narrative action than their inessential and minimal function would seem to warrant.

Variant Scene Structures. So far we have looked at how Bresson takes visual and aural motifs of a familiar sort and weaves them into parallel narrative and abstract patterns. A similar theme-and-variations method also holds true for the structuring of whole scenes. Scenes can become variants of each other through the ways that camera movements, framing, and cutting are used, as well as through more straightforward parallels in action. The following layout of the film's segments indicates what I take to be the parallel scenes. (The two main columns follow the film's chronology in a U shape; scenes paral-

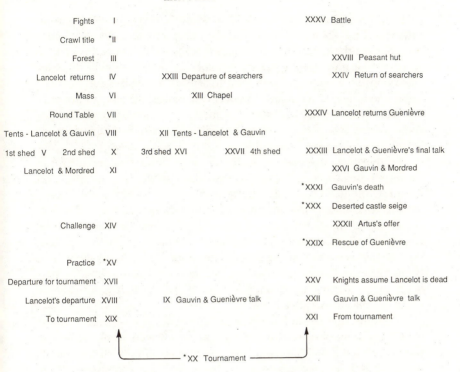

leled out of that chronological order are listed out of line, and scenes that seem to have no parallel with another scene are asterisked.)

The tournament is the film's structural center, with the other scenes forming a rough symmetry around it. It is perhaps the most obvious example of a scene that is structured by the introduction and variation of devices. The first four shots of the segment show us the basic elements that will make up the rest of the scene: a flag going up a pole (Fig. 11.2); a bagpiper playing, with a bit of the crowd visible at the rear (Fig. 11.3); a horse's legs against the ground (Fig. 11.4); and Gauvin and Artus among the onlookers (Fig. 11.5). The entire scene contains 93 of the film's 644 shots, and virtually all are variants of these four elements. There are about five framings of the group around Gauvin, all serving the same basic function. The jousts are handled in a limited and repetitious way, with the sound of the bagpipe coming from offscreen, a cut to the piper, and then a shot or two of the joust itself. A few of the bouts contain long shots, but most framings concentrate on the lower quarters of the horses, on lances striking shields, and on the reactions of the onlooking group. Even the flags have a pattern of variation, with the wind apparently reversing directions at intervals (Figs. 11.6 and 11.7). And after giving us six shots at different junctures of the piper with the same framing as in Figure 11.3, there is a cut to a new but similar framing of this action (Fig. 11.8). After this point we do not see the piper or flags again, as Bresson begins a rapid and elliptical montage of Lancelot striking down one knight after another. This kind of abstract patterning becomes more feasible here than in other scenes, since there is no dialogue as such. Only one word is spoken—"Lancelot"—but this is repeated over and over.

The tournament scene forms the film's structural center for a number of reasons. It comes about halfway through the film and provides an interruption because it is so strikingly different from the scenes around it. David Bordwell argues that in *Pickpocket*, the pickpocket scenes stand out from the rest of the film because of their relative unpredictability; moreover, their difference emphasizes the similarities among the surrounding scenes. The same thing happens in *Lancelot*, with the tournament serving as a sort of pivot to signal the parallels in scenes that precede and follow it. In short, it points up the syuzhet's formal symmetry.

On either side of this highly abstract scene comes a scene that is clearly a variant of the one on the other side: the conversations among the knights as they ride to and from the tournament. The first consists of sixteen similar medium shots, with one knight centered and facing three-quarters front left in each shot (Figs. 11.9 and 11.10). The second contains fourteen shots, beginning and ending this time with an establishing shot (Fig. 11.11) showing the whole line of knights. In between are twelve similar medium shots with the knights now facing three-quarters front right (Fig. 11.12). The actions within the two scenes are also parallel. In the first Mordred accuses Lancelot of adultery with the queen while the others defend Lancelot; in the second they tell Mordred that Lancelot's appearance at the tournament disproves the accusation. Incidentally, one might assume at first glance that Bresson has the knights face left in the first scene, and right in the second, not to achieve formal variation, but simply because they are going toward the tournament initially and away from it later. But Bresson's establishing long shot for the second scene begins with the knights riding in from right to left (i.e., riding in the same direction they had been facing in the earlier scene). Then they come around a bend in the path and ride out foreground right. (Fig. 11.11 shows this later stage of the shot, with knights riding toward the right in the front and toward the left in the rear plane.) The film demonstrates in fact that the direction the knights face in either scene is purely arbitrary in terms of any imaginary geography we may wish to construct for the road between Camelot and Escalot. Graphic considerations remain primary.

The opening and closing scenes of the film also parallel each other, the first being structured around repeated panning shots with three mounted knights, the last around repeated pans with a riderless horse running through a similar forest landscape.

But the most complex parallels and variations among scenes come with the three conversations between Lancelot and Guenièvre in the forest shed (Segments V, X, and XVI), the later scene there between Gauvin and Guenièvre (Segment XXVII), and the argument in Lancelot's castle just before he returns Guenièvre to Artus (Segment XXXIII). The subjects and settings of these scenes are fairly similar (the straw upon which Lancelot's knights sleep in his castle recalling the heaps of straw in the forest shed), but the variations Bresson works upon the stylistic constructions of these scenes has an internal formal logic quite apart from the action.

Segment V begins with a brief conversation between the lovers inside the entrance of the shed; they then go upstairs. Lancelot moves to the space he will typically occupy in these scenes, to the left of the unseen window, the light outlining his face against the dark wall (Fig. 11.13). Guenièvre sits facing him on the bench, the window just off left, with its light picking her out in similar fashion (Fig. 11.14). This shot/reverse shot pattern continues from shot 55 to 73, the end of the scene; occupying nineteen of these shots is a sustained conversation, during which he tells her of his failure to find the Grail. Early in this conversation, she asks to see his hand. He reaches out of frame right, and on the cut to Guenièvre, his hand extends in at the left. The shot spaces are thus exactly contiguous. Bresson tends to let the pace of the dialogue determine his cutting rhythms; that is, there is relatively little offscreen speech—only two instances in this scene. For the most part, one actor says a line, there follows a cut to the other actor, that actor says a line, and so on. Since Bresson's actors seldom register facial expressions, the concept of the reaction shot becomes less relevant than in a classical film. Conventional cutting usually dictates that a shot/reverse shot pattern be edited in relation to the ebb and flow of character emotion, with dialogue carrying over cuts as needed. In *Lancelot*, many of the conversations are cut with traditional shot/reverse shot framings (down to the inclusion of shoulders in the foregrounds of some shots), but the deliberate rhythm of the cuts gives the conversations a ritualistic quality that enhances the relatively flat deliveries of the actors.

Segment x, the second meeting, begins to work more complications into the simple pattern of the earlier scene. Now there is no scene downstairs to establish the situation. Rather, we first see a bird on a branch, viewed through a window, the frame of which is just visible at left and bottom (Fig. 11.15). This framing will be a familiar one later on, but this is the first time it occurs. The shot is from Lancelot's point of view (POV), but we cannot know this yet; all we hear is his voice, offscreen, saying, "Accept." A cut reveals Lancelot, apparently in a doorway, speaking to Guenièvre; we might assume at this point that he is facing her returning his gaze; rather, we move 180° to a shot from behind Lancelot (Fig. 11.17). He turns and begins to pace to the left, with the camera following (Fig. 11.18); he speaks to Guenièvre while looking at the floor. By this time we might suspect that he had not been looking at her in the previous shot, and that the bird shot had been from his POV. As in so many scenes, Bresson avoids using an establishing shot; even the apparently conventional shot/reverse shots of many of the film's scenes become more problematic when we cannot be sure of the characters' relative positions—as in this case. We hear Guenièvre's offscreen voice, refusing his plea that she release him from his oath to her. But the camera holds on him, panning to the right again as he turns and continues pacing (Fig. 11.19). He crosses the room three times in all before turning and glancing three-quarters front right at her; then he resumes pacing, crossing the room twice more. By this time the space is becoming clearer. This is the same space to the left of the window that he had occupied in the earlier scene; Guenièvre is presumably to the right on her bench again—as we discover to be the case when there is finally a cut to her.

One might assume thus far that Bresson is drawing upon that cliché of naive criticism: when the characters are emotionally separate from each other, they are not shown in the same shot together. It is true to some extent here, perhaps, and certainly in the third shed scene there is a series of two-shots as they finally embrace. But the idea is so simple as to be barely worth pointing out, and besides, it does not always hold here. For after the cut to Guenièvre on her bench, Lancelot sits beside her. A few shots later he resumes his pacing, and again the camera pans with him. Then he sits beside her again in the same two-shot framing. After several more shots, including Lancelot's return to the window and another POV of the bird, the characters move into a new shot/reverse shot setup, with three-quarters views of each (Figs. 11.20 and 11.21). But almost immediately, within the same first shot of Guenièvre, she turns her face away (Fig. 11.22), so that he and she both face to the right. This situation continues from shot 127 to 142.

During all this, Lancelot has been glancing alternatively off at her and at the floor; in shot 142 she looks up briefly at him, reestablishing the double eyeline-match characteristic of shot/reverse shot, then looks down. This play of glances within shot/reverse shot situations is characteristic of other conversation scenes in the film as well; it helps offset the expressionless performances of the actors, suggesting ongoing thought processes without specifying what shape these might take. This shot/reverse shot series continues on to shot 145, then ends as she rises, leaving the scarf on the bench with the camera holding on it after the characters exit.

The parametric structuring of these scenes becomes very apparent by the third of these parallel meetings. After a shot of Lancelot approaching the shed, there is a cut to a *plan américain* of Guenièvre standing to the left of an offscreen window, her head bowed. There then follows a medium shot of Lancelot in the doorway, looking off front right, speaking to Guenièvre. This setup reverses aspects of the second meeting. Now she is the focus of the opening shot/reverse shot; her glance is withheld, so that we understand where she is in the framings of him, but we are unsure where he is in the reverse shots of Guenièvre. Rather than pacing, as he had done, she stands absolutely still. These framings repeat twice each. After the third shot of him (Fig. 11.23), the camera returns to the same framing of her (Fig. 11.24). She says, "I wanted to see you one last time"; after a tiny pause, she raises her eyes and looks directly to the front, with a harsh birdcall from offscreen marking the moment (Fig. 11.25). This shot resolves the question of where Lancelot is; the camera is virtually in his position. As if in response to the birdcall, she looks off right (Fig. 11.26); but in fact she is looking at the stairway, and the camera pans as she moves to it, with Lancelot joining her there. They go upstairs, and a shot/reverse shot pattern interspersed with eyeline matches follows as she points out to him that the scarf is missing. She then watches as he removes his armor and tosses it on the floor; as in earlier scenes, he occupies the space to the left of the window, she to the right, by the bench.

Their embraces are framed in a way that demonstrates the careful balancing of shots that Bresson employs in these scenes—embodying on the local level the principle of balancing scenes across the film. Initially we see her on the left, holding him, as she always does, with her head on his shoulder, her face away from his (Fig. 11.27). Then she pulls away, into an over-the-shoulder shot/reverse shot situation (Fig. 11.28); a similar shot of him over her shoulder follows, and each is repeated. Then they embrace again, with her head on his other

309

shoulder, at the right (Fig. 11.29). This leads to a series of two-shots, interspersed with a pair of shots out the window, one of Mordred and his followers approaching the shed, one of them leaving; the scene ends with another, similar embrace.

Segment XXVII, Gauvin's visit to Guenièvre in the same shed, is handled more simply. Gauvin enters and joins her upstairs, but he passes along the other side of the trapdoor, thus ending by facing Guenièvre from the side of the room opposite to where Lancelot had characteristically stood (Figs. 11.30 and 11.31).

Finally, in Segment XXXIII, Lancelot and Guenièvre sit on the floor of his stronghold, arguing about whether he should turn her over to Artus. It begins simply enough, with two tracking shots following the feet of a pair of knights, the camera then holding on Lancelot and Guenièvre in medium-long shot (Fig. 11.32). A somewhat conventional shot/reverse shot pattern then begins, with Lancelot sitting still, looking off at Guenièvre (Fig. 11.33). She sits, opposite him, her face in shadow, looking variously in three directions: off and down, three-quarters front and down (Fig. 11.34), and front at him. These directions alternate from shot 555 to 562. Then, for one of the longest takes in the film, Bresson holds on Guenièvre. This time the cutting does not follow the lines of dialogue. Guenièvre and Lancelot continue to make short statements, but we now hear only his voice offscreen. This reverses the situation of their second meeting, when the camera had held on him, panning as he paced, with her lines coming from off-screen. Now she sits, glancing in different directions. One might posit a narrative function at this point—is her reaction more important than his, so that we would wish to see her face? Yet, aside from the fact that we can barely see her shadowed face—which registers no emotion during this shot—Lancelot speaks some significant lines here: "My eyes are made for the impossible"; "How to understand that the woman He made for me was not made for me, and that what is true is false." The choice of framing seems purely arbitrary in terms of what the characters say; we might just as logically hold on Lancelot for a few minutes. The long take seemingly functions primarily to complete a pattern of decoupage started in the scene of their second meeting, the to-and-fro panning movement with an avoidance of reverse shots of Guenièvre. The scene ends as Lionel enters and tells them it is time for Guenièvre to go back to Artus.

These formal variations across scenes help create narrative parallels to some extent, but the similarity of the settings, actions, and conversations would be more than enough to do that. More important, these scenes demonstrate that *Lancelot* is organized on every level, from the local to the global, on abstract formal principles that can enhance, co-exist with, or even override the narrative logic.

Other Parametric Patterns. There are two other parametric patterns that deserve mention, though they are not as pervasive as the motivic play and the variant spatiotemporal shifts: graphic matching and unclear spatial and temporal relations.

Although it has not been a characteristic of all his films, in *Lancelot* Bresson uses a surprisingly large number of close graphic matches from shot to shot. There are not a great many filmmakers in the narrative cinema who use this device extensively, although it is a staple of abstract films. *Lancelot* shares this trait with the works of Ozu and Kurosawa in particular; specifically, its several series of matches on the movements of knights arming for battle resemble the dynamic graphic matches on moving figures in *Seven Samurai*.

Segment XIX, in which Artus and his knights ride to the tournament, contains no cuts without a graphic match. Every framing presents a centered knight, seen from the waist up and facing three-quarters front left, against a moving background of the dark forest (Figs. 11.9 and 11.10). The parallel scene of the return (Segment XXI) includes a long shot at beginning and end but matches all the other shots in the same way (Fig. 11.12). One might argue that such matching serves a narrative function, but probably the only conceivable interpretation would be that Bresson is trying to suggest that these men are all similar. Yet, in fact, they are opposed to each other, and it would be difficult to demonstrate much similarity between Gauvin and Mordred or Artus. We can only conclude, once again, that these graphic patterns form a purely abstract structure alongside the narrative—a structure with its own partially independent interest.

The same principle holds true for the series of tent shots at the beginning of Segment XXV, the morning after the storm. The first shot frames a tent peak, facing to the left, with a colored flag flapping above it. Bresson then cuts to a similar shot of another tent, but facing right (Fig. 11.35) and with a differently colored flag. The next shot again shifts direction and color, with a third tent facing left (Fig. 11.36). But now the film breaks this pattern of systematic oppositions by cutting to another tent facing left—Lancelot's (Fig. 11.37). The peak and lighting match precisely with the previous tent, but the flag color is different, and the flag itself is tattered and does not flap in the wind. The cutting does differentiate Lancelot's flag a bit, but since we do not know to whom any of these flags belong until Mordred and his friend speak in the next shot, the point is a small one. On the whole, the systematic nature of the graphic shifts of color and shape comes forward. The same is true of the various scenes composed of quick shots showing knights leaping onto their horses, squires saddling horses, and knights closing their visors (Figs. 11.38 and 11.39).

The graphic matches depend on our perception of various similarities, but there is another set of devices in *Lancelot* that plays on an uncertainty in our understanding of space and time. At a number of points, Bresson presents a series of cuts or a sound/image juxtaposition that we can perhaps grasp only retrospectively, or that we must understand by inference. The use of sound at the end of Segment xxx to substitute for the battle undermines expectations. Frequently during this film Bresson uses the, by now, common device of bringing up the sound of the upcoming scene several seconds before the end of the current one. Indeed, he bares this device in the film's first dialogue, during the scene among the peasants, when the old woman tells the child that a person is doomed to die if one hears his footsteps (even his horse's) before one sees him (Segment iii). This device of sound off, sound overlaps, and sound substituting for events thus becomes one of the many ways of suggesting the fated decline of the Round Table. By the time the battle occurs, late in *Lancelot*, we will be expecting the sounds of armor and hoofbeats to carry us into a battle sequence, since Lancelot is leading his men out to attack. Instead, a straight cut takes us into a scene of the battle's aftermath. Retrospectively, the few seconds of battle sound seem to constitute a tiny separate scene, in a time we never witness, imbedded at the end of the previous scene.

Bresson plays a few spatial tricks on us as well. In Segment viii, Lancelot and Gauvin are seated in a tent, talking; the situation is initially handled in shot/reverse shot. Then Gauvin stands and moves right to the tent opening, looking through it and to the right (Fig. 11.40); Lancelot is, at that point, offscreen left. Gauvin's POV of Guenièvre's window follows (Fig. 11.41). The scene then returns to the same framing of Lancelot that had been used in the shot/reverse shot portion of the scene (Fig. 11.42); he continues to look off right. There follows a medium close-up of Gauvin, by the tent flap, now facing left (Fig. 11.43). The logical inference here is that this new framing of Gauvin is from Lancelot's POV; yet suddenly Gauvin looks through the tent flap and Lancelot stands up in the background (Fig. 11.44). We realize that Gauvin is now standing just outside the tent (having presumably moved there during the preceding shot of Lancelot). Bresson has taken advantage of the neutral backgrounds provided by the tent walls to fool us; it is impossible to tell by his surroundings whether

Gauvin is inside or outside the tent, since both positions look about the same. A similar juggling of space occurs in Segment XVII, as the knights argue before departing for the tournament. The scene looks like a conventional over-the-shoulder shot/reverse shot. But the armored shoulders and dark hair in the foreground at both sides look much alike, and Bresson makes the space considerably less clear than it might appear. In one shot, he lines Bors, Gauvin, Agravain, and Mordred up in a row (Fig. 11.45). Then he cuts to a reverse angle on Agravain and Mordred, with the same argument continuing; we must infer that the foreground shoulders belong to Gauvin on the left, Bors on the right (Fig. 11.46). Yet when the scene moves next to a new reverse shot past Agravain's shoulder, we see Lionel and Bors facing him and arguing; there is no indication where Gauvin now stands (Fig. 11.47). We have already seen how the spatial presentation of Lancelot's rescue of Guenièvre impedes our understanding of that whole scene. Such moments demand an active effort to figure out the space, time, and logic of the scene. If we simply wait to have narrative information provided to us in a straightforward way, as in the classical film, we will probably feel a confusion at the moment, then factor out what happened from our construction of a coherent chain of fabula events.[9]

CONCLUSIONS

In the mid-1960s, Bresson told interviewers Jean-Luc Godard and Michel Delahaye:

[9] Between the initial writing of this essay and its final revision, two analyses have been published which treat aspects of *Lancelot*'s parametric form. Lindley Hanlon discusses the dialogue in the film, concentrating on the use of stripped-down, repetitive sentence structures, verbal motifs, and vocal inflections. She essentially analyzes the verbal component of the film as if it were a set of poems (*Fragments: Bresson's Film Style* [Rutherford: Fairleigh Dickinson, 1986], chap. 5, "Chansons et Gestes: Voice and Verse in *Lancelot du Lac*," pp. 157–187).

André Targe takes a different approach, examining the tournament scene's layout of shots, which he says can be studied without reference to the sequence's narrative context or logic (pp. 87, 92). Targe charts the patterns of shots and finds regular alternations and symmetries running through the entire scene. At one point (p. 97) he compares the insistent repetition to Philip Glass's music for the experimental minimalist performance piece *Einstein on the Beach* ("Ici l'espace nait du temps . . . [Etude détaillée du segment central de 'Lancelot du Lac']," *Camêra Stylo* 5 [January 1985]: 87–99).

These two analyses provide additional evidence that sparse parametric repetitions govern *Lancelot*'s dominant. Targe's editing charts in particular show that the symmetries I have found between whole scenes across the film recur in miniature within a single sequence. Also, the fact that three critics independently chose to analyze subtle repetitions and variations in the same film would seem to confirm that a notion of parametric form is relevant to *Lancelot*. In addition, Hanlon and Targe use comparisons to poetry and music in characterizing *Lancelot*'s style—precisely the two art forms most heavily dependent on parametric variations.

I attach enormous importance to form. Enormous. And I believe that the form leads to the rhythms. Now the rhythms are all-powerful. That is the first thing. Even when one makes the commentary of a film, this commentary is seen, felt, at first as a rhythm. Then it is a color (it can be cold or warm); then it has a meaning. But the meaning arrives last.

Now, I believe that access to the audience is before everything else a matter of rhythm. I am persuaded of that.[10]

Whether or not one agrees with Bresson that meaning comes chronologically last among a device's effects on the spectator, the point is that he values form, and especially rhythm. And he considers rhythm, rather than meaning, the key to audience engagement with a film. We would not expect every audience member to respond to Bresson's work as he would wish; he has a reputation as a "difficult" director to all but a small number of film-goers. As is clear from his interviews, he has no wish to win a wide audience if it means having to adopt the prevailing norms of mainstream commercial filmmaking.

Rather, as with other great individualists who create their own alternative stylistic systems, Bresson must force spectators out of their normal viewing habits. His very failure to provide traditionally expressive performances and linear, clear narratives should cue us to look elsewhere for the salient aspects of the film's stylistic interest—the variations, the deliberate, playful difficulties.

But to what end should we shift our viewing habits? What interest might the graphic matches or the limited, repeated motifs hold for a spectator? To some degree, the style does have a general effect on our understanding of the narrative. By forcing an active, deflected concentration on the spectator's part, Bresson creates a sense of intensity that an ordinary film would invest entirely in the actions and expressions of conventional performances. I heard a student remark after seeing the film for the first time that she was surprised how deeply she had come by the end to care about the characters, given that she had been bothered initially by the flat performances. This sense of involvement comes, I suspect, from a complex perceptual engagement with the film as a whole—an involvement we might think of as centering around Lancelot and Guenièvre.

And perhaps our involvement with the film's form does come to some extent through the unique rhythm created by the obsessive theme-and-variations construction. Consider, for example, Penelope Gilliatt's attempt to describe what she calls the "extraordinary" final sequence.

[10] Godard and Delahaye, "The Question," p. 12.

A dark wood, in the deep watercolors that characterize the film. Two shots of a riderless horse in panic, crashing through the trees. A wounded knight. A riderless horse. A knight, crumpled: wounded, maybe dead. A riderless horse. Lancelot's knights on horseback, riding into an ambush of archers fighting for Mordred. Arrows fired by the archers who are hidden in trees. A riderless horse. King Arthur lying dead, his crown still on his helmet. A great, lone bird, high overhead, coasting in a pale-grey sky. The felled horse and his wounded rider: Lancelot, who staggers away to lean against a tree. A riderless horse. Lancelot stumbles away to a pile of dead knights in armor, who have collapsed around King Arthur. "Guinevere," says Lancelot, just before he falls. The bird again. A last movement in the monstrous pile of armor.[11]

This is generally an accurate summary of the scene's shots. But more important, Gilliatt adopts a fragmented, virtually verb-less prose style in order to convey the striking rhythms and repetitions of this sequence; it is difficult to imagine a journalistic reviewer approaching most standard narrative films this way. *Lancelot* draws us into its narrative in part by its insistent repetitions, which do not repeat literally, but vary in subtle, unpredictable ways.

Nevertheless, as we have seen, much of our involvement with the style of the film cannot be reduced to a set of narrative functions. If we assume that interpretation is the primary operation we perform when watching a film, then the permutational structure of *Lancelot* makes no sense. All those variations would have to serve the meaning or fall into a residual category like "excess"; that is, all the *systematic* aspects of style would function to create meaning in relation to the narrative, while the *non*-systematic aspects would simply be those material aspects of the image that escape thorough integration into narrative functioning (texture, color, grain, etc.). Yet clearly there are systematic stylistic structures here that operate on their own. Unless we want to deal with only parts of films like *Lancelot*, we must make different assumptions and perform other operations than interpretation. Most fundamentally, we should accept the idea that the intensity and complexity of perception itself is also an end in artistic experience—perhaps the *main* end.

This is not to say that independent formal play replaces narrative and meaning. No one would deny that many classical narrative films are deeply engaging without drawing much upon stylistic devices used for their own sakes; similarly, abstract films can provoke complex responses without the use of narratives or specific meanings. Why, then, should we not acknowledge that there exists a set of films which in a sense combine the principles of both? Narrative and abstract patterns

---

[11] Quoted in New Yorker Films's publicity flier for *Lancelot*.

for structuring stylistic devices exist side by side in such works. Either may come forward more strongly at any given time. Guenièvre's conversation with Gauvin (Figs. 11.30 and 11.31) would be an instance in which narrative dominates, while the Mondrian-like shot of tents and shields (Color Plate 1) favors the abstract. Other filmmakers who work both inside and outside mainstream commercial filmmaking institutions have blended narrative and abstract structures. While Bresson works in an alternative, less commercially oriented milieu, a filmmaker like Yasujiro Ozu used sparse parametric style while employed in one of the world's most successful commercial film industries, that of Japan. I will be analyzing similar structures in his *Late Spring* in the next chapter.

Such filmmakers' works are valuable, not simply for their originality of style or their interesting subjects, but also because this twofold working upon formal material holds such a potential for great complexity unaccompanied by thematic obfuscations. Whether sparse in style, as are the films of Bresson and Ozu, or perceptually dense, as are the works of Godard and Tati, parametric films exploit a great range of the cinematic medium's possibilities.

12

Late Spring and Ozu's
Unreasonable Style

OZU: "They don't understand—that's why they say it is Zen or something like that."
SHINBI IIDA (critic): "Yes, they make everything enigmatic."
—"A Talk with Ozu," quoted by Donald Richie in *Ozu*

STYLE AND IDEOLOGY

ODDLY ENOUGH, despite the fact that Yasujiro Ozu's films are still not commonly shown in the United States and Europe, they already need re-defamiliarization. Ozu is arguably, along with Eisenstein and Tati, one of the greatest directors in motion picture history. Yet enthusiasm for his films retains an esoteric aura, and I suspect that few scholars and devotees of the cinema have sought to view a substantial portion of his output with as much assiduity as they would give to a study of more fashionable great directors—Hitchcock, Keaton, Renoir, Kurosawa. Already clichés have encased his works: all Ozu films are variations on the same story ("Who can tell all those seasons apart?"), or, Ozu's quiet tone can really be comprehensible only if you understand Zen. From a neoformalist perspective, we can see these difficulties as having arisen because Western viewers too quickly battened onto the most obvious, but misleading, backgrounds against which to view Ozu: traditional Japanese life style and arts. These viewers often knew little about either these backgrounds or the films, but such explanations offered a blanket and convenient way of apparently understanding Ozu.

Yet if we delve a little more deeply and bother to place Ozu more precisely against specific, appropriate backgrounds, the clichés fall away. Those writers who view Ozu's films as embodying traditional

I AM GRATEFUL to David Bordwell for sharing bibliography and ideas with me; special thanks also to Jim O'Brien and Aki Miura, of the East Asian Studies Department of the University of Wisconsin-Madison, for providing information on locales and customs referred to in *Late Spring*, as well as for suggesting how a Japanese spectator might react to certain scenes.

Japanese aesthetic and ideological values will treat Ozu as far more conservative in both areas than I think he is. In particular, a view of Ozu as conservative offers an easy way of motivating the numerous odd stylistic traits of his films as being simply at the service of his ideology. If Ozu's ideology and narrative subjects arise from some sort of serene vision of a vanished world, then his restrained, minute variations on a consistent set of filmic devices become merely the objective correlative for that serenity. In short, the strange style arises, we Westerners must assume, because Japanese culture is itself alien to us; the Japanese viewer presumably grasps it. On the other hand, if it turns out that Ozu does not use traditional Japanese values in his stories, we must jettison any notion that his stylistic oddities can be explained away in this fashion. Similarly, if Japanese film practitioners and audiences find Ozu's films just as strange as do Western ones, we must seek other ways of motivating his style.

Here, rather than simply assuming that traditional Japanese culture provides the most pertinent background, I shall begin by looking at *Late Spring*'s subject matter in relation to the changes in attitudes that were occurring in the years before its production in 1949. The background of contemporary social reality reveals that Ozu's ideology tallies closely with the new, liberalized ideas that were introduced from the West, both after the war and during the 1920s and 1930s—a period of intense interest in Western culture. I shall then go on to argue that the most pertinent stylistic backgrounds for *Late Spring* are the classical Hollywood cinema and the modern parametric cinema (the latter being the same type we examined in the three previous chapters).[1]

THE NONTRADITIONAL JAPANESE FAMILY

Typically, critics in the West have viewed Ozu as essentially conservative, portraying a traditional Japanese life style. His emphasis on the family and his slow, severe style seem to some to create a nostalgia for feudal, prewar values.[2] This may be true to a certain extent in Ozu's

---

[1] The Japanese cinema of the 1930s and 1940s also serves as a pertinent background, mainly for showing that Ozu's work did not participate fully in a national or studio style. I do not have the space to pursue this line of inquiry here. David Bordwell's forthcoming British Film Institute (BFI) monograph on Ozu will offer evidence for this point by examining the contemporary Japanese cinema as a background to his work.

[2] Probably the most extreme statement of this view is given in Marc Holthof's "Ozu's Reactionary Cinema," *Jump Cut* no. 18 (1978): 20–22. There Holthof does an analysis so ethnocentric and ahistorical that there is no point in refuting it at any length. Admitting that he knows little of Japanese culture or of Japanese film, he nevertheless asserts that a Marxist analysis of Japanese culture will show Ozu to be reactionary. (Holthof's problems, I should add, stem not from his choice of a Marxist perspective, but from his lack

two wartime films, and particularly in *There Was a Father*, made under strict censorship and control. But these films are hardly typical of Ozu's work. I would argue that the postwar films like *Late Spring* offer a very different, modern view of the family. To judge the daughters and the marriage arrangements of these films by Western standards of the 1970s and 1980s gives a hopelessly skewed notion of Ozu's ideology. The mistake comes especially in the assumption that "the family" has been a single, unchanging, feudal unit in Japan; in reality, conceptions of the family have changed considerably as a result of Western influences and the war.

Before the end of World War II, the extended family unit, or *ie*, was officially considered to be structured completely around a patriarchal system (including ancestors as well as living family members). The father was the head of the *ie*, and all property and responsibility passed to the eldest son. If there was no son, one could be brought into the *ie* by adoption or by marriage. Marriage, in middle- and upper-class families at least, came about through the *miai* (an arranged meeting), and the choice of the parents usually superseded any personal desires on the parts of the young people involved; the main object of marriage was the provision of an heir for the *ie*. Marriage was considered inevitable for both sexes, and religious teachings held that to remain single was a disgrace. Love matches were considered lower-class and therefore vulgar; in fact, love was not an important value in marriage.[3] (It is notable that none of Ozu's pre-1940 films deals with this kind of traditional family.)

---

of research upon which to base such an analysis.) Holthof goes on to misdescribe *Late Spring* at several points and commits the fallacy of assuming that because some young Japanese filmmakers have considered Ozu reactionary, this view must necessarily be true.

Holthof argues that the "stability" of Ozu's shots reinforces the traditional Japanese home and therefore traditional Japanese signifying systems as well; he sees in Ozu's stylistic system an equivalent for the cinema of traditional Japanese arts, and he even goes back to the old chestnut of Ozu's having a religious conception of the sign. He claims as well that Ozu's crossings of the axis of action would only be considered wrong by a Western spectator, something we will see is not the case. Holthof concludes that Ozu's cinema is a hybrid of feudal values (in its subject matter) and capitalist economics (in its production circumstances); he sums it up as "nostalgia for a feudal signifying system and a feudal structure (the family)."

Holthof's argument arises first of all from his obvious assumption that there are only two possible types of ideology: radical and reactionary. Also, he makes no distinction between prewar and postwar conceptions of the family in Japan, assuming that there has been one long tradition of the family as a feudal (presumably meaning patriarchal) unit. But, as we shall see, the considerable changes at the war's end should nuance our view of Ozu. And if we can allow for a middle ground between radical and reactionary, we will find *Late Spring* a mildly progressive film in its historical context.

[3] Joy Hendry, *Marriage in Changing Japan* (London: Croom Helm, 1981), pp. 16–25.

Such an ideology, however, was not absolutely universal in Japan. By the 1930s, the spread of Western culture, and especially American movies, had introduced the concept of romantic love to the younger generation in Japan.

The idea of seeking happiness in marriage was a new one, and it is consistent with another new idea, that of the husband and wife setting up their own house. The movement of people to work in industry often required young couples to do this already, but the idea that it would be preferable to the old extended family was now also being expressed.

Such ideas were considered quite daring, however, and the extreme repression and insistence on duty to emperor and family during the war did not encourage their adoption. But the Japanese defeat changed this patriarchal system radically. The new constitution, designed to introduce democracy into Japan, made marriage dependent on mutual consent and on the legal equality of husband and wife with respect to inheritance, property rights, divorce, and other matters. Women received the vote in 1946, and on January 1, 1948, the new marriage laws went into effect. Young people over twenty no longer needed parental consent to marry.[4]

Of course legislation could not in itself erase deeply ingrained traditional ideology, and we are all aware by now that Japanese women still lag far behind the women of most Western countries in the struggle for equality. Sociologists have consistently found a gap in Japan between professed attitudes and actual practice. After the war and into the 1950s, polls showed that the majority of people were against *miai* marriages and in favor of love matches. Yet in practice, *miai* arrangements still predominated, and by 1961 a poll of college graduates showed 80 percent in favor of the *miai* practice. Arranged marriages have remained prevalent, although the notion of romantic love seems to have been incorporated into them, and couples often make an attempt to get to know one another before marriage.[5]

Seen in this light, Ozu's characters in *Late Spring* become almost a schematic layout of the new democratic values. The father, Somiya, observes rituals, such as in his visit to the shrine with his sister, but there is not a great deal of emphasis placed upon this. At the beginning he is apparently working on an article on European economic history, and later, in the Kyoto inn, he has a copy of *Thus Spake Zarathustra* in English—a sign *not* that he has adopted Western philosophy, but that he is aware of modern Western thought. Noriko is more

[4] Ibid., pp. 26–27.
[5] Ibid., pp. 29–30.

overtly Westernized, in that she usually wears skirts and blouses and carries a purse rather than a *furoshiki* (cloth bundle); this latter point is especially emphasized in the opening scene, when she arrives at the tea ceremony wearing a kimono but carrying a purse. She seems modernized in her love for American movies, in her resistance to her elders' advice, and in her expressed opposition to *miai*. She also speaks of marriage in terms of personal happiness, not duty to the family. Yet, as with so many young Japanese women of the postwar era, she ends by consenting to an arranged marriage.

The main point here is that the father, apparently so traditional in the eyes of Western viewers, actually represents the new notions of marriage and the family. He reinforces Noriko's ideal of love in marriage. Far from appealing to her sense of duty and telling her to go out and have children to perpetuate the *ie*, he tells her to work at forming a good marriage so that eventually she will find happiness. Here the aunt's seemingly odd comment that Noriko is a bit old-fashioned begins to make sense. Noriko clings to the notion that happiness and duty come through serving her *ie*, that is, through taking care of her father. Thus her father has to push her into the new idea of marriage as a separation from the *ie* and a move into a smaller, nuclear family. No overt mention is made of the fact that the professor's *ie* will die out with him; the emphasis is rather upon his adjustment to loneliness at the end.

Noriko's friend Aya serves in the film to reinforce and extend the idea of modern marriage. She, more than Noriko, is the complete *moga*, or "modern girl." While Noriko and her father live in a home with one Western-style room (a fairly common arrangement in Japanese houses at that time), Aya's whole house seems to be done in that style. She dresses and cooks in Western fashion and has a job taking dictation in English. Most important, in view of the fact that *Late Spring* was made about one year after the new divorce laws, she is a divorcée. She reveals in addition that her marriage had not been arranged through a *miai*; she had proposed to her husband Ken herself and had initiated the divorce herself (something unthinkable for a wife under old divorce laws except in certain extreme circumstances). She is now cynical about marriage, but there is no suggestion that she was wrong to divorce her husband; indeed, the professor admires her ability to earn her own living. Her final scene with Somiya shows her in an entirely sympathetic light, becoming a sort of substitute daughter by promising to visit him.

Aya also provides the means of bringing forward Ozu's rather jaundiced view of children. Considering the prewar focus on child-bearing in marriage, the whole notion comes off rather badly here. When Aya visits Noriko to gossip about their school reunion, she mentions that one former classmate had pretended to have only three children when she really had four—as if having children had become something shameful. The emphasis on their classmates' children in this scene functions in part, of course, to show how old Noriko is to be still unmarried (twenty-seven at a time when twenty-five would have been considered late for marriage). Yet in this conversation there is also perhaps a hint that these other women have gotten stuck in traditional marriages bound up entirely with motherhood. Certainly the one child we do see, Noriko's cousin, is a lumpish and whining specimen. Even the placid scene of Professor Onodera and Somiya contemplating the rock garden of Ryoanji suggests that raising children is not an unmixed blessing.

Perhaps the most strikingly nontraditional aspect of the film lies in the characterization of the father in relation to the traditional Japanese patriarch. The head of the feudal-style household held virtually exclusive power and could demand all sorts of services and deference from his family. This conception was by no means wiped out by the decrees of the postwar constitution. One 1947 Japanese article described ideal filial behavior toward the head of the family: "When he puts on dress, he must do it through the servant or his subordinates"; he was supposed to be fed, to be treated with ceremony upon arrival at and departure from the house, and so on. "In all other trifles of everyday life, the head of a family should enjoy special treatment, becoming his position as absolute ruler. A parent's, especially a father's, position is majestic and supreme."[6] Men could discipline their wives and daughters physically, forbid them to leave the house, and generally order every aspect of their existence in the traditional household.

With such customs still in existence, the professor's behavior in *Late Spring* clearly reflects new Western values. The notion that a man could be kind instead of stern, for example, was a new one, and Somiya behaves gently to Noriko throughout; she also mentions this to him as a quality in Hattori that would make him a good husband. Somiya also avoids forcing Noriko to do things; he defers to her to a remarkable extent in the arrangement of the marriage, resorting to subterfuge rather than to direct orders (a ploy of which *moga* Aya thoroughly approves). Indeed, Noriko seems to rule the household more than he does; the scene in which she forbids him a game of *mah-jongg*

---

[6] Quoted in Earl Herbert Cressy, *Daughters of Changing Japan* (New York: Farrar, Straus and Cudahy, 1955), p. 203.

would be almost shocking in terms of the ordinary standards of obe-
dience of daughter to father. Similarly, his willingness to fetch tea for
Noriko and Aya is a major departure from tradition. Again, the old-
fashioned aunt's remark that her brother spoils Noriko makes sense
here; from her viewpoint, it would look that way. The aunt herself is
the main representative of traditional values; she keeps referring
to the younger generation, and she discusses with her brother at
one point how offended she had been at seeing a bride who ate the
food at her own wedding reception—a reference to the traditional
etiquette that a bride should be too nervous to eat. The aunt claims
not to have eaten at her own wedding, but her brother pooh-poohs
the tradition.

For Noriko, the whole issue of marriage hinges on her belief that
her father could not, and presumably should not, fend for himself in
all the little chores of everyday life. She tells him she needs to see that
he wears clean clothes, that he shaves, that his desk is straightened,
and so on. We see her doing the most mundane and easy tasks for him:
hanging up his clothes as he changes from suit to kimono and handing
him toothpaste and water as he brushes his teeth at the Kyoto inn.
These are exactly the sorts of services a Japanese father could traditionally expect. The film specifies that the professor is an eldest son,
and hence he would have been used to such manifestations of deference all his life. Yet he says he is quite willing to do these tasks for
himself. He tells Noriko that her presence is convenient to him, but
that it is time for her to marry; he even apologizes for having kept her
so long with him to run his household. He assures her that he will
remember to take care of himself. And, in spite of Noriko's doubts,
the film does imply that Somiya will indeed get along on his own. In
a couple of scenes in which Noriko is not present, we see him folding
and hanging up a towel; in the final scene, he takes off his coat and
hangs it up—in a long-shot framing of the room reminiscent of the one
in which Noriko had performed the same action for him. There is even
a tiny motif of characters picking things up off the floor in Noriko's
room and placing them on her table; both the aunt and Somiya do
this—suggesting that Noriko is perhaps not the indispensable house-
keeper she pictures herself to be. Overall, the ideology of family life
presented in the film is not at all the traditional feudal system, but a
modern one based on newly imported Western ideas.[7] For those who
are now questioning the Western view of the family, Late Spring will

[7] Japanese critics have pointed out that Ozu has seldom portrayed the ie in traditional
ways; again, Bordwell's monograph on Ozu will deal with his ideology more extensively.

perhaps still seem conservative. But this is a view that takes no account of historical context; for 1949 Japan, the film would have been fairly progressive.

Ozu's postwar concentration on father-daughter relationships is important to this progressive ideology. In the conversation between Somiya and Onodera at the Ryoanji Temple garden, Somiya remarks that sons are better than daughters. The traditional implication of this remark would perhaps be that daughters often leave the *ie* at marriage, while sons stay on to perpetuate it. Yet the two men conclude that having sons makes no difference, since they too leave their parents. Thus, in spite of Somiya's initial traditional remark about sons being better, the scene concludes by upholding a notion of women's equality.[8]

Indeed, several of Ozu's later films develop on this notion. For example, the "remake" of *Late Spring* as *An Autumn Afternoon* changes the initial situation significantly. In *Late Spring*, Somiya has only one child and is left entirely alone at the end. In *Autumn Afternoon*, Hirayama still has his youngest son living at home after his daughter's marriage, but her departure affects him even more profoundly than Noriko's had Somiya. Ozu's exploration of the deep ties between fathers and daughters again goes against traditional beliefs concerning Japanese family life, in which the daughter is basically there to be married off. A similar, unusual concentration on the importance of daughters in the extended family figures in other Ozu films, such as *Early Summer*, in which the marriage of the daughter—and the consequent loss of her income—leads to the scattering of the family, and *Tokyo Story*, in which the childless daughter-in-law—an essentially useless person in a traditional family with four children and two grandchildren—provides the emotional support for the grandparents. The

---

[8] Kyoko Hirano's examination of the post–World War II occupation cinema has shown that there was an institutional basis for an ideology based on women's equality. According to Hirano, General Douglas MacArthur's postwar constitution was based on three principles: "civil rights, equal rights for women and renunciation of war." These ideals were officially assigned to be embodied in one project each by the three major studios, with Daiei (which specialized in period films) to make a civil rights film, Shochiku (famous for its melodramas and family films) to produce an equal rights story, and Toho (which concentrated on contemporary subjects) to do a pacifist subject. Shochiku's official women's rights film was *Emotional Flames* (released in April of 1948 and directed by Minoru Shibuya). Although Ozu was not assigned to make the official Shochiku women's rights film, it is quite possible either that he was influenced by the assignment of such a project to the studio or that the studio received the assignment because earlier films by Ozu and other Shochiku directors were perceived as conducive to such an ideological position. See Kyoko Hirano, "The Japanese Cinema Under the American Occupation Censorship: The Case of 'Between War and Peace,'" Unpublished paper, Society for Cinema Studies Conference, Montreal, 1987.

treatment of daughters in these films and others, such as *Equinox Flower* and *Late Autumn*, indicates that Ozu's vision of family life is far from the simple, traditional, nostalgic one that most Western critics attribute to him.

Another aspect of *Late Spring* that has perhaps led viewers to find the film basically conservative and traditional is its numerous references to Zen philosophy. The tea ceremony at the beginning, the prayer scene at Tsurugaoka Hachimangu shrine, and the visit to Kyoto, traditional ancient center of Japanese culture, could help foster the idea that Ozu is looking entirely backward here. Yet we should not assume such references have a monolithic and immutable meaning. The tea ceremony in particular had changed in its social function by 1949. One expert on Japanese culture has suggested that there have been three periods in the history of the tea ceremony: in the earliest (fifteenth to seventeenth centuries), tea masters in the service of rich families conducted the ceremonies; and in the second (seventeenth to nineteenth centuries), Shogunate ministers learned the tea ceremony in addition to their regular duties but did not function as professional artists. Finally, in the twentieth century,

the tea master has become an instructor. . . . The process corresponds almost exactly with that of the commercialization of the tea ceremony. The first stage in the process of commercialization occurred before the Second World War, when the study of the tea ceremony under a teacher was confined almost entirely to women of the upper classes; to be versed in the tea ceremony served as a symbol of social rank.

Later, after the war, large businesses began to sponsor cheap lessons in the tea ceremony for their women workers, and the custom became even more popularized.[9] Thus by the time *Late Spring* was made, the tea ceremony was regarded more as a social event than as a private aesthetic experience; one could argue that in the first scene Ozu may be using the ceremony to suggest quickly the characters' social status. Certainly he does not adhere to the traditional tone of the ceremony, which dictates that it take place in a small, plain room with monochromatic, subdued, and simple utensils and decorations, and without music. Ozu's cutaways to the lush gardens outside, and the music that comes up late in the scene, would seem to violate the ceremony's deliberate denial of sensuous pleasure. The scene still conjures up associations of the tea ceremony, of course, but it is a strictly Ozuian version of that tradition.

[9] Shuichi Kato, *Form, Style, Tradition: Reflections on Japanese Art and Society*, trans. John Bester (Tokyo: Kodansha International, 1981), pp. 155–157.

Moreover, Ozu avoids a completely reverential treatment of the subject of Zen by introducing humorous touches into this and other scenes. As the women wait in formal fashion for the tea ceremony to begin, the action primarily involves the aunt's instructions to Noriko about cutting down a pair of moth-eaten trousers into shorts: "Reinforce the seat." To a Japanese audience, this conversation would probably seem incongruous in this context. Similarly, the professor and aunt are praying at the shrine, but Ozu immediately switches to a comic tone as the aunt finds a wallet, promises to report it, but then scuttles away when a policeman strolls by. Even in the scene at the Kiyomizu temple in Kyoto Ozu undercuts the solemn atmosphere. Although the temple is built on a cliff, Ozu avoids showing the spectacular view of waterfalls and the city panorama at which Somiya and Mrs. Onodera are gazing from the jutting platform; instead, he concentrates on Onodera's teasing banter with Noriko over her earlier remark about his "unclean" remarriage. At the scene's end, Ozu cuts from a view of the platform (Fig. 12.1) to a medium-long shot of a temple fountain and row of dippers, with the schoolgirls seen in the previous shot now visible out of focus in the background (Fig. 12.2). The reference here is to the Shinto rite of purification through rinsing out the mouth at such fountains. Yet we do not find out whether the characters have performed this ritual. Indeed, the juxtaposition of the purification notion with the "unclean" byplay may be a little joke on Ozu's part. Only the scene in the Ryoanji garden is played in a completely contemplative fashion, with the two fathers chatting about accepting the loss of their marriageable children.

Certainly, had Ozu wished to present a very traditional view of Zen culture, he could have been far more solemn in his approach to these scenes. Indeed, he could have shown a number of things that he avoids altogether. For example, virtually any Japanese home would contain a *butsudan*, a shrine for prayer and offerings to dead family members. We never see the *butsudan* in Somiya and Noriko's house (although Ozu had placed great emphasis on the one in *There Was a Father*, a wartime film).

If we assume that Ozu's ideology is not as monolithically conservative and traditional as some have claimed, we must also toss out the notion that his style is the way it is so that it can function to support such an ideology; that is, Ozu's style is not austere because it is meant to reflect some sort of innately Japanese view of life. Certainly the styles of other Japanese directors are not similarly austere.

AN ARBITRARY STYLE

Ozu's style needs re-defamiliarization as much as did his ideology. Standard explanations have trivialized it. There has been a tendency for Western criticism of Ozu's films to deny the sparsity and uniqueness of his style, and to assume that those devices which we Occidental viewers find strange must necessarily be meaningful within some Japanese system of representation. Critics have sometimes, perversely, attempted to demonstrate this abundance of meaning by reading as symbols all objects and shots apparently superfluous to the narrative—a mode of interpretation more appropriate to a very Western mode of narrative filmmaking, the European art cinema.[10] Any device that could not conveniently be read symbolically could then be attributed to some vague sense of Zen or other Japanese traditions.[11] This approach considerably simplifies Ozu's marvelously original style and attributes all the power of his films to their creation of a contemplative vision of disappearing traditions of Japanese family life. But we have seen that this "vision" does not describe Ozu's ideology. So what explanation can we find for his style?

Some years ago, David Bordwell and I wrote an essay describing some of the unique features of Ozu's approach to the layout of space in his films, claiming that many shots and objects were included not to further or support the narrative action, but to call attention to themselves; that is, his films, like Bresson's, contained a surprisingly large proportion of artistic motivation. We argued further that Ozu's personal "rules" of editing (e.g., the shot/reverse shot series across the axis of action, the 360° shooting space, the graphic matches) were usually diametrically opposed to conventional approaches; Ozu used these

[10] Don Willis's article "Yasujiro Ozu: Emotion and Contemplation," *Sight and Sound* 48, no. 1 (Winter 1978/79): 44–49, is a good example of how boring Ozu's films can be made to sound through superficial thematic analysis. Willis explicitly compares Ozu's films to art movies such as *La Dolce Vita, The Fire Within*, and *Eclipse*. For a discussion of art cinema as a distinct mode of filmmaking, see David Bordwell, *Narration in the Fiction Film* (Madison: University of Wisconsin Press, 1985), chap. 10.

[11] Marvin Zeman's "The Zen Artistry of Yasujiro Ozu," *The Film Journal* 1, nos. 3-4 (Fall-Winter 1972): 62–71, attempts to read all of Ozu's work as fitting into a Zen approach: "The criteria that one must use for Ozu should be those of Japanese art and not cinematic art." Zeman finds everything to be narratively functional; transition shots, for example, serve simply to establish locale clearly—something Zeman can make sound convincing only because he implies that there is only one such shot per sequence, instead of series of shots.

Zeman's conception of Zen is so broad as to assure him of being able to fit anything in, but by his method, one could analyze Dreyer and many other Western filmmakers as Zen artists. Something more would be necessary to prove that this view is appropriate to Ozu.

same patterns in all types of scenes, not adapting them significantly to suit the specific action. Again, style remained resolutely noticeable in a way that did not function narratively.[12] In the intervening years, more essays on Ozu have appeared that have continued to simplify Ozu's style in one or both of the ways I have mentioned: by symbol-reading or by attributing "unreadable" stylistic flourishes to their being somehow innately Japanese.[13]

Yet I have seen no evidence that leads me to think our original argument was wrong—quite the contrary. A great many older Japanese films formerly unavailable have now been shown in the West. These reveal no directors consistently using the features characteristic of

[12] Kristin Thompson and David Bordwell, "Space and Narrative in the Films of Ozu," *Screen* 17, no. 2 (Summer 1976): 41–73.

[13] Kathe Geist's "Yasujiro Ozu: Notes on a Retrospective," *Film Quarterly* 37, no. 1 (Fall 1983): 2–9, is a good, recent example of the symbol-reading approach. Geist naturalizes Ozu's cutaways as POV shots; she offers as an example a scene in which the shots clearly are approximate POV framings, not cutaways, but she claims this is Ozu's general practice—ignoring the dozens of examples of non–POV cutaways. She also insists on reading all transition and cutaway shots symbolically, but she sometimes has to twist language to make this work out; of the many Ozu corridor shots, she says, "Hallways and alleyways are obvious symbols of passage, and most of Ozu's late films center around passages from one stage of human life to another" (p. 6). Here Geist conflates two different meanings of the word "passage" in order to impose a clichéd meaning. As with so many symbol-readers, context and function are irrelevant for Geist, and we are presumably supposed to read every one of Ozu's many corridor shots in exactly the same way. Yet Geist seems unable to interpret the fact that there are three shots instead of one of the pagoda that opens the Kyoto sequences in *Late Spring*: "The effect is visually pleasing and rhythmically satisfying" (p. 7). Joël Magny's "Le Printemps d'Ozu," *Cinéma* 81 no. 265 (January 1981): 16–27, provides a more subtle reading than Geist's. Yet Magny still psychologizes or thematizes everything, and he also has to resort to clichéd interpretations (e.g., any imbalance in a composition indicates disharmony in the diegetic world).

Robert Cohen's "Mizoguchi and Modernism: Structure, Culture, Point of View," *Sight and Sound* 47, no. 2 (Spring 1978): 110–118, takes the other tack, by denying that Ozu could have a "modernist" style (as we termed it in the *Screen* article); those aspects of Ozu's style that we found idiosyncratic, he argues, can all be explained in terms of traditional Japanese culture. Cohen never specifies in what way any of these techniques are Japanese-inspired, contenting himself with attacking the notion of "modernism" as applied to Japanese artworks. Unfortunately he makes the incorrect assumption that our analysis was done using a structuralist method, and he spends his time doing a critique of structuralist notions of modernism unconnected with what we were discussing in our article. For example, he attacks the notion of "deconstructive" style (p. 111)—a structuralist concept we did not use in our article.

Cohen basically suggests that all aspects of an artwork can be explained by cultural forces outside the art form, and that all these forces exist within the national boundaries of the artist's native land. Yet clearly Ozu was considerably influenced by Western filmmaking (as were most Japanese directors at the time he was working: for a brief discussion of this influence, see my "Notes on the Spatial System of Ozu's Early Films," *Wide Angle* 1, no. 4 [1977]: 8–17; Bordwell deals with this subject in more detail in his BFI monograph on Ozu). Moreover, there is the possibility of an artist making arbitrary stylistic choices through personal preference.

Ozu's style. Only an occasional film, like Naruse's *Floating Clouds* (1955), uses a low-height camera position or a straight-on corridor shot—and these isolated devices are probably imitations of Ozu, rather than evidence of a "naturally" Japanese approach. (Ozu was, after all, one of the two most famous and respected directors within the Japanese industry of the 1930s and 1940s, and it is no wonder that other directors would imitate his devices without picking up their functions within an overall system.) Also, the recent retrospectives of Ozu's early works have revealed a greater range of genres than most viewers had previously been aware of. It becomes apparent that the inclusion of elements for their own aesthetic interest, quite apart from narrative function, is a feature which existed throughout his career. In the early films it took a more consistently playful form, and the various comedies and gangster films of the 1930s are full of flashy stylistic passages. Gradually this use of style became more subdued and limited, but in their own restrained way, the later films also have moments of quiet humor and virtuosic style. The fact that the 360° space, the graphic matches, and the rest of Ozu's devices were applied to highly nontraditional subject matter in, say, *Dragnet Girl*, further suggests that his style does not serve a vision of vanishing Japanese family structures.

But even granting that Ozu's films do not resemble other Japanese directors' works, has he simply found a superior way of conveying traditional Japanese values to a native audience? Virtually every statement on Ozu refers to the familiar notion that he is "the most Japanese of Japanese directors," and that producers never bothered to send his films abroad, assuming that Western audiences would not be able to understand them. Does this mean that we must give up and relegate Ozu to that notorious domain of Oriental inscrutability? Certainly one does not wish to give an ethnocentric analysis of these films, but are they inevitably mysterious?

Tadao Sato, the most prominent Japanese critic of Ozu, suggests why Ozu acquired the "most Japanese" label: "On the surface he presents a modern-Japanese life-style, which to those unfamiliar with it could be boring. Since swordfighting movies are both more appealing and entertaining to foreign audiences, it is only natural that the first Japanese films to be internationally recognized were Kurosawa's period pieces."[14] Sato seems to imply that the failure to export Ozu's films was simply a matter of genre; Japanese producers perhaps as-

[14] Tadao Sato, *Currents in Japanese Cinema*, trans. Gregory Barrett (Tokyo: Kodansha International, 1982), p. 186.

329

sumed that Western audiences like the period pieces (e.g., *Rashomon*, *Ugetsu*) which had been the first big successes abroad. Note here that other directors who specialized in *gendai-geki* (stories of modern life), such as Shimizu, Gosho, and Naruse, also remained unknown in the West for decades; Ozu was simply the most prominent of this group.

More important, Sato's extensive work on Ozu suggests that his distinctive style has been very noticeable and puzzling to Japanese critics and filmmakers throughout his career. Sato's series of articles includes a number of interviews with people who worked with Ozu, as well as excerpts from interviews with Ozu. In almost all of these, the filmmakers remember having asked Ozu at various points during his life why he used a particular technique—the low camera, the lack of camera movement, the consistent crossing of the axis of action. Interviewers persistently asked such questions as well. For example, during the filming of *Equinox Flower* (1958), Ozu was asked why he used almost no tracks and pans. He replied: "It is not congenial to me. As my principle of life, I follow the general fashion in ordinary matters, and subject to the moral law in serious matters, and in respect of arts I follow myself." He simply could not use a device if he was not inclined to use it: "From this comes out my individuality, therefore I cannot leave it out of consideration. I dare to do it even if it is unreasonable."[15] Shohei Imamura, who had been an assistant director to Ozu on *Tokyo Twilight*, refused to work with him again because he could not bear Ozu's unrealistic use of actors, his shifting of props between shots, and his "incoherent" editing. In short, Ozu would not stick to conventions of filmmaking. But even while criticizing Ozu, Imamura summed up his style with a singularly happy figure: "I am inclined to think that his own taste had brought him to such a pass. There is not to be found any peculiar [i.e., particular] basis for his theory. It seems like his own breath."[16] Several anecdotes involve producers or other filmmakers who tried, in vain, to get Ozu to be more conventional. All the evidence Sato puts forth suggests that Japanese experts on film found Ozu's style distinctive, fascinating—and at times maddening.

We are left with a filmmaker whose distinctive style seems to be more a matter of personal choices than national traits. Indeed, Sato's list and discussion of what he considers Ozu's unique stylistic traits

[15] Quoted in Tadao Sato, "The Art of Yasujiro Ozu," a series of articles translated into English by Goro Iiri, in Sato's journal, *The Study of the History of the Cinema*, nos. 4-11 (1974–1978): pt. 2, pp. 83–81. These articles have not been translated into perfect English, but except for cases of obvious typographical errors or misspellings, I have not changed their wording. As the rest of the journal is in Japanese, the page numbers go from highest to lowest in these articles.

[16] Quoted in Sato, "The Art of Yasujiro Ozu," pt. 4, p. 94.

focuses upon many of the same devices that Bordwell and I discussed. At times Sato attempts to recuperate these, but often he turns right around and admits that the explanation cannot adequately account for the style. I shall refer to some of Sato's conclusions in discussing the traits of *Late Spring*.

"There is not to be found any peculiar basis for his theory"; "I dare to do it even if it is unreasonable": Ozu's stylistic choices were arbitrary, neither natural nor logical. Once chosen, his devices became a narrow set of features with which he could play within his films; they were parameters. This is not to deny that much of the power of his films comes from their extraordinary serenity of action and from the emotion generated by the characters. But these elements are readily apparent; to dwell on them to the exclusion of the films' complex stylistic patterning would be to belabor the obvious. As we saw with *Lancelot du Lac*, a film that combines elements of narrative and abstract films can multiply its interest for us. (It does not simply double that interest—narrative plus abstract—but in addition generates interest through the varying tensions between the two in the course of the film.) In this chapter, I will be looking at many of the same elements that Bordwell and I analyzed in Ozu's work, but with an eye to seeing in more detail how they function within a single film, alternately supporting and deflecting interest from the narrative. These elements require close attention, because they are the things that are not readily apparent to the viewer—as the basic narrative logic would be. Yet stylistic patterns are not for that reason negligible or incidental. I would argue that one of the reasons why we find the story of Noriko and her father so touching and why we feel them to be so intensely portrayed is precisely because we have been engaged by the complexity of every level of the film's construction. But we should not be tempted to attribute every bit of that complexity to narrative functioning, for then we would lose that additional fascination that comes from seeking to notice more and more of the maniacally precise patterns that Ozu has wrought, and that make it possible to watch his films many times—in spite of their surface sparseness—without tiring of them. Ozu's "unreasonable" style acquires a unique, self-contained logic when viewed in this way.

SELF-IMPOSED RULES

Late Spring uses most of the devices that are typical of Ozu's films in general, although it emphasizes some and downplays others. For example, a play with eyelines and point of view (POV) structures becomes central to this film, while there is almost none of the close graphic matching Bordwell and I found in *Passing Fancy, Autumn Afternoon,* and others. By looking at Ozu's self-imposed range of devices, we can judge the specific variations he works upon them in this film.

Late Spring consistently employs one of Ozu's most noticeable and famous devices, a low camera height (often mistakenly referred to as a low *angle*, although the camera remains horizontal in the majority of shots). Almost invariably commentators have claimed a realistic moti- vation for this device: because Japanese people sit on the floor, Ozu simply positions the camera as an "ideal Japanese observer," at their eye level. Sato repeats this explanation but goes beyond it as well.

This low angle, however, is not probably used merely because it was most natural for the Japanese people. The reason was that we are not always seated inside the Japanese house, but also we stand up and walk, or look up and down, or lie down and stare at the holes in the ceiling board. Yet, Yasujiro Ozu does not take such an angle at all, and sticks to low angle almost unnatu- rally. I think it was probably because he was afraid of the composition of the picture getting unstable. He avoided with scrupulous attention the same things looking changed in various shapes in accordance with the position of the camera.

Sato gives as examples Ozu's shot/reverse shots and his long views of rooms, and he concludes, "Coming thus far, it is evident that it is not natural, but it is apparently natural."[17]

Sato presents an eminently logical argument against the "ideal Jap- anese observer" notion. We are not, in fact, in the perfect position to see all actions. When characters are standing, we often see them from the shoulders or waist down, yet Ozu makes no attempt to accommo- date them by changing his framing. This happens in the Kyoto inn sequence of *Late Spring* when Noriko stands up to put out the light (Figs. 12.3 and 12.4); our attention here is drawn to the wonderful change in lighting on the back wall. Certainly in scenes in which char- acters are seated on the floor, the framing does have an "apparently natural" look (Fig. 12.5). Yet Ozu maintains this camera height even in scenes in which the characters sit in Western-style chairs (Fig. 12.6). Someone absolutely determined to find meaning in everything might claim that Ozu is here satirizing the Westernization of Japan (although there is nothing else in the film to support this interpreta- tion—aspects of Western culture are treated matter-of-factly or even pleasantly throughout the film). Yet what, then, do we make of the

---

[17] Sato, "The Art of Yasujiro Ozu," pt. 1, pp. 87–86.

low-height exterior tracking shots with walking characters (as in Fig. 12.7)? Are we to picture a Japanese observer crawling along after Noriko and Professor Somiya? Any attempt to apply a realistic motivation consistently for all instances of this device must collapse in the face of such patent absurdity. Ozu's camera height is, as Sato concludes, clearly "not natural," but an arbitrary device that he employs regardless of whether or not it fits the narrative perfectly.

The motivation for this low height is artistic, rather than realistic, transtextual, or compositional. Sato argues convincingly in relation to this and other traits of Ozu's style that he was concerned to keep the composition of each individual shot stable. Individual compositions tend to be not symmetrical, but balanced; camera movements are usually tracks at the same pace and in the same direction as the characters move, so as to maintain the general viewpoint unchanged. From shot to shot the compositions often carry some resemblances over the cut; the low height tends to place the verticals and horizontals of the walls consistently behind the characters. (Graphic matches, in the films in which Ozu emphasizes them, would of course also contribute to a consistency of composition.) Such consistency makes small formal variations stand out more immediately.

Although these low camera setups have commonly been termed "tatami shots," the phrase seems an ironic misnomer. In spite of his obsession with the compositional lines of the walls, Ozu apparently had no particular desire to emphasize floors. Masahiro Shinoda has related an anecdote from the period when he was working as an assistant on *Tokyo Twilight* (1957). Ozu ordered a cushion placed on the floor, even though no one was to sit on it. When Shinoda asked why, Ozu replied that he did not want the lines formed by the tatamis pointing in various directions. Sato emphasizes that the Japanese are used to the dark borders of the tatamis.

As for Ozu, he could not bear seeing the borderlines of tatami broadly intercrossing the picture. Therefore, in the position most effective to wiping out the lines, he had ordered him to put a cushion of no use to anybody. The space of Ozu's pictures which was apparently made up to be very natural was in reality deformed in this style.

Sato links this habit to the fact that Ozu limited the types of rooms he used; he seldom shot in the smaller rooms of a Japanese house (say, a four-and-a-half-mat room), preferring to shoot a pair of larger rooms side by side. Similarly, Ozu rarely closed off the sliding doors that are used to break up the Japanese house into rooms, but tended to shoot through open spaces. Sato links this additional restriction to the use of low camera height and the resulting stable compositions.[18]

Another famous trait of Ozu's style is his use of transitional shots between sequences: shots of landscapes near where the next scene is to occur, or of objects with only a tangential relation to the upcoming action. These shots often break our concentration on the flow of narrative cause and effect. Sometimes Ozu uses more shots than would be necessary to establish a locale; in *Late Spring*, for example, he shows a view of the Hattori building (Fig. 12.8) at the beginning of a sequence in which Noriko is shopping and meets an old friend, Professor Onodera. The initial shot serves to indicate that the area is the Ginza, since the Hattori building is perhaps the most famous of that district. But then Ozu shows another view of that same building (Fig. 12.9) which yields no new information. Only then does he cut to a long shot of Noriko crossing a street and meeting Onodera (Fig. 12.10); our view of Onodera is blocked by a pillar, so that at first we are puzzled as to why Noriko is bowing.

Late Spring uses fewer of these transitional shots than do many of Ozu's other films; *Autumn Afternoon, The Only Son*, and *End of Summer* contain lengthy series of this sort. In *Late Spring*, quite a few scenes begin without any such shots, and others are introduced by only one. A single low-angle shot of tree branches separates the scenes at the Noh drama and on the street afterwards. But a couple of sequences do spin out their openings, resulting in Ozu's characteristic play of dominants and overtones (in Eisenstein's sense) to structure a series of shots; that is, he frames one set of elements with a single one most prominent and others present but less weighted. Then Ozu will cut to other shots of the same elements, still present but shifting in importance, until the dominant element becomes an overtone and a new dominant takes over. By the time a third dominant appears, the first may be gone altogether. Thus in the opening sequence of *Late Spring*, we begin with a shot of the train station at Kitakamakura, the northern section of Kamakura, a town south of Tokyo (Fig. 12.11). The station sign, a corner of the station office at the right, and the platform steps at the left all focus our attention on the fact that this is a train station. The sound reinforces this: we hear a telegraph key tapping and, near the end of the shot, a bell begins to signal the approach of a train. Other elements are present in this shot but seem less important because they convey less narrative information: trees in the background, a telegraph pole, and a small patch of flowers in the middle

---

[18] Sato, "The Art of Yasujiro Ozu," pt. 4, p. 95.

ground. When Ozu cuts to a shot of the tracks and platform (Fig. 12.12), the relationships among the elements shift slightly. The railroad-station features—the tracks and platform—are still prominent. But as the shot continues, no train appears; the bell stops at the cut, to be replaced by quiet music. The background trees are somewhat more prominent, and there is a patch of flowers at the lower left, more noticeable than they had been in the first shot. By the next shot (Fig. 12.13), the train station elements have receded considerably: a slender signal, a bit of a slanted railing in the corner, some distant telegraph poles. By now we may suspect that no train will appear, and the station gives way in our attention to the now-dominant natural elements—the trees and prominently placed flowers. A bird call on the sound track contributes to this shift in emphasis. Then, at the next cut, the station elements disappear, and the trees take up little of the composition; a third dominant has appeared: a temple roof (Fig. 12.14), signaling the site of the first scene's action. We are still not sure that the action is going to start until the cut inside the tea house (Fig. 12.15), with its introduction of human figures, confirms that the narrative is beginning. This leisurely way of moving from one narratively significant space and time to another recurs seldom in the film; the series of scenes in Kyoto begins this way, however, with three shots of a pagoda, the last framed with wall panels placed as overtones, out of focus in the foreground at the sides of the frame; these prepare us for the cut away from the pagoda to a shot of an inn room (although we never find out if indeed Noriko and her father are staying at an inn near the pagoda).

Again, critics have attempted to force these transitional shots into one narrative function or another. Some read them symbolically, others as an expression of a severely Zen, contemplative outlook. (Admittedly, *Late Spring*'s concentration on temples and gardens tends to encourage this reading; yet other Ozu films insert shots of very non-Zen things indeed, for example, the neon signs of *Equinox Flower* and *End of Summer*, the baseball stadium lights of *Autumn Afternoon*, or the lighthouse in *Floating Weeds*.) Noël Burch has attempted to avoid such clichéd readings by positing these shots as equivalent to the empty spaces of traditional Japanese art, and specifically to the conventionalized "pillow" words used in Japanese poetry to fill out a line; indeed, he has termed such views "pillow shots," and he assumes them to be part of a Japanese aesthetic.[19]

[19] Noël Burch, *To the Distant Observer* (Berkeley: University of California Press, 1979), pp. 160–161.

Yet there is evidence that the Japanese find these shots quite as inexplicable as do Western audiences. Sato cites the film critic Keinosuke Nanbu, who "regarded these Ozu's peculiar unique sceneries that do not fail to appear at every change of scene as equivalent to the curtain used in theatrical performances, and called them curtain shots." This observation points up how alien these shots are, since the Japanese theater does not use curtains; Nanbu has resorted to a Western cultural tradition to characterize the shots—just the opposite of Burch's tactic. And Sato's reference to them as "peculiar unique sceneries" emphasizes their difference from the norms of Oriental, as well as Western, filmmaking. Indeed, Sato states that when Ozu films are shown on television in Japan, the transition shots are usually cut out.[20] So much for their function in the narrative and their accessibility for Japanese audiences.

Another device similar to these transitional shots is Ozu's use of cutaways within scenes. Again, these shots often show areas that are near the narrative action but are not essential for our understanding of what is going on. *Late Spring* employs many cutaways. During the tea ceremony at the beginning we move outside to explore the temple garden; the scene of the train ride to Tokyo consists of alternating shots of the pair inside the train and of the train, seen from the outside, moving along the tracks. In each case, the cutaway covers an ellipsis, but the characters also shift positions during the interval outside, and we may be a bit disoriented upon our return to the action. Thus this device functions in one way with the grain of the narrative and in another way against it.

Other scenes contain more limited cutaways. After one shot showing Professor Somiya brushing his teeth, with Noriko's help, at the inn at Kyoto (Fig. 12.16), there is a cut to a street with two tradespeople passing by carrying baskets (Fig. 12.17). We might expect this shot to signal the start of a new scene, but instead the next shot reveals Onodera waiting in the inn room to visit the pair (Fig. 12.18). Here the cutaway does not even have the minimal function of covering a noticeable ellipsis; Somiya and Noriko soon emerge to greet Onodera, having just finished at the sink (as we may infer by the towel Noriko carries and hangs up). Such cutaways wedge apart the smooth flow of narrative action in much the same way that the transitional shots do.

Within scenes, Ozu has a unique and rigorous approach to the laying out of space. He avoids the classical continuity approach whereby

---

[20] Sato, "The Art of Yasujiro Ozu," pt. 4, p. 88; Sato, *Currents in Japanese Cinema*, p. 190.

the camera must maintain screen direction by staying on one side of the axis of action, an imaginary line running between the main characters present.[21] Using this system, a film can maintain all characters and elements of a setting in the same general spatial relationship to each other: those on the right will remain to the right in all shots. The directions of characters' gazes also are consistent in this system, an important cue that enables the audience easily to construct a coherent overall space in the case of eyeline matches to contiguous areas.

Most directors who eschew this system, such as Dreyer, Eisenstein, and Tati, usually substitute some other, distinctive set of principles in its place. Ozu's postwar formal system is perhaps the most limited and rigorous of all; his solution to the problem of originality in film style was to work out a system that is basically the opposite of classical continuity. He treats the space of a scene as a circle, with the camera occupying points on the perimeter looking inward for general views of a room; then, for close views of a single character, or alternating views of two characters talking, the camera moves to approximately the center of the circle and points outward for shot/reverse shot patterns. In shifting from shot to shot, the framing tends to change in 45° segments, so that we may see a person from the rear, then close up in a three-quarters front view—a shift of 135°, or three 45° segments. For example, in the scene in which Noriko first visits her friend Aya at home, we see initially, from a vantage point facing a door, a Western-style interior, with no character onscreen (Fig. 12.19); then the camera shifts 180° to the other side of the circle and films Noriko at the window (Fig. 12.20). When she sits in the chair at the left, the next framing places the camera closer to her, with a slight change of angle (Fig. 12.21); the next view, of the door from a closer distance, has pivoted the camera back in nearly the opposite direction (Fig. 12.22). After another view of Noriko (Fig. 12.23), again reversing our vantage point, the final shot within the room frames the door from a position further back and to the left of the original framing, but still from the original side of the circle (Fig. 12.24). Aya enters, chats with Noriko, and takes her out through the door. Except for the cut-in, every shot change in this segment reverses our vantage point on the room; the fireplace and chairs that protrude into the sides of the frame in the first shot reverse

---

[21] For a brief summary of the continuity system, see David Bordwell and Kristin Thompson, *Film Art: An Introduction*, 2d ed. (New York: Alfred A. Knopf, 1985), chap. 7. A more detailed analysis, including the historical development of continuity, can be found in David Bordwell, Janet Staiger, and Kristin Thompson, *The Classical Hollywood Cinema: Film Style and Mode of Production to 1960* (New York: Columbia University Press, 1985), chaps. 5 and 16.

positions in the second. Were it not for these bits of furniture as cues, we might wonder if we are still in the same space, since an entirely different wall appears in the second shot. This segment has a close view of only one character, but in a shot/reverse shot pattern, the camera often rests between the characters, as in the pair of shots from the second sake-shop sequence (Figs. 12.25 and 12.26); *Late Spring* is full of such conversations.

Within this system, Ozu uses the standard continuity devices, but they come out contrary. He often films shot/reverse shots, sometimes from directly between the characters, but more often from a point just to the side of the axis—to the right of one actor, say, and to the right of the other as well. Actors end up looking off in the same direction in successive shots, though they are supposed to be facing each other in the story space. Later in the scene of Noriko's first visit to Aya, Aya serves Noriko some cake and they sit talking; Aya is framed looking off left front (Fig. 12.27) and so is Noriko (Fig. 12.28). Similarly, Ozu's meticulously correct matches on action frequently reverse screen direction. In a later shot in this scene, Noriko is visible in the foreground, reaching right to put down her cake, but we see her complete this action in the next shot, reaching toward the left. In these cases, the reversal of screen direction causes no confusion, since we have seen where the two women are sitting in an establishing shot. But, as we shall see, Ozu can play with this approach to throw us off balance.

Ozu's development of this spatial system owes little or nothing to tendencies in the Japanese cinema. There filmmakers learned the continuity rules of Hollywood films from the late 1910s and 1920s on. Sato describes this technique of discontinuity as one of the characteristic and unique features of Ozu's work. He points out that there is a specific term in Japanese for the across-the-line cut: *donden*, "a sudden reverse." According to Sato, "Although Ozu was told by studio personnel that the *donden* technique confused the directions of the gaze of the two actors, Ozu remained indifferent."[22] More than indifferent, one might add, since if Ozu did not care one way or the other, he could easily have pleased his studio by shooting the scenes "correctly." Instead, he persistently shot scenes across the line throughout his career, with his 360° method of shooting becoming more rigorous over the years.

One final device that is characteristic of Ozu's style is his use of what we termed the "hypersituated object." Ozu sometimes places within the frame objects that draw our attention far beyond their narrative

[22] Sato, *Currents in Japanese Cinema*, p. 189.

function; sometimes, indeed, they have virtually no narrative function at all. Examples in *Late Spring* would include the tiered pagoda that opens the Kyoto scenes; three shots linger over it beyond any establishing function it has. The post on the road as Hattori and Noriko cycle along has a small sign pointing to a beach, thus establishing their location (although the famous shape of Enoshima Island in the background of several shots has already done that effectively); but more eye-catching is the striking composition formed by the diamond-shaped Coke sign above, standing starkly against the blank sky (Fig. 12.29). Less prominent but more pervasive are the objects Ozu places at the sides in the foregrounds of his corridor shots: wooden stools, sake bottles, Noriko's sewing machine, and so forth. But perhaps the most famous and controversial use of a hypersituated object comes later, in the Kyoto scenes, as Noriko and her father are lying in bed. She tells him that she had found the idea of his remarriage distasteful, then glances over and sees that he is asleep. There follows a shot of her smiling face as she looks up at the ceiling, thinking (Fig. 12.30), then a cutaway to a vase in the corner of the room (Fig. 12.31), with the faint sound of snoring from offscreen. A return to the same framing of Noriko finds her no longer smiling, but shifting about, as if slightly disturbed (Fig. 12.32). The scene ends with a return to the vase (Fig. 12.33).

Donald Richie has taken this pair of cutaways to be what Noriko sees; he interprets it as a meaningful object: "into it pours our emotion," releasing the tension built up before this final moment of her acceptance.[23] Aside from the inaccuracy of description (Noriko could not see the vase—it is behind her in a corner, while she is looking up toward the ceiling) and the far-fetched pun of the vase/"pour" juxtaposition (do emotions pour?), the general function seems incorrect. This is not the emotional high point of the Kyoto scenes. Here Noriko has been regretting her remark to Onodera about his remarriage being "unclean," and she tries to tell her father that she also finds it difficult to accept the idea of his remarriage. Rather, the emotional climax comes later, when the pair is packing to leave Kyoto, and the professor finally conveys to her what marriage means and the necessity of their separating; this is when Noriko's true acceptance of the change comes. If the vase (which, incidentally, seems to have no specific traditional associations for a Japanese audience) is really there to help release our emotions in some way, why does Ozu put it in too soon? Given the film's consistent use of cutaways in a non-narrative way, it seems more

[23] Donald Richie, *Ozu* (Berkeley: University of California Press, 1974), p. 174.

reasonable to see it as a non-narrative element wedged into the action. Such wedges must have an effect on the story, assuredly, if only in the negative sense of diffusing our attention. Here we might conclude that Ozu is in fact blocking our complete concentration on Noriko in order to prevent our taking this as the emotional climax of the film; indeed, he avoids such cutaways during the packing scene, when we focus in entirely on the characters' conversation. But in any case, the choice of a vase for such a purpose is arbitrary; the shots could have shown a lantern in the garden, a tree branch, or whatever. As an emotion-charged symbol, a cut to Somiya's toothbrush and glass would have been more effective, since earlier we had seen Noriko handing these objects to her father, and this would have associated them with the pair's relationship. They have never even glanced at the vase. The very arbitrariness of the choice should warn us against simplistic readings.

These devices—low camera height, dominant/overtonal cutting, transitions and cutaways to intermediate spaces, a 360° layout of space, and the hypersituated object—constitute Ozu's basic set of rules for constructing space in *Late Spring*. (I have mentioned that graphic matches play little role in this particular film—except for the general matching of bodies in the many shot/reverse shot segments—and I will not discuss them here.) There are some other spatial and temporal guidelines at work. Ozu tends to use camera movement sparingly during this period of his career; it appears only in a few outdoor scenes in *Late Spring*. His cutting tempo is governed by a number of principles. Although his shots are varied in length, they often give a sense of a slow, steady tempo because he avoids either very short or very lengthy takes. (Even the shots of the Noh play, which seem long, are really only about a minute or less apiece.) Moreover, he generally avoids reaction shots and cuts only after the character has finished speaking. There are shots in which lines lap over, but these are distinctly in the minority. Thus the cutting of the scenes takes on the general rhythm of the spoken conversation itself, rather than of the facial expressions of the characters. This restriction means that in the few cases when the cutting speeds up to follow the exchange of short lines or when we do get a shot focusing on a reaction, the deviation stands out sharply.

Finally, Ozu eschews the use of optical effects like fades and dissolves to change scenes; rather, he usually signals the transition with music (which may or may not continue to play throughout the new scene) and transitional shots. He avoids rearranging his presentation of story events with flashbacks or flash-forwards. Indeed, the very fact that we so often must define Ozu's style by what he does *not* use indicates its sparseness. And we should remember that Ozu does not simply find functional equivalents for the devices that he avoids. In eliminating many techniques that most filmmakers use automatically, Ozu may also be eliminating the functions that those techniques usually perform. Ozu's differences from other filmmakers suggest that a distinct set of perceptual skills may be appropriate to his work. One of the most important differences lies in the films' tendency to play stylistic games with the spectator.

PLAY

Ozu's films resist all the reduction, recuperation, and naturalization that have been practiced upon them by conventionally minded critics. No matter how many symbolic readings interpreters force upon his films, there comes a point when the reading becomes too banal, too ludicrous. Were these critics correct, Ozu would emerge as a literal-minded, plodding director.

But in regard to these insistent symbol-finders, let us posit the opposite case. Assume for a moment that a filmmaker *did* deliberately want to do the sort of thing I have been describing: to insert non-narrative elements into a narrative film, purely for their own artistic interest. How could that filmmaker guide the spectator's reaction and prevent those artistic elements from being read symbolically? Short of inserting a written declaration of intent into the film itself (and there have been films that told us not to interpret them), it would be impossible. If the critic's approach dictates that analysis equals interpretation, all aspects of all films, no matter how disparate, can be forced to yield meaning. But by homogenizing films in this way, the critic often robs them of their most interesting aspects. Hence there is a great advantage in adapting one's method to the unique qualities of the work.

But if we at least admit the possibility of a mixture of narrative and non-narrative elements in a film, we can look for cues within the work that might guide us as to whether a given device functions in support of the narrative or in relative independence. In *Late Spring*, Ozu's austere, rigorous style, combined with a relatively simple story line, encourages us to notice details. The most obvious function of such attention is that everyday objects and common gestures gradually gain an importance beyond the ordinary; they are, in short, defamiliarized. After the Professor learns that Noriko has accepted Satake as her fiancé, he picks up a cup from the floor and sets it on the table. The gesture becomes one of the major moments of the scene—not a symbol, but a device of emphasis, an excuse to linger and watch him as he sits thinking. A great deal of the film's emotional impact comes from such moments.

But this function far from exhausts the fascination of Ozu's style, and the film's narrational methods suggest this. As we saw in Chapter 1, a film's narration may be more or less self-conscious and more or less communicative. Most classical films, in spite of moments when the narration flaunts itself, tend not to be overt in their usage; stylistic devices are motivated compositionally, to the degree that they generally support the narrative and serve no other apparent function. Narrative seems to saturate the film, to use up its stylistic devices. Similarly, classical narration tries for the most part to give the impression of being communicative, even when the film may withhold vital information (as in a detective film); a gap in the presentation of events usually will be motivated—by subjectivity, by a move to another event, and so on. We have seen such motivation at work in *Terror by Night* and *Stage Fright*.

Late Spring's narration seems at times to follow these classical guidelines, but for the most part it is generally more self-conscious. Ozu's stylistic "rules" themselves help make it so, in that the framing and layout of shots does not adjust itself to the action at hand. When a character stands up and goes partially out of the frame at the top, the narration's failure to accommodate the story material becomes obvious.

For the most part, the narration is communicative. The story is clear, with none of the temporal scrambling or permanent causal omissions of the art cinema. But the narration does withhold certain information, and it makes no attempt whatsoever to hide these gaps. The film ranges from scenes that linger over individual plot points to complete ellipses of vital events. In the scene at the Noh play, we simply watch the professor nod to Mrs. Miwa and then Noriko's reaction as she sits looking at her father, at Mrs. Miwa, and down into her lap. We already know she is upset at the thought of her father remarrying. Here we learn only that she infers some slight confirmation of her fears, yet the scene holds on her reaction long enough for us to absorb this fact many times over. At more crucial moments, the narration withholds fabula information; and it does so in spite of the fact that it does not restrict us to any one character's point of view. Information about Noriko and her father is balanced; we learn things about each that the other does not know, and similarly we fail to learn key things about both. We never see the scene in which the professor and his sister plot to make Noriko think he is remarrying; thus we may be as

342

deceived as she is until the surprise revelation of the deception near
the end. But this does not mean that story information will be consistently filtered through Noriko to us. At some point she has learned of
Hattori's engagement, yet we are not given this basic fact. Hence we
are likely to misconstrue the scene of the bike ride along the shore
near Enoshima Island as a signal of romantic attraction between the
two. We find out about this later, when she tells her father of the
engagement. The whole bike ride is an inessential scene in the chain
of major story events, one which exists to fool us, to create a little
suspense, and to hint at a possible romantic attraction which we never
are quite sure exists. More surprising yet, we never see either Noriko's *miai* with the prospective husband or the wedding scene itself.
Admittedly the film focuses on the separation of father and daughter,
but it is difficult to imagine a Hollywood film that did not at least give
us a look at the bridegroom (e.g., *Father of the Bride*, which treats
similar subject matter).

These ellisions and surprises do not confuse us more than momentarily. We are told fairly soon after each one what has happened. The
scene in which Somiya apparently confirms to Noriko that he plans to
remarry and urges her to attend the *miai* ends with her in tears. A
straight cut leads to a long shot of Somiya and the aunt visiting the
Tsurugaoka Hachimangu shrine; she asks, "What was her reaction?"
He replies, "She won't talk about it," and the aunt complains, "But it's
been a full week since I introduced them." The abrupt juxtaposition
flaunts the fact that the narration has skipped over this important
event, but we are more surprised than disoriented.

Certain stylistic devices contribute in an overt way to this selective
communicativeness in the narration. The transition shots and cutaways
from scenes point up the film's ability to place us somewhere other
than where the action is occurring. The opening sequence is exemplary here; as we have seen again and again in looking at formally daring films, the opening gives a strong signal to the audience of what to
watch for throughout. *Late Spring* begins with three shots of the railroad station (Figs. 12.11 to 12.13). These set the locale, North Kamakura, but it also raises our expectations that a character will arrive.
None does, and we move to the building in which a tea ceremony is
to take place. After a shot of its roof (Fig. 12.14), we see Noriko's arrival inside (Fig. 12.15). Did she come on the train we heard signaled
as approaching? Possibly, although she may live close enough to have
walked. After the conversation between Noriko and the aunt about the
worn-out trousers, Mrs. Miwa arrives. Was she the one expected at
the railroad station? Ozu bares the device of all this play with the sta-

tion shots when the aunt says, "I hoped to see you at the Shimbashi station," and Mrs. Miwa replies, "I missed my train." Ozu arbitrarily decided to show the Kitakamakura station when none of the characters—at least two of whom actually did take trains—was there. Later in this scene he cuts away from the tea ceremony twice for series of shots in the garden; the first time, he goes back inside to continue the scene, but the second cutaway proves to be the transition to the scene with the professor and Hattori. Ozu demonstrates here the arbitrariness of his stylistic choices in relation to the narrative.

Once we are alerted to this arbitrary quality of style, we can watch for further examples and find Ozu using his own rules to create a complex stylistic play to engage our perception. I have mentioned that graphic matches are used minimally here, but one set of variations that *Late Spring* works involves eyeline direction. The first sequence introduces this device with a simple ambiguity. The tea ceremony has begun during the first series of shots of the temple garden, and we are unsure of the women's relative spatial positions upon the return inside (they have shifted their seating arrangement during the interval, with Noriko, originally on her aunt's left, now on her right); a medium-long shot shows Mrs. Miwa and one of the participants in the ceremony (Fig. 12.34). At the cut to a medium close-up of Noriko looking off-screen right (Fig. 12.35), we may assume she is watching the action in the previous shot and that this is an eyeline match. But the next shot reveals the main part of the ceremony (Fig. 12.36). This, too, could be what Noriko is looking at. Certainly she does not turn her head and could not be looking at both spaces.

The train scene contains two bits of amusing byplay with eyelines. We get no establishing shot of Noriko and the professor inside the train. A medium close-up reveals them standing side by side facing the same direction (Fig. 12.37). Again, a cutaway (Fig. 12.38) covers an interval in which the characters change their positions. When we return inside the train in the next shot, we see Noriko facing right, as before (Fig. 12.39). There is a man visible, out of focus, behind her; his general appearance could lead us to assume he is the professor. But a cut reveals that Somiya now has a seat and is reading; he glances up right and asks if Noriko would like to sit (Fig. 12.40). By the logic of classical continuity, she should be standing across the aisle facing away from him, since in the reverse shot of her, she also faces right. But she glances down and right to tell him she does not need the seat (Fig. 12.41). This whole sequence is structured by repeated cutaways to exterior views of the train, but none of these are motivated by character glances. Indeed, Ozu emphasizes this lack of realistic motivation at one point. One cutaway is a tracking shot of passing buildings, taken from the moving train (Fig. 12.42). A point of view, perhaps? But the preceding shot had shown the professor and Noriko, both seated and reading now, facing away from the window (Fig. 12.43). And when, in a later shot, Noriko does glance out the window (Fig. 12.44), the cut brings us a view of the train from the side of the tracks, without camera movement (Fig. 12.45); this is impossible to take as a POV shot.

Later, Ozu begins the segment in which Noriko and Hattori meet at the Balboa Tea Shop with a shot of the famous Ginza landmark (Fig. 12.46); at that time its name was the Hattori Building, suggesting that Ozu chose to use it in order to make a little joke in relation to the character's name. Unlike the earlier shots (Figs. 12.8 and 12.9), Ozu frames this long shot through a window; but instead of moving inside this room, the sequence continues with the tea-shop sign (Fig. 12.47) before revealing the pair inside (Fig. 12.48). In the first shot, was the window frame in the tea shop? We get no clue that it was, or that the characters had been looking out.

Noriko's first visit to Aya also plays tricks with glances. The first shot of the room (see Fig. 12.19) turns out to have been taken from about where Noriko is revealed to be standing in the next shot (Fig. 12.20)—yet she is looking away from the door, and the first shot was taken from about knee level anyway. When Aya takes her upstairs for cake, the second portion of the sequence begins confusingly: a shot of Aya by the table, with no indication of where Noriko is (Fig. 12.49); a shot of Noriko, with just a bit of a chair protruding in at the right to indicate that the table is near her (Fig. 12.50); a shot with Aya glancing off right, stabilizing the space a bit (Fig. 12.51); finally a shot with Noriko visible beyond Aya, revealing that the first shot of Noriko must have been taken from where Aya is standing (Fig. 12.52). All this play with eyelines comes to a head in the scene of the wedding preparations, with Ozu showing us Noriko's glance into the mirror (Fig. 12.53), then later filming into the mirror after she has departed (Fig. 12.54). By demonstrating for us the impossibility of motivating most of the cuts and framing via eyelines, *Late Spring* continually cues us not to link all its stylistic features to character action.

With so many elements of the composition held steady, perhaps the most pervasive pattern of parametric variation comes in the layout of the scenes. Ozu's basic approach is to begin many scenes with a transitional shot, which I will here term T. Usually he follows this with an establishing long or medium-long shot that shows all the characters present; this shot I will call E. During the conversation he cuts to closer views, frontal or nearly so, of the characters' faces (though the body may be at a greater angle to the lens); A will indicate the first character thus shown, B the second. Then, at some point during the conversation, Ozu usually will shift to a "reestablishing" long or medium-long shot taken 180° from view E; this shot will be termed R. (E^1, E^2, A^1, A^2, and so on represent variations in framing of the same character or space.)

This in itself would be a rigorous pattern, eliminating as it does such common devices as crosscutting. But a closer examination of the layout of shots in *Late Spring*'s scenes reveals that Ozu creates a set of almost mathematically precise variations. For example, the two scenes in the sake shop are remarkably symmetrical.

First scene: T (the sign) E R E A (Onodera) B (Noriko) A B A E
Second scene: E R E^1 A (Somiya) B (Aya) A B A **B E B A** E T
  (restaurant interior)

The second scene is slightly longer, with four extra shots (in boldface), but the basic construction is identical. Moreover, the two transition shots act as "bookends" at opposite ends of the scenes. The first is the lighted restaurant sign outside the door (Fig. 12.55), the second, a shot of the shop interior (Fig. 12.56); when the interior light goes off in the course of this shot, we see the glow of the unseen exterior light shining against the window.

To a certain degree this pattern functions to point up the parallels between these two scenes. But those parallels are redundantly apparent, quite apart from this cutting pattern: only these two scenes take place in this locale, both involve a professor and a young woman, Noriko does not drink/Aya does, the same waiter serves them and even mentions the earlier visit to Somiya in the second scene. Thus the layouts are more precisely parallel than they need to be to draw our attention to the similarities of the scenes.

Moreover, other scenes handled with such precision of decoupage do not contain such exact parallels; rather, Ozu seems to provide at least one example of each possible variant on his basic pattern of scene layout. Thus the first scene at Somiya and Noriko's house begins with a T shot (the hillside, Fig. 12.57); continues with an E shot (Hattori and Somiya seen from the dining-room side, Fig. 12.58), one close shot of Hattori (A, Fig. 12.59), and one of Somiya (B, Fig. 12.60); then switches to a view from the garden, facing the dining room (R, Fig. 12.5). After the business with the meter man and Noriko's arrival, the scene continues with a series of shot/reverse shots among the three, always returning to R or R^1, with no return to E after its initial appearance. The next time we see this locale is when Noriko brings

Onodera home to visit. Then the opposite pattern occurs, with shots from the garden side—E, E^1, and E^2 (Fig. 12.61)—punctuating the lengthy series of closer conversation shots; finally, as Onodera and Somiya sit and joke about how confusing the geography of Kamakura is, Ozu cuts to R—a long view from the dining-room side, for the final shot of the sequence (Fig. 12.62).

This late appearance of the reverse-angle reestablishing shot not only switches the pattern of the earlier scene, but also serves to highlight a delightful baring of the device of 360° space. As the two men chat, Onodera begins asking Somiya where various landmarks are in relation to the house. He mentions the sea, the shrine, Tokyo, and the east, each time pointing, and each time Somiya corrects him by pointing off in a different direction. This goes on in shot/reverse shot for a while, and then Ozu cuts to R (Fig. 12.62). In that shot, Onodera makes his little joke about how a certain historical military leader valued this area for its confusing geography. This is the only sequence in the film in which Ozu withholds the reverse-angle view of the whole room until the last shot. Thus he points up his obsession with directions, at the same time revealing the device's playfulness.

This analysis may seem to some a bit far-fetched. Yet Sato relates a revealing anecdote: while arranging the mise-en-scene for a shot, Ozu would look through the viewfinder and set up the props before he began blocking the actors; he would have assistants stand by the furniture and move the props by tiny increments until he was satisfied with their positions. "When all the assistants grew tired, Ozu used to set them at ease by cracking a joke like, 'Toward Tokyo!' or 'For Atami!' instead of to the left or to the right."[24] The scene with Onodera and Somiya may even have been an in-joke between Ozu and his crew, referring to this habit.

A few scenes in the film do not cut to the R view at all, for example, the conversation between Noriko and Hattori in the Balboa Tea Shop and both the scenes in the downstairs room of the aunt's house. As first Somiya, then Noriko, visits the aunt, shot/reverse shots alternate with variant long views of the room, always toward the garden. (Noriko's short talk with her cousin upstairs has a simple pattern of E E R—here eliminating the notations of the closer shots.) There is no point in listing the layout of every sequence in detail. Briefly, not including the A and B conversation shots, the patterns of a few other scenes look like this: Noriko's conversation in her room with Aya over tea—E E E R E; the opening of Noriko's visit to Aya's house (analyzed already,

[24] Sato, "The Art of Yasujiro Ozu," pt. 4, p. 95.

Figs. 12.19 to 12.24—E R E^1 E^2; Onodera's visit with the pair at the Kyoto inn—E R E^1 E^2.

The major sequences involving conversations between Somiya and Noriko are worth looking at more closely, for they are extremely precise in their abstract patterning. The opening of the first is fairly complex, with Noriko folding a towel and moving about and Somiya returning home; then the two settle down to dinner, the only scene in the film shot from only one side of the axis to provide "correct" eyelines in terms of continuity. But apart from all the closer shots, the establishing views of first the study (E and R) and then the dining room (E^1, R^1, and R^2) alternate strictly: E R E^1 R^1 E^1 R^2 E^2 R^2. Admittedly this is the type of simple pattern one might expect to find in a scene, given the eccentric approach of shooting locales from opposite sides. But the next time the pair talks comes when Somiya urges Noriko to meet the marriage prospect as her aunt has arranged; here the segment of the scene that takes place downstairs has these establishing shots: E E R E^1 E^2. Once they move up to Noriko's room, the longer segment runs: E E E^1 R R^1 E E^1 E^2. Similarly, the scene at the Kyoto inn, as they pack and Somiya convinces Noriko that marriage is best for her, has this layout: E E E R E^1 E^1 E. Such obsessive precision in placing the opposing reestablishing shot(s) at the center of each scene conjures up images of Ozu and co-scenarist Kogo Noda sitting up late, surrounded by empty sake bottles, laying out these scenes for the delight and consternation of future critics.[25]

Is it possible to dredge up an interpretation of these patterns? Symbolic meaning seems impossible here. At some points, the switches to the R view of the room coincide with the entrance of a new character; thus the scene of the wedding preparations first shows Hattori and Somiya sitting in chairs in the study, viewed toward the garden. After a brief shot/reverse shot, Ozu moves to the opposite side as the maid enters from the hallway into the dining room, summoning Somiya to come and see Noriko. But of course the decision to first show the room facing the garden was arbitrary; no one enters there. Ozu could have used the R framing from the beginning, anticipating the maid's entrance. Similarly, the choice of vantage points on the scenes does not function to give us the best views of the characters; during her conversation with her aunt about marriage, Noriko sits with her back to the camera (in that sequence, as I have mentioned, the camera stays throughout on the E side), so that we cannot see her face after her

[25] Edward Branigan, fortified by Tab rather than sake, has puzzled out similar scene layouts as they occur in *Equinox Flower*; see Edward Branigan, "The Space of *Equinox Flower*," *Screen* 17, no. 2 (Summer 1976): 78–80.

aunt asks her questions. We cannot rationalize this as some sort of Japanese discretion, either, since at other moments Ozu holds on Noriko's face in medium close-up as she fights against tears or even begins crying.

These patterns of scene layout are difficult to catch exactly while viewing, but anyone who pays attention to cutting will, I think, have some sense that they are there. At least it quickly becomes apparent that within any one scene we may expect a new, opposite view of a room to appear at some point (and the anticipated reversal remains, at least subliminally, as a purely stylistic expectation). As with so many other Ozu devices, this one exists largely on its own, apart from narrative function. At most, it affects our perception of the tempo of scenes. Ozu usually allots one shot per speech, with each speech consisting of a sentence or phrase; longer speeches contain pauses. Thus scenes proceed at a steady, measured pace, and the limited, recurrent repetitions of framings can only help increase our awareness of that pace. Ozu's films are not actually slow, for there is usually something to notice both in the action and in the style, but for those unwilling to look beyond dialogue and acting, the steady tempo may lead to boredom.

Beyond the playfulness of the directional shifts and the precision of scene layout, we come to the most subtle of Ozuian tricks: minute shifts in framing.[26] Within one scene or across the entire film, Ozu repeatedly shows the same space in a framing that appears to be identical, but which actually changes slightly between repetitions. The most obvious example in *Late Spring* involves the occasional shots toward the front door of Somiya and Noriko's house as characters arrive or depart. We first see the entryway in the sequence in which Noriko returns home from the tea ceremony to find Hattori and her father at work. An oblique shot from the dining room shows the hallway beyond, but not the door itself (Fig. 12.63). At the left, a portion of a sewing machine is visible; at the right, part of the side hallway window. (This is *not* a POV shot, since the two men are in the study, not the dining room.) This same general view of the entryway, with the sewing machine at the left, recurs in six other, similar framings, yet no two are precisely the same (Figs. 12.64 to 12.69). In the scene in which the maid tells Hattori that Noriko and her father have gone to the Noh drama, for example, the maid sits in the approximate spot in the dining room from which most of the shots have been taken (Fig. 12.70); she looks up, and there follows one of the entryway shots (Fig.

---

[26] Branigan terms these "Incremental Variations" in his *Screen* article, pp. 82–86.

12.66), different from the earlier ones. This is one of the few true POV shots in the film—Hattori looking straight into the camera as he addresses the woman. In a return to the framing of Figure 12.70, she stands and goes out left toward the door (Fig. 12.71), and another variant of the entryway shot follows (Fig. 12.67). Here Ozu throws in another joke on eyelines; the woman's POV may motivate this one framing, but that just emphasizes the arbitrariness of the many shifts in framing among the other six uses of this view. Beyond this, Ozu uses a different shot down the kitchen hallway toward the entryway as an occasional substitute for this orientation. (This variation occurs five times, as in Fig. 12.72, the beginning of the scene in which the professor proposes Hattori as a husband for Noriko.) In these shots, Ozu places the same sewing machine at the right side of the frame. The shot of the hallway *without* the sewing machine—after Noriko's wedding (Fig. 12.73)—provides the payoff for this structure; it opens the scene of Somiya's return to the empty house and his loneliness without Noriko. Note, however, that the sewing machine's absence would have served the same narrative function if all the framings containing it had been identical. (Moreover, Ozu refuses to draw attention to the sewing machine by ordinary narrative means; Noriko never once uses it in the course of the film.) This sort of fascination with slight changes in the positions of objects within the frame becomes more prominent in Ozu's color films, where bottles of orange soda and brightly colored crockery seem to be performing in their own little abstract film in the lower third of conversation scenes.

Often, Ozu also varies the establishing and closing shots within conversation scenes. This is reasonable enough when characters enter or leave or move about a room; subsequent framings simply adjust minutely to re-balance the composition. But at other times there is no such function. In the scene at Kyoto in which Noriko and her father talk before going to sleep, the R view is a medium-long shot of the two, seen at an oblique angle against the closed sliding doors leading to the garden; she stands, turns off the light, and lies down (Figs. 12.3 and 12.4). After five shot/reverse shots in which she expresses regret at having been rude to Onodera, there is another medium-long shot, at an angle to the sliding doors that is just slightly less oblique. The only real difference in what we can see is that the vase at the background left (soon to be the subject of the cutaways) is less visible after Noriko turned out the light in the previous shot; now just the edge of its upper rim is silhouetted against the translucent glow of the paper wall—a tiny difference indeed.

Here we have another device with no possible narrative or symbolic function; the vast majority of viewers probably never notice it. Even when watching for the device in a Steenbeck viewing it is sometimes necessary to backtrack to confirm that a framing has really shifted. For those who do enter into this game, the pattern is purely abstract, extra-narrational—like the return of a musical motif with tiny shifts in orchestration. The changes exist in the same way that some of *Play Time*'s gags do, on the edge of perception, ready to engage the spectator more completely in the process of viewing.

Other shifts occur within the mise-en-scene, usually to maintain perfect compositions from shot to shot. Sato has commented on Ozu's love for balanced, diagonal compositions with two characters seated side by side.[27] In fact, Ozu often accentuates the diagonal line by placing one character further forward, rather than directly beside, the other (Fig. 12.58). This positioning could create problems for the 180° reverse view, but Ozu simply cheats the characters so that the other one is now further forward, and the perfect diagonal is maintained (Fig. 12.5). The same sort of shifting occurs, less obviously perhaps, in the scenes of the Noh play and the wedding preparations.

All these devices show that Ozu's playfulness is precise, but it is also unpredictable. No matter how many generalizations one makes about his self-imposed rules and variations, his films contain startling moments. In *Late Spring*, when Noriko and Onodera meet on the street, they see a poster for an exhibition of leftist artists at a Ueno Park museum. They depart, with Noriko insisting she must go shopping, and we are not sure whether they will take in the exhibit or not (Fig. 12.74). A cut-in to the poster they read (Fig. 12.75) is followed by another copy of the poster on display at the museum itself (Fig. 12.76). Still we are not sure whether the characters have gone to the exhibit, but we might expect to move inside and find them there. Instead, we next see a restaurant sign (Fig. 12.55) and a new scene begins, during which Noriko reveals that they did indeed go to the exhibit; the two poster shots substitute for their visit. (This contrasts with the concert hall and Noh play scenes later, either of which could have been shown in a similarly truncated fashion; the Noh play scene in particular is arbitrarily long.) Once again Ozu's narration flaunts its lack of communicativeness. Other scenes stand out from the pattern of variations, as with the precisely balanced cutting and camera movements of the biking scene, in which Noriko and Hattori seem at first, in terms of conventional screen direction, to be riding toward each other; or the end of the downstairs segment of Noriko's first visit to Aya (Fig.

[27] Sato, "The Art of Yasujiro Ozu," pt. 1, pp. 86–85.

12.24), when the camera holds on the empty room long enough to hear the clock chime musically but cuts away before it finishes striking the actual time. Ozu's style, sparse as it is, offered him the possibility of endless inventiveness.

Late Spring and the other films I have examined in this volume demonstrate the value of analyzing the functions of individual devices and formal patterns in pertinent contexts. Moreover, the neoformalist typology of different motivational possibilities discourages us from accounting for all films within too narrow a range of choices. While a film like *Bicycle Thieves* may privilege realistic motivation, *Late Spring* plays it down, elevating artistic motivation to a level equal with compositional motivation. Thus the same analytic *principles* may apply to all types of films, but the method adjusts itself to each film. We cannot go into an analysis assuming we know how all films work, for we will end up with the same kinds of results in every critical study. The trick is to point out each film's less obvious structures while neither reducing nor naturalizing it. Historical backgrounds permit us to point out the conventions in films, but we should not ourselves conventionalize devices by subjecting them to a clichéd reading.

Index

ILLUSTRATIONS

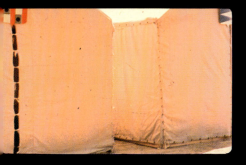

Plate 2

Plate 4

2.2

2.4

2.5

2.7

2.9

2.11

2.14

2.16

2.18

2.20

2.21

2.23

2.25

2.27

3.2

3.3

3.4

3.6

3.8

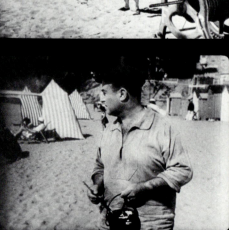

3.18

3.20

3.22

3.24

3.25

3.

4.1

4.

4.3

4.

4.5

4.

4.8

4.10

I became "the expert on the radical leftis" ...

4.12

4.14

4.15

4.17

5.1

5.3

5.6

5.8

CURTAIN

SYBIL THORNDIKE
KAY WALSH
MILES MALLESON
HECTOR MacGREGOR
JOYCE GRENFELL
ANDRE MORELL
PATRICIA HITCHCOCK
BALLARD BERKELEY

5.10

WILKIE COOPER

ART DIRECTOR
TERENCE VERITY
DIRECTED
HAROLD KING

ALFRED HITCHCOCK

5.12

5.13

5.15

5.17

6.1

3

6.4

5

6.6

7

6.8

9

6.10

6.11

6.13

6.15

6.17

6.20

6.22

6.24

6.26

7.8

7.10

8.2

8.4

8.5

8.7

8.9

8.11

8.14

8.16

Oh, we could make it a hospital benefit.

8.18

8.20

8.21

8.23

8.25

I hate to be but I just can't make it!

8.27

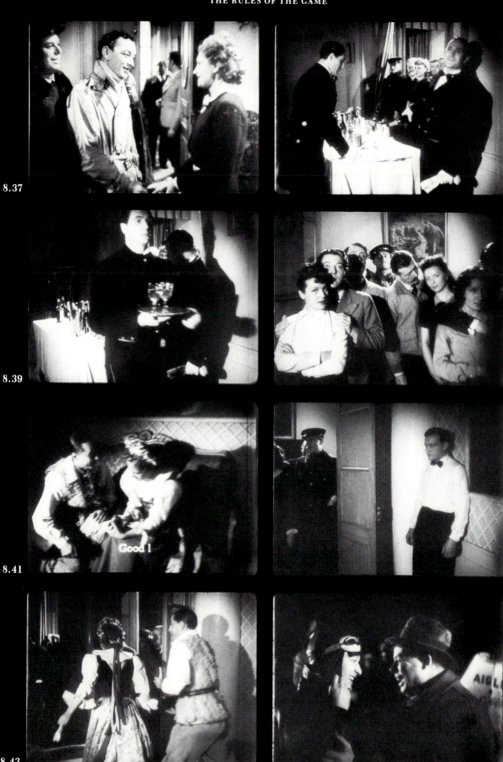

8.37

8.39

8.41

8.43

9.1

9.3

9.5

9.8

9.

9.10

9.

9.12

9.

9.14

9.